VE RI
TAS
VE RI
TAS
VE RI
TAS

THE HARVARD CLASSICS

The Five-Foot Shelf of Books

THE HARVARD CLASSICS
EDITED BY CHARLES W. ELIOT, LL.D.

English Essays

From Sir Philip Sidney *to* Macaulay

With Introductions and Notes
Volume 27

P. F. Collier & Son Corporation
NEW YORK

MANUFACTURED IN U. S. A.

CONTENTS

CONTENTS

INTRODUCTORY NOTE

SIR PHILIP SIDNEY, for three centuries the type of the English gentleman, was the son of Sir Henry Sidney, lord deputy of Ireland under Queen Elizabeth, and Lady Mary Dudley, daughter of the Duke of Northumberland. He was born at Penshurst, Kent, November 30, 1554, and was named after his godfather, Philip II of Spain, then consort of Queen Mary. He was sent to Oxford at fourteen, where he was noted as a good student; and on leaving the university he obtained the Queen's leave to travel on the Continent. He went to Paris in the train of the ambassador to France, saw much of court society there, and was in the city at the time of the massacre of St. Bartholomew. Proceeding to Germany he met, at Frankfort, the Protestant scholar Hubert Languet, with whom, though Languet was thrice his age, he formed an intimate and profitable friendship. He went on to Vienna, Hungary, Italy, and back by the Low Countries, returning to England at the age of twenty, an accomplished and courtly gentleman, with some experience of practical diplomacy, and a first-hand knowledge of the politics of the Continent.

Sidney's introduction to the court of Elizabeth took place in 1575, and within two years he was sent back to the Continent on a number of diplomatic commissions, when he used every opportunity for the furthering of the interests of Protestantism. He seems everywhere to have made the most favorable impression by both his character and his abilities. During the years between 1578 and 1585 he was chiefly at court and in Parliament, and to this period belong most of his writings. In 1585 he left England to assume the office of Governor of Flushing, and in the next year he was mortally wounded at the battle of Zutphen, dying on October 17, 1586. All England went into mourning, and the impression left by his brilliant and fascinating personality has never passed away.

Sidney's literary work was all published after his death, some of it against his express desire. The "Arcadia," an elaborate pastoral romance written in a highly ornate prose mingled with verse, was composed for the entertainment of his sister, the Countess of Pembroke. The collection of sonnets, "Astrophel and Stella," was called forth by Sidney's relation to Penelope Devereux, daughter of the Earl of Essex. While they were both little more than children, there had been some talk of a marriage between them; but evidence of any warmth of feeling appears chiefly after Penelope's unhappy marriage to Lord Rich. There has been much controversy over the question of the sincerity of these remarkable

3

poems, and over the precise nature of Sidney's sentiments toward the lady who inspired them, some regarding them as undisguised outpourings of a genuine passion, others as mere conventional literary exercises. The more recent opinion is that they express a platonic devotion such as was common in the courtly society of the day, and which was allowed by contemporary opinion to be compatible with the marriage of both parties.

In 1579 Stephen Gosson published a violent attack on the arts, called "The School of Abuse," and dedicated it without permission to Sidney. It was in answer to this that Sidney composed his "Defense of Poesy," an eloquent apology for imaginative literature, not unmingled with humor. The esthetic theories it contains are largely borrowed from Italian sources, but it is thoroughly infused with Sidney's own personality; and it may be regarded as the beginning of literary criticism in England.

THE DEFENSE OF POESY

By Sir Philip Sidney

W HEN the right virtuous Edward Wotton and I were at the Emperor's[1] court together, we gave ourselves to learn horsemanship of John Pietro Pugliano, one that with great commendation had the place of an esquire in his stable; and he, according to the fertileness of the Italian wit, did not only afford us the demonstration of his practice, but sought to enrich our minds with the contemplations therein which he thought most precious. But with none I remember mine ears were at any time more loaden, than when—either angered with slow payment, or moved with our learner-like admiration—he exercised his speech in the praise of his faculty. He said soldiers were the noblest estate of mankind, and horsemen the noblest of soldiers. He said they were the masters of war and ornaments of peace, speedy goers and strong abiders, triumphers both in camps and courts. Nay, to so unbelieved a point he proceeded, as that no earthly thing bred such wonder to a prince as to be a good horseman; skill of government was but a *pedanteria*[2] in comparison. Then would he add certain praises, by telling what a peerless beast the horse was, the only serviceable courtier without flattery, the beast of most beauty, faithfulness, courage, and such more, that if I had not been a piece of a logician before I came to him, I think he would have persuaded me to have wished myself a horse. But thus much at least with his no few words he drave into me, that self-love is better than any gilding to make that seem gorgeous wherein ourselves be parties.

Wherein if Pugliano's strong affection and weak arguments will not satisfy you, I will give you a nearer example of myself, who, I know not by what mischance, in these my not old years and idlest times, having slipped into the title of a poet, am provoked to say some-

---

[1] Maximilian II. (1527–1576).   [2] Piece of pedantry.

thing unto you in the defense of that my unelected vocation, which if I handle with more good will than good reasons, bear with me, since the scholar is to be pardoned that followeth the steps of his master. And yet I must say that, as I have just cause to make a pitiful defense of poor poetry, which from almost the highest estimation of learning is fallen to be the laughing-stock of children, so have I need to bring some more available proofs, since the former is by no man barred of his deserved credit, the silly[3] latter hath had even the names of philosophers used to the defacing of it, with great danger of civil war among the Muses.

And first, truly, to all them that, professing learning, inveigh against poetry, may justly be objected that they go very near to ungratefulness, to seek to deface that which, in the noblest nations and languages that are known, hath been the first light-giver to ignorance, and first nurse, whose milk by little and little enabled them to feed afterwards of tougher knowledges. And will they now play the hedgehog, that, being received into the den, drave out his host? Or rather the vipers, that with their birth kill their parents? Let learned Greece in any of her manifold sciences be able to show me one book before Musæus, Homer, and Hesiod, all three nothing else but poets. Nay, let any history be brought that can say any writers were there before them, if they were not men of the same skill, as Orpheus, Linus, and some other are named, who, having been the first of that country that made pens deliverers of their knowledge to their posterity, may justly challenge to be called their fathers in learning. For not only in time they had this priority—although in itself antiquity be venerable—but went before them as causes, to draw with their charming sweetness the wild untamed wits to an admiration of knowledge. So as Amphion was said to move stones with his poetry to build Thebes, and Orpheus to be listened to by beasts,—indeed stony and beastly people. So among the Romans were Livius Andronicus and Ennius; so in the Italian language the first that made it aspire to be a treasure-house of science were the poets Dante, Boccace, and Petrarch; so in our English were Gower and Chaucer, after whom, encouraged and delighted with their excellent foregoing, others have followed to

[3] Weak, poor.

beautify our mother-tongue, as well in the same kind as in other arts.

This did so notably show itself, that the philosophers of Greece durst not a long time appear to the world but under the masks of poets. So Thales, Empedocles, and Parmenides sang their natural philosophy in verses; so did Pythagoras and Phocylides their moral counsels; so did Tyrtæus in war matters, and Solon in matters of policy; or rather they, being poets, did exercise their delightful vein in those points of highest knowledge which before them lay hidden to the world. For that wise Solon was directly a poet it is manifest, having written in verse the notable fable of the Atlantic Island which was continued by Plato. And truly even Plato whosoever well considereth, shall find that in the body of his work though the inside and strength were philosophy, the skin as it were and beauty depended most of poetry. For all standeth upon dialogues; wherein he feigneth many honest burgesses of Athens to speak of such matters that, if they had been set on the rack, they would never have confessed them; besides his poetical describing the circumstances of their meetings, as the well-ordering of a banquet, the delicacy of a walk, with interlacing mere tales, as Gyges' Ring and others, which who knoweth not to be flowers of poetry did never walk into Apollo's garden.

And even historiographers, although their lips sound of things done, and verity be written in their foreheads, have been glad to borrow both fashion and perchance weight of the poets. So Herodotus entituled his history by the name of the nine Muses; and both he and all the rest that followed him either stole or usurped of poetry their passionate describing of passions, the many particularities of battles which no man could affirm, or, if that be denied me, long orations put in the mouths of great kings and captains, which it is certain they never pronounced.

So that truly neither philosopher nor historiographer could at the first have entered into the gates of popular judgments, if they had not taken a great passport of poetry, which in all nations at this day, where learning flourisheth not, is plain to be seen; in all which they have some feeling of poetry. In Turkey, besides their lawgiving divines they have no other writers but poets. In our neighbor country Ireland, where truly learning goeth very bare, yet are their poets held in a devout reverence. Even among the most barbarous and simple Indians, where no writing is, yet have they their poets, who make and sing songs (which they call *areytos*), both of their ancestors' deeds and praises of their gods,—a sufficient probability that, if ever learning come among them, it must be by having their hard dull wits softened and sharpened with the sweet delights of poetry; for until they find a pleasure in the exercise of the mind, great promises of much knowledge will little persuade them that know not the fruits of knowledge. In Wales, the true remnant of the ancient Britons, as there are good authorities to show the long time they had poets which they called bards, so through all the conquests of Romans, Saxons, Danes, and Normans, some of whom did seek to ruin all memory of learning from among them, yet do their poets even to this day last; so as it is not more notable in soon beginning, than in long continuing.

But since the authors of most of our sciences were the Romans, and before them the Greeks, let us a little stand upon their authorities, but even[4] so far as to see what names they have given unto this now scorned skill. Among the Romans a poet was called *vates*, which is as much as a diviner, foreseer, or prophet, as by his conjoined words, *vaticinium* and *vaticinari*, is manifest; so heavenly a title did that excellent people bestow upon this heart-ravishing knowledge. And so far were they carried into the admiration thereof, that they thought in the chanceable hitting upon any such verses great fore-tokens of their following fortunes were placed; whereupon grew the word of *Sortes Virgilianæ*, when by sudden opening Virgil's book they lighted upon some verse of his making. Whereof the Histories of the Emperors' Lives are full: as of Albinus, the governor of our island, who in his childhood met with this verse,

Arma amens capio, nec sat rationis in armis,

and in his age performed it. Although it were a very vain and godless superstition, as also it was to think that spirits were commanded by such verses—whereupon this word charms, derived of *carmina*, cometh—so yet serveth it to show the great reverence those wits were held in, and altogether not[5] without ground, since both the oracles of Del-

4 Only.   5 Not altogether.

phos and Sibylla's prophecies were wholly delivered in verses; for that same exquisite observing of number and measure in words, and that high-flying liberty of conceit[6] proper to the poet, did seem to have some divine force in it.

And may not I presume a little further to show the reasonableness of this word *vates,* and say that the holy David's Psalms are a divine poem? If I do, I shall not do it without the testimony of great learned men, both ancient and modern. But even the name of Psalms will speak for me, which, being interpreted, is nothing but Songs; then, that it is fully written in metre, as all learned Hebricians agree, although the rules be not yet fully found; lastly and principally, his handling his prophecy, which is merely poetical. For what else is the awaking his musical instruments, the often and free changing of persons, his notable prosopopœias, when he maketh you, as it were, see God coming in His majesty, his telling of the beasts' joyfulness and hills' leaping, but a heavenly poesy, wherein almost he showeth himself a passionate lover of that unspeakable and everlasting beauty to be seen by the eyes of the mind, only cleared by faith? But truly now having named him, I fear I seem to profane that holy name, applying it to poetry, which is among us thrown down to so ridiculous an estimation. But they that with quiet judgments will look a little deeper into it, shall find the end and working of it such as, being rightly applied, deserveth not to be scourged out of the church of God.

But now let us see how the Greeks named it and how they deemed of it. The Greeks called him ποιητήν, which name hath, as the most excellent, gone through other languages. It cometh of this word ποιεῖν, which is "to make"; wherein I know not whether by luck or wisdom we Englishmen have met with the Greeks in calling him a maker. Which name how high and incomparable a title it is, I had rather were known by marking the scope of other sciences than by any partial allegation. There is no art delivered unto mankind that hath not the works of nature for his principal object, without which they could not consist, and on which they so depend as they become actors and players, as it were, of what nature will have set forth. So doth the astronomer look upon the stars, and, by that he seeth, set down

[6] Invention.

what order nature hath taken therein. So do the geometrician and arithmetician in their divers sorts of quantities. So doth the musician in times tell you which by nature agree, which not. The natural philosopher thereon hath his name, and the moral philosopher standeth upon the natural virtues, vices, and passions of man; and "follow nature," saith he, "therein, and thou shalt not err." The lawyer saith what men have determined, the historian what men have done. The grammarian speaketh only of the rules of speech, and the rhetorician and logician, considering what in nature will soonest prove and persuade, thereon give artificial rules, which still are compassed within the circle of a question, according to the proposed matter. The physician weigheth the nature of man's body, and the nature of things helpful or hurtful unto it. And the metaphysic, though it be in the second and abstract notions, and therefore be counted supernatural, yet doth he, indeed, build upon the depth of nature.

Only the poet, disdaining to be tied to any such subjection, lifted up with the vigor of his own invention, doth grow, in effect, into another nature, in making things either better than nature bringeth forth, or, quite anew, forms such as never were in nature, as the heroes, demi-gods, cyclops, chimeras, furies, and such like; so as he goeth hand in hand with nature, not enclosed within the narrow warrant of her gifts, but freely ranging within the zodiac of his own wit. Nature never set forth the earth in so rich tapestry as divers poets have done; neither with pleasant rivers, fruitful trees, sweet-smelling flowers, nor whatsoever else may make the too-much-loved earth more lovely; her world is brazen, the poets only deliver a golden.

But let those things alone, and go to man—for whom as the other things are, so it seemeth in him her uttermost cunning is employed—and know whether she have brought forth so true a lover as Theagenes; so constant a friend as Pylades; so valiant a man as Orlando; so right a prince as Xenophon's Cyrus; so excellent a man every way as Virgil's Æneas? Neither let this be jestingly conceived, because the works of the one be essential, the other in imitation or fiction; for any understanding knoweth the skill of each artificer standeth in that idea, or fore-conceit of the work, and not in the work itself. And that the poet hath that idea is manifest, by delivering them forth in such excellency as he hath imagined them. Which delivering forth, also, is not wholly imaginative, as we are wont to say by them that build castles in the air; but so far substantially it worketh, not only to make a Cyrus, which had been but a particular excellency, as nature might have done, but to bestow a Cyrus upon the world to make many Cyruses, if they will learn aright why and how that maker made him. Neither let it be deemed too saucy a comparison to balance the highest point of man's wit with the efficacy of nature; but rather give right honor to the Heavenly Maker of that maker, who, having made man to His own likeness, set him beyond and over all the works of that second nature. Which in nothing he showeth so much as in poetry, when with the force of a divine breath he bringeth things forth far surpassing her doings, with no small argument to the incredulous of that first accursed fall of Adam,— since our erected wit maketh us know what perfection is, and yet our infected will keepeth us from reaching unto it. But these arguments will by few be understood, and by fewer granted; thus much I hope will be given me, that the Greeks with some probability of reason gave him the name above all names of learning.

Now let us go to a more ordinary opening of him, that the truth may be the more palpable; and so, I hope, though we get not so unmatched a praise as the etymology of his names will grant, yet his very description, which no man will deny, shall not justly be barred from a principal commendation.

Poesy, therefore, is an art of imitation, for so Aristotle termeth it in his word μίμησις, that is to say, a representing, counterfeiting, or figuring forth; to speak metaphorically, a speaking picture, with this end,—to teach and delight.

Of this have been three general kinds. The chief, both in antiquity and excellency, were they that did imitate the inconceivable excellencies of God. Such were David in his Psalms; Solomon in his Song of Songs, in his Ecclesiastes and Proverbs; Moses and Deborah in their Hymns; and the writer of Job; which, beside other, the learned Emanuel Tremellius and Franciscus Junius do entitle the poetical part of the Scripture. Against these none will speak that hath the Holy Ghost in due holy reverence. In this kind, though in a full wrong divinity, were Orpheus, Amphion, Homer in his Hymns, and many other, both Greeks and Romans. And this poesy must be used by whosoever will follow St. James' counsel in singing psalms when they are merry; and I know is used with the fruit of comfort by some, when, in sorrowful pangs of their death-bringing sins, they find the consolation of the never-leaving goodness.

The second kind is of them that deal with matters philosophical, either moral, as Tyrtæus, Phocylides, and Cato; or natural, as Lucretius and Virgil's Georgics; or astronomical, as Manilius and Pontanus; or historical, as Lucan; which who mislike, the fault is in their judgment quite out of taste, and not in the sweet food of sweetly uttered knowledge.

But because this second sort is wrapped within the fold of the proposed subject, and takes not the free course of his own invention, whether they properly be poets or no let grammarians dispute, and go to the third, indeed right poets, of whom chiefly this question ariseth. Betwixt whom and these second is such a kind of difference as betwixt the meaner sort of painters, who counterfeit only such faces as are set before them, and the more excellent, who having no law but wit, bestow that in colors upon you which is fittest for the eye to see,—as the constant though lamenting look of Lucretia, when she punished in herself another's fault; wherein he painteth not Lucretia, whom he never saw, but painteth the outward beauty of such a virtue. For these third be they which most properly do imitate to teach and delight; and to imitate borrow nothing of what is, hath been, or shall be; but range, only reined with learned discretion, into the divine consideration of what may be and should be. These be they that, as the first and most noble sort may justly be termed *vates,* so these are waited on in the excellentest languages and best understandings with the fore-described name of poets. For these, indeed, do merely make to imitate, and imitate both to delight and teach, and delight to move men to take that goodness in hand, which without delight they would fly as from a stranger; and teach to make them know that goodness whereunto they are moved:—which being the noblest scope to which ever any learning was directed, yet want there not idle tongues to bark at them.

These be subdivided into sundry more special denominations. The most notable be the heroic, lyric, tragic, comic, satiric, iambic, elegiac, pastoral, and certain others, some of these being termed according to the matter they deal with, some by the sort of verse they liked best to write in,—for indeed the greatest part of poets have apparelled their poetical inventions in that numberous kind of writing which is called verse. Indeed but apparelled, verse being but an ornament and no cause to poetry, since there have been many most excellent poets that never versified, and now swarm many versifiers that need never answer to the name of poets. For Xenophon, who did imitate so excellently as to give us *effigiem justi imperii*—the portraiture of a just empire under the name of Cyrus (as Cicero saith of him)—made therein an absolute heroical poem; so did Heliodorus in his sugared invention of that picture of love in Theagenes and Chariclea; and yet both these wrote in prose. Which I speak to show that it is not riming and versing that maketh a poet —no more than a long gown maketh an advocate, who, though he pleaded in armor, should be an advocate and no soldier—but it is that feigning notable images of virtues, vices, or what else, with that delightful teaching, which must be the right describing note to know a poet by. Although indeed the senate of poets hath chosen verse as their fittest raiment, meaning, as in matter they passed all in all, so in manner to go beyond them; not speaking, table-talk fashion, or like men in a dream, words as they chanceably fall from the mouth, but peizing[7] each syllable of each word by just proportion, according to the dignity of the subject.

Now, therefore, it shall not be amiss, first to weigh this latter sort of poetry by his works, and then by his parts; and if in neither of these anatomies he be condemnable, I hope we shall obtain a more favorable sentence. This purifying of wit, this enriching of memory, enabling of judgment, and enlarging of conceit, which commonly we call learning, under what name soever it come forth or to what immediate end soever it be directed, the final end is to lead and draw us to as high a perfection as our degenerate souls, made worse by their clay lodgings, can be capable of. This, according to the inclination of man, bred many-formed impressions. For some that thought this felicity principally to be gotten by knowledge, and no knowledge to be so high or heavenly as acquaintance with the stars, gave themselves to astronomy; others, persuading themselves to be

[7] Weighing.

demi-gods if they knew the causes of things, became natural and supernatural philosophers. Some an admirable delight drew to music, and some the certainty of demonstration to the mathematics; but all, one and other, having this scope:—to know, and by knowledge to lift up the mind from the dungeon of the body to the enjoying his own divine essence. But when by the balance of experience it was found that the astronomer, looking to the stars, might fall into a ditch, that the inquiring philosopher might be blind in himself, and the mathematician might draw forth a straight line with a crooked heart; then lo! did proof, the overruler of opinions, make manifest, that all these are but serving sciences, which, as they have each a private end in themselves, so yet are they all directed to the highest end of the mistress-knowledge, by the Greeks called ἀρχιτεκτονική, which stands, as I think, in the knowledge of a man's self, in the ethic and politic consideration, with the end of well-doing, and not of well-knowing only:—even as the saddler's next end is to make a good saddle, but his further end to serve a nobler faculty, which is horsemanship; so the horseman's to soldiery; and the soldier not only to have the skill, but to perform the practice of a soldier. So that the ending end of all earthly learning being virtuous action, those skills that most serve to bring forth that have a most just title to be princes over all the rest; wherein, if we can show, the poet is worthy to have it before any other competitors.

Among whom as principal challengers step forth the moral philosophers; whom, me thinketh, I see coming toward me with a sullen gravity, as though they could not abide vice by daylight; rudely clothed, for to witness outwardly their contempt of outward things; with books in their hands against glory, whereto they set their names; sophistically speaking against subtility; and angry with any man in whom they see the foul fault of anger. These men, casting largess as they go of definitions, divisions, and distinctions, with a scornful interrogative do soberly ask whether it be possible to find any path so ready to lead a man to virtue, as that which teacheth what virtue is, and teacheth it not only by delivering forth his very being, his causes and effects, but also by making known his enemy, vice, which must be destroyed, and his cumbersome servant, passion, which must be mastered; by showing the generalities that contain it, and the specialities that are derived from it; lastly, by plain setting down how it extendeth itself out of the limits of a man's own little world, to the government of families, and maintaining of public societies?

The historian scarcely giveth leisure to the moralist to say so much, but that he, loaden with old mouse-eaten records, authorizing himself for the most part upon other histories, whose greatest authorities are built upon the notable foundation of hearsay; having much ado to accord differing writers, and to pick truth out of partiality; better acquainted with a thousand years ago than with the present age, and yet better knowing how this world goeth than how his own wit runneth; curious for antiquities and inquisitive of novelties, a wonder to young folks and a tyrant in table-talk; denieth, in a great chafe,[8] that any man for teaching of virtue and virtuous actions is comparable to him. "I am *testis temporum, lux veritatis, vita memoriæ, magistra vitæ, nuntia vetustatis.*[9] The philosopher," saith he, "teacheth a disputative virtue, but I do an active. His virtue is excellent in the dangerless Academy of Plato, but mine showeth forth her honorable face in the battles of Marathon, Pharsalia, Poitiers, and Agincourt. He teacheth virtue by certain abstract considerations, but I only bid you follow the footing of them that have gone before you. Old-aged experience goeth beyond the fine-witted philosopher; but I give the experience of many ages. Lastly, if he make the song-book, I put the learner's hand to the lute; and if he be the guide, I am the light." Then would he allege you innumerable examples, confirming story by story, how much the wisest senators and princes have been directed by the credit of history, as Brutus, Alphonsus of Aragon—and who not, if need be? At length the long line of their disputation maketh[10] a point in this,—that the one giveth the precept, and the other the example.

Now whom shall we find, since the question standeth for the highest form in the school of learning, to be moderator? Truly, as me seemeth, the poet; and if not a moderator, even the man that ought to carry the title from them both, and much more from all

[8] Anger, irritation.
[9] "The witness of time, the light of truth, the life of memory, the directress of life, the herald of antiquity."—Cicero, "De Orat.," 2. 9. 36.   [10] Comes to.

other serving sciences. Therefore compare we the poet with the historian and with the moral philosopher; and if he go beyond them both, no other human skill can match him. For as for the divine, with all reverence it is ever to be excepted, not only for having his scope as far beyond any of these as eternity exceedeth a moment, but even for passing each of these in themselves. And for the lawyer, though *Jus* be the daughter of Justice, and Justice the chief of virtues, yet because he seeketh to make men good rather *formidine pœnæ*[11] than *virtutis amore*[12] or, to say righter, doth not endeavour to make men good, but that their evil hurt not others; having no care, so he be a good citizen, how bad a man he be; therefore, as our wickedness maketh him necessary, and necessity maketh him honorable, so is he not in the deepest truth to stand in rank with these, who all endeavor to take naughtiness away, and plant goodness even in the secretest cabinet of our souls. And these four are all that any way deal in that consideration of men's manners, which being the supreme knowledge, they that best breed it deserve the best commendation.

The philosopher therefore and the historian are they which would win the goal, the one by precept, the other by example; but both not having both, do both halt. For the philosopher, setting down with thorny arguments the bare rule, is so hard of utterance and so misty to be conceived, that one that hath no other guide but him shall wade in him till he be old, before he shall find sufficient cause to be honest. For his knowledge standeth so upon the abstract and general that happy is that man who may understand him, and more happy that can apply what he doth understand. On the other side, the historian, wanting the precept, is so tied, not to what should be but to what is, to the particular truth of things, and not to the general reason of things, that his example draweth no necessary consequence, and therefore a less fruitful doctrine.

Now doth the peerless poet perform both; for whatsoever the philosopher saith should be done, he giveth a perfect picture of it in some one by whom he presupposeth it was done, so as he coupleth the general notion with the particular example. A perfect picture, I say; for he yieldeth to the powers of the mind an image of that

---

[11] Fear of punishment.   [12] Love of virtue.

whereof the philosopher bestoweth but a wordish description, which doth neither strike, pierce, nor possess the sight of the soul so much as that other doth. For as, in outward things, to a man that had never seen an elephant or a rhinoceros, who should tell him most exquisitely all their shapes, color, bigness, and particular marks; or of a gorgeous palace, an architector, with declaring the full beauties, might well make the hearer able to repeat, as it were by rote, all he had heard, yet should never satisfy his inward conceit with being witness to itself of a true lively[13] knowledge; but the same man, as soon as he might see those beasts well painted, or that house well in model, should straightways grow, without need of any description, to a judicial comprehending of them; so no doubt the philosopher, with his learned definitions, be it of virtues or vices, matters of public policy or private government, replenisheth the memory with many infallible grounds of wisdom, which notwithstanding lie dark before the imaginative and judging power, if they be not illuminated or figured forth by the speaking picture of poesy.

Tully taketh much pains, and many times not without poetical helps, to make us know the force love of our country hath in us. Let us but hear old Anchises speaking in the midst of Troy's flames, or see Ulysses, in the fulness of all Calypso's delights, bewail his absence from barren and beggarly Ithaca. Anger, the Stoics said, was a short madness. Let but Sophocles bring you Ajax on a stage, killing and whipping sheep and oxen, thinking them the army of Greeks, with their chieftains Agamemnon and Menelaus, and tell me if you have not a more familiar insight into anger, than finding in the schoolmen his genus and difference. See whether wisdom and temperance in Ulysses and Diomedes, valor in Achilles, friendship in Nisus and Euryalus, even to an ignorant man carry not an apparent shining. And, contrarily, the remorse of conscience, in Œdipus; the soon-repenting pride of Agamemnon; the self-devouring cruelty in his father Atreus; the violence of ambition in the two Theban brothers; the sour sweetness of revenge in Medea; and, to fall lower, the Terentian Gnatho and our Chaucer's Pandar so expressed that we now use their names to signify their trades; and finally, all virtues, vices, and passions so in their own natural

13 Living.

states laid to the view, that we seem not to hear of them, but clearly to see through them.

But even in the most excellent determination of goodness, what philosopher's counsel can so readily direct a prince, as the feigned Cyrus in Xenophon? Or a virtuous man in all fortunes, as Æneas in Virgil? Or a whole commonwealth, as the way of Sir Thomas More's Utopia? I say the way, because where Sir Thomas More erred, it was the fault of the man, and not of the poet; for that way of patterning a commonwealth was most absolute, though he, perchance, hath not so absolutely performed it. For the question is, whether the feigned image of poesy, or the regular instruction of philosophy, hath the more force in teaching. Wherein if the philosophers have more rightly showed themselves philosophers than the poets have attained to the high top of their profession,—as in truth,

Mediocribus esse poetis
Non Dii, non homines, non concessere columnæ,—[14]

it is, I say again, not the fault of the art, but that by few men that art can be accomplished.

Certainly, even our Saviour Christ could as well have given the moral commonplaces of uncharitableness and humbleness as the divine narration of Dives and Lazarus; or of disobedience and mercy, as that heavenly discourse of the lost child and the gracious father; but that his through-searching wisdom knew the estate of Dives burning in hell, and of Lazarus in Abraham's bosom, would more constantly, as it were, inhabit both the memory and judgment. Truly, for myself, me seems I see before mine eyes the lost child's disdainful prodigality, turned to envy a swine's dinner; which by the learned divines are thought not historical acts, but instructing parables.

For conclusion, I say the philosopher teacheth, but he teacheth obscurely, so as the learned only can understand him; that is to say, he teacheth them that are already taught. But the poet is the food for the tenderest stomachs; the poet is indeed the right popular philosopher. Whereof Æsop's tales give good proof; whose pretty

---

[14] "Neither gods nor men nor booksellers permit poets to be mediocre."—Horace, "Ars Poet.," 372-3

allegories, stealing under the formal tales of beasts, make many, more beastly than beasts, begin to hear the sound of virtue from those dumb speakers.

But now it may be alleged that if this imagining of matters be so fit for the imagination, then must the historian needs surpass, who bringeth you images of true matters, such as indeed were done, and not such as fantastically[15] or falsely may be suggested to have been done. Truly, Aristotle himself, in his Discourse of Poesy, plainly determineth this question, saying that poetry is φιλοσοφώτερον and σπουδαιότερον, that is to say, it is more philosophical and more studiously serious than history. His reason is, because poesy dealeth with καθόλου, that is to say with the universal consideration, and the history with καθ' ἕκαστον, the particular.

"Now," saith he, "the universal weighs what is fit to be said or done, either in likelihood or necessity—which the poesy considereth in his imposed names; and the particular only marketh whether Alcibiades did, or suffered, this or that:" thus far Aristotle. Which reason of his, as all his, is most full of reason.

For, indeed, if the question were whether it were better to have a particular act truly or falsely set down, there is no doubt which is to be chosen, no more than whether you had rather have Vespasian's picture right as he was, or, at the painter's pleasure, nothing resembling. But if the question be for your own use and learning, whether it be better to have it set down as it should be or as it was, then certainly is more doctrinable[16] the feigned Cyrus in Xenophon than the true Cyrus in Justin; and the feigned Æneas in Virgil than the right Æneas in Dares Phrygius; as to a lady that desired to fashion her countenance to the best grace, a painter should more benefit her to portrait a most sweet face, writing Canidia upon it, than to paint Canidia as she was, who, Horace sweareth, was foul and ill-favored.

If the poet do his part aright, he will show you in Tantalus, Atreus, and such like, nothing that is not to be shunned; in Cyrus, Æneas, Ulysses, each thing to be followed. Where the historian, bound to tell things as things were, cannot be liberal—without he will be poetical—of a perfect pattern; but, as in Alexander, or Scipio him-

[15] Imaginatively.   [16] Instructive.

self, show doings, some to be liked, some to be misliked; and then how will you discern what to follow but by your own discretion, which you had without reading Quintus Curtius? And whereas a man may say, though in universal consideration of doctrine the poet prevaileth, yet that the history, in his saying such a thing was done, doth warrant a man more in that he shall follow,—the answer is manifest: that if he stand upon that *was,* as if he should argue, because it rained yesterday therefore it should rain to-day, then indeed it hath some advantage to a gross conceit. But if he know an example only informs a conjectured likelihood, and so go by reason, the poet doth so far exceed him as he is to frame his example to that which is most reasonable, be it in warlike, politic, or private matters; where the historian in his bare *was* hath many times that which we call fortune to overrule the best wisdom. Many times he must tell events whereof he can yield no cause; or if he do, it must be poetically.

For, that a feigned example hath as much force to teach as a true example—for as for to move, it is clear, since the feigned may be tuned to the highest key of passion—let us take one example wherein a poet and a historian do concur. Herodotus and Justin do both testify that Zopyrus, king Darius' faithful servant, seeing his master long resisted by the rebellious Babylonians, feigned himself in extreme disgrace of his king; for verifying of which he caused his own nose and ears to be cut off, and so flying to the Babylonians, was received, and for his known valor so far credited, that he did find means to deliver them over to Darius. Muchlike matter doth Livy record of Tarquinius and his son. Xenophon excellently feigneth such another stratagem, performed by Abradatas in Cyrus' behalf. Now would I fain know, if occasion be presented unto you to serve your prince by such an honest dissimulation, why do you not as well learn it of Xenophon's fiction as of the other's verity? and, truly, so much the better, as you shall save your nose by the bargain; for Abradatas did not counterfeit so far.

So, then, the best of the historian is subject to the poet; for whatsoever action or faction, whatsoever counsel, policy, or war-stratagem the historian is bound to recite, that may the poet, if he list, with his imitation make his own, beautifying it both for further teaching and more delighting, as it pleaseth him; having all, from Dante's Heaven to his Hell, under the authority of his pen. Which if I be asked what poets have done? so as I might well name some, yet say I, and say again, I speak of the art, and not of the artificer.

Now, to that which is commonly attributed to the praise of history, in respect of the notable learning is gotten by marking the success, as though therein a man should see virtue exalted and vice punished,—truly that commendation is peculiar to poetry and far off from history. For, indeed, poetry ever setteth virtue so out in her best colors, making Fortune her well-waiting handmaid, that one must needs be enamored of her. Well may you see Ulysses in a storm, and in other hard plights; but they are but exercises of patience and magnanimity, to make them shine the more in the near following prosperity. And, of the contrary part, if evil men come to the stage, they ever go out—as the tragedy writer answered to one that·misliked the show of such persons—so manacled as they little animate folks to follow them. But the historian, being captived to the truth of a foolish world, is many times a terror from well-doing, and an encouragement to unbridled wickedness. For see we not valiant Miltiades rot in his fetters? The just Phocion and the accomplished Socrates put to death like traitors? The cruel Severus live prosperously? The excellent Severus miserably murdered? Sylla and Marius dying in their beds? Pompey and Cicero slain then, when they would have thought exile a happiness? See we not virtuous Cato driven to kill himself, and rebel Cæsar so advanced that his name yet, after sixteen hundred years, lasteth in the highest honor? And mark but even Cæsar's own words of the forenamed Sylla—who in that only did honestly, to put down his dishonest tyranny—*literas nescivit*:[17] as if want of learning caused him to do well. He meant it not by poetry, which, not content with earthly plagues, deviseth new punishments in hell for tyrants; nor yet by

---

[17] He was without learning. Sidney here seems to miss the point of a joke of Cæsar's reported by Suetonius.

philosophy, which teacheth *occidendos esse;*[18] but, no doubt, by skill in history, for that indeed can afford you Cypselus, Periander, Phalaris, Dionysius, and I know not how many more of the same kennel, that speed well enough in their abominable injustice or usurpation.

I conclude, therefore, that he excelleth history, not only in furnishing the mind with knowledge, but in setting it forward to that which deserveth to be called and accounted good; which setting forward, and moving to well-doing, indeed setteth the laurel crown upon the poet as victorious, not only of the historian, but over the philosopher, howsoever in teaching it may be questionable. For suppose it be granted—that which I suppose with great reason may be denied—that the philosopher, in respect of his methodical proceeding, teach more perfectly than the poet, yet do I think that no man is so much φιλοφιλόσοφος[19] as to compare the philosopher in moving with the poet. And that moving is of a higher degree than teaching, it may by this appear, that it is well nigh both the cause and the effect of teaching; for who will be taught, if he be not moved with desire to be taught? And what so much good doth that teaching bring forth—I speak still of moral doctrine—as that it moveth one to do that which it doth teach? For, as Aristotle saith, it is not γνῶσις[20] but πρᾶξις[21] must be the fruit; and how πρᾶξις cannot be, without being moved to practise, it is no hard matter to consider. The philosopher showeth you the way, he informeth you of the particularities, as well of the tediousness of the way, as of the pleasant lodging you shall have when your journey is ended, as of the many by-turnings that may divert you from your way; but this is to no man but to him that will read him, and read him with attentive, studious painfulness; which constant desire whosoever hath in him, hath already passed half the hardness of the way, and therefore is beholding to the philosopher but for the other half. Nay, truly, learned men have learnedly thought, that where once reason hath so much overmastered passion as that the mind hath a free desire to do well, the inward light each mind hath in itself is as good as a philosopher's book; since in nature we know it is well to do well, and what is well and what is evil, although not in the words of art which philosophers bestow upon us; for out of natural conceit the

[18] That they are to be killed. [19] A friend to the philosopher. [20] Knowledge. [21] Practice.

philosophers drew it. But to be moved to do that which we know, or to be moved with desire to know, *hoc opus, hic labor est.*[22]

Now therein of all sciences—I speak still of human, and according to the human conceit—is our poet the monarch. For he doth not only show the way, but giveth so sweet a prospect into the way as will entice any man to enter into it. Nay, he doth, as if your journey should lie through a fair vineyard, at the very first give you a cluster of grapes, that full of that taste you may long to pass further. He beginneth not with obscure definitions, which must blur the margent[23] with interpretations, and load the memory with doubtfulness. But he cometh to you with words set in delightful proportion, either accompanied with, or prepared for, the well-enchanting skill of music; and with a tale, forsooth, he cometh unto you, with a tale which holdeth children from play, and old men from the chimney-corner, and, pretending no more, doth intend the winning of the mind from wickedness to virtue; even as the child is often brought to take most wholesome things, by hiding them in such other as to have a pleasant taste,—which, if one should begin to tell them the nature of the aloes or rhubarb they should receive, would sooner take their physic at their ears than at their mouth. So is it in men, most of which are childish in the best things, till they be cradled in their graves,—glad they will be to hear the tales of Hercules, Achilles, Cyrus, Æneas; and, hearing them, must needs hear the right description of wisdom, valor, and justice; which, if they had been barely, that is to say philosophically, set out, they would swear they be brought to school again.

That imitation whereof poetry is, hath the most conveniency to nature of all other; insomuch that, as Aristotle saith, those things which in themselves are horrible, as cruel battles, unnatural monsters, are made in poetical imitation delightful. Truly, I have known men, that even with reading Amadis de Gaule, which, God knoweth, wanteth much of a perfect poesy, have found their hearts moved to the exercise of courtesy, liberality, and especially courage. Who readeth Æneas carrying old Anchises on his back, that wisheth not it were his fortune to perform so excellent an act? Whom do not

[22] "This is the work, this the labor."—Virgil, "Æneid," VI., 129.
[23] Margin.

those words of Turnus move, the tale of Turnus having planted his
image in the imagination?

Fugientem hæc terra videbit?
Usque adeone mori miserum est?[24]

Where the philosophers, as they scorn to delight, so must they be
content little to move—saving wrangling whether virtue be the chief
or the only good, whether the contemplative or the active life do
excel—which Plato and Boethius well knew, and therefore made
Mistress Philosophy very often borrow the masking raiment of Poesy.
For even those hard-hearted evil men who think virtue a school-
name, and know no other good but *indulgere genio,*[25] and therefore
despise the austere admonitions of the philosopher, and feel not the
inward reason they stand upon, yet will be content to be delighted,
which is all the good-fellow poet seemeth to promise; and so steal
to see the form of goodness—which seen, they cannot but love—ere
themselves be aware, as if they took a medicine of cherries.

Infinite proofs of the strange effects of this poetical invention
might be alleged; only two shall serve, which are so often remembered
as I think all men know them. The one of Menenius Agrippa, who,
when the whole people of Rome had resolutely divided themselves
from the senate, with apparent show of utter ruin, though he were,
for that time, an excellent orator, came not among them upon trust
either of figurative speeches or cunning insinuations, and much less
with far-fet maxims of philosophy, which, especially if they were
Platonic, they must have learned geometry before they could well
have conceived; but, forsooth, he behaves himself like a homely and
familiar poet. He telleth them a tale, that there was a time when all
the parts of the body made a mutinous conspiracy against the belly,
which they thought devoured the fruits of each other's labor; they
concluded they would let so unprofitable a spender starve. In the
end, to be short—for the tale is notorious, and as notorious that it
was a tale—with punishing the belly they plagued themselves. This,
applied by him, wrought such effect in the people, as I never read
that ever words brought forth but then so sudden and so good an

[24] "Shall this land see him fleeing? Is it so very wretched to die?"—Virgil,
"Æneid," XII., 645–6.
[25] "To give way to one's inclination."

alteration; for upon reasonable conditions a perfect reconcilement ensued.

The other is of Nathan the prophet, who, when the holy David had so far forsaken God as to confirm adultery with murder, when he was to do the tenderest office of a friend, in laying his own shame before his eyes,—sent by God to call again so chosen a servant, how doth he it but by telling of a man whose beloved lamb was ungratefully taken from his bosom? The application most divinely true, but the discourse itself feigned; which made David (I speak of the second and instrumental cause) as in a glass to see his own filthiness, as that heavenly Psalm of Mercy well testifieth.

By these, therefore, examples and reasons, I think it may be manifest that the poet, with that same hand of delight, doth draw the mind more effectually than any other art doth. And so a conclusion not unfitly ensueth: that as virtue is the most excellent resting-place for all worldly learning to make his end of, so poetry, being the most familiar to teach it, and most princely to move towards it, in the most excellent work is the most excellent workman.

But I am content not only to decipher him by his works—although works in commendation or dispraise must ever hold a high authority —but more narrowly will examine his parts; so that, as in a man, though all together may carry a presence full of majesty and beauty, perchance in some one defectious piece we may find a blemish.

Now in his parts, kinds, or species, as you list to term them, it is to be noted that some poesies have coupled together two or three kinds,—as tragical and comical, whereupon is risen the tragi-comical; some, in the like manner, have mingled prose and verse, as Sannazzaro and Boethius; some have mingled matters heroical and pastoral; but that cometh all to one in this question, for, if severed they be good, the conjunction cannot be hurtful. Therefore, perchance forgetting some, and leaving some as needless to be remembered, it shall not be amiss in a word to cite the special kinds, to see what faults may be found in the right use of them.

Is it then the pastoral poem which is misliked?—for perchance where the hedge is lowest they will soonest leap over. Is the poor pipe disdained, which sometimes out of Meliboeus' mouth can show the misery of people under hard lords and ravening soldiers, and

again, by Tityrus, what blessedness is derived to them that lie lowest
from the goodness of them that sit highest? sometimes, under the
pretty tales of wolves and sheep, can include the whole considerations of wrong-doing and patience; sometimes show that contention
for trifles can get but a trifling victory; where perchance a man may
see that even Alexander and Darius, when they strave who should
be cock of this world's dunghill, the benefit they got was that the
after-livers may say:

> Hæc memini et victum frustra contendere Thyrsim;
> Ex illo Corydon, Corydon est tempore nobis.[26]

Or is it the lamenting elegiac, which in a kind heart would move
rather pity than blame; who bewaileth, with the great philosopher
Heraclitus, the weakness of mankind and the wretchedness of the
world; who surely is to be praised, either for compassionate ac-
companying just causes of lamentation, or for rightly painting out
how weak be the passions of wofulness?

Is it the bitter and wholesome iambic, who rubs the galled mind,
in making shame the trumpet of villainy with bold and open crying
out against naughtiness?

Or the satiric? who

> Omne vafer vitium ridenti tangit amico;[27]

who sportingly never leaveth till he make a man laugh at folly, and
at length ashamed to laugh at himself, which he cannot avoid without avoiding the folly; who, while *circum præcordia ludit,*[28] giveth
us to feel how many headaches a passionate life bringeth us to,—
how, when all is done,

> Est Ulubris, animus si nos non deficit æquus.[29]

No, perchance it is the comic; whom naughty play-makers and
stage-keepers have justly made odious. To the argument of abuse

---

[26] "Such things I remember, and that the conquered Thyrsis strove in vain. From
that time Corydon is with us the Corydon."—Virgil, "Eclogues," VII., 69–70.

[27] "The sly fellow touches every vice while he makes his friend laugh."—Condensed
from Persius, "Sat.," I., 116.

[28] "He plays about his heartstrings."—Idem.

[29] "If we do not lack the equable temper, it is in Ulubrae" [that we may find hap-
piness]. Ulubrae was noted for its desolation.—Adapted from Horace, "Epict.," I.,
11, 30.

I will answer after. Only thus much now is to be said, that the comedy in an imitation of the common errors of our life, which he representeth in the most ridiculous and scornful sort that may be, so as it is impossible that any beholder can be content to be such a one. Now, as in geometry the oblique must be known as well as the right, and in arithmetic the odd as well as the even; so in the actions of our life who seeth not the filthiness of evil, wanteth a great foil to perceive the beauty of virtue. This doth the comedy handle so, in our private and domestical matters, as with hearing it we get, as it were, an experience what is to be looked for of a niggardly Demea, of a crafty Davus, of a flattering Gnatho, of a vain-glorious Thraso; and not only to know what effects are to be expected, but to know who be such, by the signifying badge given them by the comedian. And little reason hath any man to say that men learn evil by seeing it so set out; since, as I said before, there is no man living, but by the force truth hath in nature, no sooner seeth these men play their parts, but wisheth them *in pistrinum*,[30] although perchance the sack of his own faults lie so behind his back, that he seeth not himself to dance the same measure,—whereto yet nothing can more open his eyes than to find his own actions contemptibly set forth.

So that the right use of comedy will, I think, by nobody be blamed, and much less of the high and excellent tragedy, that openeth the greatest wounds, and showeth forth the ulcers that are covered with tissue; that maketh kings fear to be tyrants, and tyrants manifest their tyrannical humors; that with stirring the effects of admiration and commiseration teacheth the uncertainty of this world, and upon how weak foundations gilden roofs are builded; that maketh us know:

> Qui sceptra sævus duro imperio regit,
> Timet timentes, metus in auctorem redit.[31]

But how much it can move, Plutarch yieldeth a notable testimony of the abominable tyrant Alexander Pheræus; from whose eyes a tragedy, well made and represented, drew abundance of tears, who without all pity had murdered infinite numbers, and some of his

---

[30] "In the mill," where slaves were sent for punishment.
[31] "The savage king who wields the sceptre with cruel sway fears those who fear him, the dread returns upon the author's head."—Seneca, "Œdipus," 705-6.

own blood; so as he that was not ashamed to make matters for tragedies, yet could not resist the sweet violence of a tragedy. And if it wrought no further good in him, it was that he, in despite of himself, withdrew himself from hearkening to that which might mollify his hardened heart. But it is not the tragedy they do mislike, for it were too absurd to cast out so excellent a representation of whatsoever is most worthy to be learned.

Is it the lyric that most displeaseth, who with his tuned lyre and well-accorded voice, giveth praise, the reward of virtue, to virtuous acts; who giveth moral precepts and natural problems; who sometimes raiseth up his voice to the height of the heavens, in singing the lauds of the immortal God? Certainly I must confess mine own barbarousness; I never heard the old song of Percy and Douglas that I found not my heart moved more than with a trumpet; and yet it is sung but by some blind crowder, with no rougher voice than rude style; which being so evil apparelled in the dust and cobwebs of that uncivil age, what would it work, trimmed in the gorgeous eloquence of Pindar? In Hungary I have seen it the manner of all feasts, and other such meetings, to have songs of their ancestors' valor, which that right soldierlike nation think the chiefest kindlers of brave courage. The incomparable Lacedæmonians did not only carry that kind of music ever with them to the field, but even at home, as such songs were made, so were they all content to be singers of them; when the lusty men were to tell what they did, the old men what they had done, and the young men what they would do. And where a man may say that Pindar many times praiseth highly victories of small moment, matters rather of sport than virtue; as it may be answered, it was the fault of the poet, and not of the poetry, so indeed the chief fault was in the time and custom of the Greeks, who set those toys at so high a price that Philip of Macedon reckoned a horserace won at Olympus among his three fearful felicities. But as the unimitable Pindar often did, so is that kind most capable and most fit to awake the thoughts from the sleep of idleness, to embrace honorable enterprises.

There rests the heroical, whose very name, I think, should daunt all backbiters. For by what conceit can a tongue be directed to speak evil of that which draweth with it no less champions than Achilles,

Cyrus, Æneas, Turnus Tydeus, Rinaldo? who doth not only teach and move to a truth, but teacheth and moveth to the most high and excellent truth; who maketh magnanimity and justice shine through all misty fearfulness and foggy desires; who, if the saying of Plato and Tully be true, that who could see virtue would be wonderfully ravished with the love of her beauty, this man setteth her out to make her more lovely, in her holiday apparel, to the eye of any that will deign not to disdain until they understand. But if anything be already said in the defense of sweet poetry, all concurreth to the maintaining the heroical, which is not only a kind, but the best and most accomplished kind of poetry. For, as the image of each action stirreth and instructeth the mind, so the lofty image of such worthies most inflameth the mind with desire to be worthy, and informs with counsel how to be worthy. Only let Æneas be worn in the tablet of your memory, how he governeth himself in the ruin of his country; in the preserving his old father, and carrying away his religious ceremonies; in obeying the god's commandment to leave Dido, though not only all passionate kindness, but even the human consideration of virtuous gratefulness, would have craved other of him; how in storms, how in sports, how in war, how in peace, how a fugitive, how victorious, how besieged, how besieging, how to strangers, how to allies, how to enemies, how to his own; lastly, how in his inward self, and how in his outward government; and I think, in a mind most prejudiced with a prejudicating humor, he will be found in excellency fruitful,—yea, even as Horace saith, *melius Chrysippo et Crantore.*[32] But truly I imagine it falleth out with these poet-whippers as with some good women who often are sick, but in faith they cannot tell where. So the name of poetry is odious to them, but neither his cause nor effects, neither the sum that contains him nor the particularities descending from him, give any fast handle to their carping dispraise.

Since, then, poetry is of all human learnings the most ancient and of most fatherly antiquity, as from whence other learnings have taken their beginnings; since it is so universal that no learned nation doth despise it, nor barbarous nation is without it; since both Roman and

---

[32] "Better than Chrysippus and Crantor"—two distinguished philosophers.—Horace, "Epict.," I. 2, 4.

Greek gave divine names unto it, the one of "prophesying," the other of "making," and that indeed that name of "making" is fit for him, considering that whereas other arts retain themselves within their subjects, and receive, as it were, their being from it, the poet only bringeth his own stuff, and doth not learn a conceit out of a matter, but maketh matter for a conceit; since neither his description nor his end containeth any evil, the thing described cannot be evil; since his effects be so good as to teach goodness, and delight the learners of it; since therein—namely in moral doctrine, the chief of all knowledges—he doth not only far pass the historian, but for instructing is well nigh comparable to the philosopher, and for moving leaveth him behind him; since the Holy Scripture, wherein there is no uncleanness, hath whole parts in it poetical, and that even our Saviour Christ vouchsafed to use the flowers of it; since all his kinds are not only in their united forms, but in their several dissections fully commendable; I think, and think I think rightly, the laurel crown appointed for triumphant captains doth worthily, of all other learnings, honor the poet's triumph.

But because we have ears as well as tongues, and that the lightest reasons that may be will seem to weigh greatly, if nothing be put in the counter-balance, let us hear, and, as well as we can, ponder, what objections be made against this art, which may be worthy either of yielding or answering.

First, truly, I note not only in these μισομούσοι, poet-haters, but in all that kind of people who seek a praise by dispraising others, that they do prodigally spend a great many wandering words in quips and scoffs, carping and taunting at each thing which, by stirring the spleen, may stay the brain from a through-beholding the worthiness of the subject. Those kind of objections, as they are full of a very idle easiness—since there is nothing of so sacred a majesty but that an itching tongue may rub itself upon it—so deserve they no other answer, but, instead of laughing at the jest, to laugh at the jester. We know a playing wit can praise the discretion of an ass, the comfortableness of being in debt, and the jolly commodity of being sick of the plague. So of the contrary side, if we will turn Ovid's verse,

Ut lateat virtus proximitate mali,

"that good lie hid in nearness of the evil," Agrippa will be as merry in showing the vanity of science, as Erasmus was in commending of folly; neither shall any man or matter escape some touch of these smiling railers. But for Erasmus and Agrippa, they had another foundation than the superficial part would promise. Marry, these other pleasant fault-finders, who will correct the verb before they understand the noun, and confute others' knowledge before they confirm their own, I would have them only remember that scoffing cometh not of wisdom; so as the best title in true English they get with their merriments is to be called good fools,—for so have our grave forefathers ever termed that humorous kind of jesters.

But that which giveth greatest scope to their scorning humor is riming and versing. It is already said, and as I think truly said, it is not riming and versing that maketh poesy. One may be a poet without versing, and a versifier without poetry. But yet presuppose it were inseparable—as indeed it seemeth Scaliger judgeth—truly it were an inseparable commendation. For if *oratio* next to *ratio,* speech next to reason, be the greatest gift bestowed upon mortality, that cannot be praiseless which doth most polish that blessing of speech; which considereth each word, not only as a man may say by his forcible quality, but by his best-measured quantity; carrying even in themselves a harmony,—without, perchance, number, measure, order, proportion be in our time grown odious.

But lay aside the just praise it hath by being the only fit speech for music—music, I say, the most divine striker of the senses—thus much is undoubtedly true, that if reading be foolish without remembering, memory being the only treasurer of knowledge, those words which are fittest for memory are likewise most convenient for knowledge. Now that verse far exceedeth prose in the knitting up of the memory, the reason is manifest; the words, besides their delight, which hath a great affinity to memory, being so set, as one cannot be lost but the whole work fails; which, accusing itself, calleth the remembrance back to itself, and so most strongly confirmeth it. Besides, one word so, as it were, begetting another, as, be it in rime or measured verse, by the former a man shall have a near guess to the follower. Lastly, even they that have taught the art of memory have showed nothing so apt for it as a certain room divided into many places, well and thoroughly known; now that hath the verse in effect perfectly, every word having his natural seat, which seat must needs make the word remembered. But what needeth more in a thing so known to all men? Who is it that ever was a scholar that doth not carry away some verses of Virgil, Horace, or Cato, which in his youth he learned, and even to his old age serve him for hourly lessons? as:

Percontatorem fugito, nam garrulus idem est.[33]

Dum sibi quisque placet, credula turba sumus.[34]

But the fitness it hath for memory is notably proved by all delivery of arts, wherein, for the most part, from grammar to logic, mathematic, physic, and the rest, the rules chiefly necessary to be borne away are compiled in verses. So that verse being in itself sweet and orderly, and being best for memory, the only handle of knowledge, it must be in jest that any man can speak against it.

Now then go we to the most important imputations laid to the poor poets; for aught I can yet learn they are these.

First, that there being many other more fruitful knowledges, a man might better spend his time in them than in this.

Secondly, that it is the mother of lies.

Thirdly, that it is the nurse of abuse, infecting us with many pestilent desires, with a siren's sweetness drawing the mind to the serpent's tail of sinful fancies,—and herein especially comedies give the largest field to ear,[35] as Chaucer saith; how, both in other nations and in ours, before poets did soften us, we were full of courage, given to martial exercises, the pillars of manlike liberty, and not lulled asleep in shady idleness with poets' pastimes.

And, lastly and chiefly, they cry out with an open mouth, as if they had overshot Robin Hood, that Plato banished them out of his Commonwealth. Truly this is much, if there be much truth in it.

First, to the first, that a man might better spend his time is a reason indeed; but it doth, as they say, but *petere principium*.[36] For

---

[33] "Avoid an inquisitive man, for he is sure to be a prattler."—Horace, "Epist.," I. 18. 69.
[34] "While each is pleasing himself, we are a credulous crowd."—Ovid, "Rem. Amoris," 686.   [35] Plough.   [36] Beg the question.

if it be, as I affirm, that no learning is so good as that which teacheth and moveth to virtue, and that none can both teach and move thereto so much as poesy, then is the conclusion manifest that ink and paper cannot be to a more profitable purpose employed. And certainly, though a man should grant their first assumption, it should follow, methinks, very unwillingly, that good is not good because better is better. But I still and utterly deny that there is sprung out of earth a more fruitful knowledge.

To the second, therefore, that they should be the principal liars, I answer paradoxically, but truly, I think truly, that of all writers under the sun the poet is the least liar; and though he would, as a poet can scarcely be a liar. The astronomer, with his cousin the geometrician, can hardly escape when they take upon them to measure the height of the stars. How often, think you, do the physicians lie, when they aver things good for sicknesses, which afterwards send Charon a great number of souls drowned in a potion before they come to his ferry? And no less of the rest which take upon them to affirm. Now for the poet, he nothing affirmeth, and therefore never lieth. For, as I take it, to lie is to affirm that to be true which is false; so as the other artists, and especially the historian, affirming many things, can, in the cloudy knowledge of mankind, hardly escape from many lies. But the poet, as I said before, never affirmeth. The poet never maketh any circles about your imagination, to conjure you to believe for true what he writeth. He citeth not authorities of other histories, but even for his entry calleth the sweet Muses to inspire into him a good invention; in troth, not laboring to tell you what is or is not, but what should or should not be. And therefore though he recount things not true, yet because he telleth them not for true he lieth not; without we will say that Nathan lied in his speech, before alleged, to David; which, as a wicked man durst scarce say, so think I none so simple would say that Æsop lied in the tales of his beasts; for who thinketh that Æsop wrote it for actually true, were well worthy to have his name chronicled among the beasts he writeth of. What child is there that, coming to a play, and seeing Thebes written in great letters upon an old door, doth believe that it is Thebes? If then a man can arrive at that child's-age, to know that the poet's persons and doings are but pictures what should be, and not stories what have been, they will never give the lie to things not affirmatively but allegorically and figuratively written. And therefore, as in history looking for truth, they may go away full-fraught with falsehood, so in poesy looking but for fiction, they shall use the narration but as an imaginative ground-plot of a profitable invention. But hereto is replied that the poets give names to men they write of, which argueth a conceit of an actual truth, and so, not being true, proveth a falsehood. And doth the lawyer lie then, when, under the names of John of the Stile, and John of the Nokes, he putteth his case? But that is easily answered: their naming of men is but to make their picture the more lively, and not to build any history. Painting men, they cannot leave men nameless. We see we cannot play at chess but that we must give names to our chess-men; and yet, me thinks, he were a very partial champion of truth that would say we lied for giving a piece of wood the reverend title of a bishop. The poet nameth Cyrus and Æneas no other way than to show what men of their fames, fortunes, and estates should do.

Their third is, how much it abuseth men's wit, training it to wanton sinfulness and lustful love. For indeed that is the principal, if not the only, abuse I can hear alleged. They say the comedies rather teach than reprehend amorous conceits. They say the lyric is larded with passionate sonnets, the elegiac weeps the want of his mistress, and that even to the heroical Cupid hath ambitiously climbed. Alas! Love, I would thou couldst as well defend thyself as thou canst offend others! I would those on whom thou dost attend could either put thee away, or yield good reason why they keep thee! But grant love of beauty to be a beastly fault, although it be very hard, since only man, and no beast, hath that gift to discern beauty; grant that lovely name of Love to deserve all hateful reproaches, although even some of my masters the philosophers spent a good deal of their lamp-oil in setting forth the excellency of it; grant, I say, whatsoever they will have granted,—that not only love, but lust, but vanity, but, if they list, scurrility, possesseth many leaves of the poets' books; yet think I when this is granted, they will find their sentence may with good manners put the last words foremost, and not say that poetry abuseth man's wit, but that man's wit abuseth poetry. For I will not deny, but that man's wit may make poesy, which should be εἰκαστική, which some learned have defined, figuring forth good things, to be φανταστική, which doth contrariwise infect the fancy with unworthy objects; as the painter that should give to the eye either some excellent perspective, or some fine picture fit for building or fortification, or containing in it some notable example, as Abraham sacrificing his son Isaac, Judith killing Holofernes, David fighting with Goliath, may leave those, and please an ill-pleased eye with wanton shows of better-hidden matters. But what! shall the abuse of a thing make the right use odious? Nay, truly, though I yield that poesy may not only be abused, but that being abused, by the reason of his sweet charming force, it can do more hurt than any other army of words, yet shall it be so far from concluding that the abuse should give reproach to the abused, that contrariwise it is a good reason, that whatsoever, being abused, doth most harm, being rightly used—and upon the right use each thing receiveth his title—doth most good. Do we not see the skill of physic, the best rampire to our often-assaulted bodies, being abused, teach poison, the most violent destroyer? Doth not knowledge of law, whose end is to even and right all things, being abused, grow the crooked fosterer of horrible injuries? Doth not, to go in the highest, God's word abused breed heresy, and his name abused become blasphemy? Truly a needle cannot do much hurt, and as truly—with leave of ladies be it spoken—it cannot do much good. With a sword thou mayst kill thy father, and with a sword thou mayst defend thy prince and country. So that, as in their calling poets the fathers of lies they say nothing, so in this their argument of abuse they prove the commendation.

They allege herewith, that before poets began to be in price our nation hath set their hearts' delight upon action, and not upon imagination; rather doing things worthy to be written, than writing things fit to be done. What that before-time was. I think scarcely Sphinx can tell; since no memory is so ancient that hath the precedence of poetry. And certain it is that, in our plainest homeliness, yet never was the Albion nation without poetry. Marry, this argument, though it be levelled against poetry, yet is it indeed a chainshot against all learning,—or bookishness, as they commonly term it.

Of such mind were certain Goths, of whom it is written that, having in the spoil of a famous city taken a fair library, one hangman—belike fit to execute the fruits of their wits—who had murdered a great number of bodies, would have set fire in it. "No," said another very gravely, "take heed what you do; for while they are busy about these toys, we shall with more leisure conquer their countries." This, indeed, is the ordinary doctrine of ignorance, and many words sometimes I have heard spent in it; but because this reason is generally against all learning, as well as poetry, or rather all learning but poetry; because it were too large a digression to handle, or at least too superfluous, since it is manifest that all government of action is to be gotten by knowledge, and knowledge best by gathering many knowledges, which is reading; I only, with Horace, to him that is of that opinion

Jubeo stultum esse libenter;[37]

for as for poetry itself, it is the freest from this objection, for poetry is the companion of the camps. I dare undertake, Orlando Furioso or honest King Arthur will never displease a soldier; but the quiddity of *ens,* and *prima materia,* will hardly agree with a corselet. And therefore, as I said in the beginning, even Turks and Tartars are delighted with poets. Homer, a Greek, flourished before Greece flourished; and if to a slight conjecture a conjecture may be opposed, truly it may seem, that as by him their learned men took almost their first light of knowledge, so their active men received their first motions of courage. Only Alexander's example may serve, who by Plutarch is accounted of such virtue, that Fortune was not his guide but his footstool; whose acts speak for him, though Plutarch did not; indeed the phœnix of warlike princes. This Alexander left his schoolmaster, living Aristotle, behind him, but took dead Homer with him. He put the philosopher Callisthenes to death for his seeming philosophical, indeed mutinous, stubbornness; but the chief thing he was ever heard to wish for was that Homer had been alive. He well found he received more bravery of mind by the pattern of Achilles, than by hearing the definition of fortitude. And therefore if Cato misliked Fulvius for carrying Ennius with him to the field,

[37] "I gladly bid him be a fool."—Adapted from Horace, "Sat.," I., 1, 63.

it may be answered that if Cato misliked it, the noble Fulvius liked
it, or else he had not done it. For it was not the excellent Cato
Uticensis, whose authority I would much more have reverenced; but
it was the former, in truth a bitter punisher of faults, but else a man
that had never sacrificed to the Graces. He misliked and cried out
upon all Greek learning; and yet, being fourscore years old, began
to learn it, belike fearing that Pluto understood not Latin. Indeed,
the Roman laws allowed no person to be carried to the wars but he
that was in the soldiers' roll. And therefore though Cato misliked
his unmustered person, he misliked not his work. And if he had,
Scipio Nasica, judged by common consent the best Roman, loved
him. Both the other Scipio brothers, who had by their virtues no
less surnames than of Asia and Afric, so loved him that they caused
his body to be buried in their sepulchre. So as Cato's authority being
but against his person, and that answered with so far greater than
himself, is herein of no validity.

But now, indeed, my burthen is great, that Plato's name is laid
upon me, whom I must confess, of all philosophers I have ever
esteemed most worthy of reverence; and with great reason, since of
all philosophers he is the most poetical; yet if he will defile the
fountain out of which his flowing streams have proceeded, let us
boldly examine with what reasons he did it.

First, truly, a man might maliciously object that Plato, being a
philosopher, was a natural enemy of poets. For, indeed, after the
philosophers had picked out of the sweet mysteries of poetry the
right discerning true points of knowledge, they forthwith, putting
it in method, and making a school-art of that which the poets did
only teach by a divine delightfulness, beginning to spurn at their
guides, like ungrateful prentices were not content to set up shops
for themselves, but sought by all means to discredit their masters;
which by the force of delight being barred them, the less they could
overthrow them the more they hated them. For, indeed, they found
for Homer seven cities strave who should have him for their citizen;
where many cities banished philosophers, as not fit members to live
among them. For only repeating certain of Euripides' verses, many
Athenians had their lives saved of the Syracusans, where the Athenians themselves thought many philosophers unworthy to live.

Certain poets as Simonides and Pindar, had so prevailed with Heiro the First, that of a tyrant they made him a just king; where Plato could do so little with Dionysius, that he himself of a philosopher was made a slave. But who should do thus, I confess, should requite the objections made against poets with like cavillations against philosophers; as likewise one should do that should bid one read Phædrus or Symposium in Plato, or the Discourse of Love in Plutarch, and see whether any poet do authorize abominable filthiness, as they do.

Again, a man might ask out of what commonwealth Plato doth banish them. In sooth, thence where he himself alloweth community of women. So as belike this banishment grew not for effeminate wantonness, since little should poetical sonnets be hurtful when a man might have what woman he listed. But I honor philosophical instructions, and bless the wits which bred them, so as they be not abused, which is likewise stretched to poetry. Saint Paul himself, who yet, for the credit of poets, allegeth twice two poets, and one of them by the name of a prophet, setteth a watchword upon philosophy,—indeed upon the abuse. So doth Plato upon the abuse, not upon poetry. Plato found fault that the poets of his time filled the world with wrong opinions of the gods, making light tales of that unspotted essence, and therefore would not have the youth depraved with such opinions. Herein may much be said; let this suffice: the poets did not induce such opinions, but did imitate those opinions already induced. For all the Greek stories can well testify that the very religion of that time stood upon many and many-fashioned gods; not taught so by the poets, but followed according to their nature of imitation. Who list may read in Plutarch the discourses of Isis and Osiris, of the Cause why Oracles ceased, of the Divine Providence, and see whether the theology of that nation stood not upon such dreams,—which the poets indeed superstitiously observed; and truly, since they had not the light of Christ, did much better in it than the philosophers, who, shaking off superstition, brought in atheism.

Plato therefore, whose authority I had much rather justly construe than unjustly resist, meant not in general of poets, in those words of which Julius Scaliger saith, *Qua authoritate barbari quidam atque*

hispidi, abuti velint ad poetas e republica exigendos;[38] but only meant
to drive out those wrong opinions of the Deity, whereof now, without
further law, Christianity hath taken away all the hurtful belief, perchance, as he thought, nourished by the then esteemed poets. And
a man need go no further than to Plato himself to know his meaning; who, in his dialogue called Ion, giveth high and rightly divine
commendation unto poetry. So as Plato, banishing the abuse, not
the thing, not banishing it, but giving due honor unto it, shall be
our patron and not our adversary. For, indeed, I had much rather,
since truly I may do it, show their mistaking of Plato, under whose
lion's skin they would make an ass-like braying against poesy, than
go about to overthrow his authority; whom, the wiser a man is, the
more just cause he shall find to have in admiration; especially since
he attributeth unto poesy more than myself do, namely to be a very
inspiring of a divine force, far above man's wit, as in the forenamed
dialogue is apparent.

Of the other side, who would show the honors have been by the
best sort of judgments granted them, a whole sea of examples would
present themselves: Alexanders, Cæsars, Scipios, all favorers of poets;
Lælius, called the Roman Socrates, himself a poet, so as part of
Heautontimoroumenos in Terence was supposed to be made by him.
And even the Greek Socrates, whom Apollo confirmed to be the
only wise man, is said to have spent part of his old time in putting
Æsop's Fables into verses; and therefore full evil should it become
his scholar, Plato, to put such words in his master's mouth against
poets. But what needs more? Aristotle writes the Art of Poesy; and
why, if it should not be written? Plutarch teacheth the use to be
gathered of them; and how, if they should not be read? And who
reads Plutarch's either history or philosophy, shall find he trimmeth
both their garments with guards[39] of poesy. But I list not to defend
poesy with the help of his underling historiography. Let it suffice
that it is a fit soil for praise to dwell upon; and what dispraise may
set upon it, is either easily overcome, or transformed into just commendation.

So that since the excellencies of it may be so easily and so justly

[38] "Which authority [*i. e.,* Plato's] some barbarous and rude persons wish to
abuse, in order to banish poets from the state."—Scaliger, "Poetics," 5. a, 1.
[39] Ornaments.

confirmed, and the low-creeping objections so soon trodden down: it not being an art of lies, but of true doctrine; not of effeminateness, but of notable stirring of courage; not of abusing man's wit, but of strengthening man's wit; not banished, but honored by Plato; let us rather plant more laurels for to engarland our poets' heads—which honor of being laureate, as besides them only triumphant captains were, is a sufficient authority to show the price they ought to be held in—than suffer the ill-savored breath of such wrong speakers once to blow upon the clear springs of poesy.

But since I have run so long a career in this matter, methinks, before I give my pen a full stop, it shall be but a little more lost time to inquire why England, the mother of excellent minds, should be grown so hard a stepmother to poets; who certainly in wit ought to pass all others, since all only proceedeth from their wit, being indeed makers of themselves, not takers of others. How can I but exclaim,

> Musa, mihi causas memora, quo numine læso?[40]

Sweet poesy! that hath anciently had kings, emperors, senators, great captains, such as, besides a thousand others, David, Adrian, Sophocles, Germanicus, not only to favor poets, but to be poets; and of our nearer times can present for her patrons a Robert, King of Sicily; the great King Francis of France; King James of Scotland; such cardinals as Bembus and Bibbiena; such famous preachers and teachers as Beza and Melancthon; so learned philosophers as Fracastorius and Scaliger; so great orators as Pontanus and Muretus; so piercing wits as George Buchanan; so grave counsellors as—besides many, but before all—that Hospital of France, than whom, I think, that realm never brought forth a more accomplished judgment more firmly builded upon virtue; I say these, with numbers of others, not only to read others' poesies but to poetize for others' reading. That poesy, thus embraced in all other places, should only find in our time a hard welcome in England, I think the very earth lamenteth it, and therefore decketh our soil with fewer laurels than it was accustomed. For heretofore poets have in England

---

[40] "O Muse, recall to me the causes by which her divine will had been insulted."— Virgil, "Æneid," I. 12.

also flourished; and, which is to be noted, even in those times when the trumpet of Mars did sound loudest. And now that an over-faint quietness should seem to strew the house for poets, they are almost in as good reputation as the mountebanks at Venice. Truly even that, as of the one side it giveth great praise to poesy, which, like Venus—but to better purpose—hath rather be troubled in the net with Mars, than enjoy the homely quiet of Vulcan; so serves it for a piece of a reason why they are less grateful to idle England, which now can scarce endure the pain of a pen. Upon this necessarily followeth, that base men with servile wits undertake it, who think it enough if they can be rewarded of the printer. And so as Epaminondas is said, with the honor of his virtue to have made an office, by his exercising it, which before was contemptible, to become highly respected; so these men, no more but setting their names to it, by their own disgracefulness disgrace the most graceful poesy. For now, as if all the Muses were got with child to bring forth bastard poets, without any commission they do post over the banks of Helicon, till they make their readers more weary than post-horses; while, in the meantime, they,

Queis meliore luto finxit præcordia Titan,[41]

are better content to suppress the outflowings of their wit, than by publishing them to be accounted knights of the same order.

But I that, before ever I durst aspire unto the dignity, am admitted into the company of the paper-blurrers, do find the very true cause of our wanting estimation is want of desert, taking upon us to be poets in despite of Pallas.[42] Now wherein we want desert were a thank-worthy labor to express; but if I knew, I should have mended myself. But as I never desired the title, so have I neglected the means to come by it; only, overmastered by some thoughts, I yielded an inky tribute unto them. Marry, they that delight in poesy itself should seek to know what they do and how they do; and especially look themselves in an unflattering glass of reason, if they be inclinable unto it. For poesy must not be drawn by the ears, it must be gently led, or rather it must lead; which was partly the cause that made the

[41] Upon hearts the Titan has formed from better clay."—Adapted from "Juvenal," XIV. 34–5.   [42] Though lacking inspiration.

ancient learned affirm it was a divine gift, and no human skill, since all other knowledges lie ready for any that hath strength of wit, a poet no industry can make if his own genius be not carried into it. And therefore is it an old proverb: *Orator fit, poeta nascitur.*[43] Yet confess I always that, as the fertilest ground must be manured,[44] so must the highest-flying wit have a Dædalus to guide him. That Dædalus, they say, both in this and in other, hath three wings to bear itself up into the air of due commendation: that is, art, imitation, and exercise. But these neither artificial rules nor imitative patterns, we much cumber ourselves withal. Exercise indeed we do, but that very fore-backwardly, for where we should exercise to know, we exercise as having known; and so is our brain delivered of much matter which never was begotten by knowledge. For there being two principal parts, matter to be expressed by words, and words to express the matter, in neither we use art or imitation rightly. Our matter is *quodlibet* indeed, though wrongly performing Ovid's verse,

Quicquid conabar dicere, versus erat;[45]

never marshalling it into any assured rank, that almost the readers cannot tell where to find themselves.

Chaucer, undoubtedly, did excellently in his Troilus and Cressida; of whom, truly, I know not whether to marvel more, either that he in that misty time could see so clearly, or that we in this clear age walk so stumblingly after him. Yet had he great wants, fit to be forgiven in so reverend antiquity. I account the Mirror of Magistrates meetly furnished of beautiful parts; and in the Earl of Surrey's lyrics many things tasting of a noble birth, and worthy of a noble mind. The Shepherd's Calendar hath much poetry in his eclogues, indeed worthy the reading, if I be not deceived. That same framing of his style to an old rustic language I dare not allow, since neither Theocritus in Greek, Virgil in Latin, nor Sannazzaro in Italian did affect it. Besides these, I do not remember to have seen but few (to speak boldly) printed, that have poetical sinews in them. For proof whereof, let but most of the verses be put in prose, and then ask the meaning, and it will be found that one verse did but beget

[43] "The orator is made, the poet is born."   [44] Cultivated.
[45] "Whatever I tried to say was poetry."—Changed from Ovid, "Tristia," IV. 10, 26.

another, without ordering at the first what should be at the last; which becomes a confused mass of words, with a tinkling sound of rime, barely accompanied with reason.

Our tragedies and comedies not without cause cried out against, observing rules neither of honest civility nor of skilful poetry, excepting Gorboduc,—again I say of those that I have seen. Which notwithstanding as it is full of stately speeches and well-sounding phrases, climbing to the height of Seneca's style, and as full of notable morality, which it doth most delightfully teach, and so obtain the very end of poesy; yet in truth it is very defectious in the circumstances, which grieveth me, because it might not remain as an exact model of all tragedies. For it is faulty both in place and time, the two necessary companions of all corporal actions. For where the stage should always represent but one place, and the uttermost time presupposed in it should be, both by Aristotle's precept and common reason, but one day; there is both many days and many places inartificially imagined.

But if it be so in Gorboduc, how much more in all the rest? where you shall have Asia of the one side, and Afric of the other, and so many other under-kingdoms, that the player, when he cometh in, must ever begin with telling where he is, or else the tale will not be conceived. Now ye shall have three ladies walk to gather flowers, and then we must believe the stage to be a garden. By and by we hear news of shipwreck in the same place, and then we are to blame if we accept it not for a rock. Upon the back of that comes out a hideous monster with fire and smoke, and then the miserable beholders are bound to take it for a cave. While in the mean time two armies fly in, represented with four swords and bucklers, and then what hard heart will not receive it for a pitched field?

Now of time they are much more liberal. For ordinary it is that two young princes fall in love; after many traverses she is got with child, delivered of a fair boy, he is lost, groweth a man, falleth in love, and is ready to get another child,—and all this in two hours' space; which how absurd it is in sense even sense may imagine, and art hath taught, and all ancient examples justified, and at this day the ordinary players in Italy will not err in. Yet will some bring in an example of Eunuchus in Terence, that containeth matter of two days, yet far short of twenty years. True it is, and so was it to be played in two days, and so fitted to the time it set forth. And though Plautus have in one place done amiss, let us hit with him, and not miss with him. But they will say, How then shall we set forth a story which containeth both many places and many times? And do they not know that a tragedy is tied to the laws of poesy, and not of history; not bound to follow the story, but having liberty either to feign a quite new matter, or to frame the history to the most tragical conveniency? Again, many things may be told which cannot be showed,—if they know the difference betwixt reporting and representing. As for example I may speak, though I am here, of Peru, and in speech digress from that to the description of Calicut; but in action I cannot represent it without Pacolet's horse. And so was the manner the ancients took, by some *Nuntius*[46] to recount things done in former time or other place.

Lastly, if they will represent a history, they must not, as Horace saith, begin *ab ovo*,[47] but they must come to the principal point of that one action which they will represent. By example this will be best expressed. I have a story of young Polydorus, delivered for safety's sake, with great riches, by his father Priamus to Polymnestor, King of Thrace, in the Trojan war time. He, after some years, hearing the overthrow of Priamus, for to make the treasure his own murdereth the child; the body of the child is taken up by Hecuba; she, the same day, findeth a sleight to be revenged most cruelly of the tyrant. Where now would one of our tragedy writers begin, but with the delivery of the child? Then should he sail over into Thrace, and so spend I know not how many years, and travel numbers of places. But where doth Euripides? Even with the finding of the body, leaving the rest to be told by the spirit of Polydorus. This needs no further to be enlarged; the dullest wit may conceive it.

But, besides these gross absurdities, how all their plays be neither right tragedies nor right comedies, mingling kings and clowns, not because the matter so carrieth it, but thrust in the clown by head and shoulders to play a part in majestical matters, with neither decency nor discretion; so as neither the admiration and commiseration, nor the right sportfulness, is by their mongrel tragi-comedy

[46] Messenger.   [47] From the egg.

obtained. I know Apuleius did somewhat so, but that is a thing recounted with space of time, not represented in one moment; and I know the ancients have one or two examples of tragi-comedies, as Plautus hath Amphytrio. But, if we mark them well, we shall find that they never, or very daintily, match hornpipes and funerals. So falleth it out that, having indeed no right comedy in that comical part of our tragedy, we have nothing but scurrility, unworthy of any chaste ears, or some extreme show of doltishness, indeed fit to lift up a loud laughter, and nothing else; where the whole tract of a comedy should be full of delight, as the tragedy should be still maintained in a well-raised admiration.

But our comedians think there is no delight without laughter, which is very wrong; for though laughter may come with delight, yet cometh it not of delight, as though delight should be the cause of laughter; but well may one thing breed both together. Nay, rather in themselves they have, as it were, a kind of contrariety. For delight we scarcely do, but in things that have a conveniency to ourselves, or to the general nature; laughter almost ever cometh of things most disproportioned to ourselves and nature. Delight hath a joy in it either permanent or present; laughter hath only a scornful tickling. For example, we are ravished with delight to see a fair woman, and yet are far from being moved to laughter. We laugh at deformed creatures, wherein certainly we cannot delight. We delight in good chances, we laugh at mischances. We delight to hear the happiness of our friends and country, at which he were worthy to be laughed at that would laugh. We shall, contrarily, laugh sometimes to find a matter quite mistaken and go down the hill against the bias, in the mouth of some such men, as for the respect of them one shall be heartily sorry he cannot choose but laugh, and so is rather pained than delighted with laughter. Yet deny I not but that they may go well together. For as in Alexander's picture well set out we delight without laughter, and in twenty mad antics we laugh without delight; so in Hercules, painted, with his great beard and furious countenance, in woman's attire, spinning at Omphale's commandment, it breedeth both delight and laughter; for the representing of so strange a power in love, procureth delight, and the scornfulness of the action stirreth laughter.

But I speak to this purpose, that all the end of the comical part be not upon such scornful matters as stir laughter only, but mixed with it that delightful teaching which is the end of poesy. And the great fault, even in that point of laughter, and forbidden plainly by Aristotle, is that they stir laughter in sinful things, which are rather execrable than ridiculous; or in miserable, which are rather to be pitied than scorned. For what is it to make folks gape at a wretched beggar or a beggarly clown, or, against law of hospitality, to jest at strangers because they speak not English so well as we do? what do we learn? since it is certain:

> Nil habet infelix paupertas durius in se,
> Quam quod ridiculos homines facit.[48]

But rather a busy loving courtier; a heartless threatening Thraso; a self-wise-seeming schoolmaster; a wry transformed traveller: these if we saw walk in stage-names, which we play naturally, therein were delightful laughter and teaching delightfulness,—as in the other, the tragedies of Buchanan do justly bring forth a divine admiration.

But I have lavished out too many words of this playmatter. I do it, because as they are excelling parts of poesy, so is there none so much used in England, and none can be more pitifully abused; which, like an unmannerly daughter, showing a bad education, causeth her mother Poesy's honesty to be called in question.

Other sorts of poetry almost have we none, but that lyrical kind of songs and sonnets, which, Lord if he gave us so good minds, how well it might be employed, and with how heavenly fruits both private and public, in singing the praises of the immortal beauty, the immortal goodness of that God who giveth us hands to write, and wits to conceive!—of which we might well want words, but never matter; of which we could turn our eyes to nothing, but we should ever have new-budding occasions.

But truly, many of such writings as come under the banner of unresistible love, if I were a mistress would never persuade me they were in love; so coldly they apply fiery speeches, as men that had

---

[48] "Unhappy poverty has nothing in it harder than this, that it makes men ridiculous."—Juvenal, "Satires," III. 152–3.

rather read lovers' writings, and so caught up certain swelling phrases—which hang together like a man which once told me the wind was at north-west and by south, because he would be sure to name winds enough—than that in truth they feel those passions, which easily, as I think, may be bewrayed by that same forcibleness, or *energia* (as the Greeks call it) of the writer. But let this be a sufficient, though short note, that we miss the right use of the material point of poesy.

Now for the outside of it, which is words, or (as I may term it) diction, it is even well worse, so is that honey-flowing matron eloquence apparelled or rather disguised, in a courtesan-like painted affectation: one time with so farfet[49] words, that many seem monsters—but must seem strangers—to any poor Englishman; another time with coursing of a letter,[50] as if they were bound to follow the method of a dictionary; another time with figures and flowers extremely winter-starved.

But I would this fault were only peculiar to versifiers, and had not as large possession among prose-printers, and, which is to be marvelled, among many scholars, and, which is to be pitied, among some preachers. Truly I could wish—if at least I might be so bold to wish in a thing beyond the reach of my capacity—the diligent imitators of Tully and Demosthenes (most worthy to be imitated) did not so much keep Nizolian paper-books of their figures and phrases, as by attentive translation, as it were devour them whole, and make them wholly theirs. For now they cast sugar and spice upon every dish that is served to the table; like those Indians, not content to wear ear-rings at the fit and natural place of the ears, but they will thrust jewels through their nose and lips, because they will be sure to be fine. Tully, when he was to drive out Catiline as it were with a thunderbolt of eloquence, often used that figure of repetition, as *Vivit. Vivit? Immo vero etiam in senatum venit,*[51] etc. Indeed, inflamed with a well-grounded rage, he would have his words, as it were, double out of his mouth; and so do that artificially, which we see men in choler do naturally. And we, having noted the grace of those words, hale them in sometime to a familiar epistle,

---

[49] Far-fetched.   [50] Alliteration.
[51] "He lives. Lives? Ay, he even comes to the Senate."—Cicero, "Catiline," I. 2.

when it were too much choler to be choleric. How well store of
similiter cadences[52] doth sound with the gravity of the pulpit, I
would but invoke Demosthenes' soul to tell, who with a rare dainti-
ness useth them. Truly they have made me think of the sophister
that with too much subtility would prove two eggs three, and though
he might be counted a sophister, had none for his labor. So these
men bringing in such a kind of eloquence, well may they obtain an
opinion of a seeming fineness, but persuade few,—which should be
the end of their fineness.

Now for similitudes in certain printed discourses, I think all
herbarists, all stories of beasts, fowls, and fishes are rifled up, that
they may come in multitudes to wait upon any of our conceits,
which certainly is as absurd a surfeit to the ears as is possible. For
the force of a similitude not being to prove any thing to a contrary
disputer, but only to explain to a willing hearer; when that is done,
the rest is a most tedious prattling, rather overswaying the memory
from the purpose whereto they were applied, than any whit informing the judgment, already either satisfied or by similitudes not to
be satisfied.

For my part, I do not doubt, when Antonius and Crassus, the
great forefathers of Cicero in eloquence, the one (as Cicero testifieth
of them) pretended not to know art, the other not to set by it, because[53] with a plain sensibleness they might win credit of popular
ears, which credit is the nearest step to persuasion, which persuasion
is the chief mark of oratory,—I do not doubt, I say, but that they
used these knacks, very sparingly; which who doth generally use
any man may see doth dance to his own music, and so be noted by
the audience more careful to speak curiously than truly. Undoubtedly (at least to my opinion undoubtedly) I have found in
divers small-learned courtiers a more sound style than in some
professors of learning; of which I can guess no other cause, but
that the courtier following that which by practice he findeth fittest
to nature, therein, though he know it not, doth according to art,
though not by art; where the other, using art to show art and not to
hide art—as in these cases he should do—flieth from nature, and indeed abuseth art.

[52] *E. g.,* rhyme.   [53] In order that.

THE DEFENSE OF POESY

But what! me thinks I deserve to be pounded for straying from poetry to oratory. But both have such an affinity in the wordish consideration, that I think this digression will make my meaning receive the fuller understanding:—which is not to take upon me to teach poets how they should do, but only, finding myself sick among the rest, to show some one or two spots of the common infection grown among the most part of writers; that, acknowledging ourselves somewhat awry, we may bend to the right use both of matter and manner: whereto our language giveth us great occasion, being, indeed, capable of any excellent exercising of it.

I know some will say it is a mingled language. And why not so much the better, taking the best of both the other? Another will say it wanteth grammar. Nay, truly, it hath that praise that it wanteth not grammar. For grammar it might have, but it needs it not; being so easy in itself, and so void of those cumbersome differences of cases, genders, moods, and tenses, which, I think, was a piece of the Tower of Babylon's curse, that a man should be put to school to learn his mother-tongue. But for the uttering sweetly and properly the conceits of the mind, which is the end of speech, that hath it equally with any other tongue in the world; and is particularly happy in compositions of two or three words together, near the Greek, far beyond the Latin,—which is one of the greatest beauties that can be in a language.

Now of versifying there are two sorts, the one ancient, the other modern. The ancient marked the quantity of each syllable, and according to that framed his verse; the modern observing only number, with some regard of the accent, the chief life of it standeth in that like sounding of the words, which we call rime. Whether of these be the more excellent would bear many speeches; the ancient no doubt more fit for music, both words and tune observing quantity; and more fit lively to express divers passions, by the low or lofty sound of the well-weighed syllable. The latter likewise with his rime striketh a certain music to the ear; and, in fine, since it doth delight, though by another way, it obtaineth the same purpose; there being in either, sweetness, and wanting in neither, majesty. Truly the English, before any other vulgar language I know, is fit for both sorts. For, for the ancient, the Italian is so full of vowels that it must ever be cumbered with elisions; the Dutch so, of the other side, with consonants, that they cannot yield the sweet sliding fit for a verse. The French in his whole language hath not one word that hath his accent in the last syllable saving two, called antepenultima, and little more hath the Spanish; and therefore very gracelessly may they use dactyls. The English is subject to none of these defects. Now for rime,[54] though we do not observe quantity, yet we observe the accent very precisely, which other languages either cannot do, or will not do so absolutely. That cæsura, or breathing-place in the midst of the verse, neither Italian nor Spanish have, the French and we never almost fail of.

Lastly, even the very rime itself the Italian cannot put in the last syllable, by the French named the masculine rime, but still in the next to the last, which the French call the female, or the next before that, which the Italians term *sdrucciola*. The example of the former is *buono: suono;* of the *sdrucciola* is *femina: semina*. The French, of the other side, hath both the male, as *bon: son,* and the female, as *plaise: taise; but the sdrucciola* he hath not. Where the English hath all three, as *due: true, father: rather, motion: potion;* with much more which might be said, but that already I find the triflingness of this discourse is much too much enlarged.

So that since the ever praiseworthy poesy is full of virtue-breeding delightfulness, and void of no gift that ought to be in the noble name of learning; since the blames laid against it are either false or feeble; since the cause why it is not esteemed in England is the fault of poet-apes, not poets; since, lastly, our tongue is most fit to honor poesy, and to be honored by poesy; I conjure you all that have had the evil luck to read this ink-wasting toy of mine, even in the name of the Nine Muses, no more to scorn the sacred mysteries of poesy; no more to laugh at the name of poets, as though they were next inheritors to fools; no more to jest at the reverend title of "a rimer"; but to believe, with Aristotle, that they were the ancient treasurers of the Grecians' divinity; to believe, with Bembus, that they were first bringers-in of all civility; to believe, with Scaliger, that no philosopher's precepts can sooner make you an honest man than the reading of Virgil; to believe, with Clauserus, the translator of

[54] Rhythm is meant.

Cornutus, that it pleased the Heavenly Deity by Hesiod and Homer, under the veil of fables, to give us all knowledge, logic, rhetoric, philosophy natural and moral, and *quid non?* to believe, with me, that there are many mysteries contained in poetry which of purpose were written darkly, lest by profane wits it should be abused; to believe, with Landino, that they are so beloved of the gods, that whatsoever they write proceeds of a divine fury; lastly, to believe themselves, when they tell you they will make you immortal by their verses.

Thus doing, your name shall flourish in the printers' shops. Thus doing, you shall be of kin to many a poetical preface. Thus doing, you shall be most fair, most rich, most wise, most all; you shall dwell upon superlatives. Thus doing, though you be *libertino patre natus,*[55] you shall suddenly grow *Herculea proles,*[56]

Si quid mea carmina possunt.[57]

Thus doing, your soul shall be placed with Dante's Beatrice or Virgil's Anchises.

But if—fie of such a but!—you be born so near the dull-making cataract of Nilus, that you cannot hear the planet-like music of poetry; if you have so earth-creeping a mind that it cannot lift itself up to look to the sky of poetry, or rather, by a certain rustical disdain, will become such a mome,[58] as to be a Momus of poetry; then, though I will not wish unto you the ass's ears of Midas, nor to be driven by a poet's verses, as Bubonax was, to hang himself; nor to be rimed to death, as is said to be done in Ireland; yet thus much curse I must send you in the behalf of all poets:—that while you live you live in love, and never get favor for lacking skill of a sonnet; and when you die, your memory die from the earth for want of an epitaph.

[55] "The son of a freedman."   [56] "Herculean offspring."
[57] "If my verses can do aught."—Virgil, "Æneid," IX. 446.
[58] Blockhead.

ON SHAKESPEARE
ON BACON

BY
BEN JONSON

INTRODUCTORY NOTE

BEN JONSON, after Shakespeare the most eminent writer for the Elizabethan stage, was born in 1573, and died in 1635. He was the founder of the so-called "Comedy of Humours," and throughout the reign of James I was the dominating personality in English letters. A large number of the younger writers were proud to confess themselves his "sons." Besides dramas of a variety of kinds, Jonson wrote much lyrical poetry, some of it of the most exquisite quality. His chief prose work appears in his posthumously published "Explorata, Timber or Discoveries, made upon men and matter," a kind of commonplace book, in which he seems to have entered quotations and translations from his reading, as well as original observations of a miscellaneous character on men and books. The volume has little or no structure or arrangement, but is impressed everywhere with the stamp of his vigorous personality. The following passages on Bacon and Shakespeare are notable as a personal estimate of these two giants by the man who, perhaps, approached them in the field of intellect more closely than any other contemporary.

BEN JONSON ON SHAKESPEARE

DE SHAKESPEARE NOSTRAT[I][1]

I REMEMBER the players have often mentioned it as an honor to Shakespeare, that in his writing, whatsoever he penned, he never blotted out a line. My answer hath been, "Would he had blotted a thousand," which they thought a malevolent speech. I had not told posterity this but for their ignorance, who chose that circumstance to commend their friend by wherein he most faulted; and to justify mine own candor, for I loved the man, and do honor his memory on this side idolatry as much as any. He was, indeed, honest, and of an open and free nature; had an excellent fancy, brave notions, and gentle expressions, wherein he flowed with that facility that sometime it was necessary he should be stopped. *"Sufflaminandus erat,"*[2] as Augustus said of Haterius. His wit was in his own power; would the rule of it had been so too. Many times he fell into those things, could not escape laughter, as when he said in the person of Cæsar, one speaking to him: "Cæsar, thou dost me wrong." He replied: "Cæsar did never wrong but with just cause;"[3] and such like, which were ridiculous. But he redeemed his vices with his virtues. There was ever more in him to be praised than to be pardoned.

[1] "Of our countryman, Shakespeare."
[2] "He should have been clogged."
[3] The speech is not found in this form in our version of Shakespeare's "Julius Cæsar."

BEN JONSON ON BACON

DOMINUS VERULAMIUS[1]

ONE, though he be excellent and the chief, is not to be imitated alone; for never no imitator ever grew up to his author; likeness is always on this side truth. Yet there happened in my time one noble speaker,[1] who was full of gravity in his speaking; his language, where he could spare or pass by a jest, was nobly censorious.[2] No man ever spake more neatly, more presly,[3] more weightily, or suffered less emptiness, less idleness, in what he uttered. No member of his speech but consisted of his own graces. His hearers could not cough, or look aside from him, without loss. He commanded where he spoke, and had his judges angry and pleased at his devotion.[4] No man had their affections more in his power. The fear of every man that heard him was lest he should make an end.

Scriptorum catalogus.[5]—Cicero is said to be the only wit that the people of Rome had equalled to their empire. *Ingenium par imperio.* We have had many, and in their several ages (to take in but the former *seculum*[6]) Sir Thomas More, the elder Wyatt, Henry Earl of Surrey, Chaloner, Smith, Eliot, B[ishop] Gardiner, were for their times admirable; and the more, because they began eloquence with us. Sir Nico[las] Bacon was singular, and almost alone, in the beginning of Queen Elizabeth's times. Sir Philip Sidney and Mr. Hooker (in different matter) grew great masters of wit and language, and in whom all vigor of invention and strength of judgment met. The Earl of Essex, noble and high; and Sir Walter Raleigh, not to be contemned, either for judgment or style; Sir Henry Savile, grave, and truly lettered; Sir Edwin Sandys, excellent in both; Lo[rd] Egerton, the Chancellor, a grave and great orator,

---

[1] Francis Bacon, Lord Verulam.   [2] Severe.   [3] Concisely.   [4] Choice, disposal.
[5] Catalogue of writers.   [6] Century.

56

and best when he was provoked; but his learned and able, though unfortunate, successor[7] is he who hath filled up all numbers, and performed that in our tongue which may be compared or preferred either to insolent Greece or haughty Rome. In short, within his view, and about his times, were all the wits born that could honor a language or help study. Now things daily fall, wits grow downward, and eloquence grows backward; so that he may be named and stand as the mark and ἀκμὴ[8] of our language.

De augmentis scientiarum.[9]—I have ever observed it to have been the office of a wise patriot, among the greatest affairs of the State, to take care of the commonwealth of learning. For schools, they are the seminaries of State; and nothing is worthier the study of a statesman than that part of the republic which we call the advancement of letters. Witness the care of Julius Cæsar, who, in the heat of the civil war, writ his books of *Analogy,* and dedicated them to Tully. This made the late Lord S[aint] Alban[10] entitle his work *Novum Organum;* which, though by the most of superficial men, who cannot get beyond the title of nominals,[11] it is not penetrated nor understood, it really openeth all defects of learning whatsoever, and is a book

Qui longum noto scriptori porriget ævum.[12]

My conceit of his person was never increased toward him by his place or honors. But I have and do reverence him for the greatness that was only proper to himself, in that he seemed to me ever, by his work, one of the greatest men, and most worthy of admiration, that had been in many ages. In his adversity I ever prayed that God would give him strength; for greatness he could not want. Neither could I condole in a word or syllable for him, as knowing no accident could do harm to virtue, but rather help to make it manifest.

[7] Bacon.　　[8] Acme.　　[9] Concerning the advancement of the sciences.　　[10] Bacon.
[11] Names of things.
[12] "Which extends to the famous author a long future."—Horace, *Ars. Poet.,* 346.

OF AGRICULTURE

BY
ABRAHAM COWLEY

INTRODUCTORY NOTE

ABRAHAM COWLEY (1618–1667) was educated at Westminster School and later at Trinity College, Cambridge, from which he was ejected with most of the Masters and Fellows for refusing to sign the Solemn League and Covenant in 1644. In the same year he crossed to France in the suite of Lord Jermyn, Queen Henrietta Maria's chief officer, and remained with the royal family in exile for twelve years. After the Restoration he became a doctor of medicine, and was one of the first members of the Royal Society. He is buried in Westminster Abbey.

Cowley's most popular work in his own day was the collection of love poems called "The Mistress," and his so-called "Pindaric Odes" were also highly esteemed. With the decline of the taste which produced the poetry of the "Metaphysical School" to which he belonged, Cowley ceased to be read; nor is it likely that the frigid ingenuity which marks his poetic style will ever again come into favor. His "Essays," on the other hand, are written with great simplicity and naturalness, and exhibit his temperament in a most pleasing light. He is one of the earliest masters of a clear and easy English prose style, and few writers of the familiar essay surpass Cowley in grace and charm. His essay "Of Agriculture" is a delightful example of his quality. "We may talk what we please," he cries in his enthusiasm for the oldest of the arts, "of lilies, and lions rampant, and spread eagles, in fields d'or or d'argent; but, if heraldry were guided by reason, a plough in a field arable would be the most noble and ancient arms."

OF AGRICULTURE

THE first wish of Virgil (as you will find anon by his verses) was to be a good philosopher, the second, a good husbandman: and God (whom he seem'd to understand better than most of the most learned heathens) dealt with him just as he did with Solomon; because he prayed for wisdom in the first place, he added all things else, which were subordinately to be desir'd. He made him one of the best philosophers and the best husbandmen; and, to adorn and communicate both those faculties, the best poet. He made him, besides all this, a rich man, and a man who desired to be no richer—

"O fortunatus nimium, et bona qui sua novit!"[1]

To be a husbandman, is but a retreat from the city; to be a philosopher, from the world; or rather, a retreat from the world, as it is man's, into the world, as it is God's.

But, since nature denies to most men the capacity or appetite, and fortune allows but to a very few the opportunities or possibility of applying themselves wholly to philosophy, the best mixture of humane[2] affairs that we can make, are the employments of a country life. It is, as Columella calls it, "Res sine dubitatione proxima, et quasi consanguinea sapientiæ," the nearest neighbour, or rather next in kindred, to philosophy. Varro says, the principles of it are the same which Ennius made to be the principles of all nature, Earth, Water, Air, and the Sun. It does certainly comprehend more parts of philosophy, than any one profession, art, or science, in the world besides: and therefore Cicero says, the pleasures of a husbandman, "mihi ad sapientis vitam proxime videntur accedere," come very nigh to those of a philosopher. There is no other sort of life

---

[1] "O fortunate exceedingly, who knew his own good fortune."—Adapted from Virgil, "Georgics," II., 458.
[2] Human.

that affords so many branches of praise to a panegyrist: the utility of it, to a man's self; the usefulness, or rather necessity, of it to all the rest of mankind; the innocence, the pleasure, the antiquity, the dignity.

The utility (I mean plainly the lucre of it) is not so great, now in our nation, as arises from merchandise and the trading of the city, from whence many of the best estates and chief honours of the kingdom are derived: we have no men now fetcht from the plow to be made lords, as they were in Rome to be made consuls and dictators; the reason of which I conceive to be from an evil custom, now grown as strong among us as if it were a law, which is, that no men put their children to be bred up apprentices in agriculture, as in other trades, but such who are so poor, that, when they come to be men, they have not wherewithal to set up in it, and so can only farm some small parcel of ground, the rent of which devours all but the bare subsistence of the tenant: whilst they who are proprietors of the land are either too proud, or, for want of that kind of education, too ignorant, to improve their estates, though the means of doing it be as easie and certain in this, as in any other track of commerce. If there were always two or three thousand youths, for seven or eight years, bound to this profession, that they might learn the whole art of it, and afterwards be enabled to be masters in it, by a moderate stock, I cannot doubt but that we should see as many aldermen's estates made in the country, as now we do out of all kind of merchandizing in the city. There are as many ways to be rich, and, which is better, there is no possibility to be poor, without such negligence as can neither have excuse nor pity; for a little ground will, without question, feed a little family, and the superfluities of life (which are now in some cases by custom made almost necessary) must be supplyed out of the superabundance of art and industry, or contemned by as great a degree of philosophy.

As for the necessity of this art, it is evident enough, since this can live without all others, and no one other without this. This is like speech, without which the society of men cannot be preserved; the others, like figures and tropes of speech, which serve only to adorn it. Many nations have lived, and some do still, without any art but this: not so elegantly, I confess, but still they live; and almost all the other arts, which are here practised, are beholding to this for most of their materials.

The innocence of this life is the next thing for which I commend it; and if husbandmen preserve not that, they are much to blame, for no men are so free from the temptations of iniquity. They live by what they can get by industry from the earth; and others, by what they can catch by craft from men. They live upon an estate given them by their mother; and others, upon an estate cheated from their brethren. They live, like sheep and kine, by the allowances of nature; and others, like wolves and foxes, by the acquisitions of rapine. And, I hope, I may affirm (without any offence to the great) that sheep and kine are very useful, and that wolves and foxes are pernicious creatures. They are, without dispute, of all men, the most quiet and least apt to be inflamed to the disturbance of the commonwealth: their manner of life inclines them, and interest binds them, to love peace: in our late mad and miserable civil wars, all other trades, even to the meanest, set forth whole troops, and raised up some great commanders, who became famous and mighty for the mischiefs they had done: but I do not remember the name of any one husbandman, who had so considerable a share in the twenty years' ruine of his country, as to deserve the curses of his countrymen.

And if great delights be joyn'd with so much innocence, I think it is ill done of men not to take them here, where they are so tame, and ready at hand, rather than hunt for them in courts and cities, where they are so wild, and the chase so troublesome and dangerous.

We are here among the vast and noble scenes of nature; we are there among the pitiful shifts of policy: we walk here in the light and open ways of the divine bounty; we grope there in the dark and confused labyrinths of humane[3] malice: our senses are here feasted with the clear and genuine taste of their objects, which are all sophisticated there, and for the most part overwhelmed with their contraries. Here, pleasure looks (methinks) like a beautiful, constant, and modest wife; it is there an impudent, fickle, and painted harlot. Here, is harmless and cheap plenty; there, guilty and expenceful luxury.

[3] Human.

I shall only instance in one delight more, the most natural and best-natured of all others, a perpetual companion of the husbandman; and that is, the satisfaction of looking round about him, and seeing nothing but the effects and improvements of his own art and diligence; to be always gathering of some fruits of it, and at the same time to behold others ripening, and others budding: to see all his fields and gardens covered with the beauteous creatures of his own industry; and to see, like God, that all his works are good:—

—— Hinc atque hinc glomerantur Orcades; ipsi
Agricolæ tacitum pertentant gaudia pectus.[4]

On his heart-string a secret joy does strike.

The antiquity of his art is certainly not be contested by any other. The three first men in the world, were a gardener, a plowman, and a grazier; and if any man object, that the second of these was a murtherer, I desire he would consider, that as soon as he was so, he quitted our profession, and turn'd builder. It is for this reason, I suppose, that Ecclesiasticus forbids us to hate husbandry; 'because (says he) the Most High has created it.' We were all born to this art, and taught by nature to nourish our bodies by the same earth out of which they were made, and to which they must return, and pay at last for their sustenance.

Behold the original and primitive nobility of all those great persons, who are too proud now, not only to till the ground, but almost to tread upon it. We may talk what we please of lillies, and lions rampant, and spread-eagles, in fields d'or or d'argent; but, if heraldry were guided by reason, a plough in a field arable would be the most noble and antient arms.

All these considerations make me fall into the wonder and complaint of Columella, how it should come to pass that all arts or sciences (for the dispute, which is an art, and which a science, does not belong to the curiosity of us husbandmen) metaphysick, physick, morality, mathematicks, logick, rhetorick, &c. which are all, I grant, good and useful faculties, (except only metaphysick which I do not know whether it be anything or no;) but even vaulting, fencing, dancing, attiring, cookery, carving, and such like vanities, should

[4] "On this side and on that gather the Orkneys; joys pervade the silent breast of the farmer."—A parody of Virgil's "Æneid," I. 500, 503.

all have publick schools and masters, and yet that we should never see or hear of any man, who took upon him the profession of teaching this so pleasant, so virtuous, so profitable, so honourable, so necessary art.

A man would think, when he's in serious humour, that it were but a vain, irrational, and ridiculous thing for a great company of men and women to run up and down in a room together, in a hundred several postures and figures, to no purpose, and with no design; and therefore dancing was invented first, and only practised antiently, in the ceremonies of the heathen religion, which consisted all in mummery and madness; the latter being the chief glory of the worship, and accounted divine inspiration: this, I say, a severe man would think; though I dare not determine so far against so customary a part, now, of good-breeding. And yet, who is there among our gentry, that does not entertain a dancing-master for his children, as soon as they are able to walk? But did ever any father provide a tutor for his son, to instruct him betimes in the nature and improvements of that land which he intended to leave him? That is at least a superfluity, and this a defect, in our manner of education; and therefore I could wish (but cannot in these times much hope to see it) that one colledge in each university were erected, and appropriated to this study, as well as there are to medicine and the civil law: there would be no need of making a body of scholars and fellows with certain endowments, as in other colledges; it would suffice, if, after the manner of halls in Oxford, there were only four professors constituted (for it would be too much work for only one master, or principal, as they call him there) to teach these four parts of it: First, Aration, and all things relating to it. Secondly, Pasturage. Thirdly, Gardens, Orchards, Vineyards, and Woods. Fourthly, all parts of Rural Oeconomy, which would contain the government of Bees, Swine, Poultry, Decoys, Ponds, &c. and all that which Varro calls *villaticas pastiones*,[5] together with the sports of the field (which ought to be looked upon not only as pleasures, but as parts of house-keeping), and the domestical conservation and uses of all that is brought in by industry abroad. The business of these professors should not be, as is commonly practised in other arts, only to read

[5] The keeping of farm animals, etc.

pompous and superficial lectures, out of Virgil's Georgicks, Pliny, Varro, or Columella; but to instruct their pupils in the whole method and course of this study, which might be run through perhaps, with diligence, in a year or two: and the continual succession of scholars, upon a moderate taxation[6] for their diet, lodging and learning, would be a sufficient constant revenue for maintenance of the house and the professors, who should be men not chosen for the ostentation of critical literature, but for solid and experimental knowledge of the things they teach; such men, so industrious and publick-spirited, as I conceive Mr. Hartlib to be, if the gentleman be yet alive: but it is needless to speak further of my thoughts of this design, unless the present disposition of the age allowed more probability of bringing it into execution. What I have further to say of the country life, shall be borrowed from the poets, who were always the most faithful and affectionate friends to it. Poetry was born among the shepherds.

> Nescio qua natale solum dulcedine Musas
> Ducit, et immemores non sinit esse sui.

> The Muses still love their own native place;
> 'T has secret charms, which nothing can deface.

The truth is, no other place is proper for their work; one might as well undertake to dance in a crowd, as to make good verses in the midst of noise and tumult.

> As well might corn, as verse, in cities grow;
> In vain the thankless glebe we plow and sow;
> Against th' unnatural soil in vain we strive;
> 'Tis not a ground, in which these plants will thrive.

It will bear nothing but the nettles and thorns of satyre, which grow most naturally in the worst earth; and therefore almost all poets, except those who were not able to eat bread without the bounty of great men, that is, without what they could get by flattering of them, have not only withdrawn themselves from the vices and vanities of the grand world,

> —— pariter vitiisque jocisque
> Altius humanis exeruere caput,[7]

[6] Charge.　[7] "They have raised their head above both human vices and vanities."—Ovid, "Fasti," I. 300.

into the innocent happiness of a retired life; but have commended and adorned nothing so much by their ever-living poems. Hesiod was the first or second poet in the world that remains yet extant (if Homer, as some think, preceded him, but I rather believe they were contemporaries); and he is the first writer too of the art of husbandry: "and he has contributed (says Columella) not a little to our profession;" I suppose, he means not a little honour, for the matter of his instructions is not very important: his great antiquity is visible through the gravity and simplicity of his stile. The most acute of all his sayings concerns our purpose very much, and is couched in the reverend obscurity of an oracle.

Πλέον ἥμισυ παντός,[8] The half is more than the whole. The occasion of the speech is this: his brother Perses had, by corrupting some great men (βασιλῆας δωροφάγους, great bribe-eaters he calls them), gotten from him the half of his estate. It is no matter (says he); they have not done me so much prejudice, as they imagine.

> Νήπιοι, οὐδ' ἴσασιν ὅσῳ πλέον ἥμισυ παντός,
> Οὐδ' ὅσον ἐν μαλαχῃ τε καὶ ασφοδέλῳ μέγ' ὄνειαρ,
> Κρύψαντες γὰρ ἔχουσι θεοὶ βίον ανθρώποισι.

> Unhappy they, to whom God ha'n't reveal'd,
> By a strong light which must their sense controul,
> That half a great estate's more than the whole.
> Unhappy, from whom still conceal'd does lye,
> Of roots and herbs, the wholesom luxury.

This I conceive to be honest Hesiod's meaning. From Homer, we must not expect much concerning our affairs. He was blind, and could neither work in the country nor enjoy the pleasures of it; his helpless poverty was likeliest to be sustained in the richest places; he was to delight the Grecians with fine tales of the wars and adventures of their ancestors; his subject removed him from all commerce with us, and yet, methinks, he made a shift to shew his goodwill a little. For, though he could do us no honour in the person of his hero Ulysses (much less of Achilles), because his whole time was consumed in wars and voyages; yet he makes his father Laertes a gardener all that while, and seeking his consolation for the absence of his son in the pleasure of planting, and even dunging his own

8 Hesiod, "Works and Days," 40.

grounds. Ye see, he did not contemn us peasants; nay, so far was he from that insolence, that he always stiles Eumaeus, who kept the hogs, with wonderful respect, δῖον ὑφορβόν, the divine swine herd; he could ha' done no more for Menelaus or Agamemnon. And Theocritus (a very antient poet, but he was one of our own tribe, for he wrote nothing but pastorals) gave the same epithete to an husbandman,— ἠμείβετο δῖος ἀγρώστες. The divine husbandman replyed to Hercules, who was but δῖος himself. These were civil Greeks, and who understood the dignity of our calling!

Among the Romans we have, in the first place, our truly divine Virgil, who, though, by the favour of Maecenas and Augustus, he might have been one of the chief men of Rome, yet chose rather to employ much of his time in the exercise, and much of his immortal wit in the praise and instructions, of a rustique life; who, though he had written, before, whole books of pastorals and georgics, could not abstain, in his great and imperial poem, from describing Evander, one of his best princes, as living just after the homely manner of an ordinary countryman. He seats him in a throne of maple, and lays him but upon a bear's skin; the kine and oxen are lowing in his court-yard; the birds under the eves of his window call him up in the morning, and when he goes abroad, only two dogs go along with him for his guard: at last, when he brings Æneas into his royal cottage, he makes him say this memorable complement, greater than even yet was spoken at the Escurial, the Louvre, or our Whitehal:

> —— Hæc (inquit) limina victor
> Alcides subiit, hæc illum regia cepit:
> Aude, hospes, contemnere opes: et te quoque dignum
> Finge Deo, rebusque veni non asper egenis.

> This humble roof, this rustick court, (said he)
> Receiv'd Alcides, crown'd with victorie:
> Scorn not, great guest, the steps where he has trod;
> But contemn wealth, and imitate a God.

The next man, whom we are much obliged to, both for his doctrine and example, is the next best poet in the world to Virgil, his dear friend Horace; who, when Augustus had desired Mæcenas to perswade him to come and live domestically and at the same table with him, and to be secretary of state of the whole world under him, or rather jointly with him, for he says, "ut nos in epistolis scribendis adjuvet,"[9] could not be tempted to forsake his Sabin, or Tiburtin mannor, for so rich and so glorious a trouble. There was never, I think, such an example as this in the world, that he should have so much moderation and courage as to refuse an offer of such greatness, and the emperor so much generosity and good-nature as not to be at all offended with his refusal, but to retain still the same kindness, and express it often to him in most friendly and familiar letters, part of which are still extant. If I should produce all the passages of this excellent author upon the several subjects which I treat of in this book, I must be obliged to translate half his works; of which I may say more truly than, in my opinion, he did of Homer.

> Qui, quid sit pulchrum, quid turpe, quid utile, quid non,
> Planius et melius Chrysippo et Crantore dicit.[10]

I shall content myself upon this particular theme with three only, one out of his *Odes,* the other out of his *Satires,* the third out of his *Epistles;* and shall forbear to collect the suffrages of all other poets, which may be found scattered up and down through all their writings, and especially in Martial's. But I must not omit to make some excuse for the bold-undertaking of my own unskilful pencil upon the beauties of a face that has been drawn before by so many great masters; especially, that I should dare to do it in Latine verses, (though of another kind), and have the confidence to translate them. I can only say that I love the matter, and that ought to cover many faults; and that I run not to contend with those before me, but follow to applaud them.

[9] "That he may assist us in writing letters."
[10] "Who says, more plainly and better than Chrysippus and Crantor, what is beautiful, what base, what useful, what the opposite of these."—Horace, "Epist." I. 2. 4. Chrysippus and Crantor were noted philosophers.

THE VISION OF MIRZA

AND

WESTMINSTER ABBEY

BY

JOSEPH ADDISON

INTRODUCTORY NOTE

JOSEPH ADDISON (1672–1719) divided his energies between literature and politics. He was educated at the Charterhouse and at Oxford with a view to holy orders, but the Earl of Halifax saw in him valuable political material, obtained for him a pension, and sent him abroad to prepare for a diplomatic career. His travels in France and Italy confirmed his classical tastes, and his critical writings show abundant traces of French influence.

On his return to England he published his "Campaign," which laid the foundation of his career. He entered Parliament, and finally rose to be Secretary of State. In spite of the bitterness of political feeling in his time, Addison kept the esteem of men of all parties, and enjoyed a universal popularity such as has been bestowed on few men of letters and fewer politicians.

Addison's fame to-day rests mainly on his writings in the "Tatler" and the "Spectator." In the essays and articles published in these two periodicals, he not only produced a succession of pieces unsurpassed in their kind, but exerted an influence as wholesome as it was powerful upon the manners and morals of society in the London of Queen Anne. His style remains the great classic example of that combination of ease and elegance which is the characteristic merit of the prose of the period; and the imaginative moralizing which is exemplified in "The Vision of Mirza" and "Westminster Abbey" reveals something of the gentle persuasiveness with which he sought to lead his generation to higher levels of living and thinking.

A more detailed account of the life and work of Addison will be found in the "Life" by Dr. Johnson in the present volume.

THE VISION OF MIRZA[1]

Omnem, quæ nunc obducta tuenti
Mortales hebetat visus tibi, et humida circum
Caligat, nubem eripiam.[2]
　　　　　　　—Virgil, "Æneid," ii. 604.

WHEN I was at Grand Cairo, I picked up several oriental manuscripts, which I have still by me. Among others I met with one entitled *"The Visions of Mirza,"* which I have read over with great pleasure. I intend to give it to the public when I have no other entertainment for them, and shall begin with the first vision, which I have translated word for word, as follows:—

"On the fifth day of the moon, which according to the custom of my forefathers I always keep holy, after having washed myself and offered up my morning devotions, I ascended the high hills of Bagdad, in order to pass the rest of the day in meditation and prayer. As I was here airing myself on the tops of the mountains, I fell into a profound contemplation on the vanity of human life, and passing from one thought to another, 'Surely,' said I, 'man is but a shadow, and life a dream.' Whilst I was thus musing, I cast my eyes towards the summit of a rock that was not far from me, where I discovered one in the habit of a shepherd, with a little musical instrument in his hand. As I looked upon him he applied it to his lips, and began to play upon it. The sound of it was exceeding sweet, and wrought into a variety of tunes that were inexpressibly melodious and altogether different from anything I had ever heard. They put me in mind of those heavenly airs that are played to the departed souls of good men upon their first arrival in Paradise, to wear out the impressions of the last agonies, and qualify them for the pleasures of that happy place. My heart melted away in secret raptures.

[1] Published in "The Spectator," September 1, 1711.
[2] "Every cloud which now drawn before thee dulls thy mortal vision and sends mists around thee, I shall snatch away."

73

"I had often been told that the rock before me was the haunt of a genius; and that several had been entertained with music who had passed by it, but never heard that the musician had before made himself visible. When he had raised my thoughts by those transporting airs which he played, to taste the pleasures of his conversation, as I looked upon him like one astonished, he beckoned to me, and by the waving of his hand directed me to approach the place where he sat. I drew near with that reverence which is due to a superior nature; and as my heart was entirely subdued by the captivating strains I had heard, I fell down at his feet and wept. The genius smiled upon me with a look of compassion and affability that familiarized him to my imagination, and at once dispelled all the fears and apprehensions with which I approached him. He lifted me from the ground, and taking me by the hand, 'Mirza,' said he, 'I have heard thee in thy soliloquies; follow me.'

"He then led me to the highest pinnacle of the rock, and placing me on the top of it, 'Cast thy eyes eastward,' said he 'and tell me what thou seest.' 'I see,' said I, 'a huge valley and a prodigious tide of water rolling through it.' 'The valley that thou seest,' said he, 'is the Vale of Misery, and the tide of water that thou seest is part of the great tide of eternity.' 'What is the reason,' said I, 'that the tide I see rises out of a thick mist at one end, and again loses itself in a thick mist at the other?' 'What thou seest,' said he, 'is that portion of eternity which is called time, measured out by the sun, and reaching from the beginning of the world to its consummation. Examine now,' said he, 'this sea that is thus bounded by darkness at both ends, and tell me what thou discoverest in it.' 'I see a bridge,' said I, 'standing in the midst of the tide.' 'The bridge thou seest,' said he, 'is human life; consider it attentively.' Upon a more leisurely survey of it I found that it consisted of more than threescore and ten entire arches, with several broken arches, which, added to those that were entire, made up the number to about a hundred. As I was counting the arches, the genius told me that this bridge consisted at first of a thousand arches; but that a great flood swept away the rest, and left the bridge in the ruinous condition I now beheld it. 'But tell me further,' said he, 'what thou discoverest on it.' 'I see multitudes of people passing over it,' said I, 'and a black cloud hanging on each end of it.' As I looked more attentively, I saw several of the passengers dropping through the bridge into the great tide that flowed underneath it; and upon further examination, perceived there were innumerable trap-doors that lay concealed in the bridge, which the passengers no sooner trod upon, but they fell through them into the tide and immediately disappeared. These hidden pitfalls were set very thick at the entrance of the bridge, so that throngs of people no sooner broke through the cloud, but many of them fell into them. They grew thinner towards the middle, but multiplied and lay closer together towards the end of the arches that were entire.

"There were indeed some persons, but their number was very small, that continued a kind of hobbling march on the broken arches, but fell through one after another, being quite tired and spent with so long a walk.

"I passed some time in the contemplation of this wonderful structure, and the great variety of objects which it presented. My heart was filled with a deep melancholy to see several dropping unexpectedly in the midst of mirth and jollity, and catching at everything that stood by them to save themselves. Some were looking up towards the heavens in a thoughtful posture, and in the midst of a speculation stumbled and fell out of sight. Multitudes were very busy in the pursuit of bubbles that glittered in their eyes and danced before them, but often when they thought themselves within the reach of them their footing failed and down they sunk. In this confusion of objects, I observed some with scimitars in their hands, and others with urinals, who ran to and fro upon the bridge, thrusting several persons on trap-doors which did not seem to lie in their way, and which they might have escaped had they not been thus forced upon them.

"The genius, seeing me indulge myself on this melancholy prospect, told me I had dwelt long enough upon it. 'Take thine eyes off the bridge,' said he, 'and tell me if thou seest anything thou dost not comprehend.' Upon looking up, 'What mean,' said I, 'those great flights of birds that are perpetually hovering about the bridge, and settling upon it from time to time? I see vultures, harpies, ravens, cormorants, and among many other feathered creatures several little winged boys that perch in great numbers upon the middle arches.' 'These,' said the genius, 'are Envy, Avarice, Superstition, Despair, Love, with the like cares and passions that infest human life.'

"I here fetched a deep sigh. 'Alas,' said I, 'man was made in vain: how is he given away to misery and mortality, tortured in life, and swallowed up in death!' The genius being moved with compassion towards me, bid me quit so uncomfortable a prospect. 'Look no more,' said he, 'on man in the first stage of his existence, in his setting out for eternity; but cast thine eye on that thick mist into which the tide bears the several generations of mortals that fall into it.' I directed my sight as I was ordered, and (whether or no the good genius strengthened it with any supernatural force, or dissipated part of the mist that was before too thick for eye to penetrate) I saw the valley opening at the farther end, and spreading forth into an immense ocean that had a huge rock of adamant running through the midst of it, and dividing it into two equal parts. The clouds still rested on one half of it, insomuch that I could discover nothing in it; but the other appeared to me a vast ocean planted with innumerable islands, that were covered with fruits and flowers, and interwoven with a thousand little shining seas that ran among them. I could see persons dressed in glorious habits with garlands upon their heads, passing among the trees, lying down by the sides of fountains, or resting on beds of flowers; and could hear a confused harmony of singing birds, falling waters, human voices, and musical instruments. Gladness grew in me upon the discovery of so delightful a scene. I wished for the wings of an eagle that I might fly away to those happy seats; but the genius told me there was no passage to them except through the gates of death that I saw opening every moment upon the bridge. 'The islands,' said he, 'that lie so fresh and green before thee, and with which the whole face of the ocean appears spotted as far as thou canst see, are more in number than the sands on the seashore; there are myriads of islands behind those which thou here discoverest, reaching farther than thine eye, or even thine imagination can extend itself. These are the mansions of good men after death, who, according to the degree and kinds of virtue in which they excelled, are distributed among these several islands, which abound with pleasures of different kinds and degrees suitable to the relishes and perfections of those who are settled in them; every island is a paradise accommodated to its respective inhabitants. Are not these, O Mirza, habitations worth contending for? Does life appear miserable that gives thee opportunities of earning such a reward? Is death to be feared that will convey thee to so happy an existence? Think not man was made in vain who has such an eternity reserved for him.' I gazed with inexpressible pleasure on these happy islands. At length, said I, 'Show me now, I beseech thee, the secrets that lie hid under those dark clouds which cover the ocean on the other side of the rock of adamant.' The genius making me no answer, I turned me about to address myself to him a second time, but I found that he had left me; I then turned again to the vision which I had been so long contemplating; but, instead of the rolling tide, the arched bridge, and the happy islands, I saw nothing but the long valley of Bagdad, with oxen, sheep, and camels grazing upon the sides of it."

The end of the first vision of Mirza.

WESTMINSTER ABBEY [1]

Pallida mors æquo palsat pede pauperam tabernas
Regumque tures, O beati Sexti,
Vitæ summa brevis spem nos vetat inchoare longam:
Jam te premet nox, fabulæque manes,
Et domus exilis Plutonia.—HOR. [2]

WHEN I am in a serious humour, I very often walk by myself in Westminster Abbey, where the gloominess of the place, and the use to which it is applied, with the solemnity of the building, and the condition of the people who lie in it, are apt to fill the mind with a kind of melancholy, or rather thoughtfulness, that is not disagreeable. I yesterday passed a whole afternoon in the churchyard, the cloisters, and the church, amusing myself with the tombstones and inscriptions that I met with in those several regions of the dead. Most of them recorded nothing else of the buried person, but that he was born upon one day, and died upon another: the whole history of his life being comprehended in those two circumstances, that are common to all mankind. I could not but look upon these registers of existence, whether of brass or marble, as a kind of satire upon the departed persons; who had left no other memorial of them, but that they were born and that they died. They put me in mind of several persons mentioned in the battles of heroic poems, who have sounding names given them, for no other reason but that they may be killed, and are celebrated for nothing but being knocked on the head.

Γλαῦκόν τε Μέδοντά τε Θερσίλοχόν τε. HOM.

Glaucumque, Medontaque, Thersilochumque. VIRG.

The life of these men is finely described in Holy Writ by "the path of an arrow," which is immediately closed up and lost.

[1] Published in "The Spectator," March 30, 1711.
[2] "Pale death knocks with impartial foot at the huts of the poor and at the towers of kings, O happy Sextus. The shortness of the span of life forbids us to cherish remote hope; already night overtakes thee, and the fabled shades, and the wretched house of Pluto."

Upon my going into the church, I entertained myself with the digging of a grave; and saw in every shovelful of it that was thrown up, the fragment of a bone or skull intermixt with a kind of fresh mouldering earth, that some time or other had a place in the composition of a human body. Upon this, I began to consider with myself what innumerable multitudes of people lay confused together under the pavement of that ancient cathedral; how men and women, friends and enemies, priests and soldiers, monks and prebendaries, were crumbled amongst one another, and blended together in the same common mass; how beauty, strength, and youth, with old age, weakness and deformity, lay undistinguished in the same promiscuous heap of matter.

After having thus surveyed this great magazine of mortality, as it were, in the lump; I examined it more particularly by the accounts which I found on several of the monuments which are raised in every quarter of that ancient fabric. Some of them were covered with such extravagant epitaphs, that, if it were possible for the dead person to be acquainted with them, he would blush at the praises which his friends have bestowed upon him. There are others so excessively modest, that they deliver the character of the person departed in Greek or Hebrew, and by that means are not understood once in a twelvemonth. In the poetical quarter, I found there were poets who had no monuments, and monuments which had no poets. I observed indeed that the present war had filled the church with many of these uninhabited monuments, which had been erected to the memory of persons whose bodies were perhaps buried in the plains of Blenheim, or in the bosom of the ocean.

I could not but be very much delighted with several modern epitaphs, which are written with great elegance of expression and justness of thought, and therefore do honour to the living as well as to the dead. As a foreigner is very apt to conceive an idea of the ignorance or politeness of a nation, from the turn of their public monuments and inscriptions, they should be submitted to the perusal of men of learning and genius, before they are put in execution. Sir Cloudesly Shovel's monument has very often given me great offence: instead of the brave rough English Admiral, which was the distinguishing character of that plain gallant man, he is represented on his tomb by the figure of a beau, dressed in a long periwig, and reposing himself upon velvet cushions under a canopy of state. The inscription is answerable to the monument; for instead of celebrating the many remarkable actions he had performed in the service of his country, it acquaints us only with the manner of his death, in which it was impossible for him to reap any honour. The Dutch, whom we are apt to despise for want of genius, show an infinitely greater taste of antiquity and politeness in their buildings and works of this nature, than what we meet with in those of our own country. The monuments of their admirals, which have been erected at the public expense, represent them like themselves; and are adorned with rostral crowns and naval ornaments, with beautiful festoons of seaweed, shells, and coral.

But to return to our subject. I have left the repository of our English kings for the contemplation of another day, when I shall find my mind disposed for so serious an amusement. I know that entertainments of this nature are apt to raise dark and dismal thoughts in timorous minds, and gloomy imaginations; but for my own part, though I am always serious, I do not know what it is to be melancholy; and can therefore take a view of nature in her deep and solemn scenes, with the same pleasure as in her most gay and delightful ones. By this means I can improve myself with those objects, which others consider with terror. When I look upon the tombs of the great, every emotion of envy dies in me; when I read the epitaphs of the beautiful, every inordinate desire goes out; when I meet with the grief of parents upon a tombstone, my heart melts with compassion; when I see the tomb of the parents themselves, I consider the vanity of grieving for those whom we must quickly follow; when I see kings lying by those who deposed them, when I consider rival wits placed side by side, or the holy men that divided the world with their contests and disputes, I reflect with sorrow and astonishment on the little competitions, factions and debates of mankind. When I read the several dates of the tombs, of some that died yesterday, and some six hundred years ago, I consider that great day when we shall all of us be contemporaries, and make our appearance together.

THE SPECTATOR CLUB
BY
SIR RICHARD STEELE

INTRODUCTORY NOTE

SIR RICHARD STEELE (1672–1729), Addison's chief collaborator in the "Tatler" and the "Spectator," was born in Dublin of an English father and an Irish mother. He made Addison's acquaintance at school, and they were at Oxford together. Steele left the University to enter the army, and opened his literary career, while still a soldier, with "The Christian Hero." In 1702 he began to write for the stage, and was of notable influence in redeeming the English drama from the indecency which had marked much of it since the Restoration. Like Addison, he combined politics with literature, and in 1715 was knighted as a reward for his services to the Hanoverian party.

The chief glory of the "Spectator" is, of course, the club, and it was in the essay which follows that Steele first sketched the characters composing it. The Spectator himself was Addison's creation, and Addison also elaborated Sir Roger, though Steele originated him. Whatever may be the respective claims of Addison and Steele to the credit for the success of the "Spectator," it is to Steele that the honor belongs of having founded its predecessor, the "Tatler," and so of originating the periodical essay.

Steele was a warm-hearted, impulsive man, full of sentiment, improvident, and somewhat weak of will. These qualities are reflected in his writings, which are inferior to Addison's in grace and finish, but are marked by greater spontaneity and invention. Probably no piece of writing of equal length has added so many portraits to the gallery of our literature as the first sketch of the Spectator Club which is here printed.

THE SPECTATOR CLUB[1]

Ast alii sex
Et plures uno conclamant ore.
—Juvenal, "Satires," vii. 166.

Six more at least join their consenting voice.

THE first of our society is a gentleman of Worcestershire, of an ancient descent, a baronet, his name Sir Roger de Coverley. His great-grandfather was inventor of that famous country-dance which is called after him. All who know that shire are very well acquainted with the parts and merits of Sir Roger. He is a gentleman that is very singular in his behavior, but his singularities proceed from his good sense, and are contradictions to the manners of the world, only as he thinks the world is in the wrong. However, this humor creates him no enemies, for he does nothing with sourness or obstinacy; and his being unconfined to modes and forms makes him but the readier and more capable to please and oblige all who know him. When he is in town he lives in Soho Square. It is said he keeps himself a bachelor by reason he was crossed in love by a perverse beautiful widow of the next county to him. Before this disappointment, Sir Roger was what you call a fine gentleman, had often supped with my Lord Rochester and Sir George Etherege, fought a duel upon his first coming to town, and kicked bully Dawson in a public coffee-house for calling him youngster. But being ill-used by the above-mentioned widow, he was very serious for a year and a half; and though, his temper being naturally jovial, he at last got over it, he grew careless of himself and never dressed afterwards. He continues to wear a coat and doublet of the same cut that were in fashion at the time of his repulse, which, in his merry humors, he tells us, has been in and out twelve times since he first wore it. It is said Sir Roger grew humble in his desires after he had forgot his cruel beauty, insomuch that it is reported he has frequently offended with beggars and

[1] Published in "The Spectator," March 1, 1711.

gypsies; but this is looked upon, by his friends, rather as matter of raillery than truth. He is now in his fifty-sixth year, cheerful, gay, and hearty; keeps a good house both in town and country; a great lover of mankind; but there is such a mirthful cast in his behavior, that he is rather beloved than esteemed. His tenants grow rich, his servants look satisfied, all the young women profess love to him, and the young men are glad of his company. When he comes into a house, he calls the servants by their names, and talks all the way upstairs to a visit. I must not omit that Sir Roger is a justice of the quorum; that he fills the chair at a quarter-session with great abilities, and three months ago gained universal applause, by ex- plaining a passage in the Game Act.

The gentleman next in esteem and authority among us is another bachelor, who is a member of the Inner Temple, a man of great probity, wit, and understanding; but he has chosen his place of residence rather to obey the direction of an old humorsome father than in pursuit of his own inclinations. He was placed there to study the laws of the land, and is the most learned of any of the house in those of the stage. Aristotle and Longinus are much better under- stood by him than Littleton or Coke. The father sends up every post questions relating to marriage-articles, leases, and tenures, in the neighborhood; all which questions he agrees with an attorney to answer and take care of in the lump. He is studying the passions themselves, when he should be inquiring into the debates among men which arise from them. He knows the argument of each of the orations of Demosthenes and Tully, but not one case in the re- ports of our own courts. No one ever took him for a fool; but none, except his intimate friends, know he has a great deal of wit. This turn makes him at once both disinterested and agreeable. As few of his thoughts are drawn from business, they are most of them fit for conversation. His taste for books is a little too just for the age he lives in; he has read all, but approves of very few. His familiarity with the customs, manners, actions, and writings of the ancients, makes him a very delicate observer of what occurs to him in the present world. He is an excellent critic, and the time of the play is his hour of business; exactly at five he passes through New-Inn, crosses through Russell-court, and takes a turn at Will's till the play begins; he has his shoes rubbed and his periwig powdered at the barber's as you go into the Rose. It is for the good of the audience when he is at the play, for the actors have an ambition to please him.

The person of next consideration is Sir Andrew Freeport, a merchant of great eminence in the city of London; a person of indefatigable industry, strong reason, and great experience. His notions of trade are noble and generous, and (as every rich man has usually some sly way of jesting, which would make no great figure were he not a rich man) he calls the sea the British Common. He is acquainted with commerce in all its parts, and will tell you that it is a stupid and barbarous way to extend dominion by arms; for true power is to be got by arts and industry. He will often argue that, if this part of our trade were well cultivated, we should gain from one nation; and if another, from another. I have heard him prove that diligence makes more lasting acquisitions than valor, and that sloth has ruined more nations than the sword. He abounds in several frugal maxims, amongst which the greatest favorite is, "A penny saved is a penny got." A general trader of good sense is pleasanter company than a general scholar; and Sir Andrew having a natural unaffected eloquence, the perspicuity of his discourse gives the same pleasure that wit would in another man. He has made his fortune himself; and says that England may be richer than other kingdoms by as plain methods as he himself is richer than other men; though at the same time I can say this of him, that there is not a point in the compass but blows home a ship in which he is an owner.

Next to Sir Andrew in the clubroom sits Captain Sentry, a gentleman of great courage, good understanding, but invincible modesty. He is one of those that deserve very well, but are very awkward at putting their talents within the observation of such as should take notice of them. He was some years a captain, and behaved himself with great gallantry in several engagements and at several sieges; but having a small estate of his own, and being next heir to Sir Roger, he has quitted a way of life in which no man can rise suitably to his merit, who is not something of a courtier as well as a soldier. I have heard him often lament that, in a profession where merit is placed in so conspicuous a view, impudence should get the better of modesty. When he has talked to this purpose, I never heard him make a sour expression, but frankly confess that he left the world because he was not fit for it. A strict honesty and an even regular behavior are in themselves obstacles to him that must press through crowds, who endeavor at the same end with himself, the favor of a commander. He will, however, in his way of talk excuse generals for not disposing according to men's dessert, or inquiring into it; for, says he, that great man who has a mind to help me has as many to break through to come to me as I have to come at him: therefore he will conclude that the man who would make a figure, especially in a military way, must get over all false modesty, and assist his patron against the importunity of other pretenders, by a proper assurance in his own vindication. He says it is a civil cowardice to be backward in asserting what you ought to expect, as it is a military fear to be slow in attacking when it is your duty. With this candor does the gentleman speak of himself and others. The same frankness runs through all his conversation. The military part of his life has furnished him with many adventures, in the relation of which he is very agreeable to the company; for he is never overbearing, though accustomed to command men in the utmost degree below him; nor ever too obsequious, from an habit of obeying men highly above him.

But that our society may not appear a set of humorists,[2] unacquainted with the gallantries and pleasures of the age, we have amongst us the gallant Will Honeycomb, a gentleman who, according to his years, should be in the decline of his life; but having ever been very careful of his person, and always had a very easy fortune, time has made but a very little impression either by wrinkles on his forehead, or traces on his brain. His person is well turned, and of a good height. He is very ready at that sort of discourse with which men usually entertain women. He has all his life dressed very well, and remembers habits as others do men. He can smile when one speaks to him, and laughs easily. He knows the history of every mode, and can inform you from which of the French king's wenches our wives and daughters had this manner of curling their hair, that way of placing their hoods; whose frailty was covered by such a

[2] Whimsical characters.

sort of a petticoat, and whose vanity to show her foot made that part of the dress so short in such a year. In a word, all his conversation and knowledge have been in the female world. As other men of his age will take notice to you what such a minister said upon such and such an occasion, he will tell you when the Duke of Monmouth danced at court, such a woman was then smitten, another was taken with him at the head of his troop in the park. In all these important relations, he has ever about the same time received a kind glance, or a blow of a fan from some celebrated beauty, mother of the present Lord Such-a-one. If you speak of a young commoner that said a lively thing in the House, he starts up, "He has good blood in his veins; Tom Mirable begot him; the rogue cheated me in that affair; that young fellow's mother used me more like a dog than any woman I ever made advances to." This way of talking of his very much enlivens the conversation among us of a more sedate turn, and I find there is not one of the company, but myself, who rarely speak at all, but speaks of him as of that sort of a man who is usually called a well-bred fine gentleman. To conclude his character, where women are not concerned, he is an honest worthy man.

I cannot tell whether I am to account him, whom I am next to speak of, as one of our company; for he visits us but seldom, but when he does, it adds to every man else a new enjoyment of himself. He is a clergyman, a very philosophic man, of general learning, great sanctity of life, and the most exact good breeding. He has the misfortune to be of a very weak constitution, and consequently cannot accept of such cares and business as preferments in his function would oblige him to; he is therefore among divines what a chamber-counsellor is among lawyers. The probity of his mind, and the integrity of his life, create him followers, as being eloquent or loud advances others. He seldom introduces the subject he speaks upon; but we are so far gone in years that he observes, when he is among us, an earnestness to have him fall on some divine topic, which he always treats with much authority, as one who has no interest in this world, as one who is hastening to the object of all his wishes, and conceives hope from his decays and infirmities. These are my ordinary companions.

HINTS TOWARDS AN ESSAY ON CONVERSATION

A TREATISE ON GOOD MANNERS AND GOOD BREEDING

A LETTER OF ADVICE TO A YOUNG POET

ON THE DEATH OF ESTHER JOHNSON [STELLA]

BY
JONATHAN SWIFT

INTRODUCTORY NOTE

JONATHAN SWIFT (1667–1745), one of the greatest of English satirists, was born in Dublin and educated for the church at Trinity College in the same city. At the age of twenty-two he became secretary to Sir William Temple, to whom he was related, and whose works he edited. During his residence with Temple he wrote his "Tale of a Tub" and the "Battle of the Books"; and on Temple's death he returned to Ireland, where he held several livings. During his secretaryship he had gained a knowledge of English politics, and in 1710 he left the Whig party and went over to the Tories, becoming their ablest pen at a time when pamphleteering was an important means of influencing politics. He was appointed Dean of St. Patrick's, Dublin, by Queen Anne in 1713, and on the fall of the Tories he retired to Ireland. He continued to write voluminously on political, literary, and ecclesiastical topics, his best known work, "Gulliver's Travels," being a political allegory. Several years before his death his brain became diseased, and he suffered terribly till his mind was almost totally eclipsed.

A fuller account of Swift's life and an estimate of his character will be found in the essay by Thackeray in another volume of the Harvard Classics.

In the first three of Swift's writings here printed will be found good examples of his treatment of social and literary questions. The ironical humor running through these frequently became, when he dealt with subjects on which he felt keenly, incredibly savage and at times extremely coarse; but for the power of his invective and the effectiveness of his sarcasm there is hardly a parallel in the language. The fourth paper deals with the death of Esther Johnson, the "Stella" of his Journal, whom he had known from the days when he lived with Temple, and to whom it has been supposed that he was married.

HINTS TOWARDS AN ESSAY
ON CONVERSATION

I HAVE observed few obvious subjects to have been so seldom, or, at least, so slightly handled as this; and, indeed, I know few so difficult to be treated as it ought, nor yet upon which there seemeth so much to be said.

Most things, pursued by men for the happiness of public or private life, our wit or folly have so refined, that they seldom subsist but in idea; a true friend, a good marriage, a perfect form of government, with some others, require so many ingredients, so good in their several kinds, and so much niceness in mixing them, that for some thousands of years men have despaired of reducing their schemes to perfection. But, in conversation, it is, or might be otherwise; for here we are only to avoid a multitude of errors, which, although a matter of some difficulty, may be in every man's power, for want of which it remaineth as mere an idea as the other. Therefore it seemeth to me, that the truest way to understand conversation, is to know the faults and errors to which it is subject, and from thence every man to form maxims to himself whereby it may be regulated, because it requireth few talents to which most men are not born, or at least may not acquire without any great genius or study. For nature hath left every man a capacity of being agreeable, though not of shining in company; and there are an hundred men sufficiently qualified for both, who, by a very few faults, that they might correct in half an hour, are not so much as tolerable.

I was prompted to write my thoughts upon this subject by mere indignation, to reflect that so useful and innocent a pleasure, so fitted for every period and condition of life, and so much in all men's power, should be so much neglected and abused.

And in this discourse it will be necessary to note those errors that are obvious, as well as others which are seldomer observed, since there are few so obvious, or acknowledged, into which most men, some time or other, are not apt to run.

For instance: Nothing is more generally exploded than the folly of talking too much; yet I rarely remember to have seen five people together, where some one among them hath not been predominant in that kind, to the great constraint and disgust of all the rest. But among such as deal in multitudes of words, none are comparable to the sober deliberate talker, who proceedeth with much thought and caution, maketh his preface, brancheth out into several digressions, findeth a hint that putteth him in mind of another story, which he promiseth to tell you when this is done; cometh back regularly to his subject, cannot readily call to mind some person's name, holding his head, complaineth of his memory; the whole company all this while in suspense; at length says, it is no matter, and so goes on. And, to crown the business, it perhaps proveth at last a story the company hath heard fifty times before; or, at best, some insipid adventure of the relater.

Another general fault in conversation is, that of those who affect to talk of themselves: Some, without any ceremony, will run over the history of their lives; will relate the annals of their diseases, with the several symptoms and circumstances of them; will enumerate the hardships and injustice they have suffered in court, in parliament, in love, or in law. Others are more dexterous, and with great art will lie on the watch to hook in their own praise: They will call a witness to remember they always foretold what would happen in such a case, but none would believe them; they advised such a man from the beginning, and told him the consequences, just as they happened; but he would have his own way. Others make a vanity of telling their faults; they are the strangest men in the world; they cannot dissemble; they own it is a folly; they have lost abundance of advantages by it; but, if you would give them the world, they cannot help it; there is something in their nature that abhors insincerity and constraint; with many other insufferable topics of the same altitude.

Of such mighty importance every man is to himself, and ready to think he is so to others; without once making this easy and obvious reflection, that his affairs can have no more weight with

other men, than theirs have with him; and how little that is, he is
sensible enough.

Where company hath met, I often have observed two persons
discover, by some accident, that they were bred together at the
same school or university, after which the rest are condemned to
silence, and to listen while these two are refreshing each other's
memory with the arch tricks and passages of themselves and their
comrades.

I know a great officer of the army, who will sit for some time
with a supercilious and impatient silence, full of anger and contempt
for those who are talking; at length of a sudden demand audience,
decide the matter in a short dogmatical way; then withdraw within
himself again, and vouchsafe to talk no more, until his spirits
circulate again to the same point.

There are some faults in conversation, which none are so subject
to as the men of wit, nor ever so much as when they are with each
other. If they have opened their mouths, without endeavouring to
say a witty thing, they think it is so many words lost: It is a torment
to the hearers, as much as to themselves, to see them upon the rack
for invention, and in perpetual constraint, with so little success. They
must do something extraordinary, in order to acquit themselves, and
answer their character, else the standers-by may be disappointed and
be apt to think them only like the rest of mortals. I have known two
men of wit industriously brought together, in order to entertain the
company, where they have made a very ridiculous figure, and provided all the mirth at their own expense.

I know a man of wit, who is never easy but where he can be
allowed to dictate and preside: he neither expecteth to be informed
or entertained, but to display his own talents. His business is to be
good company, and not good conversation; and therefore, he
chooseth to frequent those who are content to listen, and profess
themselves his admirers. And, indeed, the worst conversation I ever
remember to have heard in my life, was that at Will's coffeehouse,
where the wits (as they were called) used formerly to assemble; that
is to say, five or six men, who had writ plays, or at least prologues,
or had share in a miscellany, came thither, and entertained one
another with their trifling composures, in so important an air, as if

they had been the noblest efforts of human nature, or that the fate of kingdoms depended on them; and they were usually attended with an humble audience of young students from the inns of court, or the universities, who, at due distance, listened to these oracles, and returned home with great contempt for their law and philosophy, their heads filled with trash, under the name of politeness, criticism and *belles lettres.*

By these means the poets, for many years past, were all overrun with pedantry. For, as I take it, the word is not properly used; because pedantry is the too frequent or unseasonable obtruding our own knowledge in common discourse, and placing too great a value upon it; by which definition, men of the court or the army may be as guilty of pedantry as a philosopher or a divine; and, it is the same vice in women, when they are over copious upon the subject of their petticoats, or their fans, or their china. For which reason, although it be a piece of prudence, as well as good manners, to put men upon talking on subjects they are best versed in, yet that is a liberty a wise man could hardly take; because, beside the imputation of pedantry, it is what he would never improve by.

The great town is usually provided with some player, mimic or buffoon, who hath a general reception at the good tables; familiar and domestic with persons of the first quality, and usually sent for at every meeting to divert the company; against which I have no objection. You go there as to a farce or a puppetshow; your business is only to laugh in season, either out of inclination or civility, while this merry companion is acting his part. It is a business he hath undertaken, and we are to suppose he is paid for his day's work. I only quarrel, when in select and private meetings, where men of wit and learning are invited to pass an evening, this jester should be admitted to run over his circle of tricks, and make the whole company unfit for any other conversation, besides the indignity of confounding men's talents at so shameful a rate.

Raillery is the finest part of conversation; but, as it is our usual custom to counterfeit and adulterate whatever is too dear for us, so we have done with this, and turned it all into what is generally called repartee, or being smart; just as when an expensive fashion cometh up, those who are not able to reach it, content themselves with some paltry imitation. It now passeth for raillery to run a man down in discourse, to put him out of countenance, and make him ridiculous, sometimes to expose the defects of his person or understanding; on all which occasions he is obliged not to be angry, to avoid the imputation of not being able to take a jest. It is admirable to observe one who is dexterous at this art, singling out a weak adversary, getting the laugh on his side, and then carrying all before him. The French, from whence we borrow the word, have a quite different idea of the thing, and so had we in the politer age of our fathers. Raillery was to say something that at first appeared a reproach or reflection; but, by some turn of wit unexpected and surprising, ended always in a compliment, and to the advantage of the person it was addressed to. And surely one of the best rules in conversation is, never to say a thing which any of the company can reasonably wish we had rather left unsaid; nor can there anything be well more contrary to the ends for which people meet together, than to part unsatisfied with each other or themselves.

There are two faults in conversation, which appear very different, yet arise from the same root, and are equally blameable; I mean, an impatience to interrupt others, and the uneasiness of being interrupted ourselves. The two chief ends of conversation are to entertain and improve those we are among, or to receive those benefits ourselves; which whoever will consider, cannot easily run into either of those two errors; because when any man speaketh in company, it is to be supposed he doth it for his hearers' sake, and not his own; so that common discretion will teach us not to force their attention, if they are not willing to lend it; nor on the other side, to interrupt him who is in possession, because that is in the grossest manner to give the preference to our own good sense.

There are some people, whose good manners will not suffer them to interrupt you; but, what is almost as bad, will discover abundance of impatience, and lie upon the watch until you have done, because they have started something in their own thoughts which they long to be delivered of. Meantime, they are so far from regarding what passes, that their imaginations are wholly turned upon what they have in reserve, for fear it should slip out of their memory; and thus they confine their invention, which might otherwise range over a hundred things full as good, and that might be much more naturally introduced.

There is a sort of rude familiarity, which some people, by practising among their intimates, have introduced into their general conversation, and would have it pass for innocent freedom or humour, which is a dangerous experiment in our northern climate, where all the little decorum and politeness we have are purely forced by art, and are so ready to lapse into barbarity. This, among the Romans, was the raillery of slaves, of which we have many instances in Plautus. It seemeth to have been introduced among us by Cromwell, who, by preferring the scum of the people, made it a court entertainment, of which I have heard many particulars; and, considering all things were turned upside down, it was reasonable and judicious: Although it was a piece of policy found out to ridicule a point of honour in the other extreme, when the smallest word misplaced among gentlemen ended in a duel.

There are some men excellent at telling a story, and provided with a plentiful stock of them, which they can draw out upon occasion in all companies; and, considering how low conversation runs now among us, it is not altogether a contemptible talent; however, it is subject to two unavoidable defects; frequent repetition, and being soon exhausted; so that whoever valueth this gift in himself, hath need of a good memory, and ought frequently to shift his company, that he may not discover the weakness of his fund; for those who are thus endowed, have seldom any other revenue, but live upon the main stock.

Great speakers in public, are seldom agreeable in private conversation, whether their faculty be natural, or acquired by practice, and often venturing. Natural elocution, although it may seem a paradox, usually springeth from a barrenness of invention and of words, by which men who have only one stock of notions upon every subject, and one set of phrases to express them in, they swim upon the superfices, and offer themselves on every occasion; therefore, men of much learning, and who know the compass of a language, are generally the worst talkers on a sudden, until much practice hath inured and emboldened them, because they are confounded with plenty of matter, variety of notions, and of words, which they cannot readily choose, but are perplexed and entangled by too great a choice; which is no disadvantage in private conversation; where, on the other side, the talent of haranguing is, of all others, most insupportable.

Nothing hath spoiled men more for conversation, than the character of being wits, to support which, they never fail of encouraging a number of followers and admirers, who list themselves in their service, wherein they find their accounts on both sides, by pleasing their mutual vanity. This hath given the former such an air of superiority, and made the latter so pragmatical, that neither of them are well to be endured. I say nothing here of the itch of dispute and contradiction, telling of lies, or of those who are troubled with the disease called the wandering of the thoughts, that they are never present in mind at what passeth in discourse; for whoever labours under any of these possessions, is as unfit for conversation as a madman in Bedlam.

I think I have gone over most of the errors in conversation, that have fallen under my notice or memory, except some that are merely personal, and others too gross to need exploding; such as lewd or profane talk; but I pretend only to treat the errors of conversation in general, and not the several subjects of discourse, which would be infinite. Thus we see how human nature is most debased, by the abuse of that faculty, which is held the great distinction between men and brutes; and how little advantage we make of that which might be the greatest, the most lasting, and the most innocent, as well as useful pleasure of life. In default of which, we are forced to take up with those poor amusements of dress and visiting, or the more pernicious ones of play, drink, and vicious amours, whereby the nobility and gentry of both sexes are entirely corrupted both in body and mind, and have lost all notions of love, honour, friendship, generosity; which, under the name of fopperies, have been for some time laughed out of doors.

This degeneracy of conversation, with the pernicious consequences thereof upon our humours and dispositions, hath been owing, among other causes, to the custom arisen, for sometime past, of excluding women from any share in our society, further than in parties at play, or dancing, or in the pursuit of an amour. I take the highest period of politeness in England (and it is of the same date in France) to have been the peaceable part of King Charles the First's reign; and from what we read of those times, as well as from the accounts I have formerly met with from some who lived in that court, the methods then used for raising and cultivating conversation, were altogether different from ours. Several ladies, whom, we find celebrated by the poets of that age, had assemblies at their houses, where persons of the best understanding, and of both sexes, met to pass the evenings in discoursing upon whatever agreeable subjects were occasionally started; and although we are apt to ridicule the sublime platonic notions they had, or personated in love and friendship, I conceive their refinements were grounded upon reason, and that a little grain of the romance is no ill ingredient to preserve and exalt the dignity of human nature, without which it is apt to degenerate into everything that is sordid, vicious and low. If there were no other use in the conversation of ladies, it is sufficient that it would lay a restraint upon those odious topics of immodesty and indecencies, into which the rudeness of our northern genius is so apt to fall. And, therefore, it is observable in those sprightly gentlemen about the town, who are so very dexterous at entertaining a vizard mask in the park or the playhouse, that, in the company of ladies of virtue and honour, they are silent and disconcerted, and out of their element.

There are some people who think they sufficiently acquit themselves and entertain their company with relating of facts of no consequence, nor at all out of the road of such common incidents as happen every day; and this I have observed more frequently among the Scots than any other nation, who are very careful not to omit the minutest circumstances of time or place; which kind of discourse, if it were not a little relieved by the uncouth terms and phrases, as well as accent and gesture, peculiar to that country, would be hardly tolerable. It is not a fault in company to talk much; but to continue it long is certainly one; for, if the majority of those who are got together be naturally silent or cautious, the conversation will flag, unless it be often renewed by one among them, who can start new subjects, provided he doth not dwell upon them, but leaveth room for answers and replies.

A TREATISE ON GOOD MANNERS
AND GOOD BREEDING

GOOD manners is the art of making those people easy with whom we converse.

Whoever makes the fewest persons uneasy is the best bred in the company.

As the best law is founded upon reason, so are the best manners. And as some lawyers have introduced unreasonable things into common law, so likewise many teachers have introduced absurd things into common good manners.

One principal point of this art is to suit our behaviour to the three several degrees of men; our superiors, our equals, and those below us.

For instance, to press either of the two former to eat or drink is a breach of manners; but a farmer or a tradesman must be thus treated, or else it will be difficult to persuade them that they are welcome.

Pride, ill nature, and want of sense, are the three great sources of ill manners; without some one of these defects, no man will behave himself ill for want of experience; or of what, in the language of fools, is called knowing the world.

I defy any one to assign an incident wherein reason will not direct us what we are to say or do in company, if we are not misled by pride or ill nature.

Therefore I insist that good sense is the principal foundation of good manners; but because the former is a gift which very few among mankind are possessed of, therefore all the civilized nations of the world have agreed upon fixing some rules for common behaviour, best suited to their general customs, or fancies, as a kind of artificial good sense, to supply the defects of reason. Without which the gentlemanly part of dunces would be perpetually at cuffs, as they seldom fail when they happen to be drunk, or engaged in squabbles about women or play. And, God be thanked, there hardly happens a duel in a year, which may not be imputed to one of those three motives. Upon which account, I should be exceedingly sorry to find the legislature make any new laws against the practice of duelling; because the methods are easy and many for a wise man to avoid a quarrel with honour, or engage in it with innocence. And I can discover no political evil in suffering bullies, sharpers, and rakes, to rid the world of each other by a method of their own; where the law hath not been able to find an expedient.

As the common forms of good manners were intended for regulating the conduct of those who have weak understandings; so they have been corrupted by the persons for whose use they were contrived. For these people have fallen into a needless and endless way of multiplying ceremonies, which have been extremely troublesome to those who practise them, and insupportable to everybody else: insomuch that wise men are often more uneasy at the over civility of these refiners, than they could possibly be in the conversations of peasants or mechanics.

The impertinencies of this ceremonial behaviour are nowhere better seen than at those tables where ladies preside, who value themselves upon account of their good breeding; where a man must reckon upon passing an hour without doing any one thing he has a mind to; unless he will be so hardy to break through all the settled decorum of the family. She determines what he loves best, and how much he shall eat; and if the master of the house happens to be of the same disposition, he proceeds in the same tyrannical manner to prescribe in the drinking part: at the same time, you are under the necessity of answering a thousand apologies for your entertainment. And although a good deal of this humour is pretty well worn off among many people of the best fashion, yet too much of it still remains, especially in the country; where an honest gentleman assured me, that having been kept four days, against his will, at a friend's house, with all the circumstances of hiding his boots, locking up the stable, and other contrivances of the like nature, he could not remember, from the moment he came into the house to the moment he left it, any one thing, wherein his inclination was not directly contradicted; as if the whole family had entered into a combination to torment him.

But, besides all this, it would be endless to recount the many foolish and ridiculous accidents I have observed among these unfortunate proselytes to ceremony. I have seen a duchess fairly knocked down, by the precipitancy of an officious coxcomb running to save her the trouble of opening a door. I remember, upon a birthday at court, a great lady was utterly desperate by a dish of sauce let fall by a page directly upon her head-dress and brocade, while she gave a sudden turn to her elbow upon some point of ceremony with the person who sat next her. Monsieur Buys, the Dutch envoy, whose politics and manners were much of a size, brought a son with him, about thirteen years old, to a great table at court. The boy and his father, whatever they put on their plates, they first offered round in order, to every person in the company; so that we could not get a minute's quiet during the whole dinner. At last their two plates happened to encounter, and with so much violence, that, being china, they broke in twenty pieces, and stained half the company with wet sweetmeats and cream.

There is a pedantry in manners, as in all arts and sciences; and sometimes in trades. Pedantry is properly the overrating any kind of knowledge we pretend to. And if that kind of knowledge be a trifle in itself, the pedantry is the greater. For which reason I look upon fiddlers, dancing-masters, heralds, masters of the ceremony, &c. to be greater pedants than Lipsius, or the elder Scaliger. With these kind of pedants, the court, while I knew it, was always plentifully stocked; I mean from the gentleman usher (at least) inclusive, downward to the gentleman porter; who are, generally speaking, the most insignificant race of people that this island can afford, and with the smallest tincture of good manners, which is the only trade they profess. For being wholly illiterate, and conversing chiefly with each other, they reduce the whole system of breeding within the forms and circles of their several offices; and as they are below the notice of ministers, they live and die in court under all revolutions with great obsequiousness to those who are in any degree of favour or credit, and with rudeness or insolence to everybody else. Whence I have long concluded, that good manners are not a plant of the court growth: for if they were, those people who have understandings directly of a level for such acquirements, and who have served such long apprenticeships to nothing else, would certainly have picked them up. For as to the great officers, who attend the prince's person or councils, or preside in his family, they are a transient body, who have no better a title to good manners than their neighbours, nor will probably have recourse to gentlemen ushers for instruction. So that I know little to be learnt at court upon this head, except in the material circumstance of dress; wherein the authority of the maids of honour must indeed be allowed to be almost equal to that of a favourite actress.

I remember a passage my Lord Bolingbroke told me, that going to receive Prince Eugene of Savoy at his landing, in order to conduct him immediately to the Queen, the prince said, he was much concerned that he could not see her Majesty that night; for Monsieur Hoffman (who was then by) had assured his Highness that he could not be admitted into her presence with a tied-up periwig; that his equipage was not arrived; and that he had endeavoured in vain to borrow a long one among all his valets and pages. My lord turned the matter into a jest, and brought the Prince to her Majesty; for which he was highly censured by the whole tribe of gentlemen ushers; among whom Monsieur Hoffman, an old dull resident of the Emperor's, had picked up this material point of ceremony; and which, I believe, was the best lesson he had learned in five-and-twenty years' residence.

I make a difference between good manners and good breeding; although, in order to vary my expression, I am sometimes forced to confound them. By the first, I only understand the art of remembering and applying certain settled forms of general behaviour. But good breeding is of a much larger extent; for besides an uncommon degree of literature sufficient to qualify a gentleman for reading a play, or a political pamphlet, it takes in a great compass of knowledge; no less than that of dancing, fighting, gaming, making the circle of Italy, riding the great horse, and speaking French; not to mention some other secondary, or subaltern accomplishments, which are more easily acquired. So that the difference between good breeding and good manners lies in this, that the former cannot be attained to by the best understandings, without study and labour; whereas a tolerable degree of reason will instruct us in every part of good manners, without other assistance.

I can think of nothing more useful upon this subject, than to point out some particulars, wherein the very essentials of good manners are concerned, the neglect or perverting of which doth very much disturb the good commerce of the world, by introducing a traffic of mutual uneasiness in most companies.

First, a necessary part of good manners, is a punctual observance of time at our own dwellings, or those of others, or at third places; whether upon matter of civility, business, or diversion; which rule, though it be a plain dictate of common reason, yet the greatest minister I ever knew was the greatest trespasser against it; by which all his business doubled upon him, and placed him in a continual arrear. Upon which I often used to rally him, as deficient in point of good manners. I have known more than one ambassador, and secretary of state with a very moderate portion of intellectuals, execute their offices with good success and applause, by the mere force of exactness and regularity. If you duly observe time for the service of another, it doubles the obligation; if upon your own account, it would be manifest folly, as well as ingratitude, to neglect it. If both are concerned, to make your equal or inferior attend on you, to his own disadvantage, is pride and injustice.

Ignorance of forms cannot properly be styled ill manners; because forms are subject to frequent changes; and consequently, being not founded upon reason, are beneath a wise man's regard. Besides, they vary in every country; and after a short period of time, very frequently in the same; so that a man who travels, must needs be at first a stranger to them in every court through which he passes; and perhaps at his return, as much a stranger in his own; and after all, they are easier to be remembered or forgotten than faces or names.

Indeed, among the many impertinencies that superficial young men bring with them from abroad, this bigotry of forms is one of the principal, and more prominent than the rest; who look upon them not only as if they were matters capable of admitting of choice, but even as points of importance; and are therefore zealous on all occasions to introduce and propagate the new forms and fashions they have brought back with them. So that, usually speaking, the worst bred person in the company is a young traveller just returned from abroad.

A LETTER OF ADVICE TO A
YOUNG POET

Sir,

As I have always professed a friendship for you, and have there-fore been more inquisitive into your conduct and studies than is usually agreeable to young men, so I must own I am not a little pleased to find, by your last account, that you have entirely bent your thoughts to English poetry, with design to make it your profession and business. Two reasons incline me to encourage you in this study; one, the narrowness of your present circumstances; the other, the great use of poetry to mankind and society, and in every employment of life. Upon these views, I cannot but com-mend your wise resolution to withdraw so early from other un-profitable and severe studies, and betake yourself to that, which, if you have good luck, will advance your fortune, and make you an ornament to your friends, and your country. It may be your justi-fication, and farther encouragement, to consider, that history, ancient or modern, cannot furnish you an instance of one person, eminent in any station, who was not in some measure versed in poetry, or at least a well wisher to the professors of it. Neither would I despair to prove, if legally called thereto, that it is impossible to be a good soldier, divine, or lawyer, or even so much as an eminent bellman, or ballad-singer, without some taste of poetry, and a competent skill in versification. But I say the less of this, because the renowned Sir Philip Sidney has exhausted the subject before me, in his "De-fence of Poesie,"[1] on which I shall make no other remark but this, that he argues there as if he really believed himself.

For my own part, having never made one verse since I was at school, where I suffered too much for my blunders in poetry, to have any love to it ever since, I am not able from any experience of my own, to give you those instructions you desire; neither will I declare

[1] See the first essay in this volume.

(for I love to conceal my passions) how much I lament my neglect of poetry in those periods of my life, which were properest for improvements in that ornamental part of learning; besides, my age and infirmities might well excuse me to you, as being unqualified to be your writing-master, with spectacles on, and a shaking hand. However, that I may not be altogether wanting to you in an affair of so much importance to your credit and happiness, I shall here give you some scattered thoughts upon the subject, such as I have gathered by reading and observation.

There is a certain little instrument, the first of those in use with scholars, and the meanest, considering the materials of it, whether it be a joint of wheaten straw, (the old Arcadian pipe) or just three inches of slender wire, or a stripped feather, or a corking-pin. Furthermore, this same diminutive tool, for the posture of it, usually reclines its head on the thumb of the right hand, sustains the foremost finger upon its breast, and is itself supported by the second. This is commonly known by the name of a FESCUE; I shall here therefore condescend to be this little elementary guide, and point out some particulars which may be of use to you in your hornbook of poetry.

In the first place, I am not yet convinced, that it is at all necessary for a modern poet to *believe in God,* or have any serious sense of religion; and in this article you must give me leave to suspect your capacity; because religion being what your mother taught you, you will hardly find it possible, at least not easy, all at once to get over those early prejudices, so far as to think it better to be a *great wit* than a *good Christian,* though herein the general practice is against you; so that if, upon enquiry, you find in yourself any such softnesses, owing to the nature of your education, my advice is, that you forthwith lay down your pen, as having no further business with it in the way of poetry; unless you will be content to pass for an insipid, or will submit to be hooted at by your fraternity, or can disguise your religion, as well-bred men do their learning, in complaisance to company. For poetry, as it has been managed for some years past, by such as make a business of it, (and of such only I speak here; for I do not call him a poet that writes for his diversion, any more than that gentleman a fiddler, who amuses himself with a violin) I say our poetry of late has been altogether disengaged from the narrow notions of virtue and piety, because it has been found by experience of our professors, that the smallest quantity of religion, like a single drop of malt liquor in claret, will muddy and discompose the brightest poetical genius.

Religion supposes heaven and hell, the word of God, and sacraments, and twenty other circumstances, which, taken seriously, are a wonderful check to wit and humour, and such as a true poet cannot possibly give in to, with a saving to his poetical licence; but yet it is necessary for him, that others should believe those things seriously, that his wit may be exercised on their wisdom, for so doing: For though a wit need not have religion, religion is necessary to a wit, as an instrument is to the hand that plays upon it: And for this the moderns plead the example of their great idol Lucretius, who had not been by half so eminent a poet (as he truly was), but that he stood tiptoe on religion, *Religio pedibus subjecta,* and by that rising ground had the advantage of all the poets of his own or following times, who were not mounted on the same pedestal.

Besides, it is further to be observed, that Petronius, another of their favourites, speaking of the qualifications of a good poet, insists chiefly on the *liber spiritus;* by which I have been ignorant enough heretofore to suppose he meant, a good invention, or great compass of thought, or a sprightly imagination: But I have learned a better construction, from the opinion and practice of the moderns; and taking it literally for a free spirit, *i.e.* a spirit, or mind, free or disengaged from all prejudices concerning God, religion, and another world, it is to me a plain account why our present set of poets are, and hold themselves obliged to be, free thinkers.

But although I cannot recommend religion upon the practice of some of our most eminent English poets, yet I can justly advise you, from their example, to be conversant in the Scriptures, and, if possible, to make yourself entirely master of them: In which, however, I intend nothing less than imposing upon you a task of piety. Far be it from me to desire you to believe them, or lay any great stress upon their authority, (in that you may do as you think fit) but to read them as a piece of necessary furniture for a wit and a poet; which is a very different view from that of a Christian. For I have made it my observation, that the greatest wits have been the best textuaries. Our modern poets are, all to a man, almost as well read in the Scriptures as some of our divines, and often abound more with the phrase. They have read them historically, critically, musically, comically, poetically, and every other way, except religiously, and have found their account in doing so. For the Scriptures are undoubtedly a fund of wit, and a subject for wit. You may, according to the modern practice, be witty upon them or out of them. And to speak the truth, but for them I know not what our playwrights would do for images, allusions, similitudes, examples, or even language itself. Shut up the sacred books, and I would be bound our wit would run down like an alarum, or fall as the stocks did, and ruin half the poets in these kingdoms. And if that were the case, how would most of that tribe, (all, I think, but the immortal Addison, who made a better use of his Bible, and a few more) who dealt so freely in that fund, rejoice that they had drawn out in time, and left the present generation of poets to be the bubbles!

But here I must enter one caution, and desire you to take notice, that in this advice of reading the Scriptures, I had not the least thought concerning your qualification that way for poetical orders; which I mention, because I find a notion of that kind advanced by one of our English poets, and is, I suppose, maintained by the rest. He says to Spenser, in a pretended vision,

> ——With hands laid on, ordain me fit
> For the great cure and ministry of wit.

Which passage is, in my opinion, a notable allusion to the Scriptures; and, making (but reasonable) allowances for the small circumstances of profaneness, bordering close upon blasphemy, is inimitably fine; besides some useful discoveries made in it, as, that there are bishops in poetry, that these bishops must ordain young poets, and with laying on hands; and that poetry is a cure of souls; and, consequently speaking, those who have such cures ought to be poets, and too often are so. And indeed, as of old, poets and priests were one and the same function, the alliance of those ministerial offices is to this day happily maintained in the same persons; and this I take to be the only justifiable reason for that appellation which they so much affect, I mean the modest title of divine poets. However, having never been present at the ceremony of ordaining to the priesthood of poetry, I own I have no notion of the thing, and shall say the less of it here.

The Scriptures then being generally both the fountain and subject of modern wit, I could do no less than give them the preference in your reading. After a thorough acquaintance with them, I would advise you to turn your thoughts to human literature, which yet I say more in compliance with vulgar opinions, than according to my own sentiments.

For, indeed, nothing has surprised me more, than to see the prejudices of mankind as to this matter of human learning, who have generally thought it necessary to be a good scholar, in order to be a good poet; than which nothing is falser in fact, or more contrary to practice and experience. Neither will I dispute the matter, if any man will undertake to shew me one professed poet now in being, who is anything of what may be justly called a scholar; or is the worse poet for that, but perhaps the better, for being so little encumbered with the pedantry of learning. 'Tis true, the contrary was the opinion of our forefathers, which we of this age have devotion enough to receive from them on their own terms, and unexamined, but not sense enough to perceive 'twas a gross mistake in them. So Horace had told us:

> Scribendi recte sapere est et principium et fons,
> Rem tibi Socraticae poterunt ostendere chartae.[2]
>
> HOR. de Art. Poet. 309.

But to see the different casts of men's heads, some not inferior to that poet in understanding (if you will take their own word for it), do see no consequence in this rule, and are not ashamed to declare themselves of a contrary opinion. Do not many men write well in common account, who have nothing of that principle? Many are too wise to be poets, and others too much poets to be wise. Must a man, forsooth, be no less than a philosopher, to be a poet, when it is plain, that some of the greatest idiots of the age, are our prettiest performers that way? And for this, I appeal to the judgment and observation of mankind. Sir Philip Sidney's notable remark upon this nation, may not be improper to mention here. He says, "In our

---

[2] Good sense, that fountain of the Muse's art,
Let the strong page of Socrates impart.

neighbour country, Ireland, where true learning goes very bare, yet are their poets held in devout reverence;" which shews, that learning is no way necessary either to the making a poet, or judging of him. And further to see the fate of things, notwithstanding our learning here is as bare as ever, yet are our poets not held, as formerly in devout reverence, but are perhaps the most contemptible race of mortals now in this kingdom, which is no less to be wondered at, than lamented.

Some of the old philosophers were poets (as according to the forementioned author, Socrates and Plato were; which, however, is what I did not know before) but that does not say, that all poets are, or that any need be philosophers, otherwise than as those are so called who are a little out at the elbows. In which sense the great Shakespeare might have been a philosopher; but was no scholar, yet was an excellent poet. Neither do I think a late most judicious critic so much mistaken, as others do, in advancing this opinion, that "Shakespeare had been a worse poet, had he been a better scholar." And Sir William Davenant is another instance in the same kind. Nor must it be forgotten, that Plato was an avowed enemy to poets, which is perhaps the reason why poets have been always at enmity with his profession; and have rejected all learning and philosophy for the sake of that one philosopher. As I take the matter, neither philosophy, nor any part of learning, is more necessary to poetry, (which, if you will believe the same author, is "the sum of all learning") than to know the theory of light, and the several proportions and diversifications of it in particular colours, is to a good painter.

Whereas therefore, a certain author, called Petronius Arbiter, going upon the same mistake, has confidently declared, that one ingredient of a good poet, is, *"mens ingenti literarum flumine inundata;"*[3] I do, on the contrary, declare, that this his assertion (to speak of it in the softest terms) is no better than an invidious and unhandsome reflection on all the gentlemen-poets of these times; for, with his good leave, much less than a flood, or inundation, will serve the turn; and, to my certain knowledge, some of our greatest wits in your poetical way, have not as much real learning as would cover a sixpence in the bottom of a basin; nor do I think the worse of them.

For, to speak my private opinion, I am for every man's working

[3] "A mind flooded with a vast river of learning."

upon his own materials, and producing only what he can find within himself, which is commonly a better stock than the owner knows it to be. I think flowers of wit ought to spring, as those in a garden do, from their own root and stem, without foreign assistance. I would have a man's wit rather like a fountain, that feeds itself invisibly, than a river, that is supplied by several streams from abroad.

Or if it be necessary, as the case is with some barren wits, to take in the thoughts of others, in order to draw forth their own, as dry pumps will not play till water is thrown into them; in that necessity, I would recommend some of the approved standard authors of antiquity for your perusal, as a poet and a wit; because maggots being what you look for, as monkeys do for vermin in their keepers' heads, you will find they abound in good old authors, as in rich old cheese, not in the new; and for that reason you must have the classics, especially the most worm-eaten of them, often in your hands.

But with this caution, that you are not to use those ancients as unlucky lads do their old fathers, and make no conscience of picking their pockets and pillaging them. Your business is not to steal from them, but to improve upon them, and make their sentiments your own; which is an effect of great judgment; and though difficult, yet very possible, without the scurvy imputation of filching. For I humbly conceive, though I light my candle at my neighbour's fire, that does not alter the property, or make the wick, the wax, or the flame, or the whole candle, less my own.

Possibly you may think it a very severe task, to arrive at a competent knowledge of so many of the ancients, as excel in their way; and indeed it would be really so, but for the short and easy method lately found out of abstracts, abridgments, summaries, &c. which are admirable expedients for being very learned with little or no reading; and have the same use with burning-glasses, to collect the diffused rays of wit and learning in authors, and make them point with warmth and quickness upon the reader's imagination. And to this is nearly related that other modern device of consulting indexes, which is to read books hebraically,[4] and begin where others usually end; and this is a compendious way of coming to an acquaintance with authors. For authors are to be used like lobsters, you must look for the best meat in the tails, and lay the bodies back again in the

[4] That is, backwards.

dish. Your cunningest thieves (and what else are readers, who only read to borrow, *i.e.* to steal) use to cut off the portmanteau from behind, without staying to dive into the pockets of the owner. Lastly, you are taught thus much in the very elements of philosophy, for one of the first rules in logic is, *Finis est primus in intentione.*[5]

The learned world is therefore most highly indebted to a late painful and judicious editor of the classics, who has laboured in that new way with exceeding felicity. Every author by his management, sweats under himself, being over-loaded with his own index, and carries, like a north-country pedlar, all his substance and furniture upon his back, and with as great variety of trifles. To him let all young students make their compliments for so much time and pains saved in the pursuit of useful knowledge; for whoever shortens a road, is a benefactor to the public, and to every particular person who has occasion to travel that way.

But to proceed. I have lamented nothing more in my time, than the disuse of some ingenious little plays, in fashion with young folks, when I was a boy, and to which the great facility of that age, above ours, in composing was certainly owing; and if anything has brought a damp upon the versification of these times, we have no further than this to go for the cause of it. Now could these sports be happily revived, I am of opinion your wisest course would be to apply your thoughts to them, and never fail to make a party when you can, in those profitable diversions. For example, "Crambo" is of extraordinary use to good rhyming, and rhyming is what I have ever accounted the very essential of a good poet: And in that notion I am not singular; for the aforesaid Sir Philip Sidney has declared, "That the chief life of modern versifying, consisteth in the like sounding of words, which we call rhyme," which is an authority, either without exception, or above any reply. Wherefore, you are ever to try a good poem as you would a sound pipkin, and if it rings well upon the knuckle, be sure there is no flaw in it. Verse without rhyme, is a body without a soul, (for the "chief life consisteth in the rhyme") or a bell without a clapper; which, in strictness, is no bell, as being neither of use nor delight. And the same ever honoured knight, with so musical an ear, had that veneration for the tunableness and chiming of verse, that he speaks of a poet as one that has

[5] "In intention the end is first."

"the reverend title of a rhymer." Our celebrated Milton has done these nations great prejudice in this particular, having spoiled as many reverend rhymers, by his example, as he has made real poets.

For which reason, I am overjoyed to hear, that a very ingenious youth of this town [Dublin], is now upon the useful design (for which he is never enough to be commended) of bestowing rhyme upon Milton's Paradise Lost, which will make your poem, in that only defective, more heroic and sonorous than it has hitherto been. I wish the gentleman success in the performance; and, as it is a work in which a young man could not be more happily employed, or appear in with greater advantage to his character, so I am concerned that it did not fall out to be your province.

With much the same view, I would recommend to you the witty play of "Pictures and Mottoes," which will furnish your imagination with great store of images and suitable devices. We of these kingdoms have found our account in this diversion, as little as we consider or acknowledge it. For to this we owe our eminent felicity in posies of rings, mottoes of snuff-boxes, the humours of sign-posts with their elegant inscriptions, &c. in which kind of productions not any nation in the world, no, not the Dutch themselves, will presume to rival us.

For much the same reason, it may be proper for you to have some insight into the play called, "What is it like?" as of great use in common practice, to quicken slow capacities, and improve the quickest. But the chief end of it is, to supply the fancy with variety of similes for all subjects. It will teach you to bring things to a likeness, which have not the least imaginable conformity in nature, which is properly creation, and the very business of a poet, as his name implies; and let me tell you, a good poet can no more be without a stock of similes by him, than a shoemaker without his lasts. He should have them sized, and ranged, and hung up in order in his shop, ready for all customers, and shaped to the feet of all sorts of verse. And here I could more fully (and I long to do it) insist upon the wonderful harmony and resemblance between a poet and a shoemaker, in many circumstances common to both; such as the binding of their temples, the stuff they work upon, and the paring-knife they use, &c. but that I would not digress, nor seem to trifle in so serious a matter.

Now I say, if you apply yourself to these diminutive sports (not to mention others of equal ingenuity, such as Draw-gloves, Cross purposes, Questions and commands, and the rest) it is not to be conceived what benefit (of nature) you will find by them, and how they will open the body of your invention. To these devote your spare hours, or rather spare all your hours to them, and then you will act as becomes a wise man, and make even diversion an improvement; like the inimitable management of the bee, which does the whole business of life at once, and at the same time both feeds, and works, and diverts itself.

Your own prudence will, I doubt not, direct you to take a place every evening amongst the ingenious, in the corner of a certain coffeehouse in this town, where you will receive a turn equally right as to wit, religion, and politics: As likewise to be as frequent at the playhouse as you can afford, without selling your books. For in our chaste theatre, even Cato himself might sit to the falling of the curtain: Besides, you will sometimes meet with tolerable conversation amongst the players; they are such a kind of men, as may pass upon the same sort of capacities, for wits off the stage, as they do for fine gentlemen upon it. Besides that, I have known a factor deal in as good ware, and sell as cheap as the merchant himself that employs him.

Add to this the expediency of furnishing out your shelves with a choice collection of modern miscellanies, in the gayest edition; and of reading all sorts of plays, especially the new, and above all, those of our own growth, printed by subscription; in which article of Irish manufacture, I readily agree to the late proposal, and am altogether for "rejecting and renouncing everything that comes from England:" To what purpose should we go thither either for coals or poetry, when we have a vein within ourselves equally good and more convenient? Lastly,

A common-place book is what a provident poet cannot subsist without, for this proverbial reason, that "great wits have short memories;" and whereas, on the other hand, poets being liars by profession, ought to have good memories. To reconcile these, a book of this sort is in the nature of a supplemental memory; or a record of what occurs remarkable in every day's reading or conversation. There you enter not only your own original thoughts, (which, a hundred to one, are few and insignificant) but such of other men as you think fit to make your own by entering them there. For take this for a rule, when an author is in your books, you have the same demand upon him for his wit, as a merchant has for your money, when you are in his.

By these few and easy prescriptions (with the help of a good genius) 'tis possible you may in a short time arrive at the accomplishments of a poet, and shine in that character. As for your manner of composing, and choice of subjects, I cannot take upon me to be your director; but I will venture to give you some short hints, which you may enlarge upon at your leisure. Let me entreat you then, by no means to lay aside that notion peculiar to our modern refiners in poetry, which is, that a poet must never write or discourse as the ordinary part of mankind do, but in number and verse, as an oracle; which I mention the rather, because upon this principle, I have known heroics brought into the pulpit, and a whole sermon composed and delivered in blank verse, to the vast credit of the preacher, no less than the real entertainment and great edification of the audience.

The secret of which I take to be this. When the matter of such discourses is but mere clay, or, as we usually call it, sad stuff, the preacher, who can afford no better, wisely moulds, and polishes, and dries, and washes this piece of earthen-ware, and then bakes it with poetic fire, after which it will ring like any pancrock, and is a good dish to set before common guests, as every congregation is, that comes so often for entertainment to one place.

There was a good old custom in use, which our ancestors had, of invoking the Muses at the entrance of their poems; I suppose, by way of craving a blessing. This the graceless moderns have in a great measure laid aside, but are not to be followed in that poetical impiety; for although to nice ears, such invocations may sound harsh and disagreeable (as tuning instruments is before a concert) they are equally necessary. Again, you must not fail to dress your muse in a forehead cloth of Greek or Latin; I mean, you are always to make use of a quaint motto in all your compositions; for besides that this artifice bespeaks the reader's opinion of the writer's learning, it is otherwise useful and commendable. A bright passage in the front of a poem, is a good mark, like a star in a horse's face, and the piece will certainly go off the better for it. The *os magna sonaturum,* which, if I remember right, Horace makes one qualification of a good poet, may teach you not to gag your muse, or stint yourself in words and epithets (which cost you nothing) contrary to the practice of some few out-of-the-way writers, who use a natural and concise expression, and affect a style like unto a Shrewsbury cake, short and sweet upon the palate; they will not afford you a word more than is necessary to make them intelligible, which is as poor and niggardly, as it would be to set down no more meat than your company will be sure to eat up. Words are but lackeys to sense, and will dance attendance, without wages or compulsion; *Verba non invita sequentur.*

Farthermore, when you set about composing, it may be necessary, for your ease and better distillation of wit, to put on your worst clothes, and the worse the better; for an author, like a limbick, will yield the better for having a rag about him. Besides that, I have observed a gardener cut the outward rind of a tree, (which is the *surtout* of it), to make it bear well: And this is a natural account of the usual poverty of poets, and is an argument why wits, of all men living, ought to be ill clad. I have always a secret veneration for any one I observe to be a little out of repair in his person, as supposing him either a poet or a philosopher; because the richest minerals are ever found under the most ragged and withered surface of earth.

As for your choice of subjects, I have only to give you this caution: That as a handsome way of praising is certainly the most difficult point in writing or speaking, I would by no means advise any young man to make his first essay in panegyric, besides the danger of it: for a particular encomium is ever attended with more ill-will, than any general invective, for which I need give no reasons; wherefore, my counsel is, that you use the point of your pen, not the feather; let your first attempt be a *coup d'éclat* [6] in the way of libel, lampoon, or satire. Knock down half a score reputations, and you

---

[6] "A brilliant stroke."

will infallibly raise your own; and so it be with wit, no matter with how little justice; for fiction is your trade.

Every great genius seems to ride upon mankind, like Pyrrhus on his elephant; and the way to have the absolute ascendant of your resty nag, and to keep your seat, is, at your first mounting, to afford him the whip and spurs plentifully; after which, you may travel the rest of the day with great alacrity. Once kick the world, and the world and you will live together at a reasonable good understanding. You cannot but know, that these of your profession have been called *genus irritabile vatum;*[7] and you will find it necessary to qualify yourself for that waspish society, by exerting your talent of satire upon the first occasion, and to abandon good-nature, only to prove yourself a true poet, which you will allow to be a valuable consideration: In a word, a young robber is usually entered by a murder: A young hound is blooded when he comes first into the field: A young bully begins with killing his man: And a young poet must shew his wit, as the other his courage, by cutting and slashing, and laying about him, and banging mankind. Lastly,

It will be your wisdom to look out betimes for a good service for your muse, according to her skill and qualifications, whether in the nature of a dairymaid, a cook, or char-woman. I mean, to hire out your pen to a party, which will afford you both pay and protection; and when you have to do with the press, (as you will long to be there) take care to bespeak an importunate friend, to extort your productions with an agreeable violence; and which, according to the cue between you, you must surrender *digito male pertinaci.*[8] There is a decency in this; for it no more becomes an author, in modesty, to have a hand in publishing his own works, than a woman in labour to lay herself.

I would be very loth to give the least umbrage of offence by what I have here said, as I may do, if I should be thought to insinuate that these circumstances of good writing have been unknown to, or not observed by, the poets of this kingdom. I will do my countrymen the justice to say, they have written by the foregoing rules with great exactness, and so far, as hardly to come behind those of their pro-

---

[7] "The irritable race of poets."
[8] "With an exceedingly tenacious finger."

fession in England, in perfection of low writing. The sublime, indeed, is not so common with us; but ample amends is made for that want, in great abundance of the admirable and amazing, which appears in all our compositions. Our very good friend (the knight aforesaid) speaking of the force of poetry, mentions "rhyming to death, which" (adds he) "is said to be done in Ireland;" and truly, to our honour be it spoken, that power, in a great measure, continues with us to this day.

I would now offer some poor thoughts of mine for the encouragement of poetry in this kingdom, if I could hope they would be agreeable. I have had many an aching heart for the ill plight of that noble profession here, and it has been my late and early study how to bring it into better circumstances. And surely, considering what monstrous wits in the poetic way, do almost daily start up and surprise us in this town; what prodigious geniuses we have here (of which I could give instances without number,) and withal of what great benefit it might be to our trade to encourage that science here, (for it is plain our linen manufacture is advanced by the great waste of paper made by our present set of poets, not to mention other necessary uses of the same to shop-keepers, especially grocers, apothecaries, and pastry-cooks; and I might add, but for our writers, the nation would in a little time be utterly destitute of bumfodder, and must of necessity import the same from England and Holland, where they have it in great abundance, by the indefatigable labour of their own wits) I say, these things considered, I am humbly of opinion, it would be worth the care of our governors to cherish gentlemen of the quill, and give them all proper encouragements here. And since I am upon the subject, I shall speak my mind very freely, and if I added, saucily, it is no more than my birthright as a Briton.

Seriously then, I have many years lamented the want of a Grub Street in this our large and polite city, unless the whole may be called one. And this I have accounted an unpardonable defect in our constitution, ever since I had any opinions I could call my own. Every one knows Grub Street is a market for small ware in wit, and as necessary, considering the usual purgings of the human brain, as the nose is upon a man's face. And for the same reason we have here a court, a college, a play-house, and beautiful ladies, and fine gentlemen, and good claret, and abundance of pens, ink, and paper, (clear of taxes) and every other circumstance to provoke wit; and yet those whose province it is, have not yet thought fit to appoint a place for evacuation of it, which is a very hard case, as may be judged by comparisons.

And truly this defect has been attended with unspeakable inconveniences; for not to mention the prejudice done to the commonwealth of letters, I am of opinion we suffer in our health by it. I believe our corrupted air, and frequent thick fogs, are in a great measure owing to the common exposal of our wit; and that with good management, our poetical vapours might be carried off in a common drain, and fall into one quarter of the town, without infecting the whole, as the case is at present, to the great offence of our nobility, and gentry, and others of nice noses. When writers of all sizes, like freemen of the city, are at liberty to throw out their filth and excrementitious productions, in every street as they please, what can the consequence be, but that the town must be poisoned, and become such another jakes, as by report of great travellers, Edinburgh is at night, a thing well to be considered in these pestilential times.

I am not of the society for reformation of manners, but, without that pragmatical title, I would be glad to see some amendment in the matter before us. Wherefore I humbly bespeak the favour of the Lord Mayor, the Court of Aldermen and Common Council, together with the whole circle of arts in this town, and do recommend this affair to their most political consideration; and I persuade myself they will not be wanting in their best endeavours, when they can serve two such good ends at once, as both to keep the town sweet, and encourage poetry in it. Neither do I make any exceptions as to satirical poets and lampoon writers, in consideration of their office. For though, indeed, their business is to rake into kennels, and gather up the filth of streets and families, (in which respect they may be, for aught I know, as necessary to the town as scavengers, or chimney-sweeps) yet I have observed they too have themselves, at the same time, very foul clothes, and, like dirty persons, leave more filth and nastiness than they sweep away.

In a word: What I would be at (for I love to be plain in matters of importance to my country) is, that some private street, or blind alley of this town, may be fitted up at the charge of the public, as an apartment for the Muses, (like those at Rome and Amsterdam, for their female relations) and be wholly consigned to the uses of our wits, furnished completely with all appurtenances, such as authors, supervisors, presses, printers, hawkers, shops, and warehouses, and abundance of garrets, and every other implement and circumstance of wit; the benefit of which would obviously be this, *viz.,* That we should then have a safe repository for our best productions, which at present are handed about in single sheets or manuscripts, and may be altogether lost, (which were a pity) or at best are subject, in that loose dress, like handsome women, to great abuses.

Another point, that has cost me some melancholy reflections, is the present state of the playhouse; the encouragement of which hath an immediate influence upon the poetry of the kingdom; as a good market improves the tillage of the neighbouring country, and enriches the ploughman. Neither do we of this town seem enough to know or consider the vast benefit of a playhouse to our city and nation: That single house is the fountain of all our love, wit, dress, and gallantry. It is the school of wisdom; for there we learn to know what's what; which, however, I cannot say is always in that place sound knowledge. There our young folks drop their childish mistakes, and come first to perceive their mother's cheat of the parsley-bed; there too they get rid of natural prejudices, especially those of religion and modesty, which are great restraints to a free people. The same is a remedy for the spleen, and blushing, and several distempers occasioned by the stagnation of the blood. It is likewise a school of common swearing; my young master, who at first but minced an oath, is taught there to mouth it gracefully, and to swear, as he reads French, *ore rotundo*.[9] Profaneness was before to him in the nature of his best suit, or holiday-clothes; but upon frequenting the playhouse, swearing, cursing, and lying, become like his every-day coat, waistcoat, and breeches. Now I say, common swearing, a produce of this country, as plentiful as our corn, thus cultivated by the playhouse, might, with management, be of wonderful advantage to the nation, as a projector of the swearer's bank has proved at large. Lastly, the stage in great measure supports the

9 "With round mouth," sonorously.

pulpit; for I know not what our divines could have to say there against the corruptions of the age, but for the playhouse, which is the seminary of them. From which it is plain, the public is a gainer by the playhouse, and consequently ought to countenance it; and were I worthy to put in my word, or prescribe to my betters, I could say in what manner. I have heard that a certain gentleman has great designs to serve the public, in the way of their diversions, with due encouragement; that is, if he can obtain some concordatum-money, or yearly salary, and handsome contributions. And well he deserves the favours of the nation; for, to do him justice, he has an uncommon skill in pastimes, having altogether applied his studies that way, and travelled full many a league, by sea and land, for this his profound knowledge. With that view alone he has visited all the courts and cities in Europe, and has been at more pains than I shall speak of, to take an exact draught of the playhouse at the Hague, as a model for a new one here. But what can a private man do by himself in so public an undertaking? It is not to be doubted, but by his care and industry vast improvements may be made, not only in our play-house, (which is his immediate province) but in our gaming ordi-naries, groom-porters, lotteries, bowling-greens, ninepin-alleys, bear-gardens, cockpits, prizes, puppet and raree shows, and whatever else concerns the elegant divertisements of this town. He is truly an original genius, and I felicitate this our capital city on his residence here, where I wish him long to live and flourish, for the good of the commonwealth.

Once more: If any further applications shall be made on t'other side, to obtain a charter for a bank here, I presume to make a request, that *poetry* may be a sharer in that privilege, being a fund as real, and to the full as well grounded as our stocks; but I fear our neighbours, who envy our wit, as much as they do our wealth or trade, will give no encouragement to either. I believe also, it might be proper to erect a corporation of poets in this city. I have been idle enough in my time, to make a computation of wits here, and do find we have three hundred performing poets and upwards, in and about this town, reckoning six score to the hundred, and allowing for demies, like pint bottles; including also the several denomina-tions of imitators, translators, and familiar-letter-writers, &c. One of these last has lately entertained the town with an original piece, and such a one as, I dare say, the late British "Spectator," in his decline, would have called, "an excellent specimen of the true sublime;" or, "a noble poem;" or, "a fine copy of verses, on a subject perfectly new," (the author himself) and had given it a place amongst his latest "Lucubrations."

But as I was saying, so many poets, I am confident, are sufficient to furnish out a corporation in point of number. Then for the several degrees of subordinate members requisite to such a body, there can be no want; for although we have not one masterly poet, yet we abound with wardens and beadles, having a multitude of poetasters, poetitoes, parcel-poets, poet-apes, and philo-poets, and many of inferior attainments in wit, but strong inclinations to it, which are by odds more than all the rest. Nor shall I ever be at ease, till this project of mine (for which I am heartily thankful to myself) shall be reduced to practice. I long to see the day, when our poets will be a regular and distinct body, and wait upon our Lord Mayor on public days, like other good citizens, in gowns turned up with green instead of laurels; and when I myself, who make this proposal, shall be free of their company.

To conclude: What if our government had a poet-laureat here, as in England? What if our university had a professor of poetry here, as in England? What if our Lord Mayor had a city bard here, as in England? And, to refine upon England, what if every corporation, parish, and ward in this town, had a poet in fee, as they have *not* in England? Lastly; What if every one so qualified were obliged to add one more than usual to the number of his domestics, and besides a fool and a chaplain, (which are often united in one person) would retain a poet in his family? For, perhaps, a rhymer is as necessary amongst servants of a house, as a Dobbin with his bells, at the head of a team. But these things I leave to the wisdom of my superiors.

While I have been directing your pen, I should not forget to govern my own, which has already exceeded the bounds of a letter. I must therefore take my leave abruptly, and desire you, without farther ceremony, to believe that I am, Sir,

Your most humble servant.

ON THE DEATH OF ESTHER JOHNSON

[STELLA]

THIS day, being Sunday, January 28, 1727–8, about eight o'clock at night, a servant brought me a note, with an account of the death of the truest, most virtuous, and valuable friend, that I, or perhaps any other person, ever was blessed with. She expired about six in the evening of this day; and as soon as I am left alone, which is about eleven at night, I resolve, for my own satisfaction, to say something of her life and character.

She was born at Richmond, in Surrey, on the thirteenth day of March, in the year 1681. Her father was a younger brother of a good family in Nottinghamshire, her mother of a lower degree; and indeed she had little to boast of her birth. I knew her from six years old, and had some share in her education, by directing what books she should read, and perpetually instructing her in the principles of honour and virtue; from which she never swerved in any one action or moment of her life. She was sickly from her childhood until about the age of fifteen; but then grew into perfect health, and was looked upon as one of the most beautiful, graceful, and agreeable young women in London, only a little too fat. Her hair was blacker than a raven, and every feature of her face in perfection. She lived generally in the country, with a family, where she contracted an intimate friendship with another lady of more advanced years. I was then (to my mortification) settled in Ireland; and about a year after, going to visit my friends in England, I found she was a little uneasy upon the death of a person on whom she had some dependance. Her fortune, at that time, was in all not above fifteen hundred pounds, the interest of which was but a scanty maintenance, in so dear a country, for one of her spirit. Upon this consideration, and indeed very much for my own satisfaction, who had few friends

or acquaintance in Ireland, I prevailed with her and her dear friend
and companion, the other lady, to draw what money they had into
Ireland, a great part of their fortune being in annuities upon funds.
Money was then ten *per cent.* in Ireland, besides the advantage of
turning it, and all necessaries of life at half the price. They complied
with my advice, and soon after came over; but, I happening to continue some time longer in England, they were much discouraged
to live in Dublin, where they were wholly strangers. She was at that
time about nineteen years old, and her person was soon distinguished.
But the adventure looked so like a frolic, the censure held for some
time, as if there were a secret history in such a removal; which, however, soon blew off by her excellent conduct. She came over with
her friend on the ———— in the year 170—; and they both lived
together until this day, when death removed her from us. For some
years past, she had been visited with continual ill health; and several
times, within these two years, her life was despaired of. But, for this
twelvemonth past, she never had a day's health; and, properly
speaking, she hath been dying six months, but kept alive, almost
against nature, by the generous kindness of two physicians, and the
care of her friends. Thus far I writ the same night between eleven
and twelve.

Never was any of her sex born with better gifts of the mind, or
more improved them by reading and conversation. Yet her memory
was not of the best, and was impaired in the latter years of her life.
But I cannot call to mind that I ever once heard her make a wrong
judgment of persons, books, or affairs. Her advice was always the
best, and with the greatest freedom, mixed with the greatest decency.
She had a gracefulness, somewhat more than human, in every
motion, word, and action. Never was so happy a conjunction of
civility, freedom, easiness, and sincerity. There seemed to be a combination among all that knew her, to treat her with a dignity much
beyond her rank; yet people of all sorts were never more easy than
in her company. Mr. Addison, when he was in Ireland, being introduced to her, immediately found her out; and, if he had not soon
after left the kingdom, assured me he would have used all endeavours to cultivate her friendship. A rude or conceited coxcomb
passed his time very ill, upon the least breach of respect; for in such

a case she had no mercy, but was sure to expose him to the contempt of the standers-by; yet in such a manner as he was ashamed to complain, and durst not resent. All of us who had the happiness of her friendship, agreed unanimously, that, in an afternoon or evening's conversation, she never failed, before we parted, of delivering the best thing that was said in the company. Some of us have written down several of her sayings, or what the French call *bons mots,* wherein she excelled almost beyond belief. She never mistook the understanding of others; nor ever said a severe word, but where a much severer was deserved.

Her servants loved, and almost adored her at the same time. She would, upon occasions, treat them with freedom; yet her demeanour was so awful, that they durst not fail in the least point of respect. She chid them seldom, but it was with severity, which had an effect upon them for a long time after.

January 29. My head aches, and I can write no more.

January 30. Tuesday.

This is the night of the funeral, which my sickness will not suffer me to attend. It is now nine at night, and I am removed into another apartment, that I may not see the light in the church, which is just over against the window of my bed chamber.

With all the softness of temper that became a lady, she had the personal courage of a hero. She and her friend having removed their lodgings to a new house, which stood solitary, a parcel of rogues, armed, attempted the house, where there was only one boy. She was then about four-and-twenty; and having been warned to apprehend some such attempt, she learned the management of a pistol; and the other women and servants being half dead with fear, she stole softly to her dining-room window, put on a black hood to prevent being seen, primed the pistol fresh, gently lifted up the sash, and taking her aim with the utmost presence of mind, discharged the pistol, loaden with the bullets, into the body of one villain, who stood the fairest mark. The fellow, mortally wounded, was carried off by the rest, and died the next morning; but his companions could not be found. The Duke of Ormonde hath often drank her health to me upon that account, and had always an high esteem of her. She was indeed under some apprehensions of going in a boat, after some danger she had narrowly escaped by water, but she was reasoned thoroughly out of it. She was never known to cry out, or discover any fear, in a coach or on horseback; or any uneasiness by those sudden accidents with which most of her sex, either by weakness or affectation, appear so much disordered.

She never had the least absence of mind in conversation, nor given to interruption, or appeared eager to put in her word, by waiting impatiently until another had done. She spoke in a most agreeable voice, in the plainest words, never hesitating, except out of modesty before new faces, where she was somewhat reserved: nor, among her nearest friends, ever spoke much at a time. She was but little versed in the common topics of female chat; scandal, censure, and detraction, never came out of her mouth; yet, among a few friends, in private conversation, she made little ceremony in discovering her contempt of a coxcomb, and describing all his follies to the life; but the follies of her own sex she was rather inclined to extenuate or to pity.

When she was once convinced, by open facts, of any breach of truth or honour in a person of high station, especially in the Church, she could not conceal her indignation, nor hear them named without shewing her displeasure in her countenance; particularly one or two of the latter sort, whom she had known and esteemed, but detested above all mankind, when it was manifest that they had sacrificed those two precious virtues to their ambition, and would much sooner have forgiven them the common immoralities of the laity.

Her frequent fits of sickness, in most parts of her life, had prevented her from making that progress in reading which she would otherwise have done. She was well versed in the Greek and Roman story, and was not unskilled in that of France and England. She spoke French perfectly, but forgot much of it by neglect and sickness. She had read carefully all the best books of travels, which serve to open and enlarge the mind. She understood the Platonic and Epicurean philosophy, and judged very well of the defects of the latter. She made very judicious abstracts of the best books she had read. She understood the nature of government, and could point out all the errors of Hobbes, both in that and religion. She had a good insight into physic, and knew somewhat of anatomy; in both which she was instructed in her younger days by an eminent physician, who had her long under his care, and bore the highest esteem for her person and understanding. She had a true taste of wit and good sense, both in poetry and prose, and was a perfect good critic of style; neither was it easy to find a more proper or impartial judge, whose advice an author might better rely on, if he intended to send a thing into the world, provided it was on a subject that came within the compass of her knowledge. Yet, perhaps, she was sometimes too severe, which is a safe and pardonable error. She preserved her wit, judgment, and vivacity, to the last, but often used to complain of her memory.

Her fortune, with some accession, could not, as I have heard say, amount to much more than two thousand pounds, whereof a great part fell with her life, having been placed upon annuities in England, and one in Ireland.

In a person so extraordinary, perhaps it may be pardonable to mention some particulars, although of little moment, further than to set forth her character. Some presents of gold pieces being often made to her while she was a girl, by her mother and other friends, on promise to keep them, she grew into such a spirit of thrift, that, in about three years, they amounted to above two hundred pounds. She used to shew them with boasting; but her mother, apprehending she would be cheated of them, prevailed, in some months, and with great importunities, to have them put out to interest: when the girl lost the pleasure of seeing and counting her gold, which she never failed of doing many times in a day, and despaired of heaping up such another treasure, her humour took the quite contrary turn; she grew careless and squandering of every new acquisition, and so continued till about two-and-twenty; when by advice of some friends, and the fright of paying large bills of tradesmen, who enticed her into their debt, she began to reflect upon her own folly, and was never at rest until she had discharged all her shop-bills, and refunded herself a considerable sum she had run out. After which, by the addition of a few years, and a superior understanding, she became, and continued all her life, a most prudent economist; yet still with a strong bent to the liberal side, wherein she gratified herself by avoiding all expense in clothes (which she never despised) beyond what was merely decent. And, although her frequent returns of sickness were very chargeable, except fees to physicians, of which she met with several so generous that she could force nothing on them, (and indeed she must otherwise have been undone) yet she ever was without a considerable sum of ready money. Insomuch that, upon her death, when her nearest friends thought her very bare, her executors found in her strong box about a hundred and fifty pounds in gold. She lamented the narrowness of her fortune in nothing so much, as that it did not enable her to entertain her friends so often, and in so hospitable a manner, as she desired. Yet they were always welcome; and, while she was in health to direct, were treated with neatness and elegance, so that the revenues of her and her companion passed for much more considerable than they really were. They lived always in lodgings, their domestics consisted of two maids and one man.

She kept an account of all the family expenses, from her arrival in Ireland to some months before her death; and she would often repine, when looking back upon the annals of her household bills, that every thing necessary for life was double the price, while interest of money was sunk almost to one half; so that the addition made to her fortune was indeed grown absolutely necessary.

[I since writ as I found time.]

But her charity to the poor was a duty not to be diminished, and therefore became a tax upon those tradesmen who furnish the fopperies of other ladies. She bought clothes as seldom as possible, and those as plain and cheap as consisted with the situation she was in; and wore no lace for many years. Either her judgment or fortune was extraordinary, in the choice of those on whom she bestowed her charity; for it went further in doing good than double the sum from any other hand. And I have heard her say, she always met with gratitude from the poor; which must be owing to her skill in distinguishing proper objects, as well as her gracious manner in relieving them.

But she had another quality that much delighted her, although it may be thought a kind of check upon her bounty; however, it was a pleasure she could not resist: I mean that of making agreeable presents; wherein I never knew her equal, although it be an affair of as delicate a nature as most in the course of life. She used to define a present, That it was a gift to a friend of something he wanted, or was fond of, and which could not be easily gotten for money. I am confident, during my acquaintance with her, she hath, in these and some other kinds of liberality, disposed of to the value of several hundred pounds. As to presents made to herself, she received them with great unwillingness, but especially from those to whom she had ever given any; being on all occasions the most disinterested mortal I ever knew or heard of.

From her own disposition, at least as much as from the frequent want of health, she seldom made any visits; but her own lodgings, from before twenty years old, were frequented by many persons of the graver sort, who all respected her highly, upon her good sense, good manners, and conversation. Among these were the late Primate Lindsay, Bishop Lloyd, Bishop Ashe, Bishop Brown, Bishop Stearne, Bishop Pulleyn, with some others of later date; and indeed the greatest number of her acquaintance was among the clergy. Honour, truth, liberality, good nature, and modesty, were the virtues she chiefly possessed, and most valued in her acquaintance: and where she found them, would be ready to allow for some defects; nor valued them less, although they did not shine in learning or in wit: but would never give the least allowance for any failures in the former, even to those who made the greatest figure in either of the two latter. She had no use of any person's liberality, yet her detestation of covetous people made her uneasy if such a one was in her company; upon which occasion she would say many things very entertaining and humorous.

She never interrupted any person who spoke; she laughed at no mistakes they made, but helped them out with modesty; and if a good thing were spoken, but neglected, she would not let it fall, but set it in the best light to those who were present. She listened to all that was said, and had never the least distraction or absence of thought.

It was not safe, nor prudent, in her presence, to offend in the least word against modesty; for she then gave full employment to her wit, her contempt, and resentment, under which even stupidity and brutality were forced to sink into confusion; and the guilty person, by her future avoiding him like a bear or a satyr, was never in a way to transgress a second time.

It happened one single coxcomb, of the pert kind, was in her company, among several other ladies; and in his flippant way, began to deliver some double meanings; the rest flapped their fans, and used the other common expedients practised in such cases, of appearing not to mind or comprehend what was said. Her behaviour was very different, and perhaps may be censured. She said thus to the man: "Sir, all these ladies and I understand your meaning very well, having, in spite of our care, too often met with those of your sex who wanted manners and good sense. But, believe me, neither virtuous nor even vicious women love such kind of conversation. However, I will leave you, and report your behaviour: and whatever visit I make, I shall first enquire at the door whether you are in the house, that I may be sure to avoid you." I know not whether a majority of ladies would approve of such a proceeding; but I believe the practice of it would soon put an end to that corrupt conversation, the worst effect of dullness, ignorance, impudence, and vulgarity, and the highest affront to the modesty and understanding of the female sex.

By returning very few visits, she had not much company of her own sex, except those whom she most loved for their easiness, or esteemed for their good sense: and those, not insisting on ceremony, came often to her. But she rather chose men for her companions, the usual topics of ladies' discourse being such as she had little knowledge of, and less relish. Yet no man was upon the rack to entertain her, for she easily descended to any thing that was innocent and diverting. News, politics, censure, family management, or town-talk, she always diverted to something else; but these indeed seldom happened, for she chose her company better: and therefore many, who mistook her and themselves, having solicited her acquaintance, and finding themselves disappointed, after a few visits dropped off; and she was never known to enquire into the reason, or ask what was become of them.

She was never positive in arguing; and she usually treated those who were so, in a manner which well enough gratified that unhappy disposition; yet in such a sort as made it very contemptible, and at the same time did some hurt to the owners. Whether this proceeded from her easiness in general, or from her indifference to persons, or from her despair of mending them, or from the same practice which she much liked in Mr. Addison, I cannot determine; but when she saw any of the company very warm in a wrong opinion, she was more inclined to confirm them in it than oppose them. The excuse she commonly gave, when her friends asked the reason, was, that it prevented noise, and saved time. Yet I have known her very angry with some, whom she much esteemed, for sometimes falling into that infirmity.

She loved Ireland much better than the generality of those who owe both their birth and riches to it; and having brought over all the fortune she had in money, left the reversion of the best part of it, one thousand pounds, to Dr. Stephens's Hospital. She detested the tyranny and injustice of England, in their treatment of this kingdom. She had indeed reason to love a country, where she had the esteem and friendship of all who knew her, and the universal good report of all who ever heard of her, without one exception, if I am told the truth by those who keep general conversation. Which character is the more extraordinary, in falling to a person of so much knowledge, wit, and vivacity, qualities that are used to create envy, and consequently censure; and must be rather imputed to her great modesty, gentle behaviour, and inoffensiveness, than to her superior virtues.

Although her knowledge, from books and company, was much more extensive than usually falls to the share of her sex; yet she was so far from making a parade of it, that her female visitants, on their first acquaintance, who expected to discover it by what they call hard words and deep discourse, would be sometimes disappointed, and say, they found she was like other women. But wise men, through all her modesty, whatever they discoursed on, could easily observe that she understood them very well, by the judgment shewn in her observations as well as in her questions.

THE SHORTEST-WAY WITH THE DISSENTERS:

OR

PROPOSALS FOR THE ESTABLISHMENT OF THE CHURCH

THE EDUCATION OF WOMEN

BY

DANIEL DEFOE

INTRODUCTORY NOTE

DANIEL DEFOE (c. 1661–1731) was the son of a London butcher called Foe, a name which Daniel bore for more than forty years. He early gave up the idea of becoming a dissenting minister, and went into business. One of his earlier writings was an "Essay upon Projects," remarkable for the number of schemes suggested in it which have since been carried into practise. He won the approval of King William by his "True-born Englishman," a rough verse satire repelling the attacks on William as a foreigner. His "Shortest-Way with Dissenters," on the other hand, brought down on him the wrath of the Tories; he was fined, imprisoned, and exposed in the pillory, with the result that he became for the time a popular hero. While in prison he started a newspaper, the "Review" (1704–1713), which may in certain respects be regarded as a forerunner of the "Tatler" and "Spectator." From this time for about fourteen years he was chiefly engaged in political journalism, not always of the most reputable kind; and in 1719 he published the first volume of "Robinson Crusoe," his greatest triumph in a kind of realistic fiction in which he had already made several short essays. This was followed by a number of novels, dealing for the most part with the lives of rogues and criminals, and including "Moll Flanders," "Colonel Jack," "Roxana," and "Captain Singleton." Notable as a specially effective example of fiction disguised as truth was his "Journal of the Plague Year."

In the latter part of his career Defoe became thoroughly discredited as a politician, and was regarded as a mere hireling journalist. He wrote with almost unparalleled fluency, and a complete list of his hundreds of publications will never be made out. The specimens of his work given here show him writing vigorously and sincerely, and belong to a period when he had not yet become a government tool.

THE SHORTEST-WAY WITH
THE DISSENTERS

SIR ROGER L'ESTRANGE tells us a story in his collection of *Fables,* of the Cock and the Horses. The Cock was gotten to roost in the stable among the horses; and there being no racks or other conveniences for him, it seems, he was forced to roost upon the ground. The horses jostling about for room, and putting the Cock in danger of his life, he gives them this grave advice, "Pray, Gentlefolks! let us stand still! for fear we should tread upon one another!"

There are some people in the World, who, now they are *unperched,* and reduced to an equality with other people, and under strong and very just apprehensions of being further treated as they deserve, begin, with Esop's Cock, to preach up Peace and Union and the Christian duty of Moderation; forgetting that, when they had the Power in their hands, those Graces were strangers in their gates!

It is now, near fourteen years, [1688–1702], that the glory and peace of the purest and most flourishing Church in the world has been eclipsed, buffeted, and disturbed by a sort of men, whom, GOD in His Providence, has suffered to insult over her, and bring her down. These have been the days of her humiliation and tribulation. She has borne with an invincible patience, the reproach of the wicked: and GOD has at last heard her prayers, and delivered her from the oppression of the stranger.

And now, they find their Day is over! their power gone! and the throne of this nation possessed by a Royal, *English,* true, and ever constant member of, and friend to, the Church of England! Now, they find that they are in danger of the Church of England's just resentments! Now, they cry out, "Peace!" "Union!" "Forbearance!" and "Charity!": as if the Church had not too long harboured her enemies under her wing! and nourished the viperous brood, till they hiss and fly in the face of the Mother that cherished them!

No, Gentlemen! the time of mercy is past! your Day of Grace is over! you should have practised peace, and moderation, and charity, if you expected any yourselves!

We have heard none of this lesson, for fourteen years past! We have been huffed and bullied with your *Act of Toleration!* You have told us, *you* are the Church established by Law, as well as others! have set up your canting Synagogues at our Church doors! and the Church and her members have been loaded with reproaches, with Oaths, Associations, Abjurations, and what not! Where has been the mercy, the forbearance, the charity you have shewn to tender consciences of the Church of England that could not take Oaths *as fast as you made them?* that having sworn allegiance to their lawful and rightful King, could not dispense with that Oath, *their King being still alive;* and swear to your new hodge podge of a Dutch Government? These have been turned out of their Livings, and they and their families left to starve! their estates double taxed to carry on a war they had no hand in, and you got nothing by!

What account can you give of the multitudes you have forced to comply, against their consciences, with your new sophistical Politics, who, like New Converts in France, sin because *they cannot starve?* And now the tables are turned upon you; *you* must not be persecuted! it is not a Christian spirit!

You have butchered one King! deposed another King! and made a Mock King of a third! and yet, you could have the face to expect to be employed and trusted by the fourth! Anybody that did not know the temper of your Party, would stand amazed at the impudence as well as the folly to think of it!

Your management of your Dutch Monarch, who you reduced to a mere King of Cl[ub]s, is enough to give any future Princes such an idea of your principles, as to warn them sufficiently from coming into your clutches; and, GOD be thanked! the Queen is out of your hands! knows you! and will have a care of you!

There is no doubt but the Supreme Authority of a nation has in itself, a Power, and *a right to that Power,* to execute the Laws upon any part of that nation it governs. The execution of the known Laws of the land, and that with but a gentle hand neither, was all that the Fanatical Party of this land have ever called Persecution. This they have magnified to a height, that the sufferings of the Huguenots in France were not to be compared with them. Now to execute the known Laws of a nation upon those who transgress them, after having first been voluntarily consenting to the making of those Laws, can never be called Persecution, but Justice. But Justice is always Violence to the party offending! for every man is innocent in his own eyes.

The first execution of the Laws against Dissenters in England, was in the days of King JAMES I.; and what did it amount to? Truly, the worst they suffered was, at their own request, to let them go to New England, and erect a new colony; and give them great privileges, grants, and suitable powers; keep them under protection, and defend them against all invaders; and receive no taxes or revenue from them!

This was the cruelty of the Church of England! Fatal lenity! It was the ruin of that excellent Prince, King CHARLES I. Had King JAMES sent all the Puritans in England away to the West Indies; we had been a national unmixed Church! the Church of England had been kept undivided and entire!

To requite the lenity of the Father, they take up arms against the Son, conquer, pursue, take, imprison, and at last to death the Anointed of GOD, and destroy the very Being and Nature of Government: setting up a sordid Impostor, who had neither title to govern, nor understanding to manage, but supplied that want, with power, bloody and desperate counsels and craft, without conscience.

Had not King JAMES I. withheld the full execution of the Laws: had he given them strict justice, he had cleared the nation of them! And the consequences had been plain; his son had never been murdered by them, nor the Monarchy overwhelmed. It was too much mercy shewn them that was the ruin of his posterity, and the ruin of the nation's peace. One would think the Dissenters should not have the face to believe, that we are to be wheedled and canted into Peace and Toleration, when they know that they have once requited us with a Civil War, and once with an intolerable and unrighteous Persecution, for our former civility.

Nay, to encourage us to be easy with them, it is apparent that they never had the upper hand of the Church, but they treated her with all the severity, with all the reproach and contempt as was possible! What Peace and what Mercy did they shew the loyal Gentry of the Church of England, in the time of their triumphant Commonwealth? How did they put all the Gentry of England to ransom, whether they were actually in arms for the King or not! making people compound for their estates, and starve their families! How did they treat the Clergy of the Church of England! sequester the Ministers! devour the patrimony of the Church, and divide the spoil, by sharing the Church lands among their soldiers, and turning her Clergy out to starve! Just such measure as they have meted, should be measured to them again!

Charity and Love is the known doctrine of the Church of England, and it is plain She has put it in practice towards the Dissenters, even beyond what they ought [*deserved*], till She has been wanting to herself, and in effect unkind to her own sons: particularly, in the too much lenity of King JAMES I., mentioned before. Had he so rooted the Puritans from the face of the land, which he had an opportunity early to have done; they had not had the power to vex the Church, as since they have done.

In the days of King CHARLES II., how did the Church reward their bloody doings, with lenity and mercy! Except the barbarous Regicides of the pretended Court of Justice, not a soul suffered, for all the blood in an unnatural war! King CHARLES came in all mercy and love, cherished them, preferred them, employed them, withheld the rigour of the Law; and oftentimes, even against the advice of his Parliament, gave them Liberty of Conscience: and how did they requite him? With the villanous contrivance to depose and murder him and his successor, at the Rye [House] Plot!

King JAMES [II.], as if mercy was the inherent quality of the Family, began his reign with unusual favour to them. Nor could their joining with the Duke of MONMOUTH against him, move him to do himself justice upon them. But that mistaken Prince, thinking to win them by gentleness and love, proclaimed a Universal Liberty to them! and rather discountenanced the Church of England than them! How they requited him, all the World knows!

The late reign [*WILLIAM III.*] is too fresh in the memory of all the World to need a comment. How under pretence of joining with the Church in redressing some grievances, they pushed things to that extremity, in conjunction with some mistaken Gentlemen, as to *depose* the late King: as if the grievance of the Nation could not have been redressed but by the absolute ruin of the Prince!

Here is an instance of their Temper, their Peace, and Charity!

To what height they carried themselves during the reign of a King of their own! how they crope [*creeped*] into all Places of Trust and Profit! how they insinuated themselves into the favour of the King, and were at first preferred to the highest Places in the nation! how they engrossed the Ministry! and, above all, how pitifully they managed! is too plain to need any remarks.

But particularly, their Mercy and Charity, the spirit of Union, they tell us so much of, has been remarkable in Scotland. If any man would see the spirit of a Dissenter, let him look into Scotland! There, they made entire conquest of the Church! trampled down the sacred Orders and suppressed the Episcopal Government, with an absolute, and, as they supposed, irretrievable victory! though it is possible, *they may find themselves mistaken!*

Now it would be a very proper question to ask their impudent advocate, the *Observator*, "Pray how much mercy and favour did the members of the Episcopal Church find in Scotland, from the Scotch Presbyterian Government?" and I shall undertake for the Church of England, that the Dissenters shall still receive as much here, though they deserve but little.

In a small treatise of *The Sufferings of the Episcopal Clergy in Scotland*, it will appear what usage they met with! How they not only lost their Livings; but, in several places, were plundered and abused in their persons! the Ministers that could not conform, were turned out, with numerous families and no maintenance, and hardly charity enough left to relieve them with a bit of bread. The cruelties of the Party were innumerable, and are not to be attempted in this short Piece.

And now, to prevent the distant cloud which they perceive to hang over their heads from England, with a true Presbyterian policy, they put it for a Union of Nations! that England might unite their Church with the Kirk of Scotland, and their Assembly of Scotch canting Long-Cloaks in our Convocation. What might have been, if our Fanatic Whiggish Statesmen continued, GOD only knows! but we hope we are out of fear of that now.

It is alleged by some of the faction, and they have begun to bully us with it, that "if we won't unite with them, they will not settle the Crown with us again; but when Her Majesty dies, will choose a King for themselves!"

If they won't we must make them! and it is not the first time we have let them know that we are able! The Crowns of these Kingdoms have not so far disowned the Right of Succession, but they may retrieve it again; and if Scotland thinks to come off from a Successive to an Elective State of Government; England has not promised, not to assist the Right Heir, and put him into possession, without any regards to their ridiculous *Settlements.*

THESE are the Gentlemen! these, their ways of treating the Church, both at home and abroad!

Now let us examine the Reasons they pretend to give, why we should be favourable to them? why we should continue and tolerate them among us?

First. *They are very numerous,* they say. *They are a great part of the nation, and we cannot suppress them!*
To this, may be answered,

First. They are not so numerous as the Protestants in France: and yet the French King effectually cleared the nation of them, at once; and we don't find he misses them at home!

But I am not of the opinion, they are so numerous as is pretended. Their Party is more numerous than their Persons; and those mistaken people of the Church who are misled and deluded by their wheedling artifices to join with them, make their Party the greater: but those will open their eyes when the Government shall set heartily about the Work, and come off from them, as some animals, which they say, always desert a house when it is likely to fall.

Secondly. The more numerous, the more dangerous; and therefore the more need to suppress them! and GOD has suffered us to bear them as goads in our sides, for not utterly extinguishing them long ago.

Thirdly. If we are to allow them, only because we cannot suppress them; then it ought to be tried, Whether we can or not? And I am of opinion, it is easy to be done! and could prescribe Ways and Means, if it were proper: but I doubt not the Government will find effectual methods for the rooting of the contagion from the face of this land.

Another argument they use, which is this. *That this is a time of war, and we have need to unite against the common enemy.*

We answer, This common enemy had been no enemy, if they had not made him so! He was quiet, in peace, and no way disturbed and encroached upon us; and we know no reason we had to quarrel with him.

But further. We make no question but we are able to deal with this common enemy without their help: but why must we unite with them, because of the enemy? Will they go over to the enemy, if we do not prevent it, by a Union with them? We are very well contented [that] they should! and make no question, we shall be ready to deal with them and the common enemy too; and better without them than with them! Besides, if we have a common enemy, there is the more need to be secure against our private enemies! If there is one common enemy, we have the less need to have an enemy in our bowels!

It was a great argument some people used against suppressing the Old Money, that "it was a time of war, and it was too great a risque [*risk*] for the nation to run! If we should not master it, we should be undone!" And yet the sequel proved the hazard was not so great, but it might be mastered, and the success [*i.e., of the new coinage*] was answerable. The suppressing the Dissenters is not a harder work! nor a work of less necessity to the Public! We can never enjoy a settled uninterrupted union and tranquility in this nation, till the spirit of Whiggism, Faction, and Schism is melted down like the Old Money!

To talk of difficulty is to frighten ourselves with Chimeras and notions of a powerful Party, which are indeed a Party without power.

Difficulties often appear greater at a distance than when they are searched into with judgment, and distinguished from the vapours and shadows that attend them.

We are not to be frightened with it! This Age is wiser than that, by all our own experience, and theirs too! King CHARLES I. had early suppressed this Party, if he had taken more deliberate measures! In short, it is not worth arguing, to talk of their arms. Their MONMOUTHS, and SHAFTESBURYS, and ARGYLES are gone! Their Dutch Sanctuary is at an end! Heaven has made way for their destruction! and if we do not close with the Divine occasion, we are to blame ourselves! and may hereafter remember, that we had, once, an opportunity to serve the Church of England, by extirpating her implacable enemies; and having let slip the Minute that Heaven presented, may experimentally complain, *Post est Occasio CALVO!*

Here are some popular Objections in the way.

As First, *The Queen has promised them, to continue them in their tolerated Liberty; and has told us* She will be a religious observer of her word.

What Her Majesty will do, we cannot help! but what, as the Head of the Church, she ought to do, is another case. Her Majesty has promised to protect and defend the Church of England, and if she cannot effectually do that, without the destruction of the Dissenters; she must, of course, dispense with one promise to comply with another!

But to answer this cavil more effectually. Her Majesty did never promise to maintain the Toleration to the destruction of the Church; but it was upon supposition that it may be compatible with the well-being and safety of the Church, which she had declared she would take especial care of. Now if these two Interests clash, it is plain Her Majesty's intentions are to uphold, protect, defend, and establish the Church! and this, we conceive is impossible [*that is, while maintaining the Toleration*].

Perhaps it may be said, *That the Church is in no immediate danger from the Dissenters; and therefore it is time enough.*

But this is a weak answer. For first. If the danger be real, the distance of it is no argument against, but rather a spur to quicken us to Prevention, lest it be too late hereafter.

And secondly. Here is the opportunity, and the only one perhaps, that ever the Church had to secure herself, and destroy her enemies.

The Representatives of the Nation have now an opportunity! The Time is come, which all good men have wished for! that the Gentlemen of England may serve the Church of England, now they are protected and encouraged by a Church of England Queen!

What will you do for your Sister in the day that she shall be spoken for?

If ever you will establish the best Christian Church in the World?

If ever you will suppress the Spirit of Enthusiasm?

If ever you will free the nation from the viperous brood that have so long sucked the blood of their Mother?

If ever you will leave your Posterity free from faction and rebellion, this is the time. This is the time to pull up this heretical Weed of Sedition, that has so long disturbed the Peace of the Church, and poisoned the good corn!

But, says another hot and cold Objector, *This is renewing Fire and Faggot! reviving the* Act, De heretico comburendo! *This will be cruelty in its nature! and barbarous to all the World!*

I answer, It is cruelty to kill a snake or a toad in cold blood, but the poison of their nature makes it a charity to our neighbours, to destroy those creatures! not for any personal injury received, but for prevention; not for the evil they have done, but the evil they may do! Serpents, toads, vipers, &c., are noxious to the body, and poison the sensitive life: these poison the soul! corrupt our posterity! ensnare our children! destroy the vitals of our happiness, our future felicity! and contaminate the whole mass!

Shall any Law be given to such wild creatures! Some beasts are for sport, and the huntsmen give them the advantages of ground: but some are knocked on the head, by all possible ways of violence and surprise!

I do not prescribe Fire and Faggot! but as SCIPIO said of Carthage, *Delenda est Carthago!* They are to be rooted out of this nation, if ever we will live in peace! serve GOD! or enjoy our own! As for the manner, I leave it to those hands, who have a Right to execute GOD'S Justice on the Nation's and the Church's enemies.

But if we must be frighted from this Justice, under the[se] specious pretences, and odious sense of cruelty; nothing will be effected! It will be more barbarous to our own children and dear posterity, when they shall reproach their fathers, as we ours, and tell us [!], "You had an Opportunity to root out this cursed race from the World, under the favour and protection of a True Church of England Queen! and out of your foolish pity, you spared them: because, forsooth, you would not be cruel! And now our Church is suppressed and persecuted, our Religion trampled under foot, our estates plundered; our persons imprisoned, and dragged to gaols, gibbets, and scaffolds! Your sparing this Amalekite race is our destruction! Your mercy to them, proves cruelty to your poor posterity!"

How just will such reflections be, when our posterity shall fall under the merciless clutches of this uncharitable Generation! when our Church shall be swallowed up in Schism, Faction, Enthusiasm, and Confusion! when our Government shall be devolved upon Foreigners, and our Monarchy dwindled into a Republic!

It would be more rational for us, if we must spare this Generation, to summon our own to a general massacre: and as we have brought them into the World free, to send them out so; and not betray them to destruction by our supine negligence, and then cry "It is mercy!"

Moses was a merciful meek man; and yet with what fury did he run through the camp, and cut the throats of three and thirty thousand of his dear Israelites that were fallen into idolatry. What was the reason? It was mercy to the rest, to make these examples! to prevent the destruction of the whole army.

How many millions of future souls, [shall] we save from infection and delusion, if the present race of Poisoned Spirits were purged from the face of the land!

It is vain to trifle in this matter! The light foolish handling of them by mulcts, fines, &c.; 'tis their glory and their advantage! If the Gallows instead of the Counter, and the galleys instead of the fines; were the reward of going to a conventicle, to preach or hear, there would not be so many sufferers! The spirit of martyrdom is over! They that will go to church to be chosen Sheriffs and Mayors, would go to forty churches, rather than be hanged!

If one severe Law were made, and punctually executed, that *Whoever was found at a Conventicle should be banished the nation, and the Preacher be hanged;* we should soon see an end of the tale! They would all come to church again, and one Age [*generation*] would make us all One again!

To talk of Five Shillings a month for not coming to the Sacrament, and One Shilling per week, for not coming to Church: this is such a way of converting people as was never known! This is selling them a liberty to transgress, for so much money!

If it be not a crime, why don't we give them full license? and if it be, no price ought to compound for the committing of it! for that is selling a liberty to people to sin against GOD and the Government!

If it be a crime of the highest consequence, both against the peace and welfare of the nation, the Glory of GOD, the good of the Church, and the happiness of the soul: let us rank it among capital offences! and let it receive punishment in proportion to it!

We hang men for trifles, and banish them for things not worth naming; but that an offence against GOD and the Church, against the welfare of the World, and the dignity of Religion shall be bought off for FIVE SHILLINGS: this is such a shame to a Christian Government, that it is with regret I transmit it to posterity.

If men sin against GOD, affront His ordinances, rebel against His Church, and disobey the precepts of their superiors; let them suffer, as such capital crimes deserve! so will Religion flourish, and this divided nation be once again united.

And yet the title of *barbarous* and *cruel* will soon be taken off from this Law too. I am not supposing that all the Dissenters in England should be hanged or banished. But as in case of rebellions and insurrections, if a few of the ringleaders suffer, the multitude are dismissed; so a few obstinate people being made examples, there is no doubt but the severity of the Law would find a stop in the compliance of the multitude.

To make the reasonableness of this matter out of question, and more unanswerably plain, let us examine for what it is, that this nation is divided into Parties and factions? and let us see how they can justify a Separation? or we of the Church of England can justify our bearing the insults and inconveniences of the Party.

One of their leading Pastors, and a man of as much learning as most among them, in his *Answer* to a Pamphlet entituled *An Enquiry into the Occasional Conformity,* hath these words, *p.* 27: "Do the Religion of the Church and the Meeting Houses make two religions? Wherein do they differ? The Substance of the same Religion is common to them both, and the Modes and Accidents are the things in which only they differ." *P.* 28: "Thirty-nine *Articles* are given us for the Summary of our Religion: thirty-six contain the Substance of it, wherein we agree; three are additional Appendices, about which we have some differences."

Now, if as, by their own acknowledgment, the Church of England is a true Church; and the difference is only in a few "Modes and Accidents": why should we expect that they will suffer the gallows and galleys, corporal punishment and banishment, for these trifles? There is no question, but they will be wiser! Even their own principles won't bear them out in it!

They will certainly comply with the Laws, and with Reason! And though, at the first, severity may seem hard, the next Age will feel nothing of it! the contagion will be rooted out. The disease being cured, there will be no need of the operation! But if they should venture to transgress, and fall into the pit; all the World must condemn their obstinacy, as being without ground from their own principles.

Thus the pretence of cruelty will be taken off, and the Party actual suppressed; and the disquiets they have so often brought upon the Nation, prevented.

Their numbers and their wealth make them haughty; and that is so far from being an argument to persuade us to forbear them, that it is a warning to us, without any more delay, to reconcile them to the Unity of the Church, or remove them from us.

At present, Heaven be praised! they are not so formidable as they have been, and it is our own fault if ever we suffer them to be so! Providence and the Church of England seem to join in this particular, that now, the Destroyers of the Nation's Peace may be overturned! and to this end, the present opportunity seems to put into our hands.

To this end, Her present Majesty seems reserved to enjoy the Crown, that the Ecclesiastic as well as Civil Rights of the Nation may be restored by her hand.

To this end, the face of affairs has received such a turn in the process of a few months as never has been before. The leading men of the Nation, the universal cry of the People, the unanimous request of the Clergy agree in this, that the Deliverance of our Church is at hand!

For this end, has Providence given such a Parliament! such a Convocation! such a Gentry! and such a Queen! as we never had before.

And what may be the consequences of a neglect of such opportunities? The Succession of the Crown has but a dark prospect! Another Dutch turn may make the hopes of it ridiculous, and the practice impossible! Be the House of our future Princes ever so well inclined, they will be Foreigners! Many years will be spent in suiting the Genius of Strangers to this Crown, and the Interests of the Nation! and how many Ages it may be, before the English throne be filled with so much zeal and candour, so much tenderness and hearty affection to the Church, as we see it now covered with, who can imagine?

It is high time, then, for the friends of the Church of England to think of building up and establishing her in such a manner, that she may be no more invaded by Foreigners, nor divided by factions, schisms, and error.

If this could be done by gentle and easy methods, I should be glad! but the wound is corroded, the vitals begin to mortify, and nothing but amputation of members can complete the cure! All the ways of tenderness and compassion, all persuasive arguments have been made use of in vain!

The humour of the Dissenters has so increased among the people, that they hold the Church in defiance! and the House of GOD is an abomination among them! Nay, they have brought up their posterity in such prepossessed aversion to our Holy Religion, that the ignorant mob think we are all idolaters and worshippers of BAAL! and account it a sin to come within the walls of our churches! The primitive Christians were not more shy of a heathen temple, or of meat offered to idols; nor the Jews, of swine's flesh, than some of our Dissenters are of the church and the *Divine Service* solemnized therein.

The Obstinacy must be rooted out, with the profession of it! While the Generation are left at liberty daily to affront GOD Almighty, and dishonour His holy worship; we are wanting in our duty to GOD, and to our Mother the Church of England.

How can we answer it to GOD! to the Church! and to our posterity; to leave them entangled with Fanaticism! Error, and Obstinacy, in the bowels of the nation? to leave them an enemy in their streets, that, in time, may involve them in the same crimes, and endanger the utter extirpation of the Religion of the Nation!

What is the difference betwixt this, and being subject to the power of the Church of Rome? from whence we have reformed. If one be an extreme to the one hand, and one on another: it is equally destructive to the Truth to have errors settled among us, let them be of what nature they will! Both are enemies of our Church, and of our peace! and why should it not be as criminal to admit an Enthusiast as a Jesuit? why should the Papist with his Seven Sacraments be worse than the Quaker with no Sacraments at all? Why should Religious Houses be more intolerable than Meeting Houses?

Alas, the Church of England! What with Popery on one hand, and Schismatics on the other, how has She been crucified between two thieves. Now, LET US CRUCIFY THE THIEVES!

Let her foundations be established upon the destruction of her enemies! The doors of Mercy being always open to the returning part of the deluded people, let the obstinate be ruled with the rod of iron!

Let all true sons of so holy and oppressed a Mother, exasperated by her afflictions, harden their hearts against those who have oppressed her!

And may GOD Almighty put it into the hearts of all the friends of Truth, to lift up a Standard against Pride and ANTICHRIST! *that the Posterity of the Sons of Error may be rooted out from the face of this land, for ever!*

THE EDUCATION OF WOMEN

I HAVE often thought of it as one of the most barbarous customs in the world, considering us as a civilized and a Christian country, that we deny the advantages of learning to women. We reproach the sex every day with folly and impertinence; while I am confident, had they the advantages of education equal to us, they would be guilty of less than ourselves.

One would wonder, indeed, how it should happen that women are conversible at all; since they are only beholden to natural parts, for all their knowledge. Their youth is spent to teach them to stitch and sew or make baubles. They are taught to read, indeed, and perhaps to write their names, or so; and that is the height of a woman's education. And I would but ask any who slight the sex for their understanding, what is a man (a gentleman, I mean) good for, that is taught no more? I need not give instances, or examine the character of a gentleman, with a good estate, or a good family, and with tolerable parts; and examine what figure he makes for want of education.

The soul is placed in the body like a rough diamond; and must be polished, or the lustre of it will never appear. And 'tis manifest, that as the rational soul distinguishes us from brutes; so education carries on the distinction, and makes some less brutish than others. This is too evident to need any demonstration. But why then should women be denied the benefit of instruction? If knowledge and understanding had been useless additions to the sex, GOD Almighty would never have given them capacities; for he made nothing needless. Besides, I would ask such, What they can see in ignorance, that they should think it a necessary ornament to a woman? or how much worse is a wise woman than a fool? or what has the woman done to forfeit the privilege of being taught? Does she plague us with her pride and impertinence? Why did we not let her learn, that she might have had more wit? Shall we upbraid women with folly, when 'tis only the error of this inhuman custom, that hindered them from being made wiser?

The capacities of women are supposed to be greater, and their senses quicker than those of the men; and what they might be capable of being bred to, is plain from some instances of female wit, which this age is not without. Which upbraids us with Injustice, and looks as if we denied women the advantages of education, for fear they should *vie* with the men in their improvements. . . .

[They] should be taught all sorts of breeding suitable both to their genius and quality. And in particular, Music and Dancing; which it would be cruelty to bar the sex of, because they are their darlings. But besides this, they should be taught languages, as particularly French and Italian: and I would venture the injury of giving a woman more tongues than one. They should, as a particular study, be taught all the graces of speech, and all the necessary air of conversation; which our common education is so defective in, that I need not expose it. They should be brought to read books, and especially history; and so to read as to make them understand the world, and be able to know and judge of things when they hear of them.

To such whose genius would lead them to it, I would deny no sort of learning; but the chief thing, in general, is to cultivate the understandings of the sex, that they may be capable of all sorts of conversation; that their parts and judgements being improved, they may be as profitable in their conversation as they are pleasant.

Women, in my observation, have little or no difference in them, but as they are or are not distinguished by education. Tempers, indeed, may in some degree influence them, but the main distinguishing part is their Breeding.

The whole sex are generally quick and sharp. I believe, I may be allowed to say, generally so: for you rarely see them lumpish and heavy, when they are children; as boys will often be. If a woman be well bred, and taught the proper management of her natural wit; she proves generally very sensible and retentive.

And, without partiality, a woman of sense and manners is the finest and most delicate part of GOD's Creation, the glory of Her Maker, and the great instance of His singular regard to man, His darling creature: to whom He gave the best gift either GOD could bestow or man receive. And 'tis the sordidest piece of folly and ingratitude in the world, to withhold from the sex the due lustre which the advantages of education gives to the natural beauty of their minds.

A woman well bred and well taught, furnished with the additional accomplishments of knowledge and behaviour, is a creature *without comparison.* Her society is the emblem of sublimer enjoyments, her person is angelic, and her conversation heavenly. She is all softness and sweetness, peace, love, wit, and delight. She is every way suitable to the sublimest wish, and the man that has such a one to his portion, has nothing to do but to rejoice in her, and be thankful.

On the other hand, Suppose her to be the *very same* woman, and rob her of the benefit of education, and it follows—

> If her temper be good, want of education makes her soft and easy.
>
> Her wit, for want of teaching, makes her impertinent and talkative.
>
> Her knowledge, for want of judgement and experience, makes her fanciful and whimsical.
>
> If her temper be bad, want of breeding makes her worse; and she grows haughty, insolent, and loud.
>
> If she be passionate, want of manners makes her a termagant and a scold, *which is much at one with Lunatic.*
>
> If she be proud, want of discretion (which still is breeding) makes her conceited, fantastic, and ridiculous.
>
> And from these she degenerates to be turbulent, clamorous, noisy, nasty, the devil! . . .

The great distinguishing difference, which is seen in the world between men and women, is in their education; and this is manifested by comparing it with the difference between one man or woman, and another.

And herein it is that I take upon me to make such a bold assertion, That all the world are mistaken in their practice about women. For I cannot think that GOD Almighty ever made them so delicate, so glorious creatures; and furnished them with such charms, so agreeable and so delightful to mankind; with souls capable of the same accomplishments with men: and all, to be only Stewards of our Houses, Cooks, and Slaves.

Not that I am for exalting the female government in the least: but, in short, *I would have men take women for companions, and educate them to be fit for it.* A woman of sense and breeding will scorn as much to encroach upon the prerogative of man, as a man of sense will scorn to oppress the weakness of the woman. But if the women's souls were refined and improved by teaching, that word would be lost. To say, the *weakness* of the sex, as to judgement, would be nonsense; for ignorance and folly would be no more to be found among women than men.

I remember a passage, which I heard from a very fine woman. She had wit and capacity enough, an extraordinary shape and face, and a great fortune: but had been cloistered up all her time; and for fear of being stolen, had not had the liberty of being taught the common necessary knowledge of women's affairs. And when she came to converse in the world, her natural wit made her so sensible of the want of education, that she gave this short reflection on herself: "I am ashamed to talk with my very maids," says she, "for I don't know when they do right or wrong. I had more need go to school, than be married."

I need not enlarge on the loss the defect of education is to the sex; nor argue the benefit of the contrary practice. 'Tis a thing will be more easily granted than remedied. This chapter is but an Essay at the thing: and I refer the Practice to those Happy Days (if ever they shall be) when men shall be wise enough to mend it.

LIFE OF ADDISON

BY

SAMUEL JOHNSON

INTRODUCTORY NOTE

SAMUEL JOHNSON (1709–1784), the great literary dictator of the latter part of the eighteenth century, was the son of a bookseller at Lichfield. After leaving Oxford, he tried teaching, but soon gave it up, and came to London in 1737, where he supported himself by his pen. After years of hardship he finally rose to the head of his profession, and a pension of £300 a year from George III. made his later years free from anxiety.

Johnson attempted many forms of literature. In poetry his chief works were "London," an imitation of Juvenal, and "The Vanity of Human Wishes," a piece of dignified and impressive moralizing. Garrick produced his tragedy of "Irene" in 1749, but without much success. The great Dictionary appeared in 1755, and made an epoch in the history of English lexicography. From 1750 to 1752 he issued the "Rambler," which he wrote almost entirely himself. This periodical is regarded as the most successful of the imitations of the "Spectator," but the modern reader finds it heavy. The "Idler," a similar publication, appeared from 1758 to 1760. In 1759, when Johnson's mother died, he wrote his didactic romance of "Rasselas" in one week in order to defray the expenses of her illness and funeral. This was the most popular of his writings in his own day, and has been translated into many languages. In 1765 Johnson issued his edition of Shakespeare in eight volumes, a task in many respects inadequately performed, yet in the interpretation of obscure passages often showing Johnson's robust common sense and power of clear and vigorous expression.

It is generally agreed that none of Johnson's various works is the equal of his conversation as reported in the greatest of English biographies, Boswell's "Life of Johnson." But the "Lives of the Poets," written as prefaces to a collection of the English poets, is his most permanently valuable production, and, though limited by the standards of his time, is full of acute criticism admirably expressed. The "Life of Addison" is one of the most sympathetic of the "Lives," and gives an excellent idea of Johnson's matter and manner.

LIFE OF ADDISON

1672–1719

JOSEPH ADDISON was born on the first of May, 1672, at Milston, of which his father, Lancelot Addison, was then rector, near Ambrosbury in Wiltshire, and appearing weak and unlikely to live, he was christened the same day. After the usual domestick education, which, from the character of his father, may be reasonably supposed to have given him strong impressions of piety, he was committed to the care of Mr. Naish at Ambrosbury, and afterwards of Mr. Taylor at Salisbury.

Not to name the school or the masters of men illustrious for literature is a kind of historical fraud, by which honest fame is injuriously diminished: I would therefore trace him through the whole process of his education. In 1683, in the beginning of his twelfth year, his father being made Dean of Lichfield, naturally carried his family to his new residence, and, I believe, placed him for some time, probably not long, under Mr. Shaw, then master of the school at Lichfield, father of the late Dr. Peter Shaw. Of this interval his biographers have given no account, and I know it only from a story of a *barring-out,* told me, when I was a boy, by Andrew Corbet of Shropshire, who had heard it from Mr. Pigot his uncle.

The practice of *barring-out,* was a savage license, practised in many schools to the end of the last century, by which the boys, when the periodical vacation drew near, growing petulant at the approach of liberty, some days before the time of regular recess, took possession of the school, of which they barred the doors, and bade their master defiance from the windows. It is not easy to suppose that on such occasions the master would do more than laugh; yet, if tradition may be credited, he often struggled hard to force or surprise the garrison. The master, when Pigot was a school-boy, was *barred-out* at Lichfield, and the whole operation, as he said, was planned and conducted by Addison.

To judge better of the probability of this story, I have enquired when he was sent to the Chartreux; but, as he was not one of those who enjoyed the founder's benefaction, there is no account preserved of his admission. At the school of the Chartreux, to which he was removed either from that of Salisbury or Lichfield, he pursued his juvenile studies under the care of Dr. Ellis, and contracted that intimacy with Sir Richard Steele which their joint labours have so effectually recorded.

Of this memorable friendship the greater praise must be given to Steele. It is not hard to love those from whom nothing can be feared, and Addison never considered Steele as a rival; but Steele lived, as he confesses, under an habitual subjection to the predominating genius of Addison, whom he always mentioned with reverence, and treated with obsequiousness.

Addison, who knew his own dignity, could not always forbear to shew it, by playing a little upon his admirer; but he was in no danger of retort: his jests were endured without resistance or resentment.

But the sneer of jocularity was not the worst. Steele, whose imprudence of generosity, or vanity of profusion, kept him always incurably necessitous, upon some pressing exigence, in an evil hour borrowed a hundred pounds of his friend, probably without much purpose of repayment; but Addison, who seems to have had other notions of an hundred pounds, grew impatient of delay, and reclaimed his loan by an execution. Steele felt with great sensibility the obduracy of his creditor; but with emotions of sorrow rather than of anger.

In 1687 he was entered into Queen's College in Oxford, where, in 1689, the accidental perusal of some Latin verses gained him the patronage of Dr. Lancaster, afterwards provost of Queen's College; by whose recommendation he was elected into Magdalen College as a Demy, a term by which that society denominates those which are elsewhere called Scholars; young men, who partake of the founder's benefaction, and succeed in their order to vacant fellowships.

Here he continued to cultivate poetry and criticism, and grew first eminent by his Latin compositions, which are indeed entitled to particular praise. He has not confined himself to the imitation of any ancient author, but has formed his style from the general language, such as a diligent perusal of the productions of different ages happened to supply.

His Latin compositions seem to have had much of his fondness; for he collected a second volume of the Musæ Anglicanæ, perhaps for a convenient receptacle, in which all his Latin pieces are inserted, and where his Poem on the Peace has the first place. He afterwards presented the collection to Boileau, who from that time *conceived,* says Tickell, *an opinion of the English genius for poetry.* Nothing is better known of Boileau, than that he had an injudicious and peevish contempt of modern Latin, and therefore his profession of regard was probably the effect of his civility rather than approbation.

Three of his Latin poems are upon subjects on which perhaps he would not have ventured to have written in his own language. The Battle of the Pigmies and Cranes; The Barometer; and A Bowling-green. When the matter is low or scanty, a dead language, in which nothing is mean because nothing is familiar, affords great conveniences; and by the sonorous magnificence of Roman syllables, the writer conceals penury of thought, and want of novelty, often from the reader, and often from himself.

In his twenty-second year he first shewed his power of English poetry by some verses addressed to Dryden; and soon afterwards published a translation of the greater part of the Fourth Georgick upon Bees; after which, says Dryden, *my latter swarm is hardly worth the hiving.*

About the same time he composed the arguments prefixed to the several books of Dryden's Virgil; and produced an Essay on the Georgicks, juvenile, superficial, and uninstructive, without much either of the scholar's learning or the critick's penetration.

His next paper of verses contained a character of the principal English poets, inscribed to Henry Sacheverell, who was then, if not a poet, a writer of verses; as is shewn by his version of a small part of Virgil's Georgicks, published in the Miscellanies, and a Latin encomium on Queen Mary, in the Musæ Anglicanæ. These verses exhibit all the fondness of friendship; but on one side or the other, friendship was afterwards too weak for the malignity of faction.

In this poem is a very confident and discriminative character of Spenser, whose work he had then never read. So little sometimes is criticism the effect of judgment. It is necessary to inform the reader, that about this time he was introduced by Congreve to Montague, then Chancellor of the Exchequer: Addison was then learning the trade of a courtier, and subjoined Montague as a poetical name to those of Cowley and of Dryden.

By the influence of Mr. Montague, concurring, according to Tickell, with his natural modesty, he was diverted from his original design of entering into holy orders. Montague alleged the corruption of men who engaged in civil employments without liberal education; and declared, that, though he was represented as an enemy to the Church, he would never do it an injury by withholding Addison from it.

Soon after (in 1695) he wrote a poem to King William, with a rhyming introduction addressed to Lord Somers. King William had no regard to elegance or literature; his study was only war; yet by a choice of ministers, whose disposition was very different from his own, he procured, without intention, a very liberal patronage to poetry. Addison was caressed both by Somers and Montague.

In 1697 appeared his Latin verses on the Peace of Ryswick which he dedicated to Montague, and which was afterwards called by Smith *the best Latin poem since the Æneid*. Praise must not be too rigorously examined; but the performance cannot be denied to be vigorous and elegant.

Having yet no public employment, he obtained (in 1699) a pension of three hundred pounds a year, that he might be enabled to travel. He staid a year at Blois, probably to learn the French language; and then proceeded in his journey to Italy, which he surveyed with the eyes of a poet.

While he was travelling at leisure, he was far from being idle; for he not only collected his observations on the country, but found time to write his Dialogues on Medals, and four Acts of Cato. Such at least is the relation of Tickell. Perhaps he only collected his materials, and formed his plan.

Whatever were his other employments in Italy, he there wrote the Letter to Lord Halifax, which is justly considered as the most elegant, if not the most sublime, of his poetical productions. But in about two years he found it necessary to hasten home; being, as Swift informs us, distressed by indigence, and compelled to become the tutor of a travelling Squire, because his pension was not remitted.

At his return he published his Travels, with a dedication to Lord Somers. As his stay in foreign countries was short, his observations are such as might be supplied by a hasty view, and consist chiefly in comparisons of the present face of the country with the descriptions left us by the Roman poets, from whom he made preparatory collections, though he might have spared the trouble had he known that such collections had been made twice before by Italian authors.

The most amusing passage of his book, is his account of the minute republick of San Marino; of many parts it is not a very severe censure to say that they might have been written at home. His elegance of language, and variegation of prose and verse, however, gains upon the reader; and the book, though a while neglected, became in time so much the favourite of the publick, that before it was reprinted it rose to five times its price.

When he returned to England (in 1702), with a meanness of appearance which gave testimony of the difficulties to which he had been reduced, he found his old patrons out of power, and was therefore for a time at full leisure for the cultivation of his mind, and a mind so cultivated gives reason to believe that little time was lost.

But he remained not long neglected or useless. The victory at Blenheim (1704) spread triumph and confidence over the nation; and Lord Godolphin lamenting to Lord Halifax, that it had not been celebrated in a manner equal to the subject, desired him to propose it to some better poet. Halifax told him that there was no encouragement for genius; that worthless men were unprofitably enriched with publick money, without any care to find or employ those whose appearance might do honour to their country. To this Godolphin replied, that such abuses should in time be rectified; and that if a man could be found capable of the task then proposed, he should not want an ample recompense. Halifax then named Addison; but required that the Treasurer should apply to him in his own person. Godolphin sent the message by Mr. Boyle, afterwards Lord

Carleton; and Addison having undertaken the work, communicated it to the Treasurer, while it was yet advanced no further than the simile of the Angel, and was immediately rewarded by succeeding Mr. Locke in the place of Commissioner of Appeals.

In the following year he was at Hanover with Lord Halifax; and the year after was made under-secretary of state, first to Sir Charles Hedges, and in a few months more to the Earl of Sunderland.

About this time the prevalent taste for Italian operas inclined him to try what would be the effect of a musical Drama in our own language. He therefore wrote the opera of Rosamond, which, when exhibited on the stage, was either hissed or neglected; but trusting that the readers would do him more justice, he published it, with an inscription to the Duchess of Marlborough; a woman without skill, or pretensions to skill, in poetry or literature. His dedication was therefore an instance of servile absurdity, to be exceeded only by Joshua Barnes's dedication of a Greek Anacreon to the Duke.

His reputation had been somewhat advanced by The Tender Husband, a comedy which Steele dedicated to him, with a confession that he owed to him several of the most successful scenes. To this play Addison supplied a prologue.

When the Marquis of Wharton was appointed Lord-lieutenant of Ireland, Addison attended him as his secretary; and was made keeper of the records in Birmingham's Tower, with a salary of three hundred pounds a year. The office was little more than nominal, and the salary was augmented for his accommodation.

Interest and faction allow little to the operation of particular dispositions, or private opinions. Two men of personal characters more opposite than those of Wharton and Addison could not easily be brought together. Wharton was impious, profligate, and shameless, without regard, or appearance of regard, to right and wrong: whatever is contrary to this, may be said of Addison; but as agents of a party they were connected, and how they adjusted their other sentiments we cannot know.

Addison must, however, not be too hastily condemned. It is not necessary to refuse benefits from a bad man, when the acceptance implies no approbation of his crime; nor has the subordinate officer any obligation to examine the opinions or conduct of those under whom he acts, except that he may not be made the instrument of wickedness. It is reasonable to suppose that Addison counteracted, as far as he was able, the malignant and blasting influence of the Lieutenant, and that at least by his intervention some good was done, and some mischief prevented.

When he was in office, he made a law to himself, as Swift has recorded, never to remit his regular fees in civility to his friends: "For," said he, "I may have a hundred friends; and, if my fee be two guineas, I shall, by relinquishing my right lose two hundred guineas, and no friend gain more than two; there is therefore no proportion between the good imparted and the evil suffered."

He was in Ireland when Steele, without any communication of his design, began the publication of the Tatler; but he was not long concealed: by inserting a remark on Virgil, which Addison had given him, he discovered himself. It is indeed not easy for any man to write upon literature, or common life, so as not to make himself known to those with whom he familiarly converses, and who are acquainted with his track of study, his favourite topicks, his peculiar notions, and his habitual phrases.

If Steele desired to write in secret, he was not lucky; a single month detected him. His first Tatler was published April 22 (1709), and Addison's contribution appeared May 26. Tickell observes, that the Tatler began and was concluded without his concurrence. This is doubtless literally true; but the work did not suffer much by his unconsciousness of its commencement, or his absence at its cessation; for he continued his assistance to December 23, and the paper stopped on January 2. He did not distinguish his pieces by any signature; and I know not whether his name was not kept secret, till the papers were collected into volumes.

To the Tatler, in about two months, succeeded the Spectator; a series of essays of the same kind, but written with less levity, upon a more regular plan, and published daily. Such an undertaking shewed the writers not to distrust their own copiousness of materials or facility of composition, and their performance justified their confidence. They found, however, in their progress, many auxiliaries. To attempt a single paper was no terrifying labour: many pieces were offered, and many were received.

Addison had enough of the zeal of party, but Steele had at that time almost nothing else. The Spectator, in one of the first papers, shewed the political tenets of its authors; but a resolution was soon taken, of courting general approbation by general topicks, and subjects on which faction had produced no diversity of sentiments; such as literature, morality, and familiar life. To this practice they adhered with very few deviations. The ardour of Steele once broke out in praise of Marlborough; and when Dr. Fleetwood prefixed to some sermons a preface, overflowing with whiggish opinions, that it might be read by the Queen it was reprinted in the Spectator.

To teach the minuter decencies and inferior duties, to regulate the practice of daily conversation, to correct those depravities which are rather ridiculous than criminal, and remove those grievances which, if they produce no lasting calamities, impress hourly vexation, was first attempted by Casa in his book of Manners, and Castiglione in his Courtier; two books yet celebrated in Italy for purity and elegance, and which, if they are now less read, are neglected only because they have effected that reformation which their authors intended, and their precepts now are no longer wanted. Their usefulness to the age in which they were written is sufficiently attested by the translations which almost all the nations of Europe were in haste to obtain.

This species of instruction was continued, and perhaps advanced, by the French; among whom La Bruyere's Manners of the Age, though, as Boileau remarked, it is written without connection, certainly deserves great praise, for liveliness of description and justness of observation.

Before the Tatler and Spectator, if the writers for the theatre are excepted, England had no masters of common life. No writers had yet undertaken to reform either the savageness of neglect, or the impertinence of civility; to shew when to speak, or to be silent; how to refuse, or how to comply. We had many books to teach us our more important duties, and to settle opinions in philosophy or politicks; but an *Arbiter elegantiarum,* a judge of propriety, was yet wanting, who should survey the track of daily conversation, and free it from thorns and prickles, which teaze the passer, though they do not wound him.

For this purpose nothing is so proper as the frequent publication of short papers, which we read not as study but amusement. If the subject be slight, the treatise likewise is short. The busy may find time, and the idle may find patience.

This mode of conveying cheap and easy knowledge began among us in the Civil War, when it was much the interest of either party to raise and fix the prejudices of the people. At that time appeared Mercurius Aulicus, Mercurius Rusticus, and Mercurius Civicus. It is said, that when any title grew popular, it was stolen by the antagonist, who by this stratagem conveyed his notions to those who would not have received him had he not worn the appearance of a friend. The tumult of those unhappy days left scarcely any man leisure to treasure up occasional compositions; and so much were they neglected, that a complete collection is no where to be found.

These Mercuries were succeeded by L'Estrange's Observator, and that by Lesley's Rehearsal, and perhaps by others; but hitherto nothing had been conveyed to the people, in this commodious manner, but controversy relating to the Church or State; of which they taught many to talk, whom they could not teach to judge.

It has been suggested that the Royal Society was instituted soon after the Restoration, to divert the attention of the people from public discontent. The Tatler and the Spectator had the same tendency; they were published at a time when two parties, loud, restless, and violent, each with plausible declarations, and each perhaps without any distinct termination of its views, were agitating the nation; to minds heated with political contest, they supplied cooler and more inoffensive reflections; and it is said by Addison, in a subsequent work, that they had a perceptible influence upon the conversation of that time, and taught the frolick and the gay to unite merriment with decency; an effect which they can never wholly lose, while they continue to be among the first books by which both sexes are initiated in the elegances of knowledge.

The Tatler and Spectator adjusted, like Casa, the unsettled practice of daily intercourse by propriety and politeness; and, like La Bruyere, exhibited the *Characters and Manners of the Age*. The persons introduced in these papers were not merely ideal; they were then known and conspicuous in various stations. Of the Tatler this is told by Steele in his last paper, and of the Spectator by Budgell in the Preface to Theophrastus; a book which Addison has recommended, and which he was suspected to have revised, if he did not write it. Of those portraits, which may be supposed to be sometimes embellished, and sometimes aggravated, the originals are now partly known, and partly forgotten.

But to say that they united the plans of two or three eminent writers, is to give them but a small part of their due praise; they superadded literature and criticism, and sometimes towered far above their predecessors; and taught, with great justness of argument and dignity of language, the most important duties and sublime truths.

All these topicks were happily varied with elegant fictions and refined allegories, and illuminated with different changes of style and felicities of invention.

It is recorded by Budgell, that of the characters feigned or exhibited in the Spectator, the favourite of Addison was Sir Roger de Coverley, of whom he had formed a very delicate and discriminated idea, which he would not suffer to be violated; and therefore when Steele had shewn him innocently picking up a girl in the Temple and taking her to a tavern, he drew upon himself so much of his friend's indignation, that he was forced to appease him by a promise of forbearing Sir Roger for the time to come.

The reason which induced Cervantes to bring his hero to the grave, *para mi solo nacio Don Quixote, y yo para el,* made Addison declare, with an undue vehemence of expression, that he would kill Sir Roger; being of opinion that they were born for one another, and that any other hand would do him wrong.

It may be doubted whether Addison ever filled up his original delineation. He describes his Knight as having his imagination somewhat warped; but of this perversion he has made very little use. The irregularities in Sir Roger's conduct seem not so much the effects of a mind deviating from the beaten track of life, by the perpetual pressure of some overwhelming idea, as of habitual rusticity, and that negligence which solitary grandeur naturally generates.

The variable weather of the mind, the flying vapours of incipient madness, which from time to time cloud reason, without eclipsing it, it requires so much nicety to exhibit, that Addison seems to have been deterred from prosecuting his own design.

To Sir Roger, who, as a country gentleman, appears to be a Tory, or, as it is gently expressed, an adherent to the landed interest, is opposed Sir Andrew Freeport, a new man, a wealthy merchant, zealous for the moneyed interest, and a Whig. Of this contrariety of opinions, it is probable more consequences were at first intended, than could be produced when the resolution was taken to exclude party from the paper. Sir Andrew does but little, and that little seems not to have pleased Addison, who, when he dismissed him from the club, changed his opinions. Steele had made him, in the true spirit of unfeeling commerce, declare that he *would not build an hospital for idle people;* but at last he buys land, settles in the country, and builds not a manufactory, but an hospital for twelve old husbandmen, for men with whom a merchant has little acquaintance, and whom he commonly considers with little kindness.

Of essays thus elegant, thus instructive, and thus commodiously distributed, it is natural to suppose the approbation general and the sale numerous. I once heard it observed, that the sale may be calculated by the product of the tax, related in the last number to produce more than twenty pounds a week, and therefore stated at one and twenty pounds, or three pounds ten shillings a day: this, at a halfpenny a paper, will give sixteen hundred and eighty for the daily number.

This sale is not great; yet this, if Swift be credited, was likely to grow less; for he declares that the Spectator, whom he ridicules for his endless mention of the *fair sex,* had before his recess wearied his readers.

The next year (1713), in which Cato came upon the stage, was the grand climacterick of Addison's reputation. Upon the death of Cato, he had, as is said, planned a tragedy in the time of his travels, and had for several years the four first acts finished, which were shewn to such as were likely to spread their admiration. They were seen by Pope, and by Cibber; who relates that Steele, when he took back the copy, told him, in the despicable cant of literary modesty, that, whatever spirit his friend had shewn in the composition, he doubted whether he would have courage sufficient to expose it to the censure of a British audience.

The time however was now come, when those who affected to think liberty in danger, affected likewise to think that a stage-play might preserve it: and Addison was importuned, in the name of the tutelary deities of Britain, to shew his courage and his zeal by finishing his design.

To resume his work he seemed perversely and unaccountably unwilling; and by a request, which perhaps he wished to be denied, desired Mr. Hughes to add a fifth act. Hughes supposed him serious; and, undertaking the supplement, brought in a few days some scenes for his examination; but he had in the mean time gone to work himself, and produced half an act, which he afterward completed, but with brevity irregularly disproportionate to the foregoing parts; like a task performed with reluctance, and hurried to its conclusion.

It may yet be doubted whether Cato was made publick by any change of the author's purpose; for Dennis charged him with raising prejudices in his own favour by false positions of preparatory criticism, and with *poisoning the town* by contradicting in the Spectator the established rule of poetical justice, because his own hero, with all his virtues, was to fall before a tyrant. The fact is certain; the motives we must guess.

Addison was, I believe, sufficiently disposed to bar all avenues against all danger. When Pope brought him the prologue, which is properly accommodated to the play, there were these words, *Britons, arise, be worth like this approved;* meaning nothing more than, Britons, erect and exalt yourselves to the approbation of public virtue. Addison was frighted lest he should be thought a promoter of insurrection, and the line was liquidated to *Britons, attend.*

Now, *heavily in clouds came on the day, the great, the important day,* when Addison was to stand the hazard of the theatre. That there might, however, be left as little to hazard as was possible, on the first night Steele, as himself relates, undertook to pack an audience. This, says Pope, had been tried for the first time in favour of the Distrest Mother; and was now, with more efficacy, practised for Cato.

The danger was soon over. The whole nation was at that time on fire with faction. The Whigs applauded every line in which Liberty was mentioned, as a satire on the Tories; and the Tories echoed every clap, to shew that the satire was unfelt. The story of Bolingbroke is well known. He called Booth to his box, and gave him fifty guineas for defending the cause of Liberty so well against a perpetual dictator. The Whigs, says Pope, design a second present, when they can accompany it with as good a sentence.

The play, supported thus by the emulation of factious praise, was acted night after night for a longer time than, I believe, the publick had allowed to any drama before; and the author, as Mrs. Potter long afterwards related, wandered through the whole exhibition behind the scenes with restless and unappeasable solicitude.

When it was printed, notice was given that the Queen would be pleased if it was dedicated to her; *but as he had designed that compliment elsewhere, he found himself obliged,* says Tickell, *by his duty on the one hand, and his honour on the other, to send it into the world without any dedication.*

Human happiness has always its abatements; the brightest sunshine of success is not without a cloud. No sooner was Cato offered to the reader, than it was attacked by the acute malignity of Dennis, with all the violence of angry criticism. Dennis, though equally zealous, and probably by his temper more furious than Addison, for what they called Liberty, and though a flatterer of the Whig ministry, could not sit quiet at a successful play; but was eager to tell friends and enemies, that they had misplaced their admirations. The world was too stubborn for instruction; with the fate of the censurer of Corneille's Cid, his animadversions shewed his anger without effect, and Cato continued to be praised.

Pope had now an opportunity of courting the friendship of Addison, by vilifying his old enemy, and could give resentment its full play without appearing to revenge himself. He therefore published A Narrative of the Madness of John Dennis; a performance which left the objections to the play in their full force, and therefore discovered more desire of vexing the critick than of defending the poet.

Addison, who was no stranger to the world, probably saw the selfishness of Pope's friendship; and, resolving that he should have the consequences of his officiousness to himself, informed Dennis by Steele, that he was sorry for the insult; and that whenever he should think fit to answer his remarks, he would do it in a manner to which nothing could be objected.

The greatest weakness of the play is in the scenes of love, which are said by Pope to have been added to the original plan upon a subsequent review, in compliance with the popular practice of the stage. Such an authority it is hard to reject; yet the love is so intimately mingled with the whole action that it cannot easily be thought extrinsick and adventitious; for if it were taken away, what would be left? or how were the four acts filled in the first draught?

At the publication the Wits seemed proud to pay their attendance with encomiastick verses. The best are from an unknown hand, which will perhaps lose somewhat of their praise when the author is known to be Jeffreys.

Cato had yet other honours. It was censured as a party-play by a Scholar of Oxford, and defended in a favourable examination by Dr. Sewel. It was translated by Salvini into Italian, and acted at Florence; and by the Jesuits of St. Omer's into Latin, and played by their pupils. Of this version a copy was sent to Mr. Addison: it is to be wished that it could be found, for the sake of comparing their version of the soliloquy with that of Bland.

A tragedy was written on the same subject by Des Champs, a French poet, which was translated, with a criticism on the English play. But the translator and the critick are now forgotten.

Dennis lived on unanswered, and therefore little read: Addison knew the policy of literature too well to make his enemy important, by drawing the attention of the publick upon a criticism, which, though sometimes intemperate, was often irrefragable.

While Cato was upon the stage, another daily paper, called The Guardian, was published by Steele. To this Addison gave great assistance, whether occasionally or by previous engagement is not known.

The character of Guardian was too narrow and too serious: it might properly enough admit both the duties and the decencies of life, but seemed not to include literary speculations, and was in some degree violated by merriment and burlesque. What had the Guardian of the Lizards to do with clubs of tall or of little men, with nests of ants, or with Strada's prolusions?

Of this paper nothing is necessary to be said, but that it found many contributors, and that it was a continuation of the Spectator, with the same elegance, and the same variety, till some unlucky sparkle from a Tory paper set Steele's politics on fire, and wit at once blazed into faction. He was soon too hot for neutral topicks, and quitted the Guardian to write the Englishman.

The papers of Addison are marked in the Spectator by one of the Letters in the name of Clio, and in the Guardian by a *hand;* whether it was, as Tickell pretends to think, that he was unwilling to usurp the praise of others, or as Steele, with far greater likelihood, insinuates, that he could not without discontent impart to others any of his own. I have heard that his avidity did not satisfy itself with the air of renown, but that with great eagerness he laid hold on his proportion of the profits.

Many of these papers were written with powers truly comick, with nice discrimination of characters, and accurate observation of natural or accidental deviations from propriety; but it was not supposed that he had tried a comedy on the stage, till Steele, after his death, declared him the author of The Drummer; this, however, Steele did not know to be true by any direct testimony; for when Addison put the play into his hands, he only told him, it was the work of *a Gentleman in the Company;* and when it was received, as is confessed, with cold approbation, he was probably less willing to claim it. Tickell omitted it in his collection; but the testimony of Steele, and the total silence of any other claimant, has determined the publick to assign it to Addison, and it is now printed with his other poetry. Steele carried The Drummer to the playhouse, and afterwards to the press, and sold the copy for fifty guineas.

To the opinion of Steele may be added the proof supplied by the play itself, of which the characters are such as Addison would have delineated, and the tendency such as Addison would have promoted. That it should have been ill received would raise wonder, did we not daily see the capricious distribution of theatrical praise.

He was not all this time an indifferent spectator of publick affairs. He wrote, as different exigencies required (in 1707), The Present

State of the War, and the Necessity of an Augmentation; which, however judicious, being written on temporary topicks, and exhibiting no peculiar powers, laid hold on no attention, and has naturally sunk by its own weight into neglect. This cannot be said of the few papers entitled The Whig Examiner, in which is employed all the force of gay malevolence and humorous satire. Of this paper, which just appeared and expired, Swift remarks, with exultation, that *it is now down among the dead men*. He might well rejoice at the death of that which he could not have killed. Every reader of every party, since personal malice is past, and the papers which once inflamed the nation are read only as effusions of wit, must wish for more of the Whig Examiners; for on no occasion was the genius of Addison more vigorously exerted, and on none did the superiority of his powers more evidently appear. His Trial of Count Tariff, written to expose the Treaty of Commerce with France, lived no longer than the question that produced it.

Not long afterwards an attempt was made to revive the Spectator, at a time indeed by no means favourable to literature, when the succession of a new family to the throne filled the nation with anxiety, discord, and confusion; and either the turbulence of the times, or the satiety of the readers, put a stop to the publication, after an experiment of eighty numbers, which were afterwards collected into an eighth volume, perhaps more valuable than any one of those that went before it. Addison produced more than a fourth part, and the other contributors are by no means unworthy of appearing as his associates. The time that had passed during the suspension of the Spectator, though it had not lessened his power of humour, seems to have increased his disposition to seriousness: the proportion of his religious to his comick papers is greater than in the former series.

The Spectator, from its recommencement, was published only three times a week; and no discriminative marks were added to the papers. To Addison, Tickell has ascribed twenty-three.

The Spectator had many contributors; and Steele, whose negligence kept him always in a hurry, when it was his turn to furnish a paper, called loudly for the Letters, of which Addison, whose materials were more, made little use; having recourse to sketches and hints, the product of his former studies, which he now reviewed and completed: among these are named by Tickell the Essays on Wit, those on the Pleasures of the Imagination, and the Criticism on Milton.

When the House of Hanover took possession of the throne, it was reasonable to expect that the zeal of Addison would be suitably rewarded. Before the arrival of King George, he was made secretary to the regency, and was required by his office to send notice to Hanover that the Queen was dead, and that the throne was vacant. To do this would not have been difficult to any man but Addison, who was so overwhelmed with the greatness of the event, and so distracted by choice of expression, that the Lords, who could not wait for the niceties of criticism, called Mr. Southwell, a clerk in the house, and ordered him to dispatch the message. Southwell readily told what was necessary, in the common style of business, and valued himself upon having done what was too hard for Addison.

He was better qualified for the Freeholder, a paper which he published twice a week, from Dec. 23, 1715, to the middle of the next year. This was undertaken in defence of the established government, sometimes with argument, sometimes with mirth. In argument he had many equals; but his humour was singular and matchless. Bigotry itself must be delighted with the Tory-Fox-hunter.

There are, however, some strokes less elegant, and less decent; such as the Pretender's Journal, in which one topick of ridicule is his poverty. This mode of abuse had been employed by Milton against King Charles II.

> "— — — — — *Jacobæi.*
> Centum éxulantis viscera Marsupii regis."

And Oldmixon delights to tell of some alderman of London, that he had more money than the exiled princes; but that which might be expected from Milton's savageness, or Oldmixon's meanness, was not suitable to the delicacy of Addison.

Steele thought the humour of the Freeholder too nice and gentle for such noisy times; and is reported to have said that the ministry made use of a lute, when they should have called for a trumpet.

This year (1716) he married the Countess Dowager of Warwick, whom he had solicited by a very long and anxious courtship, perhaps with behaviour not very unlike that of Sir Roger to his disdainful widow: and who, I am afraid, diverted herself often by playing with his passion. He is said to have first known her by becoming tutor to her son. "He formed," said Tonson, "the design of getting that lady, from the time when he was first recommended into the family." In what part of his life he obtained the recommendation, or how long, and in what manner he lived in the family, I know not. His advances at first were certainly timorous, but grew bolder as his reputation and influence increased; till at last the lady was persuaded to marry him, on terms much like those on which a Turkish princess is espoused, to whom the Sultan is reported to pronounce, "Daughter, I give thee this man for thy slave." The marriage, if uncontradicted report can be credited, made no addition to his happiness; it neither found them nor made them equal. She always remembered her own rank, and thought herself entitled to treat with very little ceremony the tutor of her son. Rowe's ballad of the Despairing Shepherd is said to have been written, either before or after marriage, upon this memorable pair; and it is certain that Addison has left behind him no encouragement for ambitious love.

The year after (1717) he rose to his highest elevation, being made secretary of state. For this employment he might be justly supposed qualified by long practice of business, and by his regular ascent through other offices; but expectation is often disappointed; it is universally confessed that he was unequal to the duties of his place. In the House of Commons he could not speak, and therefore was useless to the defence of the Government. In the office, says Pope, he could not issue an order without losing his time in quest of fine expressions. What he gained in rank, he lost in credit; and, finding by experience his own inability, was forced to solicit his dismission, with a pension of fifteen hundred pounds a year. His friends palliated this relinquishment, of which both friends and enemies knew the true reason, with an account of declining health, and the necessity of recess and quiet.

He now returned to his vocation, and began to plan literary occupations for his future life. He purposed a tragedy on the death of Socrates; a story of which, as Tickell remarks, the basis is narrow, and to which I know not how love could have been appended. There would, however, have been no want either of virtue in the sentiments, or elegance in the language.

He engaged in a nobler work, a defence of the Christian Religion, of which part was published after his death; and he designed to have made a new poetical version of the Psalms.

These pious compositions Pope imputed to a selfish motive, upon the credit, as he owns, of Tonson; who having quarrelled with Addison, and not loving him, said, that, when he laid down the secretary's office, he intended to take orders, and obtain a bishop-rick; *for,* said he, *I always thought him a priest in his heart.*

That Pope should have thought this conjecture of Tonson worth remembrance is a proof, but indeed so far as I have found, the only proof, that he retained some malignity from their ancient rivalry. Tonson pretended but to guess it; no other mortal ever suspected it; and Pope might have reflected, that a man who had been secretary of state, in the ministry of Sunderland, knew a nearer way to a bishoprick than by defending Religion, or translating the Psalms.

It is related that he had once a design to make an English Dictionary, and that he considered Dr. Tillotson as the writer of highest authority. There was formerly sent to me by Mr. Locker, clerk of the Leathersellers' Company, who was eminent for curiosity and literature, a collection of examples selected from Tillotson's works, as Locker said, by Addison. It came too late to be of use, so I inspected it but slightly, and remember it indistinctly. I thought the passages too short.

Addison, however, did not conclude his life in peaceful studies; but relapsed, when he was near his end, to a political dispute.

It so happened that (1718-19) a controversy was agitated, with great vehemence, between those friends of long continuance, Addison and Steele. It may be asked, in the language of Homer, what power or what cause could set them at variance. The subject of their dispute was of great importance. The Earl of Sunderland proposed an act called the Peerage Bill, by which the number of peers should be fixed, and the King restrained from any new creation of nobility, unless when an old family should be extinct. To this the Lords would naturally agree; and the King, who was yet little acquainted with his own prerogative, and, as is now well known, almost indifferent to the possession of the Crown, had been persuaded to consent. The only difficulty was found among the Commons, who were not likely to approve the perpetual exclusion of themselves and their posterity. The bill therefore was eagerly opposed, and among others by Sir Robert Walpole, whose speech was published.

The Lords might think their dignity diminished by improper advancements, and particularly by the introduction of twelve new peers at once, to produce a majority of Tories in the last reign; an act of authority violent enough, yet certainly legal, and by no means to be compared with that contempt of national right, with which some time afterwards, by the instigation of Whiggism, the Commons, chosen by the people for three years, chose themselves for seven. But, whatever might be the disposition of the Lords, the people had no wish to increase their power. The tendency of the bill, as Steele observed in a letter to the Earl of Oxford, was to introduce an Aristocracy; for a majority in the House of Lords, so limited, would have been despotick and irresistible.

To prevent this subversion of the ancient establishment, Steele, whose pen readily seconded his political passions, endeavoured to alarm the nation by a pamphlet called The Plebeian; to this an answer was published by Addison, under the title of The Old Whig, in which it is not discovered that Steele was then known to be the advocate for the Commons. Steele replied by a second Plebeian; and, whether by ignorance or by courtesy, confined himself to his question, without any personal notice of his opponent. Nothing hitherto was committed against the laws of friendship, or proprieties of decency; but controvertists cannot long retain their kindness for each other. The Old Whig answered the Plebeian, and could not forbear some contempt of "little Dicky, whose trade it was to write pamphlets." Dicky, however, did not lose his settled veneration for his friend; but contented himself with quoting some lines of Cato, which were at once detection and reproof. The bill was laid aside during that session, and Addison died before the next, in which its commitment was rejected by two hundred and sixty-five to one hundred and seventy-seven.

Every reader surely must regret that these two illustrious friends, after so many years past in confidence and endearment, in unity of interest, conformity of opinion, and fellowship of study, should finally part in acrimonious opposition. Such a controversy was *Bellum plusquam civile,* as Lucan expresses it. Why could not faction find other advocates? But, among the uncertainties of the human state, we are doomed to number the instability of friendship.

Of this dispute I have little knowledge but from the Biographia Britannica. The Old Whig is not inserted in Addison's works, nor is it mentioned by Tickell in his Life; why it was omitted the biographers doubtless give the true reason; the fact was too recent, and those who had been heated in the contention were not yet cool.

The necessity of complying with times, and of sparing persons, is the great impediment of biography. History may be formed from permanent monuments and records; but Lives can only be written from personal knowledge, which is growing every day less, and in a short time is lost for ever. What is known can seldom be immediately told; and when it might be told, it is no longer known. The delicate features of the mind, the nice discriminations of character, and the minute peculiarities of conduct, are soon obliterated; and it is surely better that caprice, obstinacy, frolick, and folly, however they might delight in the description, should be silently forgotten, than that, by wanton merriment and unseasonable detection, a pang should be given to a widow, a daughter, a brother or a friend. As the process of these narratives is now bringing me among my contemporaries, I begin to feel myself *walking upon ashes under which the fire is not extinguished,* and coming to the time of which it will be proper rather to say *nothing that is false, than all that is true.*

The end of this useful life was now approaching.—Addison had for some time been oppressed by shortness of breath, which was now aggravated by a dropsy; and, finding his danger pressing, he prepared to die conformably to his own precepts and professions.

During this lingering decay, he sent, as Pope relates, a message by the Earl of Warwick to Mr. Gay, desiring to see him: Gay, who had not visited him for some time before, obeyed the summons, and found himself received with great kindness. The purpose for which the interview had been solicited was then discovered; Addison told him that he had injured him; but that, if he recovered, he would recompense him. What the injury was he did not explain, nor did Gay ever know; but supposed that some preferment designed for him, had, by Addison's intervention, been withheld.

Lord Warwick was a young man of very irregular life, and perhaps of loose opinions. Addison, for whom he did not want respect, had very diligently endeavoured to reclaim him; but his arguments and expostulations had no effect. One experiment, however, remained to be tried: when he found his life near its end, he directed the young Lord to be called; and when he desired, with great tenderness, to hear his last injunctions, told him, *I have sent for you that you may see how a Christian can die*. What effect this awful scene had on the Earl I know not; he likewise died himself in a short time.

In Tickell's excellent Elegy on his friend are these lines:

> He taught us how to live; and oh! too high
> The price of knowledge, taught us how to die.

In which he alludes, as he told Dr. Young, to this moving interview.

Having given directions to Mr. Tickell for the publication of his works, and dedicated them on his death-bed to his friend Mr. Craggs, he died June 17, 1719, at Holland-house, leaving no child but a daughter.

Of his virtue it is a sufficient testimony, that the resentment of party has transmitted no charge of any crime. He was not one of those who are praised only after death; for his merit was so generally acknowledged, that Swift, having observed that his election passed without a contest, adds, that if he had proposed himself for king, he would hardly have been refused.

His zeal for his party did not extinguish his kindness for the merit of his opponents: when he was secretary in Ireland, he refused to intermit his acquaintance with Swift.

Of his habits, or external manners, nothing is so often mentioned as that timorous or sullen taciturnity, which his friends called modesty by too mild a name. Steele mentions with great tenderness "that remarkable bashfulness, which is a cloak that hides and muffles merit;" and tells us, that "his abilities were covered only by modesty, which doubles the beauties which are seen, and gives credit and esteem to all that are concealed." Chesterfield affirms, that "Addison was the most timorous and aukward man that he ever saw." And Addison, speaking of his own deficience in conversation, used to say of himself, that, with respect to intellectual wealth, "he could draw bills for a thousand pounds, though he had not a guinea in his pocket."

That he wanted current coin for ready payment, and by that want was often obstructed and distressed; that he was oppressed by an improper and ungraceful timidity, every testimony concurs to prove; but Chesterfield's representation is doubtless hyperbolical. That man cannot be supposed very unexpert in the arts of conversation and practice of life, who, without fortune or alliance, by his usefulness and dexterity became secretary of state; and who died at forty-seven, after having not only stood long in the highest rank of wit and literature, but filled one of the most important offices of state.

The time in which he lived had reason to lament his obstinacy of silence; "for he was," says Steele, "above all men in that talent called humour, and enjoyed it in such perfection, that I have often reflected, after a night spent with him apart from all the world, that I had had the pleasure of conversing with an intimate acquaintance of Terence and Catullus, who had all their wit and nature, heightened with humour more exquisite and delightful than any other man ever possessed." This is the fondness of a friend; let us hear what is told us by a rival. "Addison's conversation," says Pope, "had something in it more charming than I have found in any other man. But this was only when familiar: before strangers or perhaps a single stranger, he preserved his dignity by a stiff silence."

This modesty was by no means inconsistent with a very high opinion of his own merit. He demanded to be the first name in modern wit; and, with Steele to echo him, used to depreciate Dryden, whom Pope and Congreve defended against them. There is no reason to doubt that he suffered too much pain from the prevalence of Pope's poetical reputation; nor is it without strong reason suspected, that by some disingenuous acts he endeavoured to obstruct it; Pope was not the only man whom he insidiously injured, though the only man of whom he could be afraid.

His own powers were such as might have satisfied him with conscious excellence. Of very extensive learning he has indeed given no proofs. He seems to have had small acquaintance with the sciences, and to have read little except Latin and French; but of the Latin poets his Dialogues on Medals shew that he had perused the works with great diligence and skill. The abundance of his own mind left him little need of adventitious sentiments; his wit always could suggest what the occasion demanded. He had read with critical eyes the important volume of human life, and knew the heart of man from the depths of stratagem to the surface of affectation.

What he knew he could easily communicate. "This," says Steele, "was particular in this writer, that when he had taken his resolution, or made his plan for what he designed to write, he would walk about a room, and dictate it into language with as much freedom and ease as any one could write it down, and attend to the coherence and grammar of what he dictated."

Pope, who can be less suspected of favouring his memory, declares that he wrote very fluently, but was slow and scrupulous in correcting; that many of his Spectators were written very fast, and sent immediately to the press; and that it seemed to be for his advantage not to have time for much revisal.

"He would alter," says Pope, "any thing to please his friends, before publication; but would not retouch his pieces afterwards: and I believe not one word in Cato, to which I made an objection, was suffered to stand."

The last line of Cato is Pope's, having been originally written

> And, oh! 'twas this that ended Cato's life.

Pope might have made more objections to the six concluding lines. In the first couplet the words *from hence* are improper; and the second line is taken from Dryden's Virgil. Of the next couplet, the first verse being included in the second, is therefore useless; and in the third *Discord* is made to produce *Strife*.

Of the course of Addison's familiar day, before his marriage, Pope has given a detail. He had in the house with him Budgell, and perhaps Philips. His chief companions were Steele, Budgell, Philips, Carey, Davenant, and Colonel Brett. With one or other of these he always breakfasted. He studied all morning; then dined at a tavern, and went afterwards to Button's.

Button had been a servant in the Countess of Warwick's family, who, under the patronage of Addison, kept a coffee-house on the south side of Russell-street, about two doors from Covent-garden. Here it was that the wits of that time used to assemble. It is said, that when Addison had suffered any vexation from the countess, he withdrew the company from Button's house.

From the coffee-house he went again to a tavern, where he often sat late, and drank too much wine. In the bottle, discontent seeks for comfort, cowardice for courage, and bashfulness for confidence. It is not unlikely that Addison was first seduced to excess by the manumission which he obtained from the servile timidity of his sober hours. He that feels oppression from the presence of those to whom he knows himself superior, will desire to set loose his powers of conversation; and who, that ever asked succor from Bacchus, was able to preserve himself from being enslaved by his auxiliary?

Among those friends it was that Addison displayed the elegance of his colloquial accomplishments, which may easily be supposed such as Pope represents them. The remark of Mandeville, who, when he had passed an evening in his company, declared that he was a parson in a tye-wig, can detract little from his character; he was always reserved to strangers, and was not incited to uncommon freedom by a character like that of Mandeville.

From any minute knowledge of his familiar manners, the intervention of sixty years has now debarred us. Steele once promised Congreve and the publick a complete description of his character; but the promises of authors are like the vows of lovers. Steele thought no more on his design, or thought on it with anxiety that at last disgusted him, and left his friend in the hands of Tickell.

One slight lineament of his character Swift has preserved. It was his practice when he found any man invincibly wrong, to flatter his opinions by acquiescence, and sink him yet deeper in absurdity. This artifice of mischief was admired by Stella; and Swift seems to approve her admiration.

His works will supply some information. It appears from his various pictures of the world, that, with all his bashfulness, he had conversed with many distinct classes of men, had surveyed their ways with very diligent observation, and marked with great acuteness the effects of different modes of life. He was a man in whose presence nothing reprehensible was out of danger; quick in discerning whatever was wrong or ridiculous, and not unwilling to expose it. *There are,* says Steele, *in his writings many oblique strokes upon some of the wittiest men of the age.* His delight was more to excite merriment than detestation, and he detects follies rather than crimes.

If any judgment be made, from his books, of his moral character, nothing will be found but purity and excellence. Knowledge of mankind indeed, less extensive than that of Addison, will shew, that to write, and to live, are very different. Many who praise virtue, do not more than praise it. Yet it is reasonable to believe that Addison's professions and practice were at no great variance, since, amidst that storm of faction in which most of his life was passed, though his station made him conspicuous, and his activity made him formidable, the character given him by his friends was never contradicted by his enemies: of those with whom interest or opinion united him, he had not only the esteem, but the kindness; and of others whom the violence of opposition drove against him, though he might lose the love, he retained the reverence.

It is justly observed by Tickell, that he employed wit on the side of virtue and religion. He not only made the proper use of wit himself, but taught it to others; and from his time it has been generally subservient to the cause of reason and of truth. He has dissipated the prejudice that had long connected gaiety with vice, and easiness of manners with laxity of principles. He has restored virtue to its dignity, and taught innocence not to be ashamed. This is an elevation of literary character, *above all Greek, above all Roman fame.* No greater felicity can genius attain than that of having purified intellectual pleasure, separated mirth from indecency, and wit from licentiousness; of having taught a succession of writers to bring elegance and gaiety to the aid of goodness; and, if I may use expressions yet more awful, of having *turned many to righteousness.*

Addison, in his life, and for some time afterwards, was considered by the greater part of readers as supremely excelling both in poetry and criticism. Part of his reputation may be probably ascribed to the advancement of his fortune: when, as Swift observes, he became a statesman, and saw poets waiting at his levee, it is no wonder that praise was accumulated upon him. Much likewise may be more honourably ascribed to his personal character: he who, if he had claimed it, might have obtained the diadem, was not likely to be denied the laurel.

But time quickly puts an end to artificial and accidental fame; and Addison is to pass through futurity protected only by his genius. Every name which kindness of interest once raised too high, is in danger, lest the next age should, by the vengeance of criticism, sink it in the same proportion. A great writer has lately styled him *an indifferent poet, and a worse critick*.

His poetry is first to be considered; of which it must be confessed that it has not often those felicities of diction which give lustre to sentiments, or that vigour of sentiment that animates diction: there is little of ardour, vehemence, or transport; there is very rarely the awfulness of grandeur, and not very often the splendour of elegance. He thinks justly; but he thinks faintly. This is his general character; to which, doubtless, many single passages will furnish exceptions.

Yet, if he seldom reaches supreme excellence, he rarely sinks into dulness, and is still more rarely entangled in absurdity. He did not trust his powers enough to be negligent. There is in most of his compositions a calmness and equability, deliberate and cautious, sometimes with little that delights, but seldom with any thing that offends.

Of this kind seem to be his poems to Dryden, to Somers, and to the King. His ode on St. Cecilia has been imitated by Pope, and has something in it of Dryden's vigour. Of his Account of the English Poets, he used to speak as a *poor thing;* but it is not worse than his usual strain. He has said, not very judiciously, in his character of Waller:

> Thy verse could shew ev'n Cromwell's innocence,
> And compliment the storms that bore him hence.
> O! had thy Muse not come an age too soon,
> But seen great Nassau on the British throne,
> How had his triumph glitter'd in thy page!—

What is this but to say that he who could compliment Cromwell had been the proper poet for King William? Addison, however, never printed the piece.

The *Letter from Italy* has been always praised, but has never been praised beyond its merit. It is more correct, with less appearance of labour, and more elegant, with less ambition of ornament, than any other of his poems. There is, however, one broken metaphor, of which notice may properly be taken:

> Fir'd with that name—
> I bridle in my struggling Muse with pain,
> That longs to launch into a nobler strain.

To *bridle a goddess* is no very delicate idea; but why must she be *bridled?* because she *longs to launch?* an act which was never hindered by a *bridle:* and whither will she *launch?* into a *nobler strain.* She is in the first line a *horse,* in the second a *boat;* and the care of the poet is to keep his *horse* or his *boat* from *singing.*

The next composition is the far-famed *Campaign,* which Dr. Warton has termed a Gazette in Rhyme, with harshness not often used by the good-nature of his criticism. Before a censure so severe is admitted, let us consider that War is a frequent subject of Poetry, and then enquire who has described it with more justness and force. Many of our own writers tried their powers upon this year of victory, yet Addison's is confessedly the best performance; his poem is the work of a man not blinded by the dust of learning: his images are not borrowed merely from books. The superiority which he confers upon his hero is not personal prowess, and *mighty bone,* but deliberate intrepidity, a calm command of his passions, and the power of consulting his own mind in the midst of danger. The rejection and contempt of fiction is rational and manly.

It may be observed that the last line is imitated by Pope:

> Marlb'rough's exploits appear divinely bright—
> Rais'd of themselves, their genuine charms they boast,
> And those that paint them truest, praise them most.

This Pope had in his thoughts; but, not knowing how to use what was not his own, he spoiled the thought when he had borrowed it.

The well-sung woes shall soothe my ghost;
He best can paint them who shall feel them most.

Martial exploits may be *painted;* perhaps *woes* may be *painted;* but they are surely not *painted* by being *well-sung:* it is not easy to paint in song, or to sing in colours.

No passage in the Campaign has been more often mentioned than the simile of the Angel, which is said in the Tatler to be *one of the noblest thoughts that ever entered into the heart of man,* and is therefore worthy of attentive consideration. Let it be first enquired whether it be a simile. A poetical simile is the discovery of likeness between two actions in their general nature dissimilar, or of causes terminating by different operations in some resemblance of effect. But the mention of another like consequence from a like cause, or of a like performance by a like agency, is not a simile, but an exemplification. It is not a simile to say that the Thames waters fields, as the Po waters fields; or that as Hecla vomits flames in Iceland, so Ætna vomits flames in Sicily. When Horace says of Pindar, that he pours his violence and rapidity of verse, as a river swollen with rain rushes from the mountain; or of himself, that his genius wanders in quest of poetical decorations, as the bee wanders to collect honey; he, in either case, produces a simile; the mind is impressed with the resemblance of things generally unlike, as unlike as intellect and body. But if Pindar had been described as writing with the copiousness and grandeur of Homer, or Horace had told that he reviewed and finished his own poetry with the same care as Isocrates polished his orations, instead of similitude he would have exhibited almost identity; he would have given the same portraits with different names. In the poem now examined, when the English are represented as gaining a fortified pass, by repetition of attack and perseverance of resolution; their obstinacy of courage, and vigour of onset, is well illustrated by the sea that breaks, with incessant battery, the dikes of Holland. This is a simile: but when Addison, having celebrated the beauty of Marlborough's person, tells us that *Achilles thus was formed with every grace,* here is no simile, but a mere exemplification. A simile may be compared to lines converging at a point, and is more excellent as the lines approach from greater distance: an exemplification may be considered as two parallel lines which run on together without approximation, never far separated, and never joined.

Marlborough is so like the angel in the poem, that the action of both is almost the same, and performed by both in the same manner. Marlborough *teaches the battle to rage;* the angel *directs the storm*: Marlborough is *unmoved in peaceful thought;* the angel is *calm and serene*: Marlborough stands *unmoved amidst the shock of hosts;* the angel rides *calm in the whirlwind*. The lines on Marlborough are just and noble; but the simile gives almost the same images a second time.

But perhaps this thought, though hardly a simile, was remote from vulgar conceptions, and required great labour of research, or dexterity of application. Of this, Dr. Madden, a name which Ireland ought to honour, once gave me his opinion. *If I had set,* said he, *ten school-boys to write on the battle of* Blenheim, *and eight had brought me the Angel, I should not have been surprised*.

The opera of Rosamond, though it is seldom mentioned, is one of the first of Addison's compositions. The subject is well-chosen, the fiction is pleasing, and the praise of Marlborough, for which the scene gives an opportunity, is, what perhaps every human excellence must be, the product of good-luck improved by genius. The thoughts are sometimes great, and sometimes tender; the versification is easy and gay. There is doubtless some advantage in the shortness of the lines, which there is little temptation to load with expletive epithets. The dialogue seems commonly better than the songs. The two comick characters of Sir Trusty and Grideline, though of no great value, are yet such as the poet intended. Sir Trusty's account of the death of Rosamond is, I think, too grossly absurd. The whole drama is airy and elegant; engaging in its process, and pleasing in its conclusion. If Addison had cultivated the lighter parts of poetry, he would probably have excelled.

The tragedy of Cato, which, contrary to the rule observed in selecting the works of other poets, has by the weight of its character forced its way into the late collection, is unquestionably the noblest production of Addison's genius. Of a work so much read, it is difficult to say any thing new. About things on which the public thinks long, it commonly attains to think right; and of Cato it has been not unjustly determined, that it is rather a poem in dialogue than a drama, rather a succession of just sentiments in elegant language, than a representation of natural affections, or of any state probable or possible in human life. Nothing here *excites or asswages emotion;* here is *no magical power of raising phantastick terror or wild anxiety.* The events are expected without solicitude, and are remembered without joy or sorrow. Of the agents we have no care; we consider not what they are doing, or what they are suffering; we wish only to know what they have to say. Cato is a being above our solicitude; a man of whom the gods take care, and whom we leave to their care with heedless confidence. To the rest, neither gods nor men can have much attention; for there is not one amongst them that strongly attracts either affection or esteem. But they are made the vehicles of such sentiments and such expression, that there is scarcely a scene in the play which the reader does not wish to impress upon his memory.

When Cato was shewn to Pope, he advised the author to print it, without any theatrical exhibition; supposing that it would be read more favourably than heard. Addison declared himself of the same opinion; but urged the importunity of his friends for its appearance on the stage. The emulation of parties made it successful beyond expectation, and its success has introduced or confirmed among us the use of dialogue too declamatory, of unaffecting elegance, and chill philosophy.

The universality of applause, however it might quell the censure of common mortals, had no other effect than to harden Dennis in fixed dislike; but his dislike was not merely capricious. He found and shewed many faults: he shewed them indeed with anger, but he found them with acuteness, such as ought to rescue his criticism from oblivion; though, at last, it will have no other life than it derives from the work which it endeavours to oppress.

Why he pays no regard to the opinion of the audience, he gives his reason, by remarking, that

"A deference is to be paid to a general applause, when it appears that that applause is natural and spontaneous; but that little regard is to be had to it, when it is affected and artificial. Of all the tragedies which in his memory have had vast and violent runs, not one has been excellent, few have been tolerable, most have been scandalous. When a poet writes a tragedy, who knows he has judgement, and who feels he has genius, that poet presumes upon his own merit, and scorns to make a cabal. That people come coolly to the representation of such a tragedy, without any violent expectation, or delusive imagination, or invincible prepossession; that such an audience is liable to receive the impressions which the poem shall naturally make in them, and to judge by their own reason, and their own judgements, and that reason and judgement are calm and serene, not formed by nature to make proselytes, and to controul and lord it over the imaginations of others. But that when an author writes a tragedy, who knows he has neither genius nor judgement, he has recourse to the making a party, and he endeavours to make up in industry what is wanting in talent, and to supply by poetical craft the absence of poetical art; that such an author is humbly contented to raise men's passions by a plot without doors, since he despairs of doing it by that which he brings upon the stage. That party, and passion, and prepossession, are clamorous and tumultuous things, and so much the more clamorous and tumultuous by how much the more erroneous: that they domineer and tyrannize over the imaginations of persons who want judgement, and sometimes too of those who have it; and, like a fierce and outrageous torrent, bear down all opposition before them."

He then condemns the neglect of poetical justice; which is always one of his favourite principles.

" 'Tis certainly the duty of every tragick poet, by the exact distribution of poetical justice, to imitate the Divine Dispensation, and to inculcate a particular Providence. 'Tis true, indeed, upon the stage of the world, the wicked sometimes prosper, and the guiltless suffer. But that is permitted by the Governor of the world, to shew, from the attribute of his infinite justice, that there is a compensation in futurity, to prove the immortality of the human soul, and the certainty of future rewards and punishments. But the poetical persons in tragedy exist no longer than the reading, or the representation; the whole extent of their entity is circumscribed by those; and therefore, during that reading or representation, according to their merits or demerits, they must be punished or rewarded. If this is not done, there is no impartial distribution of poetical justice, no instructive lecture of a particular Providence, and no imitation of the Divine Dispensation. And yet the author of this tragedy does not only run counter to this, in the fate of his principal character; but every where, throughout it, makes virtue suffer, and vice triumph: for not only Cato is vanquished by Cæsar, but the treachery and perfidiousness of Syphax prevails over the honest simplicity and the credulity of Juba; and the sly subtlety and dissimulation of Portius over the generous frankness and open-heartedness of Marcus."

Whatever pleasure there may be in seeing crimes punished and virtue rewarded, yet, since wickedness often prospers in real life, the poet is certainly at liberty to give it prosperity on the stage. For if poetry has an imitation of reality, how are its laws broken by exhibiting the world in its true form? The stage may sometimes gratify our wishes; but, if it be truly the *mirror of life,* it ought to shew us sometimes what we are to expect.

Dennis objects to the characters that they are not natural, or reasonable; but as heroes and heroines are not beings that are seen every day, it is hard to find upon what principles their conduct shall be tried. It is, however, not useless to consider what he says of the manner in which Cato receives the account of his son's death.

"Nor is the grief of Cato, in the Fourth Act, one jot more in nature than that of his son and Lucia in the third. Cato receives the news of his son's death not only with dry eyes, but with a sort of satisfaction; and in the same page sheds tears for the calamity of his country, and does the same thing in the next page upon the bare apprehension of the danger of his friends. Now, since the love of one's country is the love of one's countrymen, as I have shewn upon another occasion, I desire to ask these questions: Of all our countrymen, which do we love most, those whom we know, or those whom we know not? And of those whom we know, which do we cherish most, our friends or our enemies? And of our friends, which are the dearest to us? those who are related to us, or those who are not? And of all our relations, for which have we most tenderness, for those who are near to us, or for those who are remote? And of our near relations, which are the nearest, and consequently the dearest to us, our offspring or others? Our offspring, most certainly; as nature, or in other words Providence, has wisely contrived for the preservation of mankind. Now, does it not follow, from what has been said, that for a man to receive the news of his son's death with dry eyes, and to weep at the same time for the calamities of his country, is a wretched affectation, and a miserable inconsistency? Is not that, in plain English, to receive with dry eyes the news of the deaths of those for whose sake our country is a name so dear to us, and at the same time to shed tears for those for whose sakes our country is not a name so dear to us?"

But this formidable assailant is least resistible when he attacks the probability of the action, and the reasonableness of the plan. Every critical reader must remark, that Addison has, with a scrupulosity almost unexampled on the English stage, confined himself in time to a single day, and in place to rigorous unity. The scene never changes and the whole action of the play passes in the great hall of Cato's house at Utica. Much therefore is done in the hall, for which any other place had been more fit; and this impropriety affords Dennis many hints of merriment, and opportunities of triumph. The passage is long; but as such disquisitions are not common, and the objections are skilfully formed and vigorously urged, those who delight in critical controversy will not think it tedious.

"Upon the departure of Portius, Sempronius makes but one soliloquy, and immediately in comes Syphax, and then the two politicians are at it immediately. They lay their heads together, with their snuff-boxes in their hands, as Mr. Bayes has it, and league it away. But, in the midst of that wise scene, Syphax seems to give a seasonable caution to Sempronius:

> "*Syph.* But is it true, Sempronius, that your senate
> Is call'd together? Gods! thou must be cautious,
> Cato has piercing eyes.

"There is a great deal of caution shewn indeed, in meeting in a governor's own hall to carry on their plot against him. Whatever opinion they have of his eyes, I suppose they had none of his ears, or they would never have talked at this foolish rate so near.

"Gods! thou must be cautious.

"Oh! yes, very cautious: for if Cato should overhear you, and turn you off for politicians, Cæsar would never take you; no, Cæsar would never take you.

"When Cato, Act II. turns the senators out of the hall, upon pretence of acquainting Juba with the result of their debates, he appears to me to do a thing which is neither reasonable nor civil. Juba might certainly have better been made acquainted with the result of that debate in some private apartment of the palace. But the poet was driven upon this absurdity to make way for another; and that is, to give Juba an opportunity to demand Marcia of her father. But the quarrel and rage of Juba and Syphax in the same Act, the invectives of Syphax against the Romans and Cato; the advice that he gives Juba, in her father's hall, to bear away Marcia by force; and his brutal and clamorous rage upon his refusal, and at a time when Cato was scarce out of sight, and perhaps not out of hearing; at least, some of his guards or domesticks must necessarily be supposed to be within hearing; is a thing that is so far from being probable, that it is hardly possible.

"But treason is not the only thing that is carried on in this hall: that, and love, and philosophy, take their turns in it, without any manner of necessity or probability occasioned by the action, as duly and as regularly, without interrupting one another, as if there were a triple league between them, and a mutual agreement that each should give place to and make way for the other, in a due and orderly succession.

"We come now to the Third Act. Sempronius, in this Act, comes into the governor's hall, with the leaders of the mutiny: but as soon as Cato is gone, Sempronius, who but just before had acted like an unparalleled knave, discovers himself, like an egregious fool, to be an accomplice in the conspiracy.

"*Semp.* Know, villains, when such paltry slaves presume
To mix in treason, if the plot succeeds,
They're thrown neglected by: but if it fails,
They're sure to die like dogs, as you shall do.
Here, take these factious monsters, drag them forth
To sudden death.—

" 'Tis true, indeed, the second leader says, there are none there but friends; but is that possible at such a juncture? Can a parcel of rogues attempt to assassinate the governor of a town of war, in his own house, in mid-day, and after they are discovered and defeated, can there be none near them but friends? Is it not plain from these words of Sempronius,

> "Here, take these factious monsters, drag them forth
> To sudden death—

"and from the entrance of the guards upon the word of command, that those guards were within ear-shot? Behold Sempronius then palpably discovered. How comes it to pass, then, that, instead of being hanged up with the rest, he remains secure in the governor's hall, and there carries on his conspiracy against the government, the third time in the same day, with his old comrade Syphax? who enters at the same time that the guards are carrying away the leaders, big with the news of the defeat of Sempronius; though where he had his intelligence so soon is difficult to imagine. And now the reader may expect a very extraordinary scene: there is not abundance of spirit indeed, nor a great deal of passion, but there is wisdom more than enough to supply all defects.

> "*Syph*. Our first design, my friend, has prov'd abortive;
> Still there remains an after-game to play:
> My troops are mounted, their Numidian steeds
> Snuff up the winds, and long to scour the desart:
> Let but Sempronius lead us in our flight,
> We'll force the gate, where Marcus keeps his guard,
> And hew down all that would oppose our passage;
> A day will bring us into Cæsar's camp.
> "*Semp*. Confusion! I have fail'd of half my purpose;
> Marcia, the charming Marcia's left behind.

"Well! but though he tells us the half-purpose that he has failed of, he does not tell us the half that he has carried. But what does he mean by

> "Marcia, the charming Marcia's left behind?

"He is now in her own house; and we have neither seen her nor heard of her any where else since the play began. But now let us hear Syphax:

"What hinders then, but that thou find her out,
And hurry her away by manly force?

"But what does old Syphax mean by finding her out? They talk as if she were as hard to be found as a hare in a frosty morning.

"*Semp.* But how to gain admission?

"Oh! she is found out then, it seems.

"But how to gain admission? for access
Is giv'n to none, but Juba and her brothers.

"But, raillery apart, why access to Juba? For he was owned and received as a lover neither by the father nor by the daughter. Well! but let that pass. Syphax puts Sempronius out of pain immediately; and, being a Numidian, abounding in wiles, supplies him with a stratagem for admission, that, I believe, is a non-pareille:

"*Syph.* Thou shalt have Juba's dress, and Juba's guards;
The doors will open, when Numidia's prince
Seems to appear before them.

"Sempronius is, it seems, to pass for Juba in full day at Cato's house, where they were both so very well known, by having Juba's dress and his guards: as if one of the marshals of France could pass for the Duke of Bavaria, at noon-day, at Versailles, by having his dress and liveries. But how does Syphax pretend to help Sempronius to young Juba's dress? Does he serve him in a double capacity, as general and master of his wardrobe? But why Juba's guards? For the devil of any guards has Juba appeared with yet. Well! though this is a mighty politick invention, yet, methinks, they might have done without it: for, since the advice that Syphax gave to Sempronius was,

"To hurry her away by manly force,

"in my opinion, the shortest and likeliest way of coming at the lady was by demolishing, instead of putting on an impertinent disguise to circumvent two or three slaves. But Sempronius, it seems, is of another opinion. He extols to the skies the invention of old Syphax:

"*Sempr.* Heavens! what a thought was there!

"Now I appeal to the reader, if I have not been as good as my word. Did I not tell him, that I would lay before him a very wise scene?

"But now let us lay before the reader that part of the scenery of the Fourth Act, which may shew the absurdities which the author has run into, through the indiscreet observance of the Unity of Place. I do not remember that Aristotle has said any thing expressly concerning the Unity of Place. 'Tis true, implicitly he has said enough in the rules which he has laid down for the Chorus. For, by making the Chorus an essential part of Tragedy, and by bringing it on the stage immediately after the opening of the scene, and retaining it there till the very catastrophe, he has so determined and fixed the place of action, that it was impossible for an author on the Grecian stage to break through that unity. I am of opinion, that if a modern tragic poet can preserve the unity of place, without destroying the probability of the incidents, 'tis always best for him to do it; because, by the preservation of that unity, as we have taken notice above, he adds grace, and cleanness, and comeliness, to the representation. But since there are no express rules about it, and we are under no compulsion to keep it, since we have no Chorus as the Grecian poet had; if it cannot be preserved, without rendering the greater part of the incidents unreasonable and absurd, and perhaps sometimes monstrous, 'tis certainly better to break it.

"Now comes bully Sempronius, comically accoutred and equipped with his Numidian dress and his Numidian guards. Let the reader attend to him with all his ears; for the words of the wise are precious:

"*Sempr.* The deer is lodg'd, I've track'd her to her covert.

"Now I would fain know why this deer is said to be lodged, since we have not heard one word, since the play began, of her being at all out of harbour: and if we consider the discourse with which she and Lucia began the Act, we have reason to believe that they had hardly been talking of such matters in the street. However, to pleasure Sempronius, let us suppose, for once, that the deer is lodged:

"The deer is lodg'd, I've track'd her to her covert.

"If he had seen her in the open field, what occasion had he to track her, when he had so many Numidian dogs at his heels, which, with one halloo, he might have set upon her haunches? If he did not see her in the open field, how could he possibly track her? If he had seen her in the street, why did he not set upon her in the street, since through the street she must be carried at last? Now here, instead of having his thoughts upon his business, and upon the present danger; instead of meditating and contriving how he shall pass with his mistress through the southern gate, where her brother Marcus is upon the guard, and where she would certainly prove an impediment to him, which is the Roman word for the *baggage*, instead of doing this, Sempronius is entertaining himself with whimsies:

> "*Sempr.* How will the young Numidian rave to see
> His mistress lost! If aught could glad my soul,
> Beyond th' enjoyment of so bright a prize,
> 'Twould be to torture that young gay Barbarian.
> But hark! what noise? Death to my hopes, 'tis he,
> 'Tis Juba's self! There is but one way left!
> He must be murder'd, and a passage cut
> Through those his guards.

"Pray, what are *those his guards?* I thought at present, that Juba's guards had been Sempronius's tools, and had been dangling after his heels.

"But now let us sum up all these absurdities together. Sempronius goes at noonday, in Juba's clothes, and with Juba's guards, to Cato's palace, in order to pass for Juba, in a place where they were both so very well known: he meets Juba there, and resolves to murder him with his own guards. Upon the guards appearing a little bashful, he threatens them:

> "Hah! Dastards, do you tremble!
> Or act like men, or by yon azure heav'n!

"But the guards still remaining restive, Sempronius himself attacks Juba, while each of the guards is representing Mr. Spectator's sign of the Gaper, awed, it seems, and terrified by Sempronius's threats. Juba kills Sempronius, and takes his own army prisoners, and carries them in triumph away to Cato. Now I would fain know, if any part of Mr. Bayes's tragedy is so full of absurdity as this?

"Upon hearing the clash of swords, Lucia and Marcia come in. The question is, why no men come in upon hearing the noise of swords in the governor's hall? Where was the governor himself? Where were his guards? Where were his servants? Such an attempt as this, so near the person of a governor of a place of war, was enough to alarm the whole garrison: and yet, for almost half an hour after Sempronius was killed, we find none of those appear who were the likeliest in the world to be alarmed; and the noise of swords is made to draw only two poor women thither, who were most certain to run away from it. Upon Lucia and Marcia's coming in, Lucia appears in all the symptoms of an hysterical gentlewoman:

> *"Luc.* Sure 'twas the clash of swords! my troubled heart
> Is so cast down, and sunk amidst its sorrows,
> It throbs with fear, and akes at every sound!

"And immediately her old whimsy returns upon her:

> "O Marcia, should thy brothers, for my sake—
> I die away with horror at the thought.

"She fancies that there can be no cutting of throats but it must be for her. If this is tragical, I would fain know what is comical. Well! upon this they spy the body of Sempronius; and Marcia, deluded by the habit, it seems, takes him for Juba; for, says she,

> "The face is muffled up within the garment.

"Now how a man could fight, and fall with his face muffled up in his garment, is, I think, a little hard to conceive! Besides, Juba, before he killed him, knew him to be Sempronius. It was not by his garment that he knew this; it was by his face then: his face therefore was not muffled. Upon seeing this man with the muffled face, Marcia falls a-raving; and, owning her passion for the supposed defunct, begins to make his funeral oration. Upon which Juba enters listening, I suppose on tip-toe: for I cannot imagine how any one can enter listening, in any other posture. I would fain know how it came to pass, that during all this time he had sent no-body, no not so much as a candle-snuffer, to take away the dead body of Sempronius. Well! but let us regard him listening. Having left his apprehension behind him, he, at first, applies what Marcia says to Sempronius. But finding at last, with much ado, that he himself is the happy man, he quits his eves-dropping, and greedily intercepts the bliss, which was fondly designed for one who could not be the better for it. But here I must ask a question: how comes Juba to listen here, who had not listened before throughout the play? Or, how comes he to be the only person of this tragedy who listens, when love and treason were so often talked in so publick a place as a hall? I am afraid the author was driven upon all these absurdities only to introduce this miserable mistake of Marcia; which, after all, is much below the dignity of tragedy, as any thing is which is the effect or result of trick.

"But let us come to the scenery of the Fifth Act. Cato appears first upon the scene, sitting in a thoughtful posture; in his hand Plato's treatise on the Immortality of the Soul, a drawn sword on the table by him. Now let us consider the place in which this sight is presented to us. The place, forsooth, is a long hall. Let us suppose, that any one should place himself in this posture, in the midst of one of our halls in London; that he should appear *solus,* in a sullen posture, a drawn sword on the table by him; in his hand Plato's treatise on the Immortality of the Soul, translated lately by Bernard Lintot: I desire the reader to consider, whether such a person as this would pass with them who beheld him for a great patriot, a great philosopher, or a general, or for some whimsical person who fancied himself all these; and whether the people, who belonged to the family, would think that such a person had a design upon their midrifs or his own?

"In short, that Cato should sit long enough, in the aforesaid posture, in the midst of this large hall, to read over Plato's treatise on the Immortality of the Soul, which is a lecture of two long hours; that he should propose to himself to be private there upon that occasion; that he should be angry with his son for intruding there; then, that he should leave this hall upon the pretence of sleep, give himself the mortal wound in his bedchamber, and then be brought back into that hall to expire, purely to shew his good-breeding, and save his friends the trouble of coming up to his bedchamber; all this appears to me to be improbable, incredible, impossible."

Such is the censure of Dennis. There is, as Dryden expresses it, perhaps *too much horse play in his raillery;* but if his jests are coarse, his arguments are strong. Yet as we love better to be pleased than to be taught, Cato is read, and the critick is neglected.

Flushed with consciousness of these detections of absurdity in the conduct, he afterwards attacked the sentiments of Cato; but he then amused himself with petty cavils, and minute objections.

Of Addison's smaller poems, no particular mention is necessary; they have little that can employ or require a critick. The parallel of the Princes and Gods, in his verses to Kneller, is often happy, but is too well known to be quoted.

His translations, so far as I have compared them, want the exactness of a scholar. That he understood his authors cannot be doubted; but his versions will not teach others to understand them, being too licentiously paraphrastical. They are, however, for the most part, smooth and easy; and, what is the first excellence of a translator, such as may be read with pleasure by those who do not know the originals.

His poetry is polished and pure; the product of a mind too judicious to commit faults, but not sufficiently vigorous to attain excellence. He has sometimes a striking line, or a shining paragraph; but in the whole he is warm rather than fervid, and shews more dexterity than strength. He was, however, one of our earliest examples of correctness.

The versification which he had learned from Dryden, he debased rather than refined. His rhymes are often dissonant; in his Georgick he admits broken lines. He uses both triplets and alexandrines, but triplets more frequently in his translations than his other works. The mere structure of verses seems never to have engaged much of his care. But his lines are very smooth in Rosamond, and too smooth in Cato.

Addison is now to be considered as a critick; a name which the present generation is scarcely willing to allow him. His criticism is condemned as tentative or experimental, rather than scientifick, and he is considered as deciding by taste rather than by principles.

It is not uncommon for those who have grown wise by the labour of others, to add a little of their own, and overlook their masters. Addison is now despised by some who perhaps would never have seen his defects, but by the lights which he afforded them. That he always wrote as he would think it necessary to write now, cannot be affirmed; his instructions were such as the character of his readers made proper. That general knowledge which now circulates in common talk, was in his time rarely to be found. Men not professing learning were not ashamed of ignorance; and in the female world, any acquaintance with books was distinguished only to be censured. His purpose was to infuse literary curiosity, by gentle and unsuspected conveyance, into the gay, the idle, and the wealthy; he therefore presented knowledge in the most alluring form, not lofty and austere, but accessible and familiar. When he shewed them their defects, he shewed them likewise that they might be easily supplied. His attempt succeeded; enquiry was awakened, and comprehension expanded. An emulation of intellectual elegance was excited, and from his time to our own, life has been gradually exalted, and conversation purified and enlarged.

Dryden had, not many years before, scattered criticism over his Prefaces with very little parsimony; but though he sometimes condescended to be somewhat familiar, his manner was in general too scholastick for those who had yet their rudiments to learn, and found it not easy to understand their master. His observations were framed rather for those that were learning to write, than for those that read only to talk.

An instructor like Addison was now wanting, whose remarks being superficial, might be easily understood, and being just, might prepare the mind for more attainments. Had he presented Paradise Lost to the publick with all the pomp of system and severity of science, the criticism would perhaps have been admired, and the poem still have been neglected; but by the blandishments of gentleness and facility, he has made Milton an universal favourite, with whom readers of every class think it necessary to be pleased.

He descended now and then to lower disquisitions; and by a serious display of the beauties of Chevy Chase, exposed himself to the ridicule of Wagstaff, who bestowed a like pompous character on Tom Thumb, and to the contempt of Dennis, who, considering the fundamental position of his criticism, that Chevy Chase pleases, and ought to please, because it is natural, observes, "that there is a way of deviating from nature, by bombast or tumour, which soars above nature, and enlarges images beyond their real bulk; by affectation, which forsakes nature in quest of something unsuitable; and by imbecility, which degrades nature by faintness and diminution, by obscuring its appearances, and weakening its effects." In Chevy Chase there is not much of either bombast or affectation; but there is chill and lifeless imbecility. The story cannot possibly be told in a manner that shall make less impression on the mind.

Before the profound observers of the present race repose too securely on the consciousness of their superiority to Addison, let them consider his Remarks on Ovid, in which may be found specimens of criticism sufficiently subtle and refined; let them peruse likewise his Essays on Wit, and on the Pleasures of Imagination, in which he founds art on the base of nature, and draws the principles of invention from dispositions inherent in the mind of man, with skill and elegance, such as his contemners will not easily attain.

As a describer of life and manners, he must be allowed to stand perhaps the first of the first rank. His humour, which, as Steele observes, is peculiar to himself, is so happily diffused as to give the grace of novelty to domestick scenes and daily occurrences. He never *outsteps the modesty of nature,* nor raises merriment or wonder by the violation of truth. His figures neither divert by distortion, nor amaze by aggravation. He copies life with so much fidelity, that he can be hardly said to invent; yet his exhibitions have an air so much original, that it is difficult to suppose them not merely the product of imagination.

As a teacher of wisdom, he may be confidently followed. His religion has nothing in it enthusiastick or superstitious: he appears neither weakly credulous nor wantonly sceptical; his morality is neither dangerously lax, nor impracticably rigid. All the enchantment of fancy, and all the cogency of argument, are employed to recommend to the reader his real interest, the care of pleasing the Author of his being. Truth is shewn sometimes as the phantom of a vision, sometimes appears half-veiled in an allegory; sometimes attracts regard in the robes of fancy, and sometimes steps forth in the confidence of reason. She wears a thousand dresses, and in all is pleasing.

Mille habet ornatus, mille decenter habet.

His prose is the model of the middle style; on grave subjects not formal, on light occasions not groveling; pure without scrupulosity, and exact without apparent elaboration; always equable, and always easy, without glowing words or pointed sentences. Addison never deviates from his track to snatch a grace; he seeks no ambitious ornaments, and tries no hazardous innovations. His page is always luminous, but never blazes in unexpected splendour.

It was apparently his principal endeavour to avoid all harshness and severity of diction; he is therefore sometimes verbose in his transitions and connections, and sometimes descends too much to the language of conversation; yet if his language had been less idiomatical, it might have lost somewhat of its genuine Anglicism. What he attempted, he performed; he is never feeble, and he did not wish to be energetick; he is never rapid, and he never stagnates. His sentences have neither studied amplitude, nor affected brevity: his periods, though not diligently rounded, are voluble and easy. Whoever wishes to attain an English style, familiar but not coarse, and elegant but not ostentatious, must give his days and nights to the volumes of Addison.

OF THE STANDARD OF TASTE

BY

DAVID HUME

INTRODUCTORY NOTE

DAVID HUME (1711–1776) was born in Edinburgh, and was trained for the law. He early showed an eager interest in philosophy, and devoted himself to study with such intensity as to injure his health. He traveled in France more than once, and was on intimate terms with such men as d'Alembert, Turgot, and Rousseau, for the last of whom he found a pension and a temporary refuge in England.

Hume is most celebrated for his philosophical writings, in which he carried the empirical philosophy of Locke to the point of complete skepticism. He wrote also a "History of England" in eight volumes, and a large number of treatises and essays on politics, economics, ethics, and esthetics. The following essay, "Of the Standard of Taste," is a typical example of his clear thinking and admirable style. "He may be regarded," says Leslie Stephen, "as the acutest thinker in Great Britain of the eighteenth century, and the most qualified interpreter of its intellectual tendencies."

OF THE STANDARD OF TASTE

THE great variety of Taste, as well as of opinion, which prevails in the world, is too obvious not to have fallen under every one's observation. Men of the most confined knowledge are able to remark a difference of taste in the narrow circle of their acquaintance, even where the persons have been educated under the same government, and have early imbibed the same prejudices. But those, who can enlarge their view to contemplate distant nations and remote ages, are still more surprised at the great inconsistence and contrariety. We are apt to call *barbarous* whatever departs widely from our own taste and apprehension; but soon find the epithet of reproach retorted on us. And the highest arrogance and self-conceit is at last startled, on observing an equal assurance on all sides, and scruples, amidst such a contest of sentiment, to pronounce positively in its own favour.

As this variety of taste is obvious to the most careless inquirer; so will it be found, on examination, to be still greater in reality than in appearance. The sentiments of men often differ with regard to beauty and deformity of all kinds, even while their general discourse is the same. There are certain terms in every language, which import blame, and others praise; and all men, who use the same tongue, must agree in their application of them. Every voice is united in applauding elegance, propriety, simplicity, spirit in writing; and in blaming fustian, affectation, coldness, and a false brilliancy: But when critics come to particulars, this seeming unanimity vanishes; and it is found, that they had affixed a very different meaning to their expressions. In all matters of opinion and science, the case is opposite: The difference among men is there oftener found to lie in generals than in particulars; and to be less in reality than in appearance. An explanation of the terms commonly ends the controversy; and the disputants are surprised to find, that they had been quarrelling, while at bottom they agreed in their judgment.

Those who found morality on sentiment, more than on reason, are inclined to comprehend ethics under the former observation, and to maintain, that, in all questions, which regard conduct and manners, the difference among men is really greater than at first sight it appears. It is indeed obvious, that writers of all nations and all ages concur in applauding justice, humanity, magnanimity, prudence, veracity; and in blaming the opposite qualities. Even poets and other authors, whose compositions are chiefly calculated to please the imagination, are yet found, from Homer down to Fenelon, to inculcate the same moral precepts, and to bestow their applause and blame on the same virtues and vices. This great unanimity is usually ascribed to the influence of plain reason; which, in all these cases, maintains similar sentiments in all men, and prevents those controversies, to which the abstract sciences are so much exposed. So far as the unanimity is real, this account may be admitted as satisfactory: But we must also allow, that some part of the seeming harmony in morals may be accounted for from the very nature of language. The word *virtue,* with its equivalent in every tongue, implies praise; as that of *vice* does blame: And no man, without the most obvious and grossest impropriety, could affix reproach to a term, which in general acceptation is understood in a good sense; or bestow applause, where the idiom requires disapprobation. Homer's general precepts, where he delivers any such, will never be controverted; but it is obvious, that, when he draws particular pictures of manners, and represents heroism in Achilles and prudence in Ulysses, he intermixes a much greater degree of ferocity in the former, and of cunning and fraud in the latter, than Fenelon would admit of. The sage Ulysses in the Greek poet seems to delight in lies and fictions, and often employs them without any necessity or even advantage: But his more scrupulous son, in the French epic writer, exposes himself to the most imminent perils, rather than depart from the most exact line of truth and veracity.

The admirers and followers of the Alcoran insist on the excellent moral precepts interspersed through that wild and absurd performance. But it is to be supposed, that the Arabic words, which correspond to the English, equity, justice, temperance, meekness, charity, were such as, from the constant use of that tongue, must always be taken in a good sense; and it would have argued the greatest ignorance, not of morals, but of language, to have mentioned them with any epithets, besides those of applause and approbation. But would we know, whether the pretended prophet had really attained a just sentiment of morals? Let us attend to his narration; and we shall soon find, that he bestows praise on such instances of treachery, inhumanity, cruelty, revenge, bigotry, as are utterly incompatible with civilized society. No steady rule of right seems there to be attended to; and every action is blamed or praised, so far only as it is beneficial or hurtful to the true believers.

The merit of delivering true general precepts in ethics is indeed very small. Whoever recommends any moral virtues, really does no more than is implied in the terms themselves. That people, who invented the word *charity,* and used it in a good sense, inculcated more clearly and much more efficaciously, the precept, *be charitable,* than any pretended legislator or prophet, who should insert such a *maxim* in his writings. Of all expressions, those, which, together with their other meaning, imply a degree either of blame or approbation, are the least liable to be perverted or mistaken.

It is natural for us to seek a *Standard of Taste;* a rule, by which the various sentiments of men may be reconciled; at least, a decision afforded, confirming one sentiment, and condemning another.

There is a species of philosophy, which cuts off all hopes of success in such an attempt, and represents the impossibility of ever attaining any standard of taste. The difference, it is said, is very wide between judgment and sentiment. All sentiment is right; because sentiment has a reference to nothing beyond itself, and is always real, wherever a man is conscious of it. But all determinations of the understanding are not right; because they have a reference to something beyond themselves, to wit, real matter of fact; and are not always conformable to that standard. Among a thousand different opinions which different men may entertain of the same subject, there is one, and but one, that is just and true; and the only difficulty is to fix and ascertain it. On the contrary, a thousand different sentiments, excited by the same object, are all right: Because no sentiment represents what is really in the object. It only marks a certain conformity or relation between the object and the organs or faculties of the mind; and if that conformity did not really exist, the sentiment could never possibly have being. Beauty is no quality in things themselves: It exists merely in the mind which contemplates them; and each mind perceives a different beauty. One person may even perceive deformity, where another is sensible of beauty; and every individual ought to acquiesce in his own sentiment, without pretending to regulate those of others. To seek the real beauty, or real deformity is as fruitless an inquiry, as to pretend to ascertain the real sweet or real bitter. According to the disposition of the organs, the same object may be both sweet and bitter; and the proverb has justly determined it to be fruitless to dispute concerning tastes. It is very natural, and even quite necessary, to extend this axiom to mental, as well as bodily taste; and thus common sense, which is so often at variance with philosophy, especially with the sceptical kind, is found, in one instance at least, to agree in pronouncing the same decision.

But though this axiom, by passing into a proverb, seems to have attained the sanction of common sense; there is certainly a species of common sense, which opposes it, at least serves to modify and restrain it. Whoever would assert an equality of genius and elegance between Ogilby and Milton, or Bunyan and Addison, would be thought to defend no less an extravagance, than if he had maintained a mole-hill to be as high as Teneriffe, or a pond as extensive as the ocean. Though there may be found persons, who give the preference to the former authors; no one pays attention to such a taste; and we pronounce, without scruple, the sentiment of these pretended critics to be absurd and ridiculous. The principle of the natural equality of tastes is then totally forgot, and while we admit it on some occasions, where the objects seem near an equality, it appears an extravagant paradox, or rather a palpable absurdity, where objects so disproportioned are compared together.

It is evident that none of the rules of composition are fixed by reasonings *a priori,* or can be esteemed abstract conclusions of the understanding, from comparing those habitudes and relations of ideas, which are eternal and immutable. Their foundation is the same with that of all the practical sciences, experience; nor are there any thing but general observations, concerning what has been universally found to please in all countries and in all ages. Many of the beauties of poetry, and even of eloquence, are founded on falsehood and fiction, on hyperboles, metaphors, and an abuse or perversion of terms from their natural meaning. To check the sallies of the imagination, and to reduce every expression to geometrical truth and exactness, would be the most contrary to the laws of criticism; because it would produce a work, which, by universal experience, has been found the most insipid and disagreeable. But though poetry can never submit to exact truth, it must be confined by rules of art, discovered to the author either by genius or observation. If some negligent or irregular writers have pleased, they have not pleased by their transgressions of rule or order, but in spite of these transgressions: They have possessed other beauties, which were conformable to just criticism; and the force of these beauties has been able to overpower censure, and give the mind a satisfaction superior to the disgust arising from the blemishes. Ariosto pleases; but not by his monstrous and improbable fictions, by his bizarre mixture of the serious and comic styles, by the want of coherence in his stories, or by the continual interruptions of his narration. He charms by the force and clearness of his expression, by the readiness and variety of his inventions, and by his natural pictures of the passions, especially those of the gay and amorous kind: And however his faults may diminish our satisfaction, they are not able entirely to destroy it. Did our pleasure really arise from those parts of his poem, which we denominate faults, this would be no objection to criticism in general: It would only be an objection to those particular rules of criticism, which would establish such circumstances to be faults, and would represent them as universally blameable. If they are found to please, they cannot be faults; let the pleasure, which they produce, be ever so unexpected and unaccountable.

But though all the general rules of art are founded only on experience, and on the observation of the common sentiments of human nature, we must not imagine, that, on every occasion, the feelings of men will be conformable to these rules. Those finer emotions of the mind are of a very tender and delicate nature, and require the concurrence of many favourable circumstances to make them play with facility and exactness, according to their general and established principles. The least exterior hindrance to such small springs, or the least internal disorder, disturbs their motion, and confounds the operation of the whole machine. When we would make an experiment of this nature, and would try the force of any beauty or deformity, we must choose with care a proper time and place, and bring the fancy to a suitable situation and disposition. A perfect serenity of mind, a recollection of thought, a due attention to the object; if any of these circumstances be wanting, our experiment will be fallacious, and we shall be unable to judge of the catholic and universal beauty. The relation, which nature has placed between the form and the sentiment, will at least be more obscure; and it will require greater accuracy to trace and discern it. We shall be able to ascertain its influence, not so much from the operation of each particular beauty, as from the durable admiration, which attends those works, that have survived all the caprices of mode and fashion, all the mistakes of ignorance and envy.

The same Homer, who pleased at Athens and Rome two thousand years ago, is still admired at Paris and at London. All the changes of climate, government, religion, and language, have not been able to obscure his glory. Authority or prejudice may give a temporary vogue to a bad poet or orator; but his reputation will never be durable or general. When his compositions are examined by posterity or by foreigners, the enchantment is dissipated, and his faults appear in their true colours. On the contrary, a real genius, the longer his works endure, and the more wide they are spread, the more sincere is the admiration which he meets with. Envy and jealousy have too much place in a narrow circle; and even familiar acquaintance with his person may diminish the applause due to his performances: But when these obstructions are removed, the beauties, which are naturally fitted to excite agreeable sentiments, immediately display their energy; while the world endures, they maintain their authority over the minds of men.

It appears then, that, amidst all the variety and caprice of taste, there are certain general principles of approbation or blame, whose influence a careful eye may trace in all operations of the mind. Some particular forms or qualities, from the original structure of the internal fabric, are calculated to please, and others to displease; and if they fail of their effect in any particular instance, it is from some apparent defect or imperfection in the organ. A man in a fever would not insist on his palate as able to decide concerning flavours; nor would one, affected with the jaundice, pretend to give a verdict with regard to colours. In each creature, there is a sound and a defective state; and the former alone can be supposed to afford us a true standard of taste and sentiment. If, in the sound state of the organ, there be an entire or a considerable uniformity of sentiment among men, we may thence derive an idea of the perfect beauty; in like manner as the appearance of objects in day-light, to the eye of a man in health, is denominated their true and real colour, even while colour is allowed to be merely a phantasm of the senses.

Many and frequent are the defects in the internal organs, which prevent or weaken the influence of those general principles, on which depends our sentiment of beauty or deformity. Though some objects, by the structure of the mind, be naturally calculated to give pleasure, it is not to be expected, that in every individual the pleasure will be equally felt. Particular incidents and situations occur, which either throw a false light on the objects, or hinder the true from conveying to the imagination the proper sentiment and perception.

One obvious cause, why many feel not the proper sentiment of beauty, is the want of that *delicacy* of imagination, which is requisite to convey a sensibility of those finer emotions. This delicacy every one pretends to: Every one talks of it; and would reduce every kind of taste or sentiment to its standard. But as our intention in this essay is to mingle some light of the understanding with the feelings of sentiment, it will be proper to give a more accurate definition of delicacy than has hitherto been attempted. And not to draw our philosophy from too profound a source, we shall have recourse to a noted story in Don Quixote.

It is with good reason, says Sancho to the squire with the great nose, that I pretend to have a judgment in wine: This is a quality hereditary in our family. Two of my kinsmen were once called to give their opinion of a hogshead, which was supposed to be excellent, being old and of a good vintage. One of them tastes it; considers it; and, after mature reflection, pronounces the wine to be good, were it not for a small taste of leather, which he perceived in it. The other, after using the same precautions, gives also his verdict in favour of the wine; but with the reserve of a taste of iron, which he could easily distinguish. You cannot imagine how much they were both ridiculed for their judgment. But who laughed in the end? On emptying the hogshead, there was found at the bottom an old key with a leathern thong tied to it.

The great resemblance between mental and bodily taste will easily teach us to apply this story. Though it be certain, that beauty and deformity, more than sweet and bitter, are not qualities in objects, but belong entirely to the sentiment, internal or external; it must be allowed, that there are certain qualities in objects, which are fitted by nature to produce those particular feelings. Now as these qualities may be found in a small degree, or may be mixed and confounded with each other, it often happens that the taste is not affected with such minute qualities, or is not able to distinguish all the particular flavours, amidst the disorder in which they are presented. Where the organs are so fine, as to allow nothing to escape them; and at the same time so exact, as to perceive every ingredient in the composition: This we call delicacy of taste, whether we employ these terms in the literal or metaphorical sense. Here then the general rules of beauty are of use, being drawn from established models, and from the observation of what pleases or displeases, when presented singly and in a high degree: And if the same qualities, in a continued composition, and in a smaller degree, affect not the organs with a sensible delight or uneasiness, we exclude the person from all pretensions to this delicacy. To produce these general rules or avowed patterns of composition, is like finding the key with the leathern thong; which justified the verdict of Sancho's kinsmen, and confounded those pretended judges who had condemned them. Though the hogshead had never been emptied, the taste of the one was still equally delicate, and that of the other equally dull and languid: But it would have been more difficult to have proved the superiority of the former, to the conviction of every bye-stander. In like manner, though the beauties of writing had never been methodized, or reduced to general principles; though no excellent models had ever been acknowledged; the different degrees of taste would still have subsisted, and the judgment of one man been preferable to that of another; but it would not have been so easy to silence the bad critic, who might always insist upon his particular sentiment, and refuse to submit to his antagonist. But when we show him an avowed principle of art; when we illustrate this principle by examples, whose operation, from his own particular taste, he acknowledges to be conformable to the principle; when we prove that the same principle may be applied to the present case, where he did not perceive or feel its influence: He must conclude, upon the whole, that the fault lies in himself, and that he wants the delicacy, which is requisite to make him sensible of every beauty and every blemish, in any composition or discourse.

It is acknowledged to be the perfection of every sense or faculty, to perceive with exactness its most minute objects, and allow nothing to escape its notice and observation. The smaller the objects are, which become sensible to the eye, the finer is that organ, and the more elaborate its make and composition. A good palate is not tried by strong flavours, but by a mixture of small ingredients, where we are still sensible of each part, notwithstanding its minuteness and its confusion with the rest. In like manner, a quick and acute perception of beauty and deformity must be the perfection of our mental taste; nor can a man be satisfied with himself while he suspects that any excellence or blemish in a discourse has passed him unobserved. In this case, the perfection of the man, and the perfection of the sense or feeling, are found to be united. A very delicate palate, on many occasions, may be a great inconvenience both to a man himself and to his friends: But a delicate taste of wit or beauty must always be a desirable quality, because it is the source of all the finest and most innocent enjoyments of which human nature is susceptible. In this decision the sentiments of all mankind are agreed. Wherever you can ascertain a delicacy of taste, it is sure to meet with approbation; and the best way of ascertaining it is to appeal to those models and principles which have been established by the uniform consent and experience of nations and ages.

But though there be naturally a wide difference in point of delicacy between one person and another, nothing tends further to increase and improve this talent, than *practice* in a particular art, and the frequent survey or contemplation of a particular species of beauty.

When objects of any kind are first presented to the eye or imagination, the sentiment which attends them is obscure and confused; and the mind is, in a great measure, incapable of pronouncing concerning their merits or defects. The taste cannot perceive the several excellencies of the performance, much less distinguish the particular character of each excellency, and ascertain its quality and degree. If it pronounce the whole in general to be beautiful or deformed, it is the utmost that can be expected; and even this judgment, a person so unpractised will be apt to deliver with great hesitation and reserve. But allow him to acquire experience in those objects, his feeling becomes more exact and nice: He not only perceives the beauties and defects of each part, but marks the distinguishing species of each quality, and assigns it suitable praise or blame. A clear and distinct sentiment attends him through the whole survey of the objects; and he discerns that very degree and kind of approbation or displeasure which each part is naturally fitted to produce. The mist dissipates which seemed formerly to hang over the object: The organ acquires greater perfection in its operations; and can pronounce, without danger or mistake, concerning the merits of every performance. In a word, the same address and dexterity, which practice gives to the execution of any work, is also acquired by the same means, in the judging of it.

So advantageous is practice to the discernment of beauty, that, before we can give judgment on any work of importance, it will even be requisite that that very individual performance be more than once perused by us, and be surveyed in different lights with attention and deliberation. There is a flutter or hurry of thought which attends the first perusal of any piece, and which confounds the genuine sentiment of beauty. The relation of the parts is not discerned: The true characters of style are little distinguished. The several perfections and defects seem wrapped up in a species of confusion, and present themselves indistinctly to the imagination. Not to mention, that there is a species of beauty, which, as it is florid and superficial, pleases at first; but being found incompatible with a just expression either of reason or passion, soon palls upon the taste, and is then rejected with disdain, at least rated at a much lower value.

It is impossible to continue in the practice of contemplating any order of beauty, without being frequently obliged to form *comparisons* between the several species and degrees of excellence, and estimating their proportion to each other. A man, who had had no opportunity of comparing the different kinds of beauty, is indeed totally unqualified to pronounce an opinion with regard to any object presented to him. By comparison alone we fix the epithets of praise or blame, and learn how to assign the due degree of each. The coarsest daubing contains a certain lustre of colours and exactness of imitation, which are so far beauties, and would affect the mind of a peasant or Indian with the highest admiration. The most vulgar ballads are not entirely destitute of harmony or nature; and none but a person familiarised to superior beauties would pronounce their numbers harsh, or narration uninteresting. A great inferiority of beauty gives pain to a person conversant in the highest excellence of the kind, and is for that reason pronounced a deformity: As the most finished object with which we are acquainted is naturally supposed to have reached the pinnacle of perfection, and to be entitled to the highest applause. One accustomed to see, and examine, and weigh the several performances, admired in different ages and nations, can alone rate the merits of a work exhibited to his view, and assign its proper rank among the productions of genius.

But to enable a critic the more fully to execute this undertaking, he must preserve his mind free from all *prejudice,* and allow nothing to enter into his consideration but the very object which is submitted to his examination. We may observe, that every work of art, in order to produce its due effect on the mind, must be surveyed in a certain point of view, and cannot be fully relished by persons, whose situation, real or imaginary, is not conformable to that which is required by the performance. An orator addresses himself to a particular audience, and must have a regard to their particular genius, interests, opinions, passions, and prejudices; otherwise he hopes in vain to govern their resolutions, and inflame their affections. Should they even have entertained some prepossessions against him, however unreasonable, he must not overlook this disadvantage; but, before he enters upon the subject, must endeavour to conciliate their affection, and acquire their good graces. A critic of a different age or nation, who should peruse this discourse, must have all these circumstances in his eye, and must place himself in the same situation as the audience, in order to form a true judgment of the oration. In like manner, when any work is addressed to the public, though I should have a friendship or enmity with the author, I must depart from this situation; and considering myself as a man in general, forget, if possible, my individual being, and my peculiar circumstances. A person influenced by prejudice, complies not with this condition, but obstinately maintains his natural position, without placing himself in that point of view which the performance supposes. If the work be addressed to persons of a different age or nation, he makes no allowance for their peculiar views and prejudices; but, full of the manners of his own age and country, rashly condemns what seemed admirable in the eyes of those for whom alone the discourse was calculated. If the work be executed for the public, he never sufficiently enlarges his comprehension, or forgets his interest as a friend or enemy, as a rival or commentator. By this means, his sentiments are perverted; nor have the same beauties and blemishes the same influence upon him, as if he had imposed a proper violence on his imagination, and had forgotten himself for a moment. So far his taste evidently departs from the true standard, and of consequence loses all credit and authority.

It is well known, that in all questions submitted to the understanding, prejudice is destructive of sound judgment, and perverts all operations of the intellectual faculties: It is no less contrary to good taste; nor has it less influence to corrupt our sentiment of beauty. It belongs to *good sense* to check its influence in both cases; and in this respect, as well as in many others, reason, if not an essential part of taste, is at least requisite to the operations of this latter faculty. In all the nobler productions of genius, there is a mutual relation and correspondence of parts; nor can either the beauties or blemishes be perceived by him, whose thought is not capacious enough to comprehend all those parts, and compare them with each other, in order to perceive the consistence and uniformity of the whole. Every work of art has also a certain end or purpose for which it is calculated; and is to be deemed more or less perfect, as it is more or less fitted to attain this end. The object of eloquence is to persuade, of history to instruct, of poetry to please, by means of the passions and the imagination. These ends we must carry constantly in our view when we peruse any performance; and we must be able to judge how far the means employed are adapted to their respective purposes. Besides, every kind of composition, even the most poetical, is nothing but a chain of propositions and reasonings; not always indeed, the justest and most exact, but still plausible and specious, however disguised by the colouring of the imagination. The persons introduced in tragedy and epic poetry, must be represented as reasoning, and thinking, and concluding, and acting, suitably to their character and circumstances; and without judgment, as well as taste and invention, a poet can never hope to succeed in so delicate an undertaking. Not to mention, that the same excellence of faculties which contributes to the improvement of reason, the same clearness of conception, the same exactness of distinction, the same vivacity of apprehension, are essential to the operations of true taste, and are its infallible concomitants. It seldom or never happens, that a man of sense, who has experience in any art, cannot judge of its beauty; and it is no less rare to meet with a man who has a just taste without a sound understanding.

Thus, though the principles of taste be universal, and nearly, if not entirely, the same in all men; yet few are qualified to give judgment on any work of art, or establish their own sentiment as the standard of beauty. The organs of internal sensation are seldom so perfect as to allow the general principles their full play, and produce a feeling correspondent to those principles. They either labour under some defect, or are vitiated by some disorder; and by that means, excite a sentiment, which may be pronounced erroneous. When the critic has no delicacy, he judges without any distinction, and is only affected by the grosser and more palpable qualities of the object: The finer touches pass unnoticed and disregarded. Where he is not aided by practice, his verdict is attended with confusion and hesitation. Where no comparison has been employed, the most frivolous beauties, such as rather merit the name of defects, are the object of his admiration. Where he lies under the influence of prejudice, all his natural sentiments are perverted. Where good sense is wanting, he is not qualified to discern the beauties of design and reasoning,

which are the highest and most excellent. Under some or other
of these imperfections, the generality of men labour; and hence a
true judge in the finer arts is observed, even during the most polished
ages, to be so rare a character: Strong sense, united to delicate sentiment, improved by practice, perfected by comparison, and cleared of
all prejudice, can alone entitle critics to this valuable character; and
the joint verdict of such, wherever they are to be found, is the true
standard of taste and beauty.

But where are such critics to be found? By what marks are they
to be known? How distinguish them from pretenders? These questions are embarrassing; and seem to throw us back into the same
uncertainty, from which, during the course of this essay, we have
endeavoured to extricate ourselves.

But if we consider the matter aright, these are questions of fact,
not of sentiment. Whether any particular person be endowed with
good sense and a delicate imagination, free from prejudice, may
often be the subject of dispute, and be liable to great discussion and
inquiry: But that such a character is valuable and estimable, will be
agreed in by all mankind. Where these doubts occur, men can do
no more than in other disputable questions which are submitted to
the understanding: They must produce the best arguments, that their
invention suggests to them; they must acknowledge a true and
decisive standard to exist somewhere, to wit, real existence and matter
of fact; and they must have indulgence to such as differ from them
in their appeals to this standard. It is sufficient for our present
purpose, if we have proved, that the taste of all individuals is not
upon an equal footing, and that some men in general, however
difficult to be particularly pitched upon, will be acknowledged by
universal sentiment to have a preference above others.

But in reality, the difficulty of finding, even in particulars, the
standard of taste, is not so great as it is represented. Though in
speculation, we may readily avow a certain criterion in science, and
deny it in sentiment, the matter is found in practice to be much more
hard to ascertain in the former case than in the latter. Theories of
abstract philosophy, systems of profound theology, have prevailed
during one age: In a successive period, these have been universally
exploded: Their absurdity has been detected: Other theories and

systems have supplied their place, which again gave place to their successors: And nothing has been experienced more liable to the revolutions of chance and fashion than these pretended decisions of science. The case is not the same with the beauties of eloquence and poetry. Just expressions of passion and nature are sure, after a little time, to gain public applause, which they maintain for ever. Aristotle, and Plato, and Epicurus, and Descartes, may successively yield to each other: But Terence and Virgil maintain an universal, undisputed empire over the minds of men. The abstract philosophy of Cicero has lost its credit: The vehemence of his oratory is still the object of our admiration.

Though men of delicate taste be rare, they are easily to be distinguished in society by the soundness of their understanding, and the superiority of their faculties above the rest of mankind. The ascendant, which they acquire, gives a prevalence to that lively approbation, with which they receive any productions of genius, and renders it generally predominant. Many men, when left to themselves, have but a faint and dubious perception of beauty, who yet are capable of relishing any fine stroke which is pointed out to them. Every convert to the admiration of the real poet or orator is the cause of some new conversion. And though prejudices may prevail for a time, they never unite in celebrating any rival to the true genius, but yield at last to the force of nature and just sentiment. Thus, though a civilized nation may easily be mistaken in the choice of their admired philosopher, they never have been found long to err, in their affection for a favourite epic or tragic author.

But notwithstanding all our endeavours to fix a standard of taste, and reconcile the discordant apprehensions of men, there still remain two sources of variation, which are not sufficient indeed to confound all the boundaries of beauty and deformity, but will often serve to produce a difference in the degrees of our approbation or blame. The one is the different humours of particular men; the other, the particular manners and opinions of our age and country. The general principles of taste are uniform in human nature: Where men vary in their judgments, some defect or perversion in the faculties may commonly be remarked; proceeding either from prejudice, from want of practice, or want of delicacy: and there is just reason for approving one taste, and condemning another. But where there is such a diversity in the internal frame or external situation as is entirely blameless on both sides, and leaves no room to give one the preference above the other; in that case a certain degree of diversity in judgment is unavoidable, and we seek in vain for a standard, by which we can reconcile the contrary sentiments.

A young man, whose passions are warm, will be more sensibly touched with amorous and tender images, than a man more advanced in years, who takes pleasure in wise, philosophical reflections, concerning the conduct of life and moderation of the passions. At twenty, Ovid may be the favourite author; Horace at forty; and perhaps Tacitus at fifty. Vainly would we, in such cases, endeavour to enter into the sentiments of others, and divest ourselves of those propensities which are natural to us. We choose our favourite author as we do our friend, from a conformity of humour and disposition. Mirth or passion, sentiment or reflection; which ever of these most predominates in our temper, it gives us a peculiar sympathy with the writer who resembles us.

One person is more pleased with the sublime; another with the tender; a third with raillery. One has a strong sensibility to blemishes, and is extremely studious of correctness: Another has a more lively feeling of beauties, and pardons twenty absurdities and defects for one elevated or pathetic stroke. The ear of this man is entirely turned towards conciseness and energy; that man is delighted with a copious, rich, and harmonious expression. Simplicity is affected by one; ornament by another. Comedy, tragedy, satire, odes, have each its partizans, who prefer that particular species of writing to all others. It is plainly an error in a critic, to confine his approbation to one species or style of writing, and condemn all the rest. But it is almost impossible not to feel a predilection for that which suits our particular turn and disposition. Such preferences are innocent and unavoidable, and can never reasonably be the object of dispute, because there is no standard by which they can be decided.

For a like reason, we are more pleased, in the course of our reading, with pictures and characters that resemble objects which are found in our own age or country, than with those which describe a different set of customs. It is not without some effort, that we reconcile ourselves to the simplicity of ancient manners, and behold princesses carrying water from the spring, and kings and heroes dressing their own victuals. We may allow in general, that the representation of such manners is no fault in the author, nor deformity in the piece; but we are not so sensibly touched with them. For this reason, comedy is not easily transferred from one age or nation to another. A Frenchman or Englishman is not pleased with the *Andria* of Terence, or *Clitia* of Machiavel; where the fine lady, upon whom all the play turns, never once appears to the spectators, but is always kept behind the scenes, suitably to the reserved humour of the ancient Greeks and modern Italians. A man of learning and reflection can make allowance for these peculiarities of manners; but a common audience can never divest themselves so far of their usual ideas and sentiments, as to relish pictures which nowise resemble them.

But here there occurs a reflection, which may, perhaps, be useful in examining the celebrated controversy concerning ancient and modern learning; where we often find the one side excusing any seeming absurdity in the ancients from the manners of the age, and the other refusing to admit this excuse, or at least admitting it only as an apology for the author, not for the performance. In my opinion, the proper boundaries in this subject have seldom been fixed between the contending parties. Where any innocent peculiarities of manners are represented, such as those above mentioned, they ought certainly to be admitted; and a man, who is shocked with them, gives an evident proof of false delicacy and refinement. The poet's *monument more durable than brass,* must fall to the ground like common brick or clay, were men to make no allowance for the continual revolutions of manners and customs, and would admit of nothing but what was suitable to the prevailing fashion. Must we throw aside the pictures of our ancestors, because of their ruffs and fardingales? But where the ideas of morality and decency alter from one age to another, and where vicious manners are described, without being marked with the proper characters of blame and disapprobation, this must be allowed to disfigure the poem, and to be a real deformity. I cannot, nor is it proper I should, enter into such sentiments; and however I may excuse the poet, on account of the manners of his age, I never can relish the composition. The want of humanity and of decency, so conspicuous in the characters drawn by several of the ancient poets, even sometimes by Homer and the Greek tragedians, diminishes considerably the merit of their noble performances, and gives modern authors an advantage over them. We are not interested in the fortunes and sentiments of such rough heroes: We are displeased to find the limits of vice and virtue so much confounded; and whatever indulgence we may give to the writer on account of his prejudices, we cannot prevail on ourselves to enter into his sentiments, or bear an affection to characters, which we plainly discover to be blameable.

The case is not the same with moral principles as with speculative opinions of any kind. These are in continual flux and revolution. The son embraces a different system from the father. Nay there scarcely is any man, who can boast of great constancy and uniformity in this particular. Whatever speculative errors may be found in the polite writings of any age or country, they detract but little from the value of those compositions. There needs but a certain turn of thought or imagination to make us enter into all the opinions, which then prevail, and relish the sentiments or conclusions derived from them. But a very violent effort is requisite to change our judgment of manners, and excite sentiments of approbation or blame, love or hatred, different from those to which the mind, from long custom, has been familiarized. And where a man is confident of the rectitude of that moral standard, by which he judges, he is justly jealous of it, and will not pervert the sentiments of his heart for a moment, in complaisance to any writer whatsoever.

Of all speculative errors, those which regard religion are the most excusable in compositions of genius; nor is it ever permitted to judge of the civility or wisdom of any people, or even of single persons, by the grossness or refinement of their theological principles. The same good sense, that directs men in the ordinary occurrences of life, is not hearkened to in religious matters, which are supposed to be placed altogether above the cognisance of human reason. On this account, all the absurdities of the pagan system of theology must be overlooked by every critic, who would pretend to form a just notion of ancient poetry; and our posterity, in their turn, must have the same indulgence to their forefathers. No religious principles can ever be imputed as a fault to any poet, while they remain merely principles, and take not such strong possession of his heart, as to lay him under the imputation of *bigotry* or *superstition*. Where that happens, they confound the sentiments of morality, and alter the natural boundaries of vice and virtue. They are therefore eternal blemishes, according to the principle above mentioned; nor are the prejudices and false opinions of the age sufficient to justify them.

It is essential to the Roman Catholic religion to inspire a violent hatred of every other worship, and to represent all pagans, mahometans, and heretics, as the objects of Divine wrath and vengeance. Such sentiments, though they are in reality very blameable, are considered as virtues by the zealots of that communion, and are represented in their tragedies and epic poems as a kind of divine heroism. This bigotry has disfigured two very fine tragedies of the French theatre, POLIEUCTE and ATHALIA; where an intemperate zeal for particular modes of worship is set off with all the pomp imaginable, and forms the predominant character of the heroes. "What is this," says the sublime JOAD to JOSABET, finding her in discourse with MATHAN the priest of BAAL, "Does the daughter of DAVID speak to this traitor? Are you not afraid, lest the earth should open and pour forth flames to devour you both? Or lest these holy walls should fall and crush you together? What is his purpose? Why comes that enemy of GOD hither to poison the air, which we breathe, with his horrid presence?" Such sentiments are received with great applause on the theatre of Paris; but at London the spectators would be full as much pleased to hear Achilles tell Agamemnon, that he was a dog in his forehead, and a deer in his heart; or Jupiter threaten Juno with a sound drubbing, if she will not be quiet.

Religious principles are also a blemish in any polite composition, when they rise up to superstition, and intrude themselves into every sentiment, however remote from any connection with religion. It is no excuse for the poet, that the customs of his country had burthened life with so many religious ceremonies and observances, that no part of it was exempt from that yoke. It must for ever be ridiculous in Petrarch to compare his mistress, LAURA, to JESUS CHRIST. Nor is it less ridiculous in that agreeable libertine, Boccace, very seriously to give thanks to GOD ALMIGHTY and the ladies, for their assistance in defending him against his enemies.

FALLACIES OF ANTI-REFORMERS

BY

SYDNEY SMITH

INTRODUCTORY NOTE

SYDNEY SMITH (1771–1845) was an English clergyman noted as the wittiest man of his time. He was educated at Winchester and Oxford, and in 1798 went to Edinburgh as tutor to the son of an English gentleman. While there he proposed the founding of the "Edinburgh Review," and with Jeffrey, Brougham, and Francis Horner shared in its actual establishment. He superintended the first three numbers, and continued to write for it for twenty-five years. On leaving Edinburgh he lectured in London, held livings in Yorkshire and Somersetshire, was made prebendary of Bristol and Canon of St. Paul's.

The review of Bentham's "Book of Fallacies" exhibits at once the method of the Edinburgh Reviewers, Smith's vigorous, pointed, and witty style, and the general trend of his political opinions. He was a stanch Whig, and in such issues as that of Catholic Emancipation he fought for liberal opinions at the cost of injury to his personal prospects. As a clergyman he was kindly and philanthropic, a good preacher, and a hater of mysticism. No political writing of his time was more telling than his on the side of toleration and reform; and his wit, while spontaneous and exuberant, was employed in the service of good sense and with careful consideration for the feelings of others. If he lacks the terrific power of Swift, he lacks also his bitterness and savagery; his honesty and sincerity were no less, and his personality was as winning as it was amusing.

FALLACIES OF ANTI-REFORMERS[1]

THERE are a vast number of absurd and mischievous fallacies, which pass readily in the world for sense and virtue,
while in truth they tend only to fortify error and encourage
crime. Mr. Bentham has enumerated the most conspicuous of these
in the book before us.

Whether it be necessary there should be a middleman between the
cultivator and the possessor, learned economists have doubted; but
neither gods, men, nor booksellers can doubt the necessity of a
middleman between Mr. Bentham and the public. Mr. Bentham is
long; Mr. Bentham is occasionally involved and obscure; Mr. Bentham invents new and alarming expressions; Mr. Bentham loves
division and subdivision—and he loves method itself, more than its
consequences. Those only, therefore, who know his originality, his
knowledge, his vigor, and his boldness, will recur to the works themselves. The great mass of readers will not purchase improvement at
so dear a rate; but will choose rather to become acquainted with
Mr. Bentham through the medium of reviews—after that eminent
philosopher has been washed, trimmed, shaved, and forced into
clean linen. One great use of a review, indeed, is to make men wise
in ten pages, who have no appetite for a hundred pages; to condense
nourishment, to work with pulp and essence, and to guard the
stomach from idle burden and unmeaning bulk. For half a page,
sometimes for a whole page, Mr. Bentham writes with a power
which few can equal; and by selecting and omitting, an admirable
style may be formed from the text. Using this liberty, we shall
endeavor to give an account of Mr. Bentham's doctrines, for the most
part in his own words. Wherever an expression is particularly happy,
let it be considered to be Mr. Bentham's—the dulness we take to
ourselves.

[1] A review of "The Book of Fallacies: from Unfinished Papers of Jeremy Bentham.
By a Friend. London, 1824."

Our Wise Ancestors—*The Wisdom of Our Ancestors—The Wisdom of Ages—Venerable Antiquity—Wisdom of Old Times.*— This mischievous and absurd fallacy springs from the grossest perversion of the meaning of words. Experience is certainly the mother of wisdom, and the old have, of course, a greater experience than the young; but the question is who are the old? and who are the young? Of *individuals* living at the same period, the oldest has, of course, the greatest experience; but among *generations* of men the reverse of this is true. Those who come first (our ancestors) are the young people, and have the least experience. We have added to their experience the experience of many centuries; and, therefore, as far as experience goes, are wiser, and more capable of forming an opinion than they were. The real feeling should be, *not* can we be so presumptuous as to put our opinions in opposition to those of our ancestors? but can such young, ignorant, inexperienced persons as our ancestors necessarily were, be expected to have understood a subject as well as those who have seen so much more, lived so much longer, and enjoyed the experience of so many centuries? All this cant, then, about our ancestors is merely an abuse of words, by transferring phrases true of contemporary men to succeeding ages. Whereas (as we have before observed) of living men the oldest has, *cæteris paribus,*[2] the most experience; of generations, the oldest has, *cæteris paribus,* the least experience. Our ancestors, up to the Conquest, were children in arms; chubby boys in the time of Edward I; striplings under Elizabeth; men in the reign of Queen Anne; and *we* only are the white-bearded, silver-headed ancients, who have treasured up, and are prepared to profit by, all the experience which human life can supply. We are not disputing with our ancestors the palm of talent, in which they may or may not be our superiors, but the palm of experience in which it is utterly impossible they can be our superiors. And yet, whenever the Chancellor comes forward to protect some abuse, or to oppose some plan which has the increase of human happiness for its object, his first appeal is always to the wisdom of our ancestors; and he himself, and many noble lords who vote with him, are, to this hour, persuaded that all alterations and amendments on their devices are an unblushing controversy between

[2] "Other things being equal."

youthful temerity and mature experience!—and so, in truth they are—only that much-loved magistrate mistakes the young for the old, and the old for the young—and is guilty of that very sin against experience which he attributes to the lovers of innovation.

We cannot of course be supposed to maintain that our ancestors wanted wisdom, or that they were necessarily mistaken in their institutions, because their means of information were more limited than ours. But we do confidently maintain that when we find it expedient to change anything which our ancestors have enacted, we are the experienced persons, and not they. The quantity of talent is always varying in any great nation. To say that we are more or less able than our ancestors is an assertion that requires to be explained. All the able men of all ages, who have ever lived in England, probably possessed, if taken altogether, more intellect than all the able men England can now boast of. But if authority must be resorted to rather than reason, the question is, What was the wisdom of that single age which enacted the law, compared with the wisdom of the age which proposes to alter it? What are the eminent men of one and the other period? If you say that our ancestors were wiser than us, mention your date and year. If the splendor of names is equal, are the circumstances the same? If the circumstances are the same, we have a superiority of experience, of which the difference between the two periods is the measure. It is necessary to insist upon this; for upon sacks of wool, and on benches forensic, sit grave men, and agricolous persons in the Commons, crying out: "Ancestors, ancestors! *hodie non!*[3] Saxons, Danes, save us! Fiddlefrig, help us! Howel, Ethelwolf, protect us!" Any cover for nonsense—any veil for trash—any pretext for repelling the innovations of conscience and of duty!

"So long as they keep to vague generalities—so long as the two objects of comparison are each of them taken in the lump—wise ancestors in one lump, ignorant and foolish mob of modern times in the other—the weakness of the fallacy may escape detection. But let them assign for the period of superior wisdom any determinate period whatsoever, not only will the groundlessness of the notion be apparent (class being compared with class in that period and the

[3] "Not to-day!"

present one), but unless the antecedent period be comparatively speaking a very modern one, so wide will be the disparity, and to such an amount in favor of modern times, that, in comparison of the lowest class of the people in modern times (always supposing them proficient in the art of reading, and their proficiency employed in the reading of newspapers), the very highest and best-informed class of these wise ancestors will turn out to be grossly ignorant.

"Take, for example, any year in the reign of Henry VIII, from 1509 to 1546. At that time the House of Lords would probably have been in possession of by far the larger proportion of what little instruction the age afforded; in the House of Lords, among the laity, it might even then be a question whether, without exception, their lordships were all of them able so much as to read. But even supposing them all in the fullest possession of that useful art, political science being the science in question, what instruction on the subject could they meet with at that time of day?

"On no one branch of legislation was any book extant from which, with regard to the circumstances of the then present times, any useful instruction could be derived: distributive law, penal law, international law, political economy, so far from existing as sciences, had scarcely obtained a name: in all those departments under the head of *quid faciendum,* a mere blank: the whole literature of the age consisted of a meagre chronicle or two, containing short memorandums of the usual occurrences of war and peace, battles, sieges, executions, revels, deaths, births, processions, ceremonies, and other external events; but with scarce a speech or an incident that could enter into the composition of any such work as a history of the human mind—with scarce an attempt at investigation into causes, characters, or the state of the people at large. Even when at last, little by little, a scrap or two of political instruction came to be obtainable, the proportion of error and mischievous doctrine mixed up with it was so great, that whether a blank unfilled might not have been less prejudicial than a blank thus filled, may reasonably be matter of doubt.

"If we come down to the reign of James I, we shall find that Solomon of his time eminently eloquent as well as learned, not only among crowned but among uncrowned heads, marking out for prohibition and punishment the practices of devils and witches, and without the slightest objection on the part of the great characters of that day in their high situations, consigning men to death and torment for the misfortune of not being so well acquainted as he was with the composition of the Godhead.

"Under the name of exorcism the Catholic liturgy contains a form of procedure for driving out devils;—even with the help of this instrument, the operation cannot be performed with the desired success, but by an operator qualified by holy orders for the working of this as well as so many other wonders. In our days and in our country the same object is attained, and beyond comparison more effectually, by so cheap an instrument as a common newspaper; before this talisman, not only devils but ghosts, vampires, witches, and all their kindred tribes, are driven out of the land, never to return again! The touch of holy water is not so intolerable to them as the bare smell of printers' ink." [4]

FALLACY OF IRREVOCABLE LAWS.—A law, says Mr. Bentham (no matter to what effect) is proposed to a legislative assembly, who are called upon to reject it, upon the single ground that by those who in some former period exercised the same power, a regulation was made, having for its object to preclude forever, or to the end of an unexpired period, all succeeding legislators from enacting a law to any such effect as that now proposed.

Now it appears quite evident that, at every period of time, every legislature must be endowed with all those powers which the exigency of the times may require; and any attempt to infringe on this power is inadmissible and absurd. The sovereign power, at any one period, can only form a blind guess at the measures which may be necessary for any future period; but by this principle of immutable laws, the government is transferred from those who are necessarily the best judges of what they want, to others who can know little or nothing about the matter. The thirteenth century decides for the fourteenth. The fourteenth makes laws for the fifteenth. The fifteenth hermetically seals up the sixteenth, which tyrannizes over the seventeenth,

[4] From Bentham, pp. 74–77.

which again tells the eighteenth how it is to act, under circumstances which cannot be foreseen, and how it is to conduct itself in exigencies which no human wit can anticipate.

"Men who have a century more experience to ground their judgments on, surrender their intellect to men who had a century less experience, and who, unless that deficiency constitutes a claim, have no claim to preference. If the prior generation were, in respect of intellectual qualification, ever so much superior to the subsequent generation—if it understood so much better than the subsequent generation itself the interest of that subsequent generation—could it have been in an equal degree anxious to promote that interest, and consequently equally attentive to those facts with which, though in order to form a judgment it ought to have been, it is impossible that it should have been, acquainted? In a word, will its love for that subsequent generation be quite so great as that same generation's love for itself?

"Not even here, after a moment's deliberate reflection, will the assertion be in the affirmative. And yet it is their prodigious anxiety for the welfare of their posterity that produces the propensity of these sages to tie up the hands of this same posterity forever more—to act as guardians to its perpetual and incurable weakness, and take its conduct forever out of its own hands.

"If it be right that the conduct of the nineteenth century should be determined not by its own judgment but by that of the eighteenth, it will be equally right that the conduct of the twentieth century should be determined not by its own judgment but by that of the nineteenth. And if the same principle were still pursued, what at length would be the consequence?—that in process of time the practice of legislation would be at an end. The conduct and fate of all men would be determined by those who neither knew nor cared anything about the matter; and the aggregate body of the living would remain forever in subjection to an inexorable tyranny, exercised as it were by the aggregate body of the Dead." [5]

The despotism, as Mr. Bentham well observes, of Nero or Caligula would be more tolerable than an "irrevocable law." The despot, through fear or favor, or in a lucid interval, might relent; but how

[5] *Ibid.*, pp. 84–86.

are the Parliament who made the Scotch Union, for example, to be awakened from that dust in which they repose—the jobber and the patriot, the speaker and the doorkeeper, the silent voters and the men of rich allusions, Cannings and cultivators, Barings and beggars— making irrevocable laws for men who toss their remains about with spades, and use the relics of these legislators to give breadth to broc- coli, and to aid the vernal eruption of asparagus?

If the law be good, it will support itself; if bad, it should not be supported by "irrevocable theory," which is never resorted to but as the veil of abuses. All living men must possess the supreme power over their own happiness at every particular period. To suppose that there is anything which a whole nation cannot do, which they deem to be essential to their happiness, and that they cannot do it, because *another* generation, long ago dead and gone, said it must not be done, is mere nonsense. While you are captain of the vessel, do what you please; but the moment you quit the ship I become as omnipotent as you. You may leave me as much *advice* as you please, but you can- not leave me *commands;* though, in fact, this is the only meaning which can be applied to what are called irrevocable laws. It appeared to the legislature for the time being to be of immense importance to make such and such a law. Great good was gained, or great evil avoided, by enacting it. Pause before you alter an institution which has been deemed to be of so much importance. This is prudence and common-sense; the rest is the exaggeration of fools, or the artifice of knaves, who eat up fools. What endless nonsense has been talked of our navigation laws! What wealth has been sacrificed to either before they were repealed! How impossible it appeared to Noodle- dom to repeal them! They were considered of the irrevocable class— a kind of law over which the dead only were omnipotent, and the living had no power. Frost, it is true, cannot be put off by act of Parliament, nor can spring be accelerated by any majority of both houses. It is, however, quite a mistake to suppose that any alteration of any of the articles of union is as much out of the jurisdiction of Parliament as these meteorological changes. In every year, and every day of that year, living men have a right to make their own laws and manage their own affairs; to break through the tyranny of the antespirants—the people who breathed before them—and to do what they please for themselves. Such supreme power cannot indeed be well exercised by the people at large; it must be exercised therefore by the delegates, or Parliament, whom the people choose; and such Parliament, disregarding the superstitious reverence for "irrevocable laws," can have no other criterion of wrong and right than that of public utility.

When a law is considered as immutable, and the immutable law happens at the same time to be too foolish and mischievous to be endured, instead of being repealed, it is clandestinely evaded, or openly violated; and thus the authority of all law is weakened.

Where a nation has been ancestorially bound by foolish and improvident treaties, ample notice must be given of their termination. Where the State has made ill-advised grants, or rash bargains with individuals, it is necessary to grant proper compensation. The most difficult case, certainly, is that of the union of nations, where a smaller number of the weaker nation is admitted into the larger senate of the greater nation, and will be overpowered if the question come to a vote; but the lesser nation must run this risk; it is not probable that any violation of articles will take place till they are absolutely called for by extreme necessity. But let the danger be what it may, no danger is so great, no supposition so foolish, as to consider any human law as irrevocable. The shifting attitude of human affairs would often render such a condition an intolerable evil to all parties. The absurd jealousy of our countrymen at the Union secured heritable jurisdiction to the owners; nine and thirty years afterward they were abolished, in the very teeth of the Act of Union, and to the evident promotion of the public good.

CONTINUITY OF A LAW BY OATH.—The sovereign of England at his coronation takes an oath to maintain the laws of God, the true profession of the Gospel, and the Protestant religion, as established by law, and to preserve to the bishops and clergy of this realm the rights and privileges which by law appertain to them, and to preserve inviolate the doctrine, discipline, worship, and the government of the Church. It has been suggested that by this oath the King stands precluded from granting those indulgences to the Irish Catholics which are included in the bill for their emancipation. The true meaning of these provisions is of course to be decided, if doubtful, by the same legislative authority which enacted them. But a different notion it seems is now afloat. The King for the time being (we are putting an imaginary case) thinks as an individual that he is not maintaining the doctrine, discipline, and rights of the Church of England, if he grant any extension of civil rights to those who are not members of that Church; that he is violating his oath by so doing. This oath, then, according to this reasoning, is the great palladium of the Church. As long as it remains inviolate the Church is safe. How, then, can any monarch who has taken it ever consent to repeal it? How can he, consistently with his oath for the preservation of the privileges of the Church, contribute his part to throw down so strong a bulwark as he deems his oath to be! The oath, then, cannot be altered. It must remain under all circumstances of society the same. The King who has taken it is bound to continue it, and to refuse his sanction to any bill for its future alteration, because it prevents him, and, he must needs think, will prevent others, from granting dangerous immunities to the enemies of the Church.

Here, then, is an irrevocable law—a piece of absurd tyranny exercised by the rulers of Queen Anne's time upon the government of 1825—a certain art of potting and preserving a kingdom in one shape, attitude, and flavor—and in this way it is that an institution appears like old ladies' sweetmeats and made wines—Apricot Jam 1822—Currant Wine 1819—Court of Chancery 1427—Penal Laws against Catholics 1676. The difference is, that the ancient woman is a better judge of mouldy commodities than the illiberal part of his majesty's ministers. The potting lady goes sniffing about and admitting light and air to prevent the progress of decay; while to him of the wool-sack all seems doubly dear in proportion as it is antiquated, worthless, and unusable.

It ought not to be in the power of the sovereign to tie up his own hands, much less the hands of his successors. If the sovereign were to oppose his own opinion to that of the two other branches of the legislature, and himself to decide what he considers to be for the benefit of the Protestant Church, and what not a king who has spent his whole life in the frivolous occupation of a court may by perversion of understanding conceive measures most salutary to the Church to be most pernicious, and, persevering obstinately in his own error, may frustrate the wisdom of his parliament, and perpetuate the most inconceivable folly! If Henry VIII had argued in this manner we should have had no Reformation. If George III had always argued in this manner the Catholic code would never have been relaxed. And thus a King, however incapable of forming an opinion upon serious subjects, has nothing to do but pronounce the word "Conscience," and the whole power of the country is at his feet.

Can there be greater absurdity than to say that a man is acting contrary to his conscience who surrenders his opinion upon any subject to those who must understand the subject better than himself? I think my ward has a claim to the estate; but the best lawyers tell me he has none. I think my son capable of undergoing the fatigues of a military life; but the best physicians say he is much too weak. My Parliament say this measure will do the Church no harm; but I think it very pernicious to the Church. Am I acting contrary to my conscience because I apply much higher intellectual powers than my own to the investigation and protection of these high interests?

"According to the form in which it is conceived, any such engagement is in effect either a check or a license:—a license under the appearance of a check, and for that very reason but the more efficiently operative.

"Chains to the man in power? Yes:—but only such as he figures with on the stage; to the spectators as imposing, to himself as light as possible. Modelled by the wearer to suit his own purposes, they serve to rattle but not to restrain.

"Suppose a king of Great Britain and Ireland to have expressed his fixed determination, in the event of any proposed law being tendered to him for his assent, to refuse such assent, and this not on the persuasion that the law would not be 'for the utility of the subjects,' but that by his coronation oath he stands precluded from so doing, the course proper to be taken by Parliament, the course pointed out by principle and precedent, would be a vote of abdication—a vote declaring the king to have abdicated his royal authority, and that, as in case of death or incurable mental derangement, now is the time for the person next in succession to take his place. In the celebrated case in which a vote to this effect was actually passed, the declaration of abdication was, in lawyers' language, a fiction—in plain truth, a falsehood, and that falsehood a mockery; not a particle of his power was it the wish of James to abdicate, to part with, but to increase it to a maximum was the manifest object of all his efforts. But in the case here supposed, with respect to a part, and that a principal part of the royal authority, the will and purpose to abdicate is actually declared; and this being such a part, without which the remainder cannot, 'to the utility of the subjects,' be exercised, the remainder must of necessity be, on their part and for their sake, added." [6]

SELF-TRUMPETER's FALLACY.—Mr. Bentham explains the self-trumpeter's fallacy as follows:

"There are certain men in office who, in discharge of their functions, arrogate to themselves a degree of probity, which is to exclude all imputations and all inquiry. Their assertions are to be deemed equivalent to proof, their virtues are guaranties for the faithful discharge of their duties, and the most implicit confidence is to be reposed in them on all occasions. If you expose any abuse, propose any reform, call for securities, inquiry, or measures to promote publicity, they set up a cry of surprise, amounting almost to indignation, as if their integrity were questioned or their honor wounded. With all this, they dexterously mix up intimations that the most exalted patriotism, honor, and perhaps religion, are the only sources of all their actions." [7]

Of course every man will try what he can effect by these means; but (as Mr. Bentham observes) if there be any one maxim in politics more certain than another, it is that no possible degree of virtue in the governor can render it expedient for the governed to dispense with good laws and good institutions. Madame De Staël (to her disgrace) said to the Emperor of Russia: "Sire, your character is a constitution for your country, and your conscience its guaranty." His reply was: *"Quand cela serait, je ne serais jamais qu'un accident heureux;"* [8] and this we think one of the truest and most brilliant replies ever made by monarch.

LAUDATORY PERSONALITIES.—"The object of laudatory personalities

---

[6] *Ibid.*, pp. 110, 111.
[7] *Ibid.*, p. 120.   [8] "If that were so, I should be only a happy accident."

is to effect the rejection of a measure on account of the alleged good character of those who oppose it, and the argument advanced is: 'The measure is rendered unnecessary by the virtues of those who are in power—their opposition is a sufficient authority for the rejection of the measure. The measure proposed implies a distrust of the members of his Majesty's Government; but so great is their integrity, so complete their disinterestedness, so uniformly do they prefer the public advantage to their own, that such a measure is altogether unnecessary. Their disapproval is sufficient to warrant an opposition; precautions can only be requisite where danger is apprehended; here the high character of the individuals in question is a sufficient guaranty against any ground of alarm.' " [9]

The panegyric goes on increasing with the dignity of the lauded person. All are honorable and delightful men. The person who opens the door of the office is a person of approved fidelity; the junior clerk is a model of assiduity; all the clerks are models—seven years' models, eight years' models, nine years' models, and upward. The first clerk is a paragon, and ministers the very perfection of probity and intelligence; and as for the highest magistrate of the State, no adulation is equal to describe the extent of his various merits! It is too condescending, perhaps, to refute such folly as this. But we would just observe that, if the propriety of the measure in question be established by direct arguments, these must be at least as conclusive against the character of those who oppose it as their character can be against the measure.

The effect of such an argument is to give men of good or reputed good character the power of putting a negative on any question not agreeable to their inclinations.

"In every public trust the legislator should for the purpose of prevention, suppose the trustee disposed to break the trust in every imaginable way in which it would be possible for him to reap from the breach of it any personal advantage. This is the principle on which public institutions ought to be formed, and when it is applied to all men indiscriminately, it is injurious to none. The practical inference is to oppose to such possible (and what will always be probable) breaches of trust every bar that can be opposed consistently

[9] *Ibid.*, pp. 123, 124.

with the power requisite for the efficient and due discharge of the trust. Indeed, these arguments, drawn from the supposed virtues of men in power, are opposed to the first principles on which all laws proceed.

"Such allegations of individual virtue are never supported by specific proof, are scarce ever susceptible of specific disproof, and specific disproof, if offered, could not be admitted in either House of Parliament. If attempted elsewhere, the punishment would fall not on the unworthy trustee, but on him by whom the unworthiness has been proved." [10]

FALLACIES OF PRETENDED DANGER.—*Imputations of Bad Design; of Bad Character; of Bad Motives; of Inconsistency; of Suspicious Connections.*—The object of this class of fallacies is to draw aside attention from the measure to the man, and this in such a manner that, for some real or supposed defect in the author of the measure, a corresponding defect shall be imputed to the measure itself. Thus, "the author of the measure entertains a bad design; therefore the measure is bad. His character is bad, therefore the measure is bad; his motive is bad, I will vote against the measure. On former occasions this same person who proposed the measure was its enemy, therefore the measure is bad. He is on a footing of intimacy with this or that dangerous man, or has been seen in his company, or is suspected of entertaining some of his opinions, therefore the measure is bad. He bears a name that at a former period was borne by a set of men now no more, by whom bad principles were entertained, therefore the measure is bad!"

Now, if the measure be really inexpedient, why not at once show it to be so? If the measure be good, is it bad because a bad man is its author? If bad, is it good because a good man has produced it? What are these arguments but to say to the assembly who are to be the judges of any measure, that their imbecility is too great to allow them to judge of the measure by its own merits, and that they must have recourse to distant and feebler probabilities for that purpose?

"In proportion to the degree of efficiency with which a man suffers these instruments of deception to operate upon his mind, he enables bad men to exercise over him a sort of power, the thought of which

[10] *Ibid.*, pp. 125, 126.

ought to cover him with shame. Allow this argument the effect of a conclusive one, you put it into the power of any man to draw you at pleasure from the support of every measure which in your own eyes is good, to force you to give your support to any and every measure which in your own eyes is bad. Is it good?—the bad man embraces it, and by the supposition, you reject it. Is it bad?—he vituperates it, and that suffices for driving you into its embrace. You split upon the rocks because he has avoided them; you miss the harbor because he has steered into it! Give yourself up to any such blind antipathy, you are no less in the power of your adversaries than if, by a correspondently irrational sympathy and obsequiousness, you put yourself into the power of your friends." [11]

"Besides, nothing but laborious application and a clear and comprehensive intellect can enable a man on any given subject to employ successfully relevant arguments drawn from the subject itself. To employ personalities, neither labor nor intellect is required. In this sort of contest the most idle and the most ignorant are quite on a par with, if not superior to, the most industrious and the most highly gifted individuals. Nothing can be more convenient for those who would speak without the trouble of thinking. The same ideas are brought forward over and over again, and all that is required is to vary the turn of expression. Close and relevant arguments have very little hold on the passions, and serve rather to quell than to inflame them; while in personalities there is always something stimulant, whether on the part of him who praises or him who blames. Praise forms a kind of connection between the party praising and the party praised, and vituperation gives an air of courage and independence to the party who blames.

"Ignorance and indolence, friendship and enmity, concurring and conflicting interest, servility and independence, all conspire to give personalities the ascendency they so unhappily maintain. The more we lie under the influence of our own passions, the more we rely on others being affected in a similar degree. A man who can repel these injuries with dignity may often convert them into triumph: 'Strike me, but hear,' says he, and the fury of his antagonist redounds to his own discomfiture." [12]

[11] *Ibid.*, pp. 132, 133.   [12] *Ibid.*, pp. 141, 142.

No Innovation!—To say that all things new are bad is to say that all old things were bad in their commencement: for of all the old things ever seen or heard of there is not one that was not once new. Whatever is now establishment was once innovation. The first inventor of pews and parish clerks was no doubt considered as a Jacobin in his day. Judges, juries, criers of the court, are all the inventions of ardent spirits, who filled the world with alarm, and were considered as the great precursors of ruin and dissolution. No inoculation, no turnpikes, no reading, no writing, no popery! The fool sayeth in his heart and crieth with his mouth, "I will have nothing new!"

Fallacy of Distrust!—"What's at the Bottom?"—This fallacy begins with a virtual admission of the propriety of the measure considered in itself, and thus demonstrates its own futility, and cuts up from under itself the ground which it endeavours to make. A measure is to be rejected for something that, by bare possibility, may be found amiss in some other measure! This is vicarious reprobation; upon this principle Herod instituted his massacre. It is the argument of a driveller to other drivellers, who says: "We are not able to decide upon the evil when it arises; our only safe way is to act upon the general apprehension of evil."

Official Malefactor's Screen—"Attack Us, You Attack Government."—If this notion is acceded to, everyone who derives at present any advantage from misrule has it in fee-simple, and all abuses, present and future, are without remedy. So long as there is anything amiss in conducting the business of government, so long as it can be made better, there can be no other mode of bringing it nearer to perfection than the indication of such imperfections as at the time being exist.

"But so far is it from being true that a man's aversion or contempt for the hands by which the powers of government, or even for the system under which they are exercised, is a proof of his aversion or contempt toward government itself, that, even in proportion to the strength of that aversion or contempt, it is a proof of the opposite affection. What, in consequence of such contempt or aversion, he wishes for is not that there be no hands at all to exercise these powers, but that the hands may be better regulated;—not that those powers should not be exercised at all, but that they should be better exercised;—not that in the exercise of them no rules at all should be pursued, but that the rules by which they are exercised should be a better set of rules.

"All government is a trust, every branch of government is a trust, and immemorially acknowledged so to be; it is only by the magnitude of the scale that public differ from private trusts. I complain of the conduct of a person in the character of guardian, as domestic guardian, having the care of a minor or insane person. In so doing do I say that guardianship is a bad institution? Does it enter into the head of anyone to suspect me of so doing? I complain of an individual in the character of a commercial agent or assignee of the effects of an insolvent. In so doing do I say that commercial agency is a bad thing? that the practice of vesting in the hands of trustees or assignees the effects of an insolvent for the purpose of their being divided among his creditors is a bad practice? Does any such conceit ever enter into the head of man as that of suspecting me of so doing." [13]

There are no complaints against government in Turkey—no motions in Parliament, no "Morning Chronicles," and no "Edinburgh Reviews": yet of all countries in the world it is that in which revolts and revolutions are the most frequent.

It is so far from true that no good government can exist consistently with such disclosure, that no good government can exist without it. It is quite obvious to all who are capable of reflection that by no other means than by lowering the governors in the estimation of the people can there be hope or chance of beneficial change. To infer from this wise endeavor to lessen the existing rulers in the estimation of the people, a wish of dissolving the government, is either artifice or error. The physician who intentionally weakens the patient by bleeding him has no intention he should perish.

The greater the quantity of respect a man receives, independently of good conduct, the less good is his behavior likely to be. It is the interest, therefore, of the public in the case of each to see that the respect paid to him should, as completely as possible, depend upon the goodness of his behavior in the execution of his trust. But it is, on

[13] *Ibid.*, pp. 162, 163.

the contrary, the interest of the trustee that the respect, the money, or any other advantage he receives in virtue of his office, should be as great, as secure, and as independent of conduct as possible. Soldiers expect to be shot at; public men must expect to be attacked, and sometimes unjustly. It keeps up the habit of considering their conduct as exposed to scrutiny; on the part of the people at large it keeps alive the expectation of witnessing such attacks, and the habit of looking out for them. The friends and supporters of government have always greater facility in keeping and raising it up than its adversaries have for lowering it.

ACCUSATION-SCARER'S DEVICE—*"Infamy Must Attach Somewhere."*—This fallacy consists in representing the character of a calumniator as necessarily and justly attaching upon him who, having made a charge of misconduct against any person possessed of political power or influence, fails of producing evidence sufficient for their conviction.

"If taken as a general proposition, applying to all public accusations, nothing can be more mischievous as well as fallacious. Supposing the charge unfounded, the delivery of it may have been accompanied with *mala fides* (consciousness of its injustice), with *temerity* only, or it may have been perfectly blameless. It is in the first case alone that infamy can with propriety attach upon him who brings it forward. A charge really groundless may have been honestly *believed* to be well founded, *i. e.,* believed with a sort of provisional credence, sufficient for the purpose of engaging a man to do his part toward the bringing about an investigation, but without sufficient reasons. But a charge may be perfectly groundless without attaching the smallest particle of blame upon him who brings it forward. Suppose him to have heard from one or more, presenting themselves to him in the character of percipient witnesses, a story which, either *in toto,* or perhaps only in *circumstances,* though in circumstances of the most material importance, should prove false and mendacious, how is the person who hears this and acts accordingly to blame? What sagacity can enable a man previously to legal investigation, a man who has no power that can enable him to insure correctness or completeness on the part of this extrajudicial testimony, to guard against deception in such a case?" [14]

[14] *Ibid.,* pp. 185, 186.

FALLACY OF FALSE CONSOLATION—"*What is the Matter with You?* *—What Would You Have?—Look at the People There, and There; Think how much Better Off You Are than They Are—Your Prosperity and Liberty are Objects of Their Envy; Your Institutions, Models of Their Imitation.*"—It is not the desire to look to the bright side that is blamed, but when a particular suffering, produced by an assigned cause, has been pointed out, the object of many apologists is to turn the eyes of inquirers and judges into any other quarter in preference. If a man's tenants were to come with a general encomium on the prosperity of the country instead of a specified sum, would it be accepted? In a court of justice in an action for damages did ever any such device occur as that of pleading assets in the hands of a third person? There is in fact no country so poor and so wretched in every element of prosperity, in which matter for this argument might not be found. Were the prosperity of the country tenfold as great as at present, the absurdity of the argument would not in the least degree be lessened. Why should the smallest evil be endured which can be cured because others suffer patiently under greater evils? Should the smallest improvement attainable be neglected because others remain contented in a state of still greater inferiority?

"Seriously and pointedly in the character of a bar to any measure of relief, no, nor to the most trivial improvement, can it ever be employed. Suppose a bill brought in for converting an impassable road anywhere into a passable one, would any man stand up to oppose it who could find nothing better to urge against it than the multitude and goodness of the roads we have already? No: when in the character of a serious bar to the measure in hand, be that measure what it may, an argument so palpably inapplicable is employed, it can only be for the purpose of creating a diversion;—of turning aside the minds of men from the subject really in hand to a picture which, by its beauty, it is hoped, may engross the attention of the assembly, and make them forget for the moment for what purpose they came there." [15]

THE QUIETEST, OR NO COMPLAINT.—"A new law of measure being proposed in the character of a remedy for some incontestable

[15] *Ibid.,* pp. 196, 197.

abuse or evil, an objection is frequently started to the following effect:—'The measure is unnecessary. Nobody complains of disorder in that shape, in which it is the aim of your measure to propose a remedy to it. But even when *no* cause of complaint has been found to exist, especially under governments which admit of complaints, men have in general not been slow to complain; much less where any just cause of complaint has existed.' The argument amounts to this:—Nobody complains, therefore nobody suffers. It amounts to a veto on all measures of precaution or prevention, and goes to establish a maxim in legislation directly opposed to the most ordinary prudence of common life; it enjoins us to build no parapets to a bridge till the number of accidents has raised a universal clamor." [16]

PROCRASTINATOR'S ARGUMENT—"*Wait a Little; This is Not the Time.*"—This is the common argument of men who, being in reality hostile to a measure, are ashamed or afraid of appearing to be so. *To-day* is the plea—*eternal exclusion* commonly the object. It is the same sort of quirk as a plea of abatement in law—which is never employed but on the side of a dishonest defendant, whose hope it is to obtain an ultimate triumph, by overwhelming his adversary with despair, impoverishment, and lassitude. Which is the properest day to do good? which is the properest day to remove a nuisance? We answer, the very first day a man can be found to propose the removal of it; and whoever opposes the removal of it on that day will (if he dare) oppose it on every other. There is in the minds of many feeble friends to virtue and improvement, an imaginary period for the removal of evils, which it would certainly be worth while to wait for, if there was the smallest chance of its ever arriving—a period of unexampled peace and prosperity, when a patriotic king and an enlightened mob united their ardent efforts for the amelioration of human affairs; when the oppressor is as delighted to give up the oppression, as the oppressed is to be liberated from it; when the difficulty and the unpopularity would be to continue the evil, not to abolish it! These are the periods when fair-weather philosophers are willing to venture out and hazard a little for the general good. But the history of human nature is so contrary to all this, that almost

[16] *Ibid.*, pp. 190, 191.

all improvements are made after the bitterest resistance, and in the midst of tumults and civil violence—the worst period at which they can be made, compared to which any period is eligible, and should be seized hold of by the friends of salutary reform.

SNAIL'S PACE ARGUMENT—*"One Thing at a Time!—Not Too Fast!—Slow and Sure!*—Importance of the business—extreme difficulty of the business—danger of innovation—need of caution and circumspection—impossibility of foreseeing all consequences—danger of precipitation—everything should be gradual—one thing at a time—this is not the time—great occupation at present—wait for more leisure—people well satisfied—no petitions presented—no complaints heard—no such mischief has yet taken place—stay till it has taken place! Such is the prattle which the magpie in office, who, understanding nothing, yet understands that he must have something to say on every subject, shouts out among his auditors as a succedaneum to thought." [17]

VAGUE GENERALITIES.—Vague generalities comprehend a numerous class of fallacies resorted to by those who, in preference to the determinate expressions which they might use, adopt others more vague and indeterminate.

Take, for instance, the terms government, laws, morals, religion. Everybody will admit that there are in the world bad governments, bad laws, bad morals, and bad religions. The bare circumstance, therefore, of being engaged in exposing the defects of government, law, morals, and religion does not of itself afford the slightest presumption that a writer is engaged in anything blamable. If his attack be only directed against that which is bad in each, his efforts may be productive of good to any extent. This essential distinction, however, the defender of abuses uniformly takes care to keep out of sight; and boldly imputes to his antagonists an intention to subvert all *government, law, morals, and religion.* Propose anything with a view to the improvement of the existing practice, in relation to law, government, and religion, he will treat you with an oration upon the necessity and utility of law, government, and religion. Among the several cloudy appellatives which have been commonly employed as cloaks for misgovernment, there is none more conspicuous in this

[17] *Ibid.*, pp. 203, 204.

atmosphere of illusion than the word order. As often as any measure is brought forward which has for its object to lessen the sacrifice made by the many to the few, *social order* is the phrase commonly opposed to its progress.

"By a defalcation made from any part of the mass of fictitious delay, vexation, and expense, out of which, and in proportion to which, lawyers' profit is made to flow—by any defalcation made from the mass of needless and worse than useless emolument to office, with or without service or pretence of service—by any addition endeavored to be made to the quantity, or improvement in the quality of service rendered, or time bestowed in service rendered in return for such emolument—by every endeavor that has for its object the persuading the people to place their fate at the disposal of any other agents than those in whose hands breach of trust is certain, due fulfilment of it morally and physically impossible—*social order* is said to be endangered, and threatened to be destroyed." [18]

In the same way "Establishment" is a word in use to protect the bad parts of establishments, by charging those who wish to remove or alter them, with a wish to subvert all good establishments.

Mischievous fallacies also circulate from the convertible use of what Mr. B. is pleased to call dyslogistic and eulogistic terms. Thus, a vast concern is expressed for the "liberty of the press," and the utmost abhorrence of its "licentiousness": but then, by the licentiousness of the press is meant every disclosure by which any abuse is brought to light and exposed to shame—by the "liberty of the press" is meant only publications from which no such inconvenience is to be apprehended; and the fallacy consists in employing the sham approbation of liberty as a mask for the real opposition to all free discussion. To write a pamphlet so ill that nobody will read it; to animadvert in terms so weak and insipid upon great evils, that no disgust is excited at the vice, and no apprehension in the evil-doer, is a fair use of the liberty of the press, and is not only pardoned by the friends of government, but draws from them the most fervent eulogium. The licentiousness of the press consists in doing the thing boldly and well, in striking terror into the guilty, and in rousing the attention of the public to the defence of their highest interests. This

[18] *Ibid.*, p. 234.

is the licentiousness of the press held in the greatest horror by timid and corrupt men, and punished by semi-animous, semi-cadaverous judges, with a captivity of many years. In the same manner the dyslogistic and eulogistic fallacies are used in the case of reform.

"Between all abuses whatsoever there exists that connection—between all persons who see, each of them, any one abuse in which an advantage results to himself, there exists, in point of interest, that close and sufficiently understood connection, of which intimation has been given already. To no one abuse can correction be administered without endangering the existence of every other.

"If, then, with this inward determination not to suffer, so far as depends upon himself, the adoption of any reform which he is able to prevent, it should seem to him necessary or advisable to put on for a cover the profession or appearance of a desire to contribute to such reform—in pursuance of the device or fallacy here in question, he will represent that which goes by the name of reform as distinguishable into two species; one of them a fit subject for approbation, the other for disapprobation. That which he thus professes to have marked for approbation, he will accordingly for the expression of such approbation, characterize by some adjunct of the *eulogistic* cast, such as moderate, for example, or temperate, or practical, or practicable.

"To the other of these nominally distinct species, he will, at the same time, attach some adjunct of the *dyslogistic* cast, such as violent, intemperate, extravagant, outrageous, theoretical, speculative, and so forth.

"Thus, then, in profession and to appearance, there are in his conception of the matter two distinct and opposite species of reform, to one of which his approbation, to the other his disapprobation, is attached. But the species to which his approbation is attached is an *empty* species—a species in which no individual is, or is intended to be, contained.

"The species to which his disapprobation is attached is, on the contrary, a crowded species, a receptacle in which the whole contents of the *genus*—of the *genus* 'Reform'—are intended to be included." [19]

[19] *Ibid.*, pp. 277, 278.

ANTI-RATIONAL FALLACIES.—When reason is in opposition to a man's interests his study will naturally be to render the faculty itself, and whatever issues from it, an object of hatred and contempt. The sarcasm and other figures of speech employed on the occasion are directed not merely against reason but against thought, as if there were something in the faculty of thought that rendered the exercise of it incompatible with useful and successful practice. Sometimes a plan, which would not suit the official person's interest, is without more ado pronounced a speculative one; and, by this observation, all need of rational and deliberate discussion is considered to be superseded. The first effort of the corruptionist is to fix the epithet speculative upon any scheme which he thinks may cherish the spirit of reform. The expression is hailed with the greatest delight by bad and feeble men, and repeated with the most unwearied energy; and to the word "speculative," by way of reinforcement, are added: *theoretical, visionary, chimerical, romantic, Utopian.*

"Sometimes a distinction is taken, and thereupon a concession made. The plan is good in theory, but it would be bad in practice, *i. e.,* its being good in theory does not hinder its being bad in practice.

"Sometimes, as if in consequence of a further progress made in the art of irrationality, the plan is pronounced to be "too good to be practicable"; and its being so good as it is, is thus represented as the very cause of its being bad in practice.

"In short, such is the perfection at which this art is at length arrived, that the very circumstance of a plan's being susceptible of the appellation of a *plan,* has been gravely stated as a circumstance sufficient to warrant its being rejected—rejected, if not with hatred, at any rate with a sort of accompaniment which, to the million, is commonly felt still more galling—with contempt." [20]

There is a propensity to push theory too far; but what is the just inference? not that theoretical propositions (*i. e.,* all propositions of any considerable comprehension or extent) should, from such their extent, be considered to be false *in toto,* but only that, in the particular case, should inquiry be made whether, supposing the proposition to be in the character of a rule generally true, an exception ought to

[20] *Ibid.,* p. 296.

be taken out of it. It might almost be imagined that there was something wicked or unwise in the exercise of thought; for everybody feels a necessity for disclaiming it. "I am not given to speculation, I am no friend to theories." Can a man disclaim theory, can he disclaim speculation, without disclaiming thought?

The description of persons by whom this fallacy is chiefly employed are those who, regarding a plan as adverse to their interests, and not finding it on the ground of general utility exposed to any preponderant objection, have recourse to this objection in the character of an instrument of contempt, in the view of preventing those from looking into it who might have been otherwise disposed. It is by the fear of seeing it practised that they are drawn to speak of it as impracticable. "Upon the face of it (exclaims some feeble or pensioned gentleman) it carries that air of plausibility, that, if you were not upon your guard, might engage you to bestow more or less attention upon it; but were you to take the trouble, you would find that (as it is with all these plans which promise so much) practicability would at last be wanting to it. To save yourself from this trouble, the wisest course you can take is to put the plan aside, and to think no more about the matter." This is always accompanied with a peculiar grin of triumph.

The whole of these fallacies may be gathered together in a little oration, which we will denominate the "Noodle's Oration":—

"What would our ancestors say to this, Sir? How does this measure tally with their institutions? How does it agree with their experience? Are we to put the wisdom of yesterday in competition with the wisdom of centuries? [*Hear! hear!*] Is beardless youth to show no respect for the decisions of mature age? [*Loud cries of hear! hear!*] If this measure be right, would it have escaped the wisdom of those Saxon progenitors to whom we are indebted for so many of our best political institutions? Would the Dane have passed it over? Would the Norman have rejected it? Would such a notable discovery have been reserved for these modern and degenerate times? Besides, Sir, if the measure itself is good, I ask the honorable gentleman if this is the time for carrying it into execution—whether, in fact, a more unfortunate period could have been selected than that which he has chosen? If this were an ordinary measure I should not oppose it with so much vehemence; but, Sir, it calls in question the wisdom of an irrevocable law—of a law passed at the memorable period of the Revolution. What right have we, Sir, to break down this firm column on which the great men of that age stamped a character of eternity? Are not all authorities against this measure—Pitt, Fox, Cicero, and the Attorney- and Solicitor-General? The proposition is new, Sir; it is the first time it was ever heard in this House. I am not prepared, Sir—this House is not prepared—to receive it. The measure implies a distrust of his Majesty's Government; their disapproval is sufficient to warrant opposition. Precaution only is requisite where danger is apprehended. Here the high character of the individuals in question is a sufficient guarantee against any ground of alarm. Give not, then, your sanction to this measure; for, whatever be its character, if you do give your sanction to it, the same man by whom this is proposed will propose to you others to which it will be impossible to give your consent. I care very little, Sir, for the ostensible measure; but what is there behind? What are the honorable gentleman's future schemes? If we pass this bill, what fresh concessions may he not require? What further degradation is he planning for his country? Talk of evil and inconvenience, Sir! look to other countries—study other aggregations and societies of men, and then see whether the laws of this country demand a remedy or deserve a panegyric. Was the honorable gentleman (let me ask him) always of this way of thinking? Do I not remember when he was the advocate, in this House, of very opposite opinions? I not only quarrel with his present sentiments, Sir, but I declare very frankly I do not like the party with which he acts. If his own motives were as pure as possible, they cannot but suffer contamination from those with whom he is politically associated. This measure may be a boon to the Constitution, but I will accept no favor to the Constitution from such hands. [*Loud cries of hear! hear!*] I profess myself, Sir, an honest and upright member of the British Parliament, and I am not afraid to profess myself an enemy to all change and all innovation. I am satisfied with things as they are; and it will be my pride and pleasure to hand down this country to my children as I received it from those who preceded me. The honorable gentleman pretends to justify the severity with which he has attacked the noble lord who presides in the Court of Chancery. But I say such attacks are pregnant with mischief to government itself. Oppose ministers, you oppose government; disgrace ministers, you disgrace government; bring ministers into contempt, you bring government into contempt; and anarchy and civil war are the consequences. Besides, sir, the measure is unnecessary. Nobody complains of disorder in that shape in which it is the aim of your measure to propose a remedy to it. The business is one of the greatest importance; there is need of the greatest caution and circumspection. Do not let us be precipitate, Sir; it is impossible to foresee all consequences. Everything should be gradual; the example of a neighboring nation should fill us with alarm! The honorable gentleman has taxed me with illiberality, Sir; I deny the charge. I hate innovation, but I love improvement. I am an enemy to the corruption of government, but I defend its influence. I dread reform, but I dread it only when it is intemperate. I consider the liberty of the press as the great palladium of the Constitution; but, at the same time, I hold the licentiousness of the press in the greatest abhorrence. Nobody is more conscious than I am of the splendid abilities of the honorable mover, but I tell him at once his scheme is too good to be practicable. It savors of Utopia. It looks well in theory, but it won't do in practice. It will not do, I repeat, Sir, in practice; and so the advocates of the measure will find, if, unfortunately, it should find its way through Parliament. [*Cheers.*] The source of that corruption to which the honorable member alludes is in the minds of the people; so rank and extensive is that corruption, that no political reform can have any effect in removing it. Instead of reforming others—instead of reforming the State, the Constitution, and everything that is most excellent, let each man reform himself! let him look at home, he will find there enough to do without looking abroad and aiming at what is out of his power. [*Loud cheers.*] And now, Sir, as it is frequently the custom in this House to end with a quotation, and as the gentleman who preceded me in the debate has anticipated me in my favorite quotation of the 'Strong pull and the long pull,' I shall end with the memorable words of the assembled barons: '*Nolumus leges Angliæ mutari.*' [21]

"Upon the whole, the following are the characters which appertain

---

[21] "We do not wish the laws of England to be changed."

in common to all the several arguments here distinguished by the name of fallacies:—

"1. Whatsoever be the measure in hand, they are, with relation to it, irrelevant.

"2. They are all of them such, that the application of these irrelevant arguments affords a presumption either of the weakness or total absence of relevant arguments on the side of which they are employed.

"3. To any good purpose they are all of them unnecessary.

"4. They are all of them not only capable of being applied, but actually in the habit of being applied, and with advantage, to bad purposes, viz.: to the obstruction and defeat of all such measures as have for their object the removal of the abuses or other imperfections still discernible in the frame and practice of the government.

"5. By means of the irrelevancy, they all of them consume and misapply time, thereby obstructing the course and retarding the progress of all necessary and useful business.

"6. By that irritative quality which, in virtue of their irrelevancy, with the improbity or weakness of which it is indicative, they possess, all of them, in a degree more or less considerable, but in a more particular degree such of them as consist in personalities, are productive of ill-humor, which in some instances has been productive of bloodshed, and is continually productive, as above, of waste of time and hindrance of business.

"7. On the part of those who, whether in spoken or written discourses, give utterance to them, they are indicative either of improbity or intellectual weakness, or of a contempt for the understanding of those on whose minds they are destined to operate.

"8. On the part of those on whom they operate, they are indicative of intellectual weakness; and on the part of those in and by whom they are pretended to operate, they are indicative of improbity, viz., in the shape of insincerity.

"The practical conclusion is, that in proportion as the acceptance, and thence the utterance, of them can be prevented, the understanding of the public will be strengthened, the morals of the public will be purified, and the practice of government improved." [22]

[22] From Bentham, pp. 359, 360.

ON POESY OR ART

BY
SAMUEL TAYLOR COLERIDGE

INTRODUCTORY NOTE

SAMUEL TAYLOR COLERIDGE (1772–1834) was the tenth child of a Devonshire clergyman, and the most distinguished member of one of the most intellectual stocks in modern England. His life was devoted to literary and philosophical pursuits, but an inherent weakness of will and lack of practical sense made him depend upon friends and benefactors for a large part of the support of himself and his family. In poetry he achieved his greatest distinction, and the best of his work stands at the head of its class. But he was constantly planning great schemes which he usually abandoned before they were carried out, and in spite of the extraordinary nature of his endowments he never fulfilled his promise.

In prose his chief work was in philosophy and esthetics. He was one of the first to introduce into England the philosophy of Kant, and in literary criticism he stands in the front rank. Probably no interpreter of Shakespeare has said so many memorable and penetrating things in illumination of the characters of the great dramas; and in the present essay he shows his power of dealing with profound philosophic insight with the fundamental principles of art.

ON POESY OR ART[1]

MAN communicates by articulation of sounds, and paramountly by the memory in the ear; nature by the impression of bounds and surfaces on the eye, and through the eye it gives significance and appropriation, and thus the conditions of memory, or the capability of being remembered, to sounds, smells, etc. Now Art, used collectively for painting, sculpture, architecture, and music, is the mediatress between, and reconciler of nature and man. It is, therefore, the power of humanizing nature, of infusing the thoughts and passions of man into everything which is the object of his contemplation; color, form, motion, and sound, are the elements which it combines, and it stamps them into unity in the mould of a moral idea.

The primary art is writing;—primary, if we regard the purpose abstracted from the different modes of realizing it, those steps of progression of which the instances are still visible in the lower degrees of civilization. First, there is mere gesticulation; then rosaries or wampum; then picture-language; then hieroglyphics, and finally alphabetic letters. These all consist of a translation of man into nature, of a substitution of the visible for the audible.

The so-called music of savage tribes as little deserves the name of art for the understanding as the ear warrants it for music. Its lowest state is a mere expression of passion by sounds which the passion itself necessitates;—the highest amounts to no more than a voluntary reproduction of these sounds in the absence of the occasioning causes, so as to give the pleasure of contrast—for example, by the various outcries of battle in the song of security and triumph. Poetry also is purely human; for all its materials are from the mind, and all its products are for the mind. But it is the apotheosis of the former state, in which by excitement of the associative power passion itself imitates order, and the order resulting produces a

[1] Delivered as a lecture in 1818.

255

pleasurable passion, and thus it elevates the mind by making its feelings the object of its reflection. So likewise, while it recalls the sights and sounds that had accompanied the occasions of the original passions, poetry impregnates them with an interest not their own by means of the passions, and yet tempers the passion by the calming power which all distinct images exert on the human soul. In this way poetry is the preparation for art, inasmuch as it avails itself of the forms of nature to recall, to express, and to modify the thoughts and feelings of the mind.

Still, however, poetry can only act through the intervention of articulate speech, which is so peculiarly human that in all languages it constitutes the ordinary phrase by which man and nature are contradistinguished. It is the original force of the word "brute," and even "mute" and "dumb" do not convey the absence of sound, but the absence of articulated sounds.

As soon as the human mind is intelligibly addressed by an outward image exclusively of articulate speech, so soon does art commence. But please to observe that I have laid particular stress on the words "human mind"—meaning to exclude thereby all results common to man and all other sentient creatures, and consequently confining myself to the effect produced by the congruity of the animal impression with the reflective powers of the mind; so that not the thing presented, but that which is re-presented by the thing, shall be the source of the pleasure. In this sense nature itself is to a religious observer the art of God; and for the same cause art itself might be defined as of a middle quality between a thought and a thing, or as I said before, the union and reconciliation of that which is nature with that which is exclusively human. It is the figured language of thought, and is distinguished from nature by the unity of all the parts in one thought or idea. Hence nature itself would give us the impression of a work of art, if we could see the thought which is present at once in the whole and in every part; and a work of art will be just in proportion as it adequately conveys the thought, and rich in proportion to the variety of parts which it holds in unity.

If, therefore, the term "mute" be taken as opposed not to sound but to articulate speech, the old definition of painting will in fact be the true and best definition of the fine arts in general, that is, *muta poesis,* mute poesy, and so of course poesy. And, as all languages perfect themselves by a gradual process of desynonymizing words originally equivalent, I have cherished the wish to use the word "poesy" as the generic or common term, and to distinguish that species of poesy which is not *muta poesis* by its usual name "poetry"; while of all the other species which collectively form the fine arts, there would remain this as the common definition—that they all, like poetry, are to express intellectual purposes, thoughts, conceptions, and sentiments which have their origin in the human mind—not, however, as poetry does, by means of articulate speech, but as nature or the divine art does, by form, color, magnitude, proportion, or by sound, that is, silently or musically.

Well! it may be said—but who has ever thought otherwise? We all know that art is the imitatress of nature. And, doubtless, the truths which I hope to convey would be barren truisms, if all men meant the same by the words "imitate" and "nature." But it would be flattering mankind at large, to presume that such is the fact. First, to imitate. The impression on the wax is not an imitation, but a copy, of the seal; the seal itself is an imitation. But, further, in order to form a philosophic conception, we must seek for the kind, as the heat in ice, invisible light, etc., whilst, for practical purposes, we must have reference to the degree. It is sufficient that philosophically we understand that in all imitation two elements must coexist, and not only coexist, but must be perceived as coexisting. These two constituent elements are likeness and unlikeness, or sameness and difference, and in all genuine creations of art there must be a union of these disparates. The artist may take his point of view where he pleases, provided that the desired effect be perceptibly produced—that there be likeness in the difference, difference in the likeness, and a reconcilement of both in one. If there be likeness to nature without any check of difference, the result is disgusting, and the more complete the delusion, the more loathsome the effect. Why are such simulations of nature, as wax-work figures of men and women, so disagreeable? Because not finding the motion and the life which we expected, we are shocked as by a falsehood, every circumstance of detail, which before induced us to be interested, making the distance from truth more palpable. You set out with a supposed reality and are disappointed and disgusted with the deception; while, in respect to a work of genuine imitation, you begin with an acknowledged total difference, and then every touch of nature gives you the pleasure of an approximation to truth. The fundamental principle of all this is undoubtedly the horror of falsehood and the love of truth inherent in the human breast. The Greek tragic dance rested on these principles, and I can deeply sympathize in imagination with the Greeks in this favorite part of their theatrical exhibitions, when I call to mind the pleasure I felt in beholding the combat of the Horatii and Curiatii most exquisitely danced in Italy to the music of Cimarosa.

Secondly, as to nature. We must imitate nature! yes, but what in nature—all and everything? No, the beautiful in nature. And what then is the beautiful? What is beauty? It is, in the abstract, the unity of the manifold, the coalescence of the diverse; in the concrete, it is the union of the shapely (*formosum*) with the vital. In the dead organic it depends on regularity of form, the first and lowest species of which is the triangle with all its modifications, as in crystals, architecture, etc.; in the living organic it is not mere regularity of form, which would produce a sense of formality; neither is it subservient to anything beside itself. It may be present in a disagreeable object, in which the proportion of the parts constitutes a whole; it does not arise from association, as the agreeable does, but sometimes lies in the rupture of association; it is not different to different individuals and nations, as has been said, nor is it connected with the ideas of the good, or the fit, or the useful. The sense of beauty is intuitive, and beauty itself is all that inspires pleasure without, and aloof from, and even contrarily to, interest.

If the artist copies the mere nature, the *natura naturata,* what idle rivalry! If he proceeds only from a given form, which is supposed to answer to the notion of beauty, what an emptiness, what an unreality there always is in his productions, as in Cipriani's pictures! Believe me, you must master the essence, the *natura naturans,* which presupposes a bond between nature in the higher sense and the soul of man.

The wisdom in nature is distinguished from that in man by the co-instantaneity of the plan and the execution; the thought and the product are one, or are given at once; but there is no reflex act, and hence there is no moral responsibility. In man there is reflection, freedom, and choice; he is, therefore, the head of the visible creation. In the objects of nature are presented, as in a mirror, all the possible elements, steps, and processes of intellect antecedent to consciousness, and therefore to the full development of the intelligential act; and man's mind is the very focus of all the rays of intellect which are scattered throughout the images of nature. Now, so to place these images, totalized and fitted to the limits of the human mind, as to elicit from, and to superinduce upon, the forms themselves the moral reflections to which they approximate, to make the external internal, the internal external, to make nature thought, and thought nature—this is the mystery of genius in the fine arts. Dare I add that the genius must act on the feeling, that body is but a striving to become mind—that it is mind in its essence?

In every work of art there is a reconcilement of the external with the internal; the conscious is so impressed on the unconscious as to appear in it; as compare mere letters inscribed on a tomb with figures themselves constituting the tomb. He who combines the two is the man of genius; and for that reason he must partake of both. Hence there is in genius itself an unconscious activity; nay, that is the genius in the man of genius. And this is the true exposition of the rule that the artist must first eloign himself from nature in order to return to her with full effect. Why this? Because if he were to begin by mere painful copying, he would produce masks only, not forms breathing life. He must out of his own mind create forms according to the severe laws of the intellect, in order to generate in himself that co-ordination of freedom and law, that involution of obedience in the prescript, and of the prescript in the impulse to obey, which assimilates him to nature, and enables him to understand her. He merely absents himself for a season from her, that his own spirit, which has the same ground with nature, may learn her unspoken language in its main radicals, before he approaches to her endless compositions of them. Yes, not to acquire cold notions— lifeless technical rules—but living and life-producing ideas, which shall contain their own evidence, the certainty that they are essentially one with the germinal causes in nature—his consciousness being the focus and mirror of both—for this does the artist for a time abandon the external real in order to return to it with a complete sympathy with its internal and actual. For of all we see, hear, feel, and touch the substance is and must be in ourselves; and therefore there is no alternative in reason between the dreary (and thank heaven! almost impossible) belief that everything around us is but a phantom, or that the life which is in us is in them likewise; and that to know is to resemble, when we speak of objects out of ourselves, even as within ourselves to learn is, according to Plato, only to recollect;—the only effective answer to which, that I have been fortunate to meet with, is that which Pope has consecrated for future use in the line—

"And coxcombs vanquish Berkeley with a grin!"

The artist must imitate that which is within the thing, that which is active through form and figure, and discourses to us by symbols—the *Natur-geist,* or spirit of nature, as we unconsciously imitate those whom we love; for so only can he hope to produce any work truly natural in the object and truly human in the effect. The idea which puts the form together cannot itself be the form. It is above form, and is its essence, the universal in the individual, or the individuality itself—the glance and the exponent of the indwelling power.

Each thing that lives has its moment of self-exposition, and so has each period of each thing, if we remove the disturbing forces of accident. To do this is the business of ideal art, whether in images of childhood, youth, or age, in man or in woman. Hence a good portrait is the abstract of the personal; it is not the likeness for actual comparison, but for recollection. This explains why the likeness of a very good portrait is not always recognized; because some persons never abstract, and among these are especially to be numbered the near relations and friends of the subject, in consequence of the constant pressure and check exercised on their minds by the actual presence of the original. And each thing that only appears to live has also its possible position of relation to life, as nature herself testifies, who, where she cannot be, prophesies her being in the crystallized metal, or the inhaling plant.

The charm, the indispensable requisite, of sculpture is unity of effect. But painting rests in a material remoter from nature, and its compass is therefore greater. Light and shade give external, as well internal, being even with all its accidents, while sculpture is confined to the latter. And here I may observe that the subjects chosen for works of art, whether in sculpture or painting, should be such as really are capable of being expressed and conveyed within the limits of those arts. Moreover, they ought to be such as will affect the spectator by their truth, their beauty, or their sublimity, and therefore they may be addressed to the judgment, the senses, or the reason. The peculiarity of the impression which they may make may be derived either from color and form, or from proportion and fitness, or from the excitement of the moral feelings; or all these may be combined. Such works as do combine these sources of effect must have the preference in dignity.

Imitation of the antique may be too exclusive, and may produce an injurious effect on modern sculpture:—first, generally, because such an imitation cannot fail to have a tendency to keep the attention fixed on externals rather than on the thought within;—secondly, because, accordingly, it leads the artist to rest satisfied with that which is always imperfect, namely, bodily form, and circumscribes his views of mental expression to the ideas of power and grandeur only;—thirdly, because it induces an effort to combine together two incongruous things, that is to say, modern feelings in antique forms;—fourthly, because it speaks in a language, as it were, learned and dead; the tones of which, being unfamiliar, leave the common spectator cold and unimpressed;—and lastly, because it necessarily causes a neglect of thoughts, emotions, and images of profounder interest and more exalted dignity, as motherly, sisterly, and brotherly love, piety, devotion, the divine become human—the Virgin, the Apostle, the Christ. The artist's principle in the statue of a great man should be the illustration of departed merit; and I cannot but think that a skilful adoption of modern habiliments would, in many instances, give a variety and force of effect which a bigoted adherence to Greek or Roman costume precludes. It is, I believe, from artists finding Greek models unfit for several important modern purposes that we see so many allegorical figures on monuments and elsewhere. Painting was, as it were, a new art, and being un-shackled by old models it chose its own subjects, and took an eagle's flight. And a new field seems opened for modern sculpture in the symbolical expression of the ends of life, as in Guy's monu-ment, Chantrey's children in Worcester Cathedral, etc.

Architecture exhibits the greatest extent of the difference from nature which may exist in works of art. It involves all the powers of design, and is sculpture and painting inclusively. It shows the greatness of man, and should at the same time teach him humility.

Music is the most entirely human of the fine arts, and has the fewest *analoga* in nature. Its first delightfulness is simple accord-ance with the ear; but it is an associated thing, and recalls the deep emotions of the past with an intellectual sense of proportion. Every human feeling is greater and larger than the exciting cause—a proof, I think, that man is designed for a higher state of existence; and this is deeply implied in music in which there is always something more and beyond the immediate expression.

With regard to works in all the branches of the fine arts, I may remark that the pleasure arising from novelty must of course be allowed its due place and weight. This pleasure consists in the iden-tity of two opposite elements—that is to say, sameness and variety. If in the midst of the variety there be not some fixed object for the attention, the unceasing succession of the variety will prevent the mind from observing the difference of the individual objects; and the only thing remaining will be the succession, which will then produce precisely the same effect as sameness. This we experience when we let the trees or hedges pass before the fixed eye during a rapid movement in a carriage, or, on the other hand, when we suffer a file of soldiers or ranks of men in procession to go on before us without resting the eye on anyone in particular. In order to derive pleasure from the occupation of the mind, the principle of unity must always be present, so that in the midst of the multeity the centripetal force be never suspended, nor the sense be fatigued by the predominance of the centrifugal force. This unity in multeity I have elsewhere stated as the principle of beauty. It is equally the source of pleasure in variety, and in fact a higher term including both. What is the seclusive or distinguishing term between them?

Remember that there is a difference between form as proceeding, and shape as superinduced;—the latter is either the death or the imprisonment of the thing;—the former is its self-witnessing and self-effected sphere of agency. Art would or should be the abridgment of nature. Now the fulness of nature is without character, as water is purest when without taste, smell, or color; but this is the highest, the apex only—it is not the whole. The object of art is to give the whole *ad hominem;* hence each step of nature hath its ideal, and hence the possibility of a climax up to the perfect form of a harmonized chaos.

To the idea of life victory or strife is necessary; as virtue consists not simply in the absence of vices, but in the overcoming of them. So it is in beauty. The sight of what is subordinated and conquered heightens the strength and the pleasure; and this should be exhibited by the artist either inclusively in his figure, or else out of it, and beside it to act by way of supplement and contrast. And with a view to this, remark the seeming identity of body and mind in infants, and thence the loveliness of the former; the commencing separation in boyhood, and the struggle of equilibrium in youth: thence onward the body is first simply indifferent; then demanding the translucency of the mind not to be worse than indifferent; and finally all that presents the body as body becoming almost of an excremental nature.[2]

[2] The discussion, like so much of Coleridge's work, seems to have been left incomplete.

OF PERSONS ONE WOULD WISH
TO HAVE SEEN

BY
WILLIAM HAZLITT

INTRODUCTORY NOTE

WILLIAM HAZLITT (1778–1830) was the son of a Unitarian minister. He went to Paris in his youth with the aim of becoming a painter, but gradually convinced himself that he could not excel in this art. He then turned to journalism and literature, and came into close association with Wordsworth, Coleridge, Lamb, Hunt, and others of the Romantic School. He was, however, of a sensitive and difficult temperament, and sooner or later quarreled with most of his friends. Though a worshiper of Napoleon, whose life he wrote, he was a strong liberal in politics, and supposed himself persecuted for his opinions.

Of all Hazlitt's voluminous writings, those which retain most value to-day are his literary criticisms and his essays on general topics. His clear and vivacious style rose at times to a rare beauty; and when the temper of his work was not marred by his touchiness and egotism he wrote with great charm and a delicate fancy.

The following essay shows in a high degree the tact and grace of Hazlitt's best writing, and his power of creating a distinctive atmosphere. It would be difficult to find a paper of this length which conveys so much of the special quality of the literary circle which added so much to the glory of English letters in the first quarter of the nineteenth century.

OF PERSONS ONE WOULD WISH
TO HAVE SEEN[1]

"Come like shadows—so depart."

LAMB it was, I think, who suggested this subject, as well as the defence of Guy Fawkes, which I urged him to execute. As, however, he would undertake neither, I suppose I must do both, a task for which he would have been much fitter, no less from the temerity than the felicity of his pen—

> "Never so sure our rapture to create
> As when it touch'd the brink of all we hate." [2]

Compared with him, I shall, I fear, make but a commonplace piece of business of it; but I should be loth the idea was entirely lost, and, besides, I may avail myself of some hints of his in the progress of it. I am sometimes, I suspect, a better reporter of the ideas of other people than expounder of my own. I pursue the one too far into paradox or mysticism; the others I am not bound to follow farther than I like, or than seems fair and reasonable.

On the question being started, Ayrton[3] said, "I suppose the two first persons you would choose to see would be the two greatest names in English literature, Sir Isaac Newton and Mr. Locke?" In this Ayrton, as usual, reckoned without his host. Everyone burst out a-laughing at the expression on Lamb's face, in which impatience was restrained by courtesy. "Yes, the greatest names," he stammered out hastily; "but they were not persons—not persons." "Not persons," said Ayrton, looking wise and foolish at the same time, afraid his triumph might be premature. "That is," re-

---

[1] Originally published in the "New Monthly Magazine," January, 1826. The conversation described is supposed to take place at one of Charles Lamb's "Wednesdays," at 16 Mitre Court Buildings, London.
[2] Pope, "Moral Essays," II., 51.   [3] William Ayrton, a musician.

267

joined Lamb, "not characters, you know. By Mr. Locke and Sir Isaac Newton, you mean the 'Essay on the Human Understanding,' and the 'Principia,' which we have to this day. Beyond their contents there is nothing personally interesting in the men. But what we want to see anyone *bodily* for, is when there is something peculiar, striking in the individuals, more than we can learn from their writings, and yet are curious to know. I dare say Locke and Newton were very like Kneller's portraits of them. But who could paint Shakespeare?" "Ay," retorted Ayrton, "there it is; then I suppose you would prefer seeing him and Milton instead?" "No," said Lamb, "neither. I have seen so much of Shakespeare on the stage and on book-stalls, in frontispieces and on mantelpieces, that I am quite tired of the everlasting repetition: and as to Milton's face, the impressions that have come down to us of it I do not like; it is too starched and puritanical; and I should be afraid of losing some of the manna of his poetry in the leaven of his countenance and the precisian's band and gown." "I shall guess no more," said Ayrton. "Who is it, then, you would like to see 'in his habit as he lived,' if you had your choice of the whole range of English literature?" Lamb then named Sir Thomas Browne and Fulke Greville, the friend of Sir Philip Sidney, as the two worthies whom he should feel the greatest pleasure to encounter on the floor of his apartment in their nightgowns and slippers and to exchange friendly greeting with them. At this Ayrton laughed outright, and conceived Lamb was jesting with him; but as no one followed his example, he thought there might be something in it, and waited for an explanation in a state of whimsical suspense. Lamb then (as well as I can remember a conversation that passed twenty years ago—how time slips!) went on as follows: "The reason why I pitch upon these two authors is, that their writings are riddles, and they themselves the most mysterious of personages. They resemble the soothsayers of old, who dealt in dark hints and doubtful oracles; and I should like to ask them the meaning of what no mortal but themselves, I should suppose, can fathom. There is Dr. Johnson: I have no curiosity, no strange uncertainty about him; he and Boswell together have pretty well let me into the secret of what passed through his mind. He and other writers like him are sufficiently explicit; my friends, whose repose I should be tempted to disturb (were it in my power), are implicit, inextricable, inscrutable.

> " 'And call up him who left half-told
> The story of Cambuscan bold.' [4]

"When I look at that obscure but gorgeous prose composition, the 'Urn-burial,' I seem to myself to look into a deep abyss, at the bottom of which are hid pearls and rich treasure; or it is like a stately labyrinth of doubt and withering speculation, and I would invoke the spirit of the author to lead me through it. Besides, who would not be curious to see the lineaments of a man who, having himself been twice married, wished that mankind were propagated like trees! [5] As to Fulke Greville, he is like nothing but one of his own 'Prologues spoken by the ghost of an old king of Ormus,' a truly formidable and inviting personage: his style is apocalyptical, cabalistical, a knot worthy of such an apparition to untie; and for the unravelling a passage or two, I would stand the brunt of an encounter with so portentous a commentator!" "I am afraid, in that case," said Ayrton, "that if the mystery were once cleared up, the merit might be lost;" and turning to me, whispered a friendly apprehension, that while Lamb continued to admire these old crabbed authors, he would never become a popular writer. Dr. Donne was mentioned as a writer of the same period, with a very interesting countenance, whose history was singular, and whose meaning was often quite as "uncomeatable," without a personal citation from the dead, as that of any of his contemporaries. The volume was produced; and while someone was expatiating on the exquisite simplicity and beauty of the portrait prefixed to the old edition, Ayrton got hold of the poetry, and exclaiming "What have we here?" read the following:

> " 'Here lies a She-Sun and a He-Moon there,
> She gives the best light to his sphere
> Or each is both and all, and so
> They unto one another nothing owe.' " [6]

There was no resisting this, till Lamb, seizing the volume, turned to the beautiful "Lines to His Mistress," dissuading her from ac-

---

[4] Milton, "Il Penseroso," 109.   [5] "Religio Medici," II., ix.
[6] "Epithalamion on the Lady Elizabeth and Count Palatine."

companying him abroad, and read them with suffused features and
a faltering tongue:

    " 'By our first strange and fatal interview,
    By all desires which thereof did ensue,
    By our long starving hopes, by that remorse
    Which my words' masculine perswasive force
    Begot in thee, and by the memory
    Of hurts, which spies and rivals threatened me,
    I calmely beg. But by thy father's wrath,
    By all paines which want and divorcement hath,
    I conjure thee; and all the oathes which I
    And thou have sworne to seale joynt constancy
    Here I unsweare, and overswear them thus—
    Thou shalt not love by ways so dangerous.
    Temper, O fair love! love's impetuous rage,
    Be my true mistris still, not my faign'd Page;
    I'll goe, and, by thy kinde leave, leave behinde
    Thee! onely worthy to nurse it in my minde.
    Thirst to come backe; O, if thou die before,
    My soule, from other lands to thee shall soare.
    Thy (else almighty) beautie cannot move
    Rage from the seas, nor thy love teach them love,
    Nor tame wild Boreas' harshnesse: thou hast reade
    How roughly hee in peeces shivered
    Fair Orithea, whom he swore he lov'd.
    Fair ill or good, 'tis madness to have prov'd
    Dangers unurg'd: Feed on this flattery,
    That absent lovers one in th' other be.
    Dissemble nothing, not a boy; nor change
    Thy bodie's habite, not minde; be not strange
    To thyeselfe onely. All will spie in thy face
    A blushing, womanly, discovering grace.
    Richly-cloath'd apes are call'd apes, and as soon
    Eclips'd as bright, we call the moone the moon.
    Men of France, changeable camelions,
    Spittles of diseases, shops of fashions,
    Love's fuellers, and the rightest company
    Of players, which upon the world's stage be,
    Will quickly know thee . . . O stay here! for thee
    England is onely a worthy gallerie,
    To walke in expectation; till from thence
    Our greatest King call thee to his presence.
    When I am gone, dreame me some happinesse,

Nor let thy lookes our long-hid love confesse,
Nor praise, nor dispraise me; nor blesse, nor curse
Openly love's force, nor in bed fright thy nurse
With midnight's startings, crying out, Oh, oh,
Nurse, oh my love is slaine, I saw him goe
O'er the white Alpes alone! I saw him, I,
Assail'd, fight, taken, stabb'd, bleed, fall, and die.
Augure me better chance, except dread Jove
Thinke it enough for me to have had thy love.' "

Someone then inquired of Lamb if we could not see from the
window the Temple-walk in which Chaucer used to take his
exercise; and on his name being put to the vote, I was pleased to find
that there was a general sensation in his favor in all but Ayrton,
who said something about the ruggedness of the metre, and even
objected to the quaintness of the orthography. I was vexed at this
superficial gloss, pertinaciously reducing everything to its own
trite level, and asked, "If he did not think it would be worth while
to scan the eye that had first greeted the Muse in that dim twilight
and early dawn of English literature; to see the head round which
the visions of fancy must have played like gleams of inspiration or
a sudden glory; to watch those lips that 'lisped in numbers, for the
numbers came'—as by a miracle, or as if the dumb should speak?
Nor was it alone that he had been the first to tune his native tongue
(however imperfectly to modern ears); but he was himself a noble,
manly character, standing before his age and striving to advance it;
a pleasant humorist withal, who has not only handed down to us the
living manners of his time, but had, no doubt, store of curious and
quaint devices, and would make as hearty a companion as mine
host of the Tabard. His interview with Petrarch is fraught with
interest. Yet I would rather have seen Chaucer in company with
the author of the 'Decameron,' and have heard them exchange
their best stories together—the 'Squire's Tale' against the story of
the 'Falcon,' the 'Wife of Bath's Prologue' against the 'Adventures of
Friar Albert.' How fine to see the high mysterious brow which
learning then wore, relieved by the gay, familiar tone of men of the
world, and by the courtesies of genius! Surely, the thoughts and
feelings which passed through the minds of these great revivers
of learning, these Cadmuses who sowed the teeth of letters, must

have stamped an expression on their features as different from the moderns as their books, and well worth the perusal. Dante," I continued, "is as interesting a person as his own Ugolino, one whose lineaments curiosity would as eagerly devour in order to penetrate his spirit, and the only one of the Italian poets I should care much to see. There is a fine portrait of Ariosto by no less a hand than Titian's; light, Moorish, spirited, but not answering our idea. The same artist's large colossal profile of Peter Aretine is the only likeness of the kind that has the effect of conversing with 'the mighty dead'; and this is truly spectral, ghastly, necromantic." Lamb put it to me if I should like to see Spenser as well as Chaucer; and I answered, without hesitation, "No; for that his beauties were ideal, visionary, not palpable or personal, and therefore connected with less curiosity about the man. His poetry was the essence of romance, a very halo round the bright orb of fancy; and the bringing in the individual might dissolve the charm. No tones of voice could come up to the mellifluous cadence of his verse; no form but of a winged angel could vie with the airy shapes he has described. He was (to our apprehensions) rather a 'creature of the element, that lived in the rainbow and played in the plighted clouds,' than an ordinary mortal. Or if he did appear, I should wish it to be as a mere vision, like one of his own pageants, and that he should pass by unquestioned like a dream or sound—

> " '——*That* was Arion crown'd:
> So went he playing on the wat'ry plain.' " [7]

Captain Burney muttered something about Columbus, and Martin Burney hinted at the Wandering Jew; but the last was set aside as spurious, and the first made over to the New World.

"I should like," said Mrs. Reynolds, "to have seen Pope talk with Patty Blount; and I *have* seen Goldsmith." Everyone turned round to look at Mrs. Reynolds, as if by so doing they could get a sight at Goldsmith.

"Where," asked a harsh, croaking voice, "was Dr. Johnson in the years 1745-46? He did not write anything that we know of, nor is there any account of him in Boswell during those two years. Was

[7] "The Faerie Queene," IV., xi. 23.

he in Scotland with the Pretender? He seems to have passed through the scenes in the Highlands in company with Boswell, many years after, 'with lack-lustre eye,' yet as if they were familiar to him, or associated in his mind with interests that he durst not explain. If so, it would be an additional reason for my liking him; and I would give something to have seen him seated in the tent with the youthful Majesty of Britain, and penning the Proclamation to all true subjects and adherents of the legitimate government."

"I thought," said Ayrton, turning short round upon Lamb, "that you of the Lake School did not like Pope?" "Not like Pope! My dear sir, you must be under a mistake—I can read him over and over forever!" "Why, certainly, the 'Essay on Man' must be allowed to be a masterpiece." "It may be so, but I seldom look into it." "Oh! then it's his satires you admire?" "No, not his satires, but his friendly epistles and his compliments." "Compliments! I did not know he ever made any." "The finest," said Lamb, "that were ever paid by the wit of man. Each of them is worth an estate for life—nay, is an immortality. There is that superb one to Lord Cornbury:

> " 'Despise low joys, low gains;
> Disdain whatever Cornbury disdains;
> Be virtuous, and be happy for your pains.' [8]

Was there ever more artful insinuation of idolatrous praise? And then that noble apotheosis of his friend Lord Mansfield (however little deserved), when, speaking of the House of Lords, he adds:

> " 'Conspicuous scene! another yet is nigh,
> (More silent far) where kings and poets lie;
> Where Murray (long enough his country's pride)
> Shall be no more than Tully or than Hyde!' [9]

And with what a fine turn of indignant flattery he addresses Lord Bolingbroke:

> " 'Why rail they then, if but one wreath of mine,
> O all-accomplish'd St. John, deck thy shrine?' [10]

Or turn," continued Lamb, with a slight hectic on his cheek and his eyes glistening, "to his list of early friends:

[8] "Imitations of Horace, Epistles," I., vi. 60–2.   [9] *Ibid.*, 50–3.
[10] "Epil. to Satires," II., 138–9.

> " 'But why then publish? Granville the polite,
>   And knowing Walsh, would tell me I could write;
>   Well-natured Garth inflamed with early praise,
>   And Congreve loved, and Swift endured my lays:
>   The courtly Talbot, Somers, Sheffield read,
>   Ev'n mitred Rochester would nod the head;
>   And St. John's self (great Dryden's friend before)
>   Received with open arms one poet more.
>   Happy my studies, if by these approved!
>   Happier their author, if by these beloved!
>   From these the world will judge of men and books,
>   Not from the Burnets, Oldmixons, and Cooks.' " [11]

Here his voice totally failed him, and throwing down the book, he said, "Do you think I would not wish to have been friends with such a man as this?"

"What say you to Dryden?" "He rather made a show of himself, and courted popularity in that lowest temple of fame, a coffee-shop, so as in some measure to vulgarize one's idea of him. Pope, on the contrary, reached the very *beau ideal* of what a poet's life should be; and his fame while living seemed to be an emanation from that which was to circle his name after death. He was so far enviable (and one would feel proud to have witnessed the rare spectacle in him) that he was almost the only poet and man of genius who met with his reward on this side of the tomb, who realized in friends, fortune, the esteem of the world, the most sanguine hopes of a youthful ambition, and who found that sort of patronage from the great during his lifetime which they would be thought anxious to bestow upon him after his death. Read Gay's verses to him on his supposed return from Greece, after his translation of Homer was finished, and say if you would not gladly join the bright procession that welcomed him home, or see it once more land at Whitehall stairs." "Still," said Mrs. Reynolds, "I would rather have seen him talking with Patty Blount, or riding by in a coronet-coach with Lady Mary Wortley Montague!"

Erasmus Phillips, who was deep in a game of piquet at the other end of the room, whispered to Martin Burney to ask if "Junius" would not be a fit person to invoke from the dead. "Yes," said Lamb, "provided he would agree to lay aside his mask."

[11] "Prol. to Satires," 135–146.

We were now at a stand for a short time, when Fielding was mentioned as a candidate; only one, however, seconded the proposition. "Richardson?" "By all means, but only to look at him through the glass door of his back shop, hard at work upon one of his novels (the most extraordinary contrast that ever was presented between an author and his works); not to let him come behind his counter, lest he should want you to turn customer, or to go upstairs with him, lest he should offer to read the first manuscript of 'Sir Charles Grandison,' which was originally written in eight-and-twenty volumes octavo, or get out the letters of his female correspondents, to prove that Joseph Andrews was low."

There was but one statesman in the whole of English history that anyone expressed the least desire to see—Oliver Cromwell, with his fine, frank, rough, pimply face and wily policy; and one enthusiast, John Bunyan, the immortal author of the "Pilgrim's Progress." It seemed that if he came into the room, dreams would follow him, and that each person would nod under his golden cloud, "nigh-sphered in heaven," a canopy as strange and stately as any in Homer.

Of all persons near our own time, Garrick's name was received with the greatest enthusiasm, who was proposed by Barron Field. He presently superseded both Hogarth and Handel, who had been talked of, but then it was on condition that he should act in tragedy and comedy, in the play and the farce, Lear and Wildair and Abel Drugger. What a "sight for sore eyes" that would be! Who would not part with a year's income at least, almost with a year of his natural life, to be present at it? Besides, as he could not act alone, and recitations are unsatisfactory things, what a troop he must bring with him—the silver-tongued Barry, and Quin, and Shuter and Weston, and Mrs. Clive and Mrs. Pritchard, of whom I have heard my father speak as so great a favorite when he was young. This would indeed be a revival of the dead, the restoring of art; and so much the more desirable, as such is the lurking scepticism mingled with our overstrained admiration of past excellence, that though we have the speeches of Burke, the portraits of Reynolds, the writings of Goldsmith, and the conversation of Johnson, to show what people could do at that period, and to confirm the universal testimony to the merits of Garrick; yet, as it was before our time, we have our misgivings, as if he was probably, after all, little better than a Bartlemy-fair actor, dressed out to play Macbeth in a scarlet coat and laced cocked-hat. For one, I should like to have seen and heard with my own eyes and ears. Certainly, by all accounts, if anyone was ever moved by the true histrionic *æstus,* it was Garrick. When he followed the Ghost in "Hamlet," he did not drop the sword, as most actors do, behind the scenes, but kept the point raised the whole way round, so fully was he possessed with the idea, or so anxious not to lose sight of his part for a moment. Once at a splendid dinner-party at Lord ———'s, they suddenly missed Garrick, and could not imagine what was become of him, till they were drawn to the window by the convulsive screams and peals of laughter of a young negro boy, who was rolling on the ground in an ecstasy of delight to see Garrick mimicking a turkey-cock in the courtyard, with his coat-tail stuck out behind, and in a seeming flutter of feathered rage and pride. Of our party only two persons present had seen the British Roscius; and they seemed as willing as the rest to renew their acquaintance with their old favorite.

We were interrupted in the hey-day and mid-career of this fanciful speculation, by a grumbler in a corner, who declared it was a shame to make all this rout about a mere player and farce-writer, to the neglect and exclusion of the fine old dramatists, the contemporaries and rivals of Shakespeare. Lamb said he had anticipated this objection when he had named the author of "Mustapha" and "Alaham"; and, out of caprice, insisted upon keeping him to represent the set, in preference to the wild, hare-brained enthusiast, Kit Marlowe; to the sexton of St. Ann's, Webster, with his melancholy yew-trees and death's-heads; to Decker, who was but a garrulous proser; to the voluminous Heywood; and even to Beaumont and Fletcher, whom we might offend by complimenting the wrong author on their joint productions. Lord Brooke, on the contrary, stood quite by himself, or, in Cowley's words, was "a vast species alone." Someone hinted at the circumstance of his being a lord, which rather startled Lamb, but he said a ghost would perhaps dispense with strict etiquette, on being regularly addressed by his title. Ben Jonson divided our suffrages pretty equally. Some were afraid he would begin to traduce Shakespeare, who was not present to defend himself. "If he grows disagreeable," it was whispered aloud, "there is Godwin can match him." At length, his romantic visit to Drummond of Hawthornden was mentioned, and turned the scale in his favor.

Lamb inquired if there was anyone that was hanged that I would choose to mention? And I answered, Eugene Aram.[12] The name of the "Admirable Crichton" was suddenly started as a splendid example of waste talents, so different from the generality of his countrymen. This choice was mightily approved by a North-Briton present, who declared himself descended from that prodigy of learning and accomplishment, and said he had family plate in his possession as vouchers for the fact, with the initials A. C.—"Admirable Crichton"! Hunt laughed, or rather roared, as heartily at this as I should think he has done for many years.

The last-named Mitre-courtier[13] then wished to know whether there were any metaphysicians to whom one might be tempted to apply the wizard spell? I replied, there were only six in modern times deserving the name—Hobbes, Berkeley, Butler, Hartley, Hume, Leibnitz; and perhaps Jonathan Edwards, a Massachusetts man.[14] As to the French, who talked fluently of having created this science, there was not a tittle in any of their writings that was not to be found literally in the authors I had mentioned. [Horne Tooke, who might have a claim to come in under the head of grammar, was still living.] None of these names seemed to excite much interest, and I did not plead for the reappearance of those who might be thought best fitted by the abstracted nature of their studies for the present spiritual and disembodied state, and who, even while on this living stage, were nearly divested of common flesh and blood. As Ayrton, with an uneasy, fidgety face, was about to put some question about Mr. Locke and Dugald Stewart, he was prevented by

[12] See "Newgate Calendar" for 1758.—H.

[13] Lamb at this time occupied chambers in Mitre Court, Fleet Street.—H.

[14] Bacon is not included in this list, nor do I know where he should come in. It is not easy to make room for him and his reputation together. This great and celebrated man in some of his works recommends it to pour a bottle of claret into the ground of a morning, and to stand over it, inhaling the perfumes. So he sometimes enriched the dry and barren soil of speculation with the fine aromatic spirit of his genius. His essays and his "Advancement of Learning" are works of vast depth and scope of observation. The last, though it contains no positive discoveries, is a noble chart of the human intellect, and a guide to all future inquirers.—H.

Martin Burney, who observed, "If J——— was here, he would undoubtedly be for having up those profound and redoubted socialists, Thomas Aquinas and Duns Scotus." I said this might be fair enough in him who had read, or fancied he had read, the original works, but I did not see how we could have any right to call up these authors to give an account of themselves in person till we had looked into their writings.

By this time it should seem that some rumor of our whimsical deliberation had got wind, and had disturbed the *irritabile genus* in their shadowy abodes, for we received messages from several candidates that we had just been thinking of. Gray declined our invitation, though he had not yet been asked; Gay offered to come, and bring in his hand the Duchess of Bolton, the original Polly; Steele and Addison left their cards as Captain Sentry and Sir Roger de Coverley; Swift came in and sat down without speaking a word, and quitted the room as abruptly; Otway and Chatterton were seen lingering on the opposite side of the Styx, but could not muster enough between them to pay Charon his fare; Thomson fell asleep in the boat, and was rowed back again; and Burns sent a low fellow, one John Barleycorn, an old companion of his, who had conducted him to the other world, to say that he had during his lifetime been drawn out of his retirement as a show, only to be made an exciseman of, and that he would rather remain where he was. He desired, however, to shake hands by his representative—the hand, thus held out, was in a burning fever, and shook prodigiously.

The room was hung round with several portraits of eminent painters. While we were debating whether we should demand speech with these masters of mute eloquence, whose features were so familiar to us, it seemed that all at once they glided from their frames, and seated themselves at some little distance from us. There was Leonardo, with his majestic beard and watchful eye, having a bust of Archimedes before him; next him was Raphael's graceful head turned round to the Fornarina; and on his other side was Lucretia Borgia, with calm, golden locks; Michael Angelo had placed the model of St. Peter's on the table before him; Correggio had an angel at his side; Titian was seated with his mistress between himself and Giorgione; Guido was accompanied by his own Aurora,

who took a dice-box from him; Claude held a mirror in his hand;
Rubens patted a beautiful panther (led in by a satyr) on the head;
Vandyke appeared as his own Paris, and Rembrandt was hid under
furs, gold chains, and jewels, which Sir Joshua eyed closely, holding
his hand so as to shade his forehead. Not a word was spoken; and
as we rose to do them homage, they still presented the same surface
to the view. Not being *bona-fide* representations of living people, we
got rid of the splendid apparitions by signs and dumb show. As soon
as they had melted into thin air, there was a loud noise at the outer
door, and we found it was Giotto, Cimabue, and Ghirlandajo, who
had been raised from the dead by their earnest desire to see their
illustrious successors—

> "Whose names on earth
> In Fame's eternal record live for aye!"

Finding them gone, they had no ambition to be seen after them, and
mournfully withdrew. "Egad!" said Lamb, "these are the very
fellows I should like to have had some talk with, to know how
they could see to paint when all was dark around them."

"But shall we have nothing to say," interrogated G. J——, "to the
'Legend of Good Women'?" "Name, name, Mr. J——," cried
Hunt in a boisterous tone of friendly exultation, "name as many as
you please, without reserve or fear of molestation!" J—— was perplexed between so many amiable recollections, that the name of the
lady of his choice expired in a pensive whiff of his pipe; and Lamb
impatiently declared for the Duchess of Newcastle. Mrs. Hutchinson
was no sooner mentioned, than she carried the day from the Duchess.
We were the less solicitous on this subject of filling up the post-
humous lists of good women, as there was already one in the room
as good, as sensible, and in all respects as exemplary, as the best of
them could be for their lives! "I should like vastly to have seen
Ninon de l'Enclos," said that incomparable person; and this immediately put us in mind that we had neglected to pay honor due
to our friends on the other side of the Channel: Voltaire, the patri-
arch of levity, and Rousseau, the father of sentiment; Montaigne and
Rabelais (great in wisdom and in wit); Molière and that illustrious
group that are collected round him (in the print of that subject) to

hear him read his comedy of the "Tartuffe" at the house of Ninon; Racine, La Fontaine, Rochefoucauld, St. Evremont, etc.

"There is one person," said a shrill, querulous voice, "I would rather see than all these—Don Quixote!"

"Come, come!" said Hunt; "I thought we should have no heroes, real or fabulous. What say you, Mr. Lamb? Are you for eking out your shadowy list with such names as Alexander, Julius Cæsar, Tamerlane, or Genghis Khan?" "Excuse me," said Lamb; "on the subject of characters in active life, plotters and disturbers of the world, I have a crotchet of my own, which I beg leave to reserve." "No, no! come out with your worthies!" "What do you think of Guy Fawkes and Judas Iscariot?" Hunt turned an eye upon him like a wild Indian, but cordial and full of smothered glee. "Your most exquisite reason!" was echoed on all sides; and Ayrton thought that Lamb had now fairly entangled himself. "Why, I cannot but think," retorted he of the wistful countenance, "that Guy Fawkes, that poor, fluttering, annual scarecrow of straw and rags, is an ill-used gentleman. I would give something to see him sitting pale and emaciated, surrounded by his matches and his barrels of gunpowder, and expecting the moment that was to transport him to Paradise for his heroic self-devotion; but if I say any more, there is that fellow Godwin will make something of it. And as to Judas Iscariot, my reason is different. I would fain see the face of him who, having dipped his hand in the same dish with the Son of Man, could afterwards betray him. I have no conception of such a thing; nor have I ever seen any picture (not even Leonardo's very fine one) that gave me the least idea of it." "You have said enough, Mr. Lamb, to justify your choice."

"Oh! ever right, Menenius—ever right!"

"There is only one other person I can ever think of after this," continued Lamb;[15] but without mentioning a name that once put on a semblance of mortality. "If Shakespeare was to come into the room, we should all rise up to meet him; but if that person was to come into it, we should all fall down and try to kiss the hem of his garment!"

As a lady present seemed now to get uneasy at the turn the con-

[15] In the original form of the essay, this speech is given to Hunt.

versation had taken, we rose up to go. The morning broke with that dim, dubious light by which Giotto, Cimabue, and Ghirlandajo must have seen to paint their earliest works; and we parted to meet again and renew similar topics at night, the next night, and the night after that, till that night overspread Europe which saw no dawn. The same event, in truth, broke up our little congress that broke up the great one. But that was to meet again: our deliberations have never been resumed.

DEATHS OF LITTLE CHILDREN

ON THE REALITIES OF IMAGINATION

BY

LEIGH HUNT

INTRODUCTORY NOTE

JAMES HENRY LEIGH HUNT (1784–1859) was the son of a clergyman from the West Indies. Like Lamb and Coleridge, he was educated at Christ's Hospital in London, and began writing poetry while still a boy. He attracted attention early by his theatrical criticisms; and in 1808 he joined his brother in founding a weekly newspaper, the "Examiner." During the thirteen years for which he contributed to this paper he exerted a wholesome influence in journalism, raising the tone of the press, showing great independence and tolerance, and fighting vigorously for liberal principles. He earned the distinction of two years' imprisonment for telling plain truths about the Prince Regent; and his prosecution by the Government made him many distinguished friends. Some years later he went to Italy to join Shelley and Byron in the establishment of a new magazine; and it was on returning from Leghorn, where he had gone to meet Hunt, that Shelley was drowned. The new magazine was soon abandoned, Hunt returned to England, engaged in various periodical and other literary enterprises from which he seldom earned enough to meet his expenses, and struggled on cheerfully and courageously to the age of seventy-five.

Hunt's poetry is pretty, fanciful, and musical, but, with the exception of one or two pieces, is now little read. Much of his prose work is merely high-toned journalism, the interest of which has passed with its occasion. But among his familiar essays, from which the two papers here printed are taken, there are many little masterpieces, suffused with his cheerful optimistic spirit, and expressed always gracefully and sometimes exquisitely. "No man," says James Russell Lowell, "has ever understood the delicacies and luxuries of language better than he; and his thoughts often have all the rounded grace and shifting luster of a dove's neck. . . . He was as pure-minded a man as ever lived, and a critic whose subtlety of discrimination and whose soundness of judgment, supported as it was on a broad basis of truly liberal scholarship, have hardly yet won fitting appreciation."

DEATHS OF LITTLE CHILDREN

A GRECIAN philosopher being asked why he wept for the death of his son, since the sorrow was in vain, replied, "I weep on that account." And his answer became his wisdom. It is only for sophists to contend that we, whose eyes contain the fountains of tears, need never give way to them. It would be unwise not to do so on some occasions. Sorrow unlocks them in her balmy moods. The first bursts may be bitter and overwhelming; but the soil on which they pour would be worse without them. They refresh the fever of the soul—the dry misery which parches the countenance into furrows, and renders us liable to our most terrible "flesh-quakes."

There are sorrows, it is true, so great, that to give them some of the ordinary vents is to run a hazard of being overthrown. These we must rather strengthen ourselves to resist, or bow quietly and drily down, in order to let them pass over us, as the traveller does the wind of the desert. But where we feel that tears would relieve us, it is false philosophy to deny ourselves at least that first refreshment; and it is always false consolation to tell people that because they cannot help a thing, they are not to mind it. The true way is, to let them grapple with the unavoidable sorrow, and try to win it into gentleness by a reasonable yielding. There are griefs so gentle in their very nature that it would be worse than false heroism to refuse them a tear. Of this kind are the deaths of infants. Particular circumstances may render it more or less advisable to indulge in grief for the loss of a little child; but, in general, parents should be no more advised to repress their first tears on such an occasion, than to repress their smiles towards a child surviving, or to indulge in any other sympathy. It is an appeal to the same gentle tenderness; and such appeals are never made in vain. The end of them is an acquittal from the harsher bonds of affliction—from the tying down of the spirit to one melancholy idea.

It is the nature of tears of this kind, however strongly they may gush forth, to run into quiet waters at last. We cannot easily, for the whole course of our lives, think with pain of any good and kind person whom we have lost. It is the divine nature of their qualities to conquer pain and death itself; to turn the memory of them into pleasure; to survive with a placid aspect in our imaginations. We are writing at this moment just opposite a spot which contains the grave of one inexpressibly dear to us. We see from our window the trees about it, and the church spire. The green fields lie around. The clouds are travelling overhead, alternately taking away the sunshine and restoring it. The vernal winds, piping of the flowery summer-time, are nevertheless calling to mind the far-distant and dangerous ocean, which the heart that lies in that grave had many reasons to think of. And yet the sight of this spot does not give us pain. So far from it, it is the existence of that grave which doubles every charm of the spot; which links the pleasures of our child-hood and manhood together; which puts a hushing tenderness in the winds, and a patient joy upon the landscape; which seems to unite heaven and earth, mortality and immortality, the grass of the tomb and the grass of the green field; and gives a more maternal aspect to the whole kindness of nature. It does not hinder gaiety it-self. Happiness was what its tenant, through all her troubles, would have diffused. To diffuse happiness, and to enjoy it, is not only carrying on her wishes, but realising her hopes; and gaiety, freed from its only pollutions, malignity and want of sympathy, is but a child playing about the knees of its mother.

The remembered innocence and endearments of a child stand us instead of virtues that have died older. Children have not exercised the voluntary offices of friendship; they have not chosen to be kind and good to us; nor stood by us, from conscious will, in the hour of adversity. But they have shared their pleasures and pains with us as well as they could; the interchange of good offices between us has, of necessity, been less mingled with the troubles of the world; the sorrow arising from their death is the only one which we can asso-ciate with their memories. These are happy thoughts that cannot die. Our loss may always render them pensive; but they will not always be painful. It is a part of the benignity of Nature that pain does not survive like pleasure, at any time, much less where the cause of it is an innocent one. The smile will remain reflected by memory, as the moon reflects the light upon us when the sun has gone into heaven.

When writers like ourselves quarrel with earthly pain (we mean writers of the same intentions, without implying, of course, anything about abilities or otherwise), they are misunderstood if they are supposed to quarrel with pains of every sort. This would be idle and effeminate. They do not pretend, indeed, that humanity might not wish, if it could, to be entirely free from pain; for it endeavours, at all times, to turn pain into pleasure: or at least to set off the one with the other, to make the former a zest and the latter a refreshment. The most unaffected dignity of suffering does this, and, if wise, acknowledges it. The greatest benevolence towards others, the most unselfish relish of their pleasures, even at its own expense, does but look to increasing the general stock of happiness, though content, if it could, to have its identity swallowed up in that splendid contemplation. We are far from meaning that this is to be called selfishness. We are far, indeed, from thinking so, or of so confounding words. But neither is it to be called pain when most unselfish, if disinterestedness be truly understood. The pain that is in it softens into pleasure, as the darker hue of the rainbow melts into the brighter. Yet even if a harsher line is to be drawn between the pain and pleasure of the most unselfish mind (and ill-health, for instance, may draw it), we should not quarrel with it if it contributed to the general mass of comfort, and were of a nature which general kindliness could not avoid. Made as we are, there are certain pains without which it would be difficult to conceive certain great and overbalancing pleasures. We may conceive it possible for beings to be made entirely happy; but in our composition something of pain seems to be a necessary ingredient, in order that the materials may turn to as fine account as possible, though our clay, in the course of ages and experience, may be refined more and more. We may get rid of the worst earth, though not of earth itself.

Now the liability to the loss of children—or rather what renders us sensible of it, the occasional loss itself—seems to be one of these necessary bitters thrown into the cup of humanity. We do not mean

that every one must lose one of his children in order to enjoy the rest;
or that every individual loss afflicts us in the same proportion. We
allude to the deaths of infants in general. These might be as few
as we could render them. But if none at all ever took place, we
should regard every little child as a man or woman secured; and it
will easily be conceived what a world of endearing cares and hopes
this security would endanger. The very idea of infancy would lose
its continuity with us. Girls and boys would be future men and
women, not present children. They would have attained their full
growth in our imaginations, and might as well have been men and
women at once. On the other hand, those who have lost an infant,
are never, as it were, without an infant child. They are the only persons who, in one sense, retain it always, and they furnish their
neighbours with the same idea. The other children grow up to
manhood and womanhood, and suffer all the changes of mortality.
This one alone is rendered an immortal child. Death has arrested
it with his kindly harshness, and blessed it into an eternal image
of youth and innocence.

Of such as these are the pleasantest shapes that visit our fancy
and our hopes. They are the ever-smiling emblems of joy; the
prettiest pages that wait upon imagination. Lastly, "Of these are
the kingdom of heaven." Wherever there is a province of that
benevolent and all-accessible empire, whether on earth or elsewhere,
such are the gentle spirits that must inhabit it. To such simplicity,
or the resemblance of it, must they come. Such must be the ready
confidence of their hearts and creativeness of their fancy. And so
ignorant must they be of the "knowledge of good and evil," losing
their discernment of that self-created trouble, by enjoying the garden
before them, and not being ashamed of what is kindly and innocent.

ON THE REALITIES OF
IMAGINATION

THERE is not a more unthinking way of talking than to say such and such pains and pleasures are only imaginary, and therefore to be got rid of or under-valued accordingly. There is nothing imaginary in the common acceptation of the word. The logic of Moses in the *Vicar of Wakefield* is good argument here:—"Whatever is, is." Whatever touches us, whatever moves us, does touch and does move us. We recognise the reality of it, as we do that of a hand in the dark. We might as well say that a sight which makes us laugh, or a blow which brings tears into our eyes, is imaginary, as that anything else is imaginary which makes us laugh or weep. We can only judge of things by their effects. Our perception constantly deceives us, in things with which we suppose ourselves perfectly conversant; but our reception of their effect is a different matter. Whether we are materialists or immaterialists, whether things be about us or within us, whether we think the sun is a substance, or only the image of a divine thought, an idea, a thing imaginary, we are equally agreed as to the notion of its warmth. But on the other hand, as this warmth is felt differently by different temperaments, so what we call imaginary things affect different minds. What we have to do is not to deny their effect, because we do not feel in the same proportion, or whether we even feel it at all; but to see whether our neighbours may not be moved. If they are, there is, to all intents and purposes, a moving cause. But we do not see it? No;—neither perhaps do they. They only feel it; they are only sentient,—a word which implies the sight given to the imagination by the feelings. But what do you mean, we may ask in return, by seeing? Some rays of light come in contact with the eye; they bring a sensation to it; in a word, they touch it; and the impression left by this touch we call sight. How far does this differ in effect from the impression left by any other touch, however mysterious? An ox knocked down by a butcher, and a man knocked down by a fit of apoplexy, equally feel themselves compelled to drop. The tickling of a straw and of a comedy equally move the muscles about the mouth. The look of a beloved eye will so thrill the frame, that old philosophers have had recourse to a doctrine of beams and radiant particles flying from one sight to another. In fine, what is contact itself, and why does it affect us? There is no one cause more mysterious than another, if we look into it.

Nor does the question concern us like moral causes. We may be content to know the earth by its fruits; but how to increase and improve them is a more attractive study. If, instead of saying that the causes which moved in us this or that pain or pleasure were imaginary, people were to say that the causes themselves were removable, they would be nearer the truth. When a stone trips us up, we do not fall to disputing its existence: we put it out of the way. In like manner, when we suffer from what is called an imaginary pain, our business is not to canvass the reality of it. Whether there is any cause or not in that or any other perception, or whether everything consist not in what is called effect, it is sufficient for us that the effect is real. Our sole business is to remove those second causes, which always accompany the original idea. As in deliriums, for instance, it would be idle to go about persuading the patient that he did not behold the figures he says he does. He might reasonably ask us, if he could, how we know anything about the matter; or how we can be sure that in the infinite wonders of the universe certain realities may not become apparent to certain eyes, whether diseased or not. Our business would be to put him into that state of health in which human beings are not diverted from their offices and comforts by a liability to such imaginations. The best reply to his question would be, that such a morbidity is clearly no more a fit state for a human being than a disarranged or incomplete state of works is for a watch; and that seeing the general tendency of nature to this completeness or state of comfort, we naturally conclude that the imaginations in question, whether substantial or not, are at least not of the same lasting or prevailing description.

We do not profess metaphysics. We are indeed so little conversant with the masters of that art, that we are never sure whether we are using even its proper terms. All that we may know on the subject comes to us from some reflection and some experience; and this all may be so little as to make a metaphysician smile; which, if he be a true one, he will do good-naturedly. The pretender will take occasion, from our very confession, to say that we know nothing. Our faculty, such as it is, is rather instinctive than reasoning; rather physical than metaphysical; rather sentient because it loves much, than because it knows much; rather calculated by a certain retention of boyhood, and by its wanderings in the green places of thought, to light upon a piece of the old golden world, than to tire ourselves, and conclude it unattainable, by too wide and scientific a search. We pretend to see farther than none but the worldly and the malignant. And yet those who see farther may not see so well. We do not blind our eyes with looking upon the sun in the heavens. We believe it to be there, but we find its light upon earth also; and we would lead humanity, if we could, out of misery and coldness into the shine of it. Pain might still be there; must be so, as long as we are mortal;

"For oft we still must weep, since we are human:"

but it should be pain for the sake of others, which is noble; not unnecessary pain inflicted by or upon them, which it is absurd not to remove. The very pains of mankind struggle towards pleasures; and such pains as are proper for them have this inevitable accompaniment of true humanity,—that they cannot but realise a certain gentleness of enjoyment. Thus the true bearer of pain would come round to us; and he would not grudge us a share of his burden, though in taking from his trouble it might diminish his pride. Pride is but a bad pleasure at the expense of others. The great object of humanity is to enrich everybody. If it is a task destined not to succeed, it is a good one from its very nature; and fulfils at least a glad destiny of its own. To look upon it austerely is in reality the reverse of austerity. It is only such an impatience of the want of pleasure as leads us to grudge it in others; and this impatience itself, if the sufferer knew how to use it, is but another impulse, in the general yearning, towards an equal wealth of enjoyment.

But we shall be getting into other discussions.—The ground-work of all happiness is health. Take care of this ground; and the doleful imaginations that come to warn us against its abuse will avoid it. Take care of this ground, and let as many glad imaginations throng to it as possible. Read the magical works of the poets, and they will come. If you doubt their existence, ask yourself whether you feel pleasure at the idea of them; whether you are moved into delicious smiles, or tears as delicious. If you are, the result is the same to you, whether they exist or not. It is not mere words to say that he who goes through a rich man's park, and sees things in it which never bless the mental eyesight of the possessor, is richer than he. He is richer. More results of pleasure come home to him. The ground is actually more fertile to him: the place haunted with finer shapes. He has more servants to come at his call, and administer to him with full hands. Knowledge, sympathy, imagination, are all divining-rods, with which he discovers treasure. Let a painter go through the grounds, and he will see not only the general colours of green and brown, but their combinations and contrasts, and the modes in which they might again be combined and contrasted. He will also put figures in the landscape if there are none there, flocks and herds, or a solitary spectator, or Venus lying with her white body among the violets and primroses. Let a musician go through, and he will hear "differences discreet" in the notes of the birds and the lapsing of the water-fall. He will fancy a serenade of wind instruments in the open air at a lady's window, with a voice rising through it; or the horn of the hunter; or the musical cry of the hounds,

> "Matched in mouth like bells,
> Each under each;"

or a solitary voice in a bower, singing for an expected lover; or the chapel organ, waking up like the fountain of the winds. Let a poet go through the grounds and he will heighten and increase all these sounds and images. He will bring the colours from heaven, and put an unearthly meaning into the voice. He will have stories of the sylvan inhabitants; will shift the population through infinite varieties; will put a sentiment upon every sight and sound; will be human, romantic, supernatural; will make all nature send tribute into that spot.

We may say of the love of nature what Shakespeare says of another love, that it

> "Adds a precious seeing to the eye."

And we may say also, upon the like principle, that it adds a precious hearing to the ear. This and imagination, which ever follows upon it, are the two purifiers of our sense, which rescue us from the deafening babble of common cares, and enable us to hear all the affectionate voices of earth and heaven. The starry orbs, lapsing about in their smooth and sparkling dance, sing to us. The brooks talk to us of solitude. The birds are the animal spirits of nature, carolling in the air, like a careless lass.

> "The gentle gales,
> Fanning their odoriferous wings, dispense
> Native perfumes; and whisper whence they stole
> Those balmy spoils."—*Paradise Lost,* book iv.

The poets are called creators, because with their magical words they bring forth to our eyesight the abundant images and beauties of creation. They put them there, if the reader pleases; and so are literally creators. But whether put there or discovered, whether created or invented (for invention means nothing but finding out), there they are. If they touch us, they exist to as much purpose as anything else which touches us. If a passage in *King Lear* brings the tears into our eyes, it is real as the touch of a sorrowful hand. If the flow of a song of Anacreon's intoxicates us, it is as true to a pulse within us as the wine he drank. We hear not their sounds with ears, nor see their sights with eyes; but we hear and see both so truly, that we are moved with pleasure; and the advantage, nay even the test, of seeing and hearing, at any time, is not in the seeing and hearing, but in the ideas we realise, and the pleasure we derive. Intellectual objects, therefore, inasmuch as they come home to us, are as true a part of the stock of nature as visible ones; and they are infinitely more abundant. Between the tree of a country clown and the tree of a Milton or Spenser, what a difference in point of productiveness! Between the plodding of a sexton through a church-yard and the walk of a Gray, what a difference! What a difference

between the Bermudas of a ship-builder and the Bermoothes of
Shakespeare! the isle

> "Full of noises,
> Sounds, and sweet airs, that give delight, and hurt not;"

the isle of elves and fairies, that chased the tide to and fro on the
sea-shore; of coral-bones and the knell of sea-nymphs; of spirits
dancing on the sands, and singing amidst the hushes of the wind;
of Caliban, whose brute nature enchantment had made poetical;
of Ariel, who lay in cowslip bells, and rode upon the bat; of Miranda,
who wept when she saw Ferdinand work so hard, and begged him,
to let her help; telling him,

> "I am your wife, if you will marry me;
> If not, I'll die your maid. To be your fellow
> You may deny me; but I'll be your servant,
> Whether you will or no."

Such are the discoveries which the poets make for us; worlds to
which that of Columbus was but a handful of brute matter. America
began to be richer for us the other day, when Humboldt came back
and told us of its luxuriant and gigantic vegetation; of the myriads
of shooting lights, which revel at evening in the southern sky; and
of that grand constellation, at which Dante seems to have made so
remarkable a guess (*Purgatorio,* cant. i., v. 22). The natural warmth
of the Mexican and Peruvian genius, set free from despotism, will
soon do all the rest for it; awaken the sleeping riches of its eyesight,
and call forth the glad music of its affections.

Imagination enriches everything. A great library contains not
only books, but

> "The assembled souls of all that men held wise."
> —Davenant.

The moon is Homer's and Shakespeare's moon, as well as the one
we look at. The sun comes out of his chamber in the east, with a
sparkling eye, "rejoicing like a bridegroom." The commonest thing
becomes like Aaron's rod, that budded. Pope called up the spirits of
the Cabala to wait upon a lock of hair, and justly gave it the honours
of a constellation; for he has hung it, sparkling for ever in the eyes

of posterity. A common meadow is a sorry thing to a ditcher or a coxcomb; but by the help of its dues from imagination and the love of nature, the grass brightens for us, the air soothes us, we feel as we did in the daisied hours of childhood. Its verdures, its sheep, its hedge-row elms,—all these, and all else which sight, and sound, and associations can give it, are made to furnish a treasure of pleasant thoughts. Even brick and mortar are vivified, as of old, at the harp of Orpheus. A metropolis becomes no longer a mere collection of houses or of trades. It puts on all the grandeur of its history, and its literature; its towers, and rivers; its art, and jewellery, and foreign wealth; its multitude of human beings all intent upon excitement, wise or yet to learn; the huge and sullen dignity of its canopy of smoke by day; the wide gleam upwards of its lighted lustre at night-time; and the noise of its many chariots, heard at the same hour, when the wind sets gently towards some quiet suburb.

ON THE TRAGEDIES OF SHAKSPERE

BY

CHARLES LAMB

INTRODUCTORY NOTE

CHARLES LAMB (1775–1834) was born in the Temple, London, where his father was a clerk to one of the benchers. He was a schoolmate of Coleridge's at Christ's Hospital, and shortly after leaving school he entered the India House, on the staff of which he worked for thirty-three years. He never married, but lived with his sister Mary as her guardian on account of her inherited tendency to insanity. His friends included (besides Coleridge) Wordsworth, Hunt, Hazlitt, Southey, and many others, and his letters as well as the works he published reveal one of the most attractive personalities in literature.

Lamb wrote a handful of poems marked by delicate sentiment, and made some rather unsuccessful attempts at drama. But his name rests on his essays,—the familiar essays on a great variety of subjects, whimsical, humorous, graceful, quaint; the critical essays, sensitive, illuminating, in the best sense appreciative. He did much for the revival of interest in the Elizabethan drama; and the essay "On the Tragedies of Shakspere," is the most distinguished single piece of critical writing that came from his pen. The main thesis of the paper—"that the plays of Shakespeare are less calculated for performance on a stage than those of almost any dramatist whatever"—is, of course, paradoxical; but Lamb's method was not logical or philosophical as his friend Coleridge's aimed at being. His criticism is a frank expression of his personal feelings; it is in the proper sense "impressionistic" criticism; and it gets its value from the quality and flavor of the author's taste and personality. It is thus pure literature—the expression of the man himself—rather than scientific analysis; and in this branch of writing there is nothing in English more delightful.

ON THE TRAGEDIES OF
SHAKSPERE

CONSIDERED WITH REFERENCE TO THEIR FITNESS FOR
STAGE REPRESENTATION

TAKING a turn the other day in the Abbey, I was struck
with the affected attitude of a figure, which I do not remember to have seen before, and which upon examination proved
to be a whole-length of the celebrated Mr. Garrick. Though I would
not go so far with some good Catholics abroad as to shut players
altogether out of consecrated ground, yet I own I was not a little
scandalised at the introduction of theatrical airs and gestures into a
place set apart to remind us of the saddest realities. Going nearer,
I found inscribed under this harlequin figure the following
lines:—

> To paint fair Nature, by divine command,
> Her magic pencil in his glowing hand,
> A Shakspere rose: then, to expand his fame
> Wide o'er this breathing world, a Garrick came.
> Though sunk in death the forms the Poet drew,
> The Actor's genius made them breathe anew;
> Though, like the bard himself, in night they lay,
> Immortal Garrick call'd them back to day:
> And till Eternity with power sublime
> Shall mark the mortal hour of hoary Time,
> Shakspere and Garrick like twin-stars shall shine,
> And earth irradiate with a beam divine.

It would be an insult to my readers' understandings to attempt
anything like a criticism on this farrago of false thoughts and nonsense. But the reflection it led me into was a kind of wonder, how,
from the days of the actor here celebrated to our own, it should have
been the fashion to compliment every performer in his turn, that has
had the luck to please the town in any of the great characters of

Shakspere, with a notion of possessing a *mind congeniai to the poet's;* how people should come thus unaccountably to confound the power of originating poetical images and conceptions with the faculty of being able to read or recite the same when put into words;[1] or what connection that absolute mastery over the heart and soul of man, which a great dramatic poet possesses, has with those low tricks upon the eye and ear, which a player by observing a few general effects, which some common passion, as grief, anger, etc., usually has upon the gestures and exterior, can easily compass. To know the internal workings and movements of a great mind, of an Othello or a Hamlet, for instance, the *when* and the *why* and the *how far* they should be moved; to what pitch a passion is becoming; to give the reins and to pull in the curb exactly at the moment when the drawing in or the slacking is most graceful; seems to demand a reach of intellect of a vastly different extent from that which is employed upon the bare imitation of the signs of these passions in the countenance or gesture, which signs are usually observed to be most lively and emphatic in the weaker sort of minds, and which signs can after all but indicate some passion, as I said before, anger, or grief, generally; but of the motives and grounds of the passion, wherein it differs from the same passion in low and vulgar natures, of these the actor can give no more idea by his face or gesture than the eye (without a metaphor) can speak, or the muscles utter intelligible sounds. But such is the instantaneous nature of the impressions which we take in at the eye and ear at a playhouse, compared with the slow apprehension oftentimes of the understanding in reading, that we are apt not only to sink the play-writer in the consideration which we pay to the actor, but even to identify in our minds in a perverse manner, the actor with the character which he represents. It is difficult for a frequent play-goer to disembarrass the idea of Hamlet from the person and voice of Mr. K. We speak of Lady Macbeth, while we are in reality thinking of Mrs. S. Nor is this confusion incidental alone to unlettered persons, who, not possessing

[1] It is observable that we fall into this confusion only in *dramatic* recitations. We never dream that the gentleman who reads Lucretius in public with great applause, is therefore a great poet and philosopher; nor do we find that Tom Davies, the bookseller, who is recorded to have recited the "Paradise Lost" better than any man in England in his day (though I cannot help thinking there must be some mistake in this tradition) was therefore, by his intimate friends, set upon a level with Milton.

the advantage of reading, are necessarily dependent upon the stage-player for all the pleasure which they can receive from the drama, and to whom the very idea of *what an author is* cannot be made comprehensible without some pain and perplexity of mind: the error is one from which persons otherwise not meanly lettered find it almost impossible to extricate themselves.

Never let me be so ungrateful as to forget the very high degree of satisfaction which I received some years back from seeing for the first time a tragedy of Shakspere performed, in which these two great performers sustained the principal parts. It seemed to embody and realise conceptions which had hitherto assumed no distinct shape. But dearly do we pay all our life afterwards for this juvenile pleasure, this sense of distinctness. When the novelty is past, we find to our cost that, instead of realising an idea, we have only materialised and brought down a fine vision to the standard of flesh and blood. We have let go a dream, in quest of an unattainable substance.

How cruelly this operates upon the mind, to have its free conceptions thus cramped and pressed down to the measure of a strait-lacing actuality, may be judged from that delightful sensation of freshness, with which we turn to those plays of Shakspere which have escaped being performed, and to those passages in the acting plays of the same writer which have happily been left out of the performance. How far the very custom of hearing anything *spouted,* withers and blows upon a fine passage, may be seen in those speeches from *Henry the Fifth,* etc., which are current in the mouths of school-boys from their being to be found in *Enfield Speakers,* and such kind of books. I confess myself utterly unable to appreciate that celebrated soliloquy in *Hamlet,* beginning "To be, or not to be," or to tell whether it be good, bad, or indifferent, it has been so handled and pawed about by declamatory boys and men, and torn so inhumanly from its living place and principle of continuity in the play, till it is become to me a perfect dead member.

It may seem a paradox, but I cannot help being of opinion that the plays of Shakspere are less calculated for performance on a stage than those of almost any other dramatist whatever. Their distinguished excellence is a reason that they should be so. There is so much in them, which comes not under the province of acting, with which eye, and tone, and gesture, have nothing to do.

The glory of the scenic art is to personate passion, and the turns of passion; and the more coarse and palpable the passion is, the more hold upon the eyes and ears of the spectators the performer obviously possesses. For this reason, scolding scenes, scenes where two persons talk themselves into a fit of fury, and then in a surprising manner talk themselves out of it again, have always been the most popular upon our stage. And the reason is plain, because the spectators are here most palpably appealed to, they are the proper judges in this war of words, they are the legitimate ring that should be formed round such "intellectual prize-fighters." Talking is the direct object of the imitation here. But in the best dramas, and in Shakspere above all, how obvious it is, that the form of *speaking,* whether it be in soliloquy or dialogue, is only a medium, and often a highly artificial one, for putting the reader or spectator into possession of that knowledge of the inner structure and workings of mind in a character, which he could otherwise never have arrived at *in that form of composition* by any gift short of intuition. We do here as we do with novels written in the *epistolary form.* How many improprieties, perfect solecisms in letter-writing, do we put up with in "Clarissa" and other books, for the sake of the delight which that form upon the whole gives us.

But the practice of stage representation reduces everything to a controversy of elocution. Every character, from the boisterous blasphemings of Bajazet to the shrinking timidity of womanhood, must play the orator. The love-dialogues of *Romeo and Juliet,* those silver-sweet sounds of lovers' tongues by night; the more intimate and sacred sweetness of nuptial colloquy between an Othello or a Posthumus with their married wives, all those delicacies which are so delightful in the reading, as when we read of those youthful dalliances in Paradise—

As beseem'd
Fair couple link'd in happy nuptial league,
Alone:

by the inherent fault of stage representation, how are these things sullied and turned from their very nature by being exposed to a large assembly; when such speeches as Imogen addresses to her lord, come drawling out of the mouth of a hired actress, whose courtship, though nominally addressed to the personated Posthumus, is manifestly aimed at the spectators, who are to judge of her endearments and her returns of love.

The character of Hamlet is perhaps that by which, since the days of Betterton, a succession of popular performers have had the greatest ambition to distinguish themselves. The length of the part may be one of their reasons. But for the character itself, we find it in a play, and therefore we judge it a fit subject of dramatic representation. The play itself abounds in maxims and reflections beyond any other, and therefore we consider it as a proper vehicle for conveying moral instruction. But Hamlet himself—what does he suffer meanwhile by being dragged forth as a public schoolmaster, to give lectures to the crowd! Why, nine parts in ten of what Hamlet does, are transactions between himself and his moral sense, they are the effusions of his solitary musings, which he retires to holes and corners and the most sequestered parts of the palace to pour forth; or rather, they are the silent meditations with which his bosom is bursting, reduced to *words* for the sake of the reader, who must else remain ignorant of what is passing there. These profound sorrows, these light-and-noise-abhorring ruminations, which the tongue scarce dares utter to deaf walls and chambers, how can they be represented by a gesticulating actor, who comes and mouths them out before an audience, making four hundred people his confidants at once? I say not that it is the fault of the actor so to do; he must pronounce them *ore rotundo*, he must accompany them with his eye, he must insinuate them into his auditory by some trick of eye, tone, or gesture, or he fails. *He must be thinking all the while of his appearance, because he knows that all the while the spectators are judging of it.* And this is the way to represent the shy, negligent, retiring Hamlet.

It is true that there is no other mode of conveying a vast quantity of thought and feeling to a great portion of the audience, who otherwise would never learn it for themselves by reading, and the intellectual acquisition gained this way may, for aught I know, be inestimable; but I am not arguing that *Hamlet* should not be acted, but how much *Hamlet* is made another thing by being acted. I have heard much of the wonders which Garrick performed in this part; but as I never saw him, I must have leave to doubt whether the representation of such a character came within the province of his art. Those who tell me of him, speak of his eye, of the magic of his eye, and of his commanding voice: physical properties, vastly desirable in an actor, and without which he can never insinuate meaning into an auditory,—but what have they to do with Hamlet? what have they to do with intellect? In fact, the things aimed at in theatrical representation, are to arrest the spectator's eye upon the form and the gesture, and so to gain a more favourable hearing to what is spoken: it is not what the character is, but how he looks; not what he says, but how he speaks it. I see no reason to think that if the play of Hamlet were written over again by some such writer as Banks or Lillo, retaining the process of the story, but totally omitting all the poetry of it, all the divine features of Shakspere, his stupendous intellect; and only taking care to give us enough of passionate dialogue, which Banks or Lillo were never at a loss to furnish; I see not how the effect could be much different upon an audience, nor how the actor has it in his power to represent Shakspere to us differently from his representation of Banks or Lillo. Hamlet would still be a youthful accomplished prince, and must be gracefully personated; he might be puzzled in his mind, wavering in his conduct, seemingly cruel to Ophelia, he might see a ghost, and start at it, and address it kindly when he found it to be his father; all this in the poorest and most homely language of the servilest creeper after nature that ever consulted the palate of an audience; without troubling Shakspere for the matter; and I see not but there would be room for all the power which an actor has, to display itself. All the passions and changes of passion might remain; for those are much less difficult to write or act than is thought; it is a trick easy to be attained, it is but rising or falling a note or two in the voice, a whisper with a significant foreboding look to announce its approach, and so contagious the counterfeit appearance of any emotion is, that let the words be what they will, the look and tone shall carry it off and make it pass for deep skill in the passions.

It is common for people to talk of Shakspere's plays being *so natural,* that everybody can understand him. They are natural indeed, they are grounded deep in nature, so deep that the depth of them lies out of the reach of most of us. You shall hear the same persons say that *George Barnwell* is very natural, and *Othello* is very natural, that they are both very deep; and to them they are the same kind of thing. At the one they sit and shed tears, because a good sort of young man is tempted by a naughty woman to commit a *trifling peccadillo,* the murder of an uncle or so,[2] that is all, and so comes to an untimely end, which is *so moving;* and at the other, because a blackamoor in a fit of jealousy kills his innocent white wife: and the odds are that ninety-nine out of a hundred would willingly behold the same catastrophe happen to both the heroes, and have thought the rope more due to Othello than to Barnwell. For of the texture of Othello's mind, the inward construction marvellously laid open with all its strengths and weaknesses, its heroic confidences and its human misgivings, its agonies of hate springing from the depths of love, they see no more than the spectators at a cheaper rate, who pay their pennies apiece to look through the man's telescope in Leicester Fields, see into the inward plot and topography of the moon. Some dim thing or other they see, they see an actor personating a passion, of grief, or anger, for instance, and they recognise it as a copy of the usual external effects of such passions; or at least as being true to *that symbol of the emotion which passes current at the theatre for it,* for it is often no more than that: but of the grounds of the passion, its correspondence to a great or heroic nature, which is the only worthy object of tragedy,—that common auditors know anything of this, or can have any such notions dinned into them by the mere strength of an actor's lungs,—that apprehensions foreign to them should be thus infused into them by storm, I can neither believe, nor understand how it can be possible.

[2] If this note could hope to meet the eye of any of the Managers, I would entreat and beg of them, in the name of both the galleries, that this insult upon the morality of the common people of London should cease to be eternally repeated in the holiday weeks. Why are the 'Prentices of this famous and well-governed city, instead of an amusement, to be treated over and over again with a nauseous sermon of George Barnwell? Why *at the end of their vistas* are we to place the *gallows?* Were I an uncle, I should not much like a nephew of mine to have such an example placed before his eyes. It is really making uncle-murder too trivial to exhibit it as done upon such slight motives;—it is attributing too much to such characters as Millwood; it is putting things into the heads of good young men, which they would never otherwise have dreamed of. Uncles that think anything of their lives, should fairly petition the Chamberlain against it.

We talk of Shakspere's admirable observation of life, when we should feel that not from a petty inquisition into those cheap and every-day characters which surrounded him, as they surround us, but from his own mind, which was, to borrow a phrase of Ben Jonson's, the very "sphere of humanity," he fetched those images of virtue and of knowledge, of which every one of us recognising a part, think we comprehend in our natures the whole; and oftentimes mistake the powers which he positively creates in us for nothing more than indigenous faculties of our own minds, which only waited the application of corresponding virtues in him to return a full and clear echo of the same.

To return to Hamlet.—Among the distinguishing features of that wonderful character, one of the most interesting (yet painful) is that soreness of mind which makes him treat the intrusions of Polonius with harshness, and that asperity which he puts on in his interviews with Ophelia. These tokens of an unhinged mind (if they be not mixed in the latter case with a profound artifice of love, to alienate Ophelia by affected discourtesies, so to prepare her mind for the breaking off of that loving intercourse, which can no longer find a place amidst business so serious as that which he has to do) are parts of his character, which to reconcile with our admiration of Hamlet, the most patient consideration of his situation is no more than necessary; they are what we *forgive afterwards,* and explain by the whole of his character, but *at the time* they are harsh and unpleasant. Yet such is the actor's necessity of giving strong blows to the audience, that I have never seen a player in this character, who did not exaggerate and strain to the utmost these ambiguous features,—these temporary deformities in the character. They make him express a vulgar scorn at Polonius which utterly degrades his gentility, and which no explanation can render palatable; they make him show contempt, and curl up the nose at Ophelia's father,—contempt in its very grossest and most hateful form; but they get applause by it: it is natural, people say; that is, the words are scornful, and the actor expresses scorn, and that they can judge of: but why so much scorn, and of that sort, they never think of asking.

So to Ophelia.—All the Hamlets that I have ever seen, rant and rave at her as if she had committed some great crime, and the audience are highly pleased, because the words of the part are satirical, and they are enforced by the strongest expression of satirical indignation of which the face and voice are capable. But then, whether Hamlet is likely to have put on such brutal appearances to a lady whom he loved so dearly, is never thought on. The truth is, that in all such deep affections as had subsisted between Hamlet and Ophelia, there is a stock of *supererogatory love* (if I may venture to use the expression), which in any great grief of heart, especially where that which preys upon the mind cannot be communicated, confers a kind of indulgence upon the grieved party to express itself, even to its heart's dearest object, in the language of a temporary alienation; but it is not alienation, it is a distraction purely, and so it always makes itself to be felt by that object: it is not anger, but grief assuming the appearance of anger,—love awkwardly counterfeiting hate, as sweet countenances when they try to frown: but such sternness and fierce disgust as Hamlet is made to show, is no counterfeit, but the real face of absolute aversion,—of irreconcilable alienation. It may be said he puts on the madman; but then he should only so far put on this counterfeit lunacy as his own real distraction will give him leave; that is, incompletely, imperfectly; not in that confirmed, practised way, like a master of his art, or as Dame Quickly would say, "like one of those harlotry players."

I mean no disrespect to any actor, but the sort of pleasure which Shakspere's plays give in the acting seems to me not at all to differ from that which the audience receive from those of other writers; and, *they being in themselves essentially so different from all others,* I must conclude that there is something in the nature of acting which levels all distinctions. And in fact, who does not speak indifferently of the *Gamester* and of *Macbeth* as fine stage performances, and praise the Mrs. Beverley in the same way as the Lady Macbeth of Mrs. S.? Belvidera, and Calista, and Isabella, and Euphrasia, are they less liked than Imogen, or than Juliet, or than Desdemona? Are they not spoken of and remembered in the same way? Is not the female performer as great (as they call it) in one as in the other? Did not Garrick shine, and was he not ambitious of shining in every drawling tragedy that his wretched day produced,—the productions of the Hills and the Murphys and the Browns,—and shall he have

that honour to dwell in our minds for ever as an inseparable con-
comitant with Shakspere? A kindred mind! O who can read that
affecting sonnet of Shakspere which alludes to his profession as a
player:—

> Oh for my sake do you with Fortune chide,
> The guilty goddess of my harmful deeds,
> That did not better for my life provide
> Than public means which public manners breeds—
> Thence comes it that my name receives a brand;
> And almost thence my nature is subdued
> To what it works in, like the dyer's hand——

Or that other confession;—

> Alas! 'tis true, I have gone here and there,
> And made myself a motley to the view,
> Gored mine own thoughts, sold cheap what is most dear—

Who can read these instances of jealous self-watchfulness in our
sweet Shakspere, and dream of any congeniality between him and
one that, by every tradition of him, appears to have been as mere a
player as ever existed; to have had his mind tainted with the lowest
player's vices,—envy and jealousy, and miserable cravings after
applause; one who in the exercise of his profession was jealous even
of the women-performers that stood in his way; a manager full of
managerial tricks and stratagems and finesse: that any resemblance
should be dreamed of between him and Shakspere,—Shakspere who,
in the plenitude and consciousness of his own powers, could with
that noble modesty, which we can neither imitate nor appreciate,
express himself thus of his own sense of his own defects:—

> Wishing me like to one more rich in hope,
> Featured like him, like him with friends possess'd:
> Desiring *this man's art, and that man's scope.*

I am almost disposed to deny to Garrick the merits of being an
admirer of Shakspere. A true lover of his excellences he certainly was
not; for would any true lover of them have admitted into his matchless scenes such ribald trash as Tate and Cibber, and the rest of
them, that

> With their darkness durst affront his light,

have foisted into the acting plays of Shakspere? I believe it impossible that he could have had a proper reverence for Shakspere, and have condescended to go through that interpolated scene in *Richard the Third,* in which Richard tries to break his wife's heart by telling her he loves another woman, and says, "if she survives this she is immortal." Yet I doubt not he delivered this vulgar stuff with as much anxiety of emphasis as any of the genuine parts: and for acting, it is as well calculated as any. But we have seen the part of Richard lately produce great fame to an actor by his manner of playing it, and it lets us into the secret of acting, and of popular judgments of Shakspere derived from acting. Not one of the spectators who have witnessed Mr. C.'s exertions in that part, but has come away with a proper conviction that Richard is a very wicked man, and kills little children in their beds, with something like the pleasure which the giants and ogres in children's books are represented to have taken in that practice; moreover, that he is very close and shrewd, and devilish cunning, for you could see that by his eye.

But is in fact this the impression we have in reading the Richard of Shakspere? Do we feel anything like disgust, as we do at that butcher-like representation of him that passes for him on the stage? A horror at his crimes blends with the effect which we feel, but how is it qualified, how is it carried off, by the rich intellect which he displays, his resources, his wit, his buoyant spirits, his vast knowledge and insight into characters, the poetry of his part—not an atom of all which is made perceivable in Mr. C.'s way of acting it. Nothing but his crimes, his actions, is visible; they are prominent and staring; the murderer stands out, but where is the lofty genius, the man of vast capacity,—the profound, the witty, accomplished Richard?

The truth is, the characters of Shakspere are so much the objects of meditation rather than of interest or curiosity as to their actions, that while we are reading any of his great criminal characters,—Macbeth, Richard, even Iago,—we think not so much of the crimes which they commit, as of the ambition, the aspiring spirit, the intellectual activity which prompts them to overleap those moral fences. Barnwell is a wretched murderer; there is a certain fitness between his neck and the rope; he is the legitimate heir to the gallows; nobody who thinks at all can think of any alleviating circumstances in his case to make him a fit object of mercy. Or to take an instance from the higher tragedy, what else but a mere assassin is Glenalvon! Do we think of anything but of the crime which he commits, and the rack which he deserves? That is all which we really think about him. Whereas in corresponding characters in Shakspere so little do the actions comparatively affect us, that while the impulses, the inner mind in all its perverted greatness, solely seems real and is exclusively attended to, the crime is comparatively nothing. But when we see these things represented, the acts which they do are comparatively everything, their impulses nothing. The state of sublime emotion into which we are elevated by those images of night and horror which Macbeth is made to utter, that solemn prelude with which he entertains the time till the bell shall strike which is to call him to murder Duncan,—when we no longer read it in a book, when we have given up that vantage-ground of abstraction which reading possesses over seeing, and come to see a man in his bodily shape before our eyes actually preparing to commit a murder, if the acting be true and impressive, as I have witnessed it in Mr. K.'s performance of that part, the painful anxiety about the act, the natural longing to prevent it while it yet seems unperpetrated, the too close pressing semblance of reality, give a pain and an uneasiness which totally destroy all the delight which the words in the book convey, where the deed doing never presses upon us with the painful sense of presence: it rather seems to belong to history,—to something past and inevitable, if it has anything to do with time at all. The sublime images, the poetry alone, is that which is present to our minds in the reading.

So to see Lear acted,—to see an old man tottering about the stage with a walking-stick, turned out of doors by his daughters in a rainy night, has nothing in it but what is painful and disgusting. We want to take him into shelter and relieve him. That is all the feeling which the acting of Lear ever produced in me. But the Lear of Shakspere cannot be acted. The contemptible machinery by which they mimic the storm which he goes out in, is not more inadequate to represent the horrors of the real elements, than any actor can be to represent Lear: they might more easily propose to personate the

fervent youth, I saw (dimly relieved upon the dark background of my dreams) the imperfect lineaments of the awful sisters. These sisters—by what name shall we call them? If I say simply, "The Sorrows," there will be a chance of mistaking the term; it might be understood of individual sorrow,—separate cases of sorrow,—whereas I want a term expressing the mighty abstractions that incarnate themselves in all individual sufferings of man's heart; and I wish to have these abstractions presented as impersonations, that is, as clothed with human attributes of life, and with functions pointing to flesh. Let us call them, therefore, *Our Ladies of Sorrow.* I know them thoroughly, and have walked in all their kingdoms. Three sisters they are, of one mysterious household; and their paths are wide apart; but of their dominion there is no end. Them I saw often conversing with Levana, and sometimes about myself. Do they talk, then? O, no! mighty phantoms like these disdain the infirmities of language. They may utter voices through the organs of man when they dwell in human hearts, but amongst themselves there is no voice nor sound; eternal silence reigns in *their* kingdoms. *They* spoke not, as they talked with Levana; *they* whispered not; *they* sang not; though oftentimes methought they *might* have sung, for I upon earth had heard their mysteries oftentimes deciphered by harp and timbrel, by dulcimer and organ. Like God, whose servants they are, they utter their pleasure, not by sounds that perish, or by words that go astray, but by signs in heaven, by changes on earth, by pulses in secret rivers, heraldries painted on darkness, and hiero-glyphics written on the tablets of the brain. *They* wheeled in mazes; *I* spelled the steps. *They* telegraphed from afar; *I* read the signals. *They* conspired together; and on the mirrors of darkness *my* eye traced the plots. *Theirs* were the symbols; *mine* are the words.

What is it the sisters are? What is it that they do? Let me describe their form, and their presence: if form it were that still fluctuated in its outline, or presence it were that for ever advanced to the front, or for ever receded amongst shades.

The eldest of the three is named *Mater Lachrymarum,* Our Lady of Tears. She it is that night and day raves and moans, calling for vanished faces. She stood in Rama, where a voice was heard of lamentation,—Rachel weeping for her children, and refusing to be comforted. She it was that stood in Bethlehem on the night when Herod's sword swept its nurseries of Innocents, and the little feet were stiffened for ever, which, heard at times as they tottered along floors overhead, woke pulses of love in household hearts that were not unmarked in heaven.

Her eyes are sweet and subtle, wild and sleepy, by turns; often-times rising to the clouds, oftentimes challenging the heavens. She wears a diadem round her head. And I knew by childish memories that she could go abroad upon the winds, when she heard the sob-bing of litanies or the thundering of organs, and when she beheld the mustering of summer clouds. This sister, the eldest, it is that carries keys more than papal at her girdle, which open every cottage and every palace. She, to my knowledge, sat all last summer by the bedside of the blind beggar, him that so often and so gladly I talked with, whose pious daughter, eight years old, with the sunny counte-nance, resisted the temptations of play and village mirth to travel all day long on dusty roads with her afflicted father. For this did God send her a great reward. In the spring-time of the year, and whilst yet her own Spring was budding, he recalled her to himself. But her blind father mourns for ever over *her;* still he dreams at midnight that the little guiding hand is locked within his own; and still he wakens to a darkness that is *now* within a second and a deeper darkness. This *Mater Lachrymarum* has also been sitting all this winter of 1844-5 within the bed-chamber of the Czar, bringing before his eyes a daughter (not less pious) that vanished to God not less suddenly, and left behind her a darkness not less profound. By the power of the keys it is that Our Lady of Tears glides a ghostly intruder into the chambers of sleepless men, sleepless women, sleep-less children, from Ganges to Nile, from Nile to Mississippi. And her, because she is the first-born of her house, and has the widest empire, let us honour with the title of "Madonna!"

The second sister is called *Mater Suspiriorum*—Our Lady of Sighs. She never scales the clouds, nor walks abroad upon the winds. She wears no diadem. And her eyes, if they were ever seen, would be neither sweet nor subtle; no man could read their story; they would be found filled with perishing dreams, and with wrecks of forgotten delirium. But she raises not her eyes; her head, on which sits a dilapidated turban, droops for ever, for ever fastens on the dust. She weeps not. She groans not. But she sighs inaudibly at intervals. Her sister, Madonna, is oftentimes stormy and frantic, raging in the highest against heaven, and demanding back her darlings. But Our Lady of Sighs never clamours, never defies, dreams not of rebellious aspirations. She is humble to abjectness. Hers is the meekness that belongs to the hopeless. Murmur she may, but it is in her sleep. Whisper she may, but it is to herself in the twilight. Mutter she does at times, but it is in solitary places that are desolate as she is desolate, in ruined cities, and when the sun has gone down to his rest. This sister is the visitor of the Pariah, of the Jew, of the bondsman to the oar in the Mediterranean galleys; and of the English criminal in Norfolk Island, blotted out from the books of remembrance in sweet far-off England; of the baffled penitent reverting his eyes for ever upon a solitary grave, which to him seems the altar overthrown of some past and bloody sacrifice, on which altar no oblations can now be availing, whether towards pardon that he might implore, or towards reparation that he might attempt. Every slave that at noon-day looks up to the tropical sun with timid reproach, as he points with one hand to the earth, our general mother, but for *him* a step-mother,—as he points with the other hand to the Bible, our general teacher, but against *him* sealed and sequestered;—every woman sitting in darkness, without love to shelter her head, or hope to illumine her solitude, because the heaven-born instincts kindling in her nature germs of holy affections which God implanted in her womanly bosom, having been stifled by social necessities, now burn sullenly to waste, like sepulchral lamps amongst the ancients; every nun defrauded of her unreturning May-time by wicked kinsman, whom God will judge; every captive in every dungeon; all that are betrayed and all that are rejected outcasts by traditionary law, and children of *hereditary* disgrace,—all these walk with Our Lady of Sighs. She also carries a key; but she needs it little. For her kingdom is chiefly amongst the tents of Shem, and the houseless vagrant of every clime. Yet in the very highest walks of man she finds chapels of her own; and even in glorious England there are some that, to the world, carry their heads as proudly as the reindeer, who yet secretly have received her mark upon their foreheads. But the third sister, who is also the youngest——! Hush, whisper whilst we talk of *her!* Her kingdom is not large, or else no flesh should live; but within that kingdom all power is hers. Her head, turreted like that of Cybele, rises almost beyond the reach of sight. She droops not; and her eyes rising so high *might* be hidden by distance; but, being what they are, they cannot be hidden; through the treble veil of crape which she wears, the fierce light of a blazing misery, that rests not for matins or for vespers, for noon of day or noon of night, for ebbing or for flowing tide, may be read from the very ground. She is the defier of God. She is also the mother of lunacies, and the suggestress of suicides. Deep lie the roots of her power; but narrow is the nation that she rules. For she can approach only those in whom a profound nature has been upheaved by central convulsions; in whom the heart trembles, and the brain rocks under conspiracies of tempest from without and tempest from within. Madonna moves with uncertain steps, fast or slow, but still with tragic grace. Our Lady of Sighs creeps timidly and stealthily. But this youngest sister moves with incalculable motions, bounding, and with tiger's leaps. She carries no key; for, though coming rarely amongst men, she storms all doors at which she is permitted to enter at all. And *her* name is *Mater Tenebrarum*—Our Lady of Darkness.

These were the *Semnai Theai,* or Sublime Goddesses, these were the *Eumenides,* or Gracious Ladies (so called by antiquity in shuddering propitiation), of my Oxford dreams. Madonna spoke. She spoke by her mysterious hand. Touching my head, she said to Our Lady of Sighs; and *what* she spoke, translated out of the signs which (except in dreams) no man reads, was this:—

"Lo! here is he, whom in childhood I dedicated to my altars. This is he that once I made my darling. Him I led astray, him I beguiled, and from heaven I stole away his young heart to mine. Through me did he become idolatrous; and through me it was, by languishing desires, that he worshipped the worm, and prayed to the wormy grave. Holy was the grave to him; lovely was its darkness; saintly its corruption. Him, this young idolater, I have seasoned for thee, dear gentle Sister of Sighs! Do thou take him now to *thy* heart, and season him for our dreadful sister. And thou,"—

turning to the *Mater Tenebrarum,* she said,—"wicked sister, that temptest and hatest, do thou take him from *her.* See that thy sceptre lie heavy on his head. Suffer not woman and her tenderness to sit near him in his darkness. Banish the frailties of hope, wither the relenting of love, scorch the fountain of tears, curse him as only thou canst curse. So shall he be accomplished in the furnace, so shall he see the things that ought not to be seen, sights that are abominable, and secrets that are unutterable. So shall he read elder truths, sad truths, grand truths, fearful truths. So shall he rise again *before* he dies, and so shall our commission be accomplished which from God we had,—to plague his heart until we had unfolded the capacities of his spirit."

A DEFENCE OF POETRY

BY

PERCY BYSSHE SHELLEY

INTRODUCTORY NOTE

A SHORT sketch of the life of Percy Bysshe Shelley will be found pre-fixed to his drama of the "Cenci" in the volume of modern English Drama in the Harvard Classics.

The "Defence of Poetry" is by far the most important of Shelley's prose writings, and is of great value in supplementing and correcting the picture of his mind which is given by his lyrical poetry; for we can perceive from this brilliant piece of philosophical discussion that Shelley had intellect as well as imagination.

The immediate occasion of the essay was the publication of Thomas Love Peacock's "Four Ages of Poetry," to which Shelley's work was originally a reply. In this, as in other notable respects, the treatise is parallel with Sidney's. In its present form Shelley has eliminated much of the controversial matter; and it stands as one of the most eloquent and inspiring assertions of the "ideal nature and essential value of poetry."

A DEFENCE OF POETRY

ACCORDING to one mode of regarding those two classes of mental action, which are called reason and imagination, the former may be considered as mind contemplating the relations borne by one thought to another, however produced, and the latter, as mind acting upon those thoughts so as to color them with its own light, and composing from them, as from elements, other thoughts, each containing within itself the principle of its own integrity. The one is the τὸ ποιεῖν, or the principle of synthesis, and has for its objects those forms which are common to universal nature and existence itself; the other is the τὸ λογίζειν, or principle of analysis, and its action regards the relations of things simply as relations; considering thoughts, not in their integral unity, but as the algebraical representations which conduct to certain general results. Reason is the enumeration of qualities already known; imagination is the perception of the value of those qualities, both separately and as a whole. Reason respects the differences, and imagination the similitudes of things. Reason is to imagination as the instrument to the agent, as the body to the spirit, as the shadow to the substance.

Poetry, in a general sense, may be defined to be "the expression of the imagination": and poetry is connate with the origin of man. Man is an instrument over which a series of external and internal impressions are driven, like the alternations of an ever-changing wind over an Æolian lyre, which move it by their motion to ever-changing melody. But there is a principle within the human being, and perhaps within all sentient beings, which acts otherwise than in the lyre, and produces not melody alone, but harmony, by an internal adjustment of the sounds or motions thus excited to the impressions which excite them. It is as if the lyre could accommodate its chords to the motions of that which strikes them, in a determined proportion of sound; even as the musician can accommodate his voice to the sound of the lyre. A child at play by itself will express its delight by its voice and motions; and every inflexion of tone and every gesture will bear exact relation to a corresponding antitype in the pleasurable impressions which awakened it; it will be the reflected image of that impression; and as the lyre trembles and sounds after the wind has died away, so the child seeks, by prolonging in its voice and motions the duration of the effect, to prolong also a consciousness of the cause. In relation to the objects which delight a child these expressions are what poetry is to higher objects. The savage (for the savage is to ages what the child is to years) expresses the emotions produced in him by surrounding objects in a similar manner; and language and gesture, together with plastic or pictorial imitation, become the image of the combined effect of those objects, and of his apprehension of them. Man in society, with all his passions and his pleasures, next becomes the object of the passions and pleasures of man; an additional class of emotions produces an augmented treasure of expressions; and language, gesture, and the imitative arts, become at once the representation and the medium, the pencil and the picture, the chisel and the statue, the chord and the harmony. The social sympathies, or those laws from which, as from its elements, society results, begin to develop themselves from the moment that two human beings coexist; the future is contained within the present, as the plant within the seed; and equality, diversity, unity, contrast, mutual dependence, become the principles alone capable of affording the motives according to which the will of a social being is determined to action, inasmuch as he is social; and constitute pleasure in sensation, virtue in sentiment, beauty in art, truth in reasoning, and love in the intercourse of kind. Hence men, even in the infancy of society, observe a certain order in their words and actions, distinct from that of the objects and the impressions represented by them, all expression being subject to the laws of that from which it proceeds. But let us dismiss those more general considerations which might involve an inquiry into the principles of society itself, and restrict our view to the manner in which the imagination is expressed upon its forms.

In the youth of the world, men dance and sing and imitate natural objects, observing in these actions, as in all others, a certain rhythm or order. And, although all men observe a similar, they observe not the same order, in the motions of the dance, in the melody of the song, in the combinations of language, in the series of their imitations of natural objects. For there is a certain order or rhythm belonging to each of these classes of mimetic representation, from which the hearer and the spectator receive an intenser and purer pleasure than from any other: the sense of an approximation to this order has been called *taste* by modern writers. Every man in the infancy of art observes an order which approximates more or less closely to that from which this highest delight results: but the diversity is not sufficiently marked, as that its gradations should be sensible, except in those instances where the predominance of this faculty of approximation to the beautiful (for so we may be permitted to name the relation between this highest pleasure and its cause) is very great. Those in whom it exists in excess are poets, in the most universal sense of the word; and the pleasure resulting from the manner in which they express the influence of society or nature upon their own minds, communicates itself to others, and gathers a sort of reduplication from that community. Their language is vitally metaphorical; that is, it marks the before unapprehended relations of things and perpetuates their apprehension, until the words which represent them, become, through time, signs for portions or classes of thoughts instead of pictures of integral thoughts; and then if no new poets should arise to create afresh the associations which have been thus disorganized, language will be dead to all the nobler purposes of human intercourse. These similitudes or relations are finely said by Lord Bacon to be "the same footsteps of nature impressed upon the various subjects of the world"[1] and he considers the faculty which perceives them as the storehouse of axioms common to all knowledge. In the infancy of society every author is necessarily a poet, because language itself is poetry; and to be a poet is to apprehend the true and the beautiful, in a word, the good which exists in the relation, subsisting, first between existence and perception, and secondly between perception and expression. Every original language near to its source is in itself the chaos of a cyclic poem: the copiousness of lexicography and the distinctions

[1] "De Augment. Scient.," cap. 1, lib. iii.

of grammar are the works of a later age, and are merely the catalogue and the form of the creations of poetry.

But poets, or those who imagine and express this indestructible order, are not only the authors of language and of music, of the dance, and architecture, and statuary, and painting: they are the institutors of laws, and the founders of civil society, and the inventors of the arts of life, and the teachers, who draw into a certain propinquity with the beautiful and the true that partial apprehension of the agencies of the invisible world which is called religion. Hence all original religions are allegorical, or susceptible of allegory, and, like Janus, have a double face of false and true. Poets, according to the circumstances of the age and nation in which they appeared, were called, in the earlier epochs of the world, legislators, or prophets: a poet essentially comprises and unites both these characters. For he not only beholds intensely the present as it is, and discovers those laws according to which present things ought to be ordered, but he beholds the future in the present, and his thoughts are the germs of the flower and the fruit of latest time. Not that I assert poets to be prophets in the gross sense of the word, or that they can foretell the form as surely as they foreknow the spirit of events: such is the pretence of superstition, which would make poetry an attribute of prophecy, rather than prophecy an attribute of poetry. A poet participates in the eternal, the infinite, and the one; as far as relates to his conceptions, time and place and number are not. The grammatical forms which express the moods of time, and the difference of persons, and the distinction of place, are convertible with respect to the highest poetry without injuring it as poetry; and the choruses of Æschylus, and the book of Job, and Dante's "Paradise" would afford, more than any other writings, examples of this fact, if the limits of this essay did not forbid citation. The creations of sculpture, painting, and music are illustrations still more decisive.

Language, color, form, and religious and civil habits of action, are all the instruments and materials of poetry; they may be called poetry by that figure of speech which considers the effect as a synonym of the cause. But poetry in a more restricted sense expresses those arrangements of language, and especially metrical language, which are created by that imperial faculty, whose throne is curtained within the invisible nature of man. And this springs from the nature itself of language, which is a more direct representation of the actions and passions of our internal being, and is susceptible of more various and delicate combinations, than color, form, or motion, and is more plastic and obedient to the control of that faculty of which it is the creation. For language is arbitrarily produced by the imagination, and has relation to thoughts alone; but all other materials, instruments, and conditions of art have relations among each other, which limit and interpose between conception and expression. The former is as a mirror which reflects, the latter as a cloud which enfeebles, the light of which both are mediums of communication. Hence the fame of sculptors, painters, and musicians, although the intrinsic powers of the great masters of these arts may yield in no degree to that of those who have employed language as the hieroglyphic of their thoughts, has never equalled that of poets in the restricted sense of the term; as two performers of equal skill will produce unequal effects from a guitar and a harp. The fame of legislators and founders of religions, so long as their institutions last, alone seems to exceed that of poets in the restricted sense; but it can scarcely be a question, whether, if we deduct the celebrity which their flattery of the gross opinions of the vulgar usually conciliates, together with that which belonged to them in their higher character of poets, any excess will remain.

We have thus circumscribed the word poetry within the limits of that art which is the most familiar and the most perfect expression of the faculty itself. It is necessary, however, to make the circle still narrower, and to determine the distinction between measured and unmeasured language; for the popular division into prose and verse is inadmissible in accurate philosophy.

Sounds as well as thoughts have relation both between each other and towards that which they represent, and a perception of the order of those relations has always been found connected with a perception of the order of the relations of thoughts. Hence the language of poets has ever affected a certain uniform and harmonious recurrence of sound, without which it were not poetry, and which is scarcely less indispensable to the communication of its influence, than the words themselves, without reference to that peculiar order.

Hence the vanity of translation; it were as wise to cast a violet into
a crucible that you might discover the formal principle of its color
and odor, as seek to transfuse from one language into another the
creations of a poet. The plant must spring again from its seed,
or it will bear no flower—and this is the burden of the curse of
Babel.

An observation of the regular mode of the recurrence of harmony
in the language of poetical minds, together with its relation to music,
produced metre, or a certain system of traditional forms of harmony
and language. Yet it is by no means essential that a poet should
accommodate his language to this traditional form, so that the
harmony, which is its spirit, be observed. The practice is indeed
convenient and popular, and to be preferred, especially in such
composition as includes much action: but every great poet must
inevitably innovate upon the example of his predecessors in the
exact structure of his peculiar versification. The distinction between
poets and prose writers is a vulgar error. The distinction between
philosophers and poets has been anticipated. Plato was essentially a
poet—the truth and splendor of his imagery, and the melody of his
language, are the most intense that it is possible to conceive. He
rejected the measure of the epic, dramatic, and lyrical forms, because he sought to kindle a harmony in thoughts divested of shape
and action, and he forebore to invent any regular plan of rhythm
which would include, under determinate forms, the varied pauses of
his style. Cicero sought to imitate the cadence of his periods, but with
little success. Lord Bacon was a poet.[2] His language has a sweet
and majestic rhythm, which satisfies the sense, no less than the almost superhuman wisdom of his philosophy satisfies the intellect; it
is a strain which distends, and then bursts the circumference of the
reader's mind, and pours itself forth together with it into the universal element with which it has perpetual sympathy. All the
authors of revolutions in opinion are not only necessarily poets as
they are inventors, nor even as their words unveil the permanent
analogy of things by images which participate in the life of truth;
but as their periods are harmonious and rhythmical, and contain
in themselves the elements of verse; being the echo of the eternal

[2] See the "Filum Labyrinthi," and the "Essay on Death" particularly.—S.

music. Nor are those supreme poets, who have employed traditional forms of rhythm on account of the form and action of their subjects, less capable of perceiving and teaching the truth of things, than those who have omitted that form. Shakespeare, Dante, and Milton (to confine ourselves to modern writers) are philosophers of the very loftiest power.

A poem is the very image of life expressed in its eternal truth. There is this difference between a story and a poem, that a story is a catalogue of detached facts, which have no other connection than time, place, circumstance, cause and effect; the other is the creation of actions according to the unchangeable forms of human nature, as existing in the mind of the Creator, which is itself the image of all other minds. The one is partial, and applies only to a definite period of time, and a certain combination of events which can never again recur; the other is universal, and contains within itself the germ of a relation to whatever motives or actions have place in the possible varieties of human nature. Time, which destroys the beauty and the use of the story of particular facts, stripped of the poetry which should invest them, augments that of poetry, and forever develops new and wonderful applications of the eternal truth which it contains. Hence epitomes have been called the moths of just history; they eat out the poetry of it. A story of particular facts is as a mirror which obscures and distorts that which should be beautiful; poetry is a mirror which makes beautiful that which is distorted.

The parts of a composition may be poetical, without the composition as a whole being a poem. A single sentence may be considered as a whole, though it may be found in the midst of a series of unassimilated portions; a single word even may be a spark of inextinguishable thought. And thus all the great historians, Herodotus, Plutarch, Livy, were poets; and although the plan of these writers, especially that of Livy, restrained them from developing this faculty in its highest degree, they made copious and ample amends for their subjection, by filling all the interstices of their subjects with living images.

Having determined what is poetry, and who are poets, let us proceed to estimate its effects upon society.

Poetry is ever accompanied with pleasure: all spirits on which it falls open themselves to receive the wisdom which is mingled with its delight. In the infancy of the world, neither poets themselves nor their auditors are fully aware of the excellence of poetry: for it acts in a divine and unapprehended manner, beyond and above consciousness; and it is reserved for future generations to contemplate and measure the mighty cause and effect in all the strength and splendor of their union. Even in modern times, no living poet ever arrived at the fulness of his fame; the jury which sits in judgment upon a poet, belonging as he does to all time, must be composed of his peers: it must be impanelled by Time from the selectest of the wise of many generations. A poet is a nightingale, who sits in darkness and sings to cheer its own solitude with sweet sounds; his auditors are as men entranced by the melody of an unseen musician, who feel that they are moved and softened, yet know not whence or why. The poems of Homer and his contemporaries were the delight of infant Greece; they were the elements of that social system which is the column upon which all succeeding civilization has reposed. Homer embodied the ideal perfection of his age in human character; nor can we doubt that those who read his verses were awakened to an ambition of becoming like to Achilles, Hector, and Ulysses: the truth and beauty of friendship, patriotism, and persevering devotion to an object, were unveiled to the depths in these immortal creations: the sentiments of the auditors must have been refined and enlarged by a sympathy with such great and lovely impersonations, until from admiring they imitated, and from imitation they identified themselves with the objects of their admiration. Nor let it be objected that these characters are remote from moral perfection, and that they can by no means be considered as edifying patterns for general imitation. Every epoch, under names more or less specious, has deified its peculiar errors; Revenge is the naked idol of the worship of a semi-barbarous age; and Self-deceit is the veiled image of unknown evil, before which luxury and satiety lie prostrate. But a poet considers the vices of his contemporaries as the temporary dress in which his creations must be arrayed, and which cover without concealing the eternal proportions of their beauty. An epic or dramatic personage is understood to wear them around his soul, as he may the ancient armor or the modern uniform around his body; whilst it is easy to conceive a dress more graceful than either. The beauty of the internal nature cannot be so far concealed by its accidental vesture, but that the spirit of its form shall communicate itself to the very disguise, and indicate the shape it hides from the manner in which it is worn. A majestic form and graceful motions will express themselves through the most barbarous and tasteless costume. Few poets of the highest class have chosen to exhibit the beauty of their conceptions in its naked truth and splendor; and it is doubtful whether the alloy of costume, habit, etc., be not necessary to temper this planetary music for mortal ears.

The whole objection, however, of the immorality of poetry rests upon a misconception of the manner in which poetry acts to produce the moral improvement of man. Ethical science arranges the elements which poetry has created, and propounds schemes and proposes examples of civil and domestic life: nor is it for want of admirable doctrines that men hate, and despise, and censure, and deceive, and subjugate one another. But poetry acts in another and diviner manner. It awakens and enlarges the mind itself by rendering it the receptacle of a thousand unapprehended combinations of thought. Poetry lifts the veil from the hidden beauty of the world, and makes familiar objects be as if they were not familiar; it reproduces all that it represents, and the impersonations clothed in its' Elysian light stand thenceforward in the minds of those who have once contemplated them, as memorials of that gentle and exalted content which extends itself over all thoughts and actions with which it coexists. The great secret of morals is love; or a going out of our nature, and an identification of ourselves with the beautiful which exists in thought, action, or person, not our own. A man, to be greatly good, must imagine intensely and comprehensively; he must put himself in the place of another and of many others; the pains and pleasures of his species must become his own. The great instrument of moral good is the imagination; and poetry administers to the effect by acting upon the cause. Poetry enlarges the circumference of the imagination by replenishing it with thoughts of ever new delight, which have the power of attracting and assimilating to their own nature all other thoughts, and which form new intervals and interstices whose void forever craves fresh food. Poetry strengthens the faculty which is the organ of the moral nature of man, in the same manner as exercise strengthens a limb. A poet therefore would do ill to embody his own conceptions of right and wrong, which are usually those of his place and time, in his poetical creations, which participate in neither. By this assumption of the inferior office of interpreting the effect, in which perhaps after all he might acquit himself but imperfectly, he would resign a glory in a participation in the cause. There was little danger that Homer, or any of the eternal poets, should have so far misunderstood themselves as to have abdicated this throne of their widest dominion. Those in whom the poetical faculty, though great, is less intense, as Euripides, Lucan, Tasso, Spenser, have frequently affected a moral aim, and the effect of their poetry is diminished in exact proportion to the degree in which they compel us to advert to this purpose.

Homer and the cyclic poets were followed at a certain interval by the dramatic and lyrical poets of Athens, who flourished contemporaneously with all that is most perfect in the kindred expressions of the poetical faculty; architecture, painting, music, the dance, sculpture, philosophy, and, we may add, the forms of civil life. For although the scheme of Athenian society was deformed by many imperfections which the poetry existing in chivalry and Christianity has erased from the habits and institutions of modern Europe; yet never at any other period has so much energy, beauty, and virtue been developed; never was blind strength and stubborn form so disciplined and rendered subject to the will of man, or that will less repugnant to the dictates of the beautiful and the true, as during the century which preceded the death of Socrates. Of no other epoch in the history of our species have we records and fragments stamped so visibly with the image of the divinity in man. But it is poetry alone, in form, in action, or in language, which has rendered this epoch memorable above all others, and the store-house of examples to everlasting time. For written poetry existed at that epoch simultaneously with the other arts, and it is an idle inquiry to demand which gave and which received the light, which all, as from a common focus, have scattered over the darkest periods of succeeding time. We know no more of cause and effect than a constant conjunction of events:

poetry is ever found to coexist with whatever other arts contribute to the happiness and perfection of man. I appeal to what has already been established to distinguish between the cause and the effect.

It was at the period here adverted to that the drama had its birth; and however a succeeding writer may have equalled or surpassed those few great specimens of the Athenian drama which have been preserved to us, it is indisputable that the art itself never was under-stood or practised according to the true philosophy of it, as at Athens. For the Athenians employed language, action, music, painting, the dance, and religious institutions, to produce a common effect in the representation of the highest idealism of passion and of power; each division in the art was made perfect in its kind of artists of the most consummate skill, and was disciplined into a beautiful proportion and unity one towards the other. On the modern stage a few only of the elements capable of expressing the image of the poet's concep-tion are employed at once. We have tragedy without music and dancing; and music and dancing without the highest impersonations of which they are the fit accompaniment, and both without religion and solemnity. Religious institution has indeed been usually ban-ished from the stage. Our system of divesting the actor's face of a mask, on which the many expressions appropriated to his dramatic character might be moulded into one permanent and unchanging expression, is favorable only to a partial and inharmonious effect; it is fit for nothing but a monologue, where all the attention may be directed to some great master of ideal mimicry. The modern prac-tice of blending comedy with tragedy, though liable to great abuse in point of practice, is undoubtedly an extension of the dramatic circle; but the comedy should be as in "King Lear," universal, ideal, and sublime. It is perhaps the intervention of this principle which determines the balance in favor of "King Lear" against the "Œdipus Tyrannus" or the "Agamemnon," or, if you will, the trilogies with which they are connected; unless the intense power of the choral poetry, especially that of the latter, should be considered as restoring the equilibrium. "King Lear," if it can sustain this comparison, may be judged to be the most perfect specimen of the dramatic art existing in the world; in spite of the narrow conditions to which the poet was subjected by the ignorance of the philosophy of the drama which has prevailed in modern Europe. Calderon, in his religious *autos,* has attempted to fulfil some of the high conditions of dramatic representation neglected by Shakespeare; such as the establishing a relation between the drama and religion, and the accommodating them to music and dancing; but he omits the observation of conditions still more important, and more is lost than gained by the substitution of the rigidly defined and ever-repeated idealisms of a distorted superstition for the living impersonations of the truth of human passion.

But I digress. The connection of scenic exhibitions with the improvement or corruption of the manners of men has been universally recognized; in other words, the presence or absence of poetry in its most perfect and universal form has been found to be connected with good and evil in conduct or habit. The corruption which has been imputed to the drama as an effect, begins, when the poetry employed in its constitution ends: I appeal to the history of manners whether the periods of the growth of the one and the decline of the other have not corresponded with an exactness equal to any example of moral cause and effect.

The drama at Athens, or wheresoever else it may have approached to its perfection, ever coexisted with the moral and intellectual greatness of the age. The tragedies of the Athenian poets are as mirrors in which the spectator beholds himself, under a thin disguise of circumstance, stripped of all but that ideal perfection and energy which everyone feels to be the internal type of all that he loves, admires, and would become. The imagination is enlarged by a sympathy with pains and passions so mighty, that they distend in their conception the capacity of that by which they are conceived; the good affections are strengthened by pity, indignation, terror, and sorrow; and an exalted calm is prolonged from the satiety of this high exercise of them into the tumult of familiar life: even crime is disarmed of half its horror and all its contagion by being represented as the fatal consequence of the unfathomable agencies of nature; error is thus divested of its wilfulness; men can no longer cherish it as the creation of their choice. In a drama of the highest order there is little food for censure or hatred; it teaches rather self-knowledge and self-respect. Neither the eye nor the mind can see itself, unless reflected upon that which it resembles. The drama, so long as it continues to express poetry, is as a prismatic and many-sided mirror, which collects the brightest rays of human nature and divides and reproduces them from the simplicity of these elementary forms, and touches them with majesty and beauty, and multiplies all that it reflects, and endows it with the power of propagating its like wherever it may fall.

But in periods of the decay of social life, the drama sympathizes with that decay. Tragedy becomes a cold imitation of the form of the great masterpieces of antiquity, divested of all harmonious accompaniment of the kindred arts; and often the very form misunderstood, or a weak attempt to teach certain doctrines, which the writer considers as moral truths; and which are usually no more than specious flatteries of some gross vice or weakness, with which the author, in common with his auditors, are infected. Hence what has been called the classical and domestic drama. Addison's "Cato" is a specimen of the one; and would it were not superfluous to cite examples of the other! To such purposes poetry cannot be made subservient. Poetry is a sword of lightning, ever unsheathed, which consumes the scabbard that would contain it. And thus we observe that all dramatic writings of this nature are unimaginative in a singular degree; they affect sentiment and passion, which, divested of imagination, are other names for caprice and appetite. The period in our own history of the grossest degradation of the drama is the reign of Charles II, when all forms in which poetry had been accustomed to be expressed became hymns to the triumph of kingly power over liberty and virtue. Milton stood alone illuminating an age unworthy of him. At such periods the calculating principle pervades all the forms of dramatic exhibition, and poetry ceases to be expressed upon them. Comedy loses its ideal universality: wit succeeds to humor; we laugh from self-complacency and triumph, instead of pleasure; malignity, sarcasm, and contempt succeed to sympathetic merriment; we hardly laugh, but we smile. Obscenity, which is ever blasphemy against the divine beauty in life, becomes, from the very veil which it assumes, more active if less disgusting: it is a monster for which the corruption of society forever brings forth new food, which it devours in secret.

The drama being that form under which a greater number of modes of expression of poetry are susceptible of being combined than any other, the connection of poetry and social good is more observable in the drama than in whatever other form. And it is indisputable that the highest perfection of human society has ever corresponded with the highest dramatic excellence; and that the corruption or the extinction of the drama in a nation where it has once flourished is a mark of a corruption of manners, and an extinction of the energies which sustain the soul of social life. But, as Machiavelli says of political institutions, that life may be preserved and renewed, if men should arise capable of bringing back the drama to its principles. And this is true with respect to poetry in its most extended sense: all language, institution, and form require not only to be produced but to be sustained: the office and character of a poet participate in the divine nature as regards providence, no less than as regards creation.

Civil war, the spoils of Asia, and the fatal predominance first of the Macedonian, and then of the Roman arms, were so many symbols of the extinction or suspension of the creative faculty in Greece. The bucolic writers, who found patronage under the lettered tyrants of Sicily and Egypt, were the latest representatives of its most glorious reign. Their poetry is intensely melodious; like the odor of the tuberose, it overcomes and sickens the spirit with excess of sweetness; whilst the poetry of the preceding age was as a meadow-gale of June, which mingles the fragrance of all the flowers of the field, and adds a quickening and harmonizing spirit of its own which endows the sense with a power of sustaining its extreme delight. The bucolic and erotic delicacy in written poetry is correlative with that softness in statuary, music, and the kindred arts, and even in manners and institutions, which distinguished the epoch to which I now refer. Nor is it the poetical faculty itself, or any misapplication of it, to which this want of harmony is to be imputed. An equal sensibility to the influence of the senses and the affections is to be found in the writings of Homer and Sophocles: the former, especially, has clothed sensual and pathetic images with irresistible attractions. Their superiority over these succeeding writers consists in the presence of those thoughts which belong to the inner faculties of our nature, not in the absence of those which are connected with the external; their incomparable perfection consists in a harmony of the union of all. It is not what the erotic poets have, but what they have not, in which their imperfection consists. It is not inasmuch as they were poets, but inasmuch as they were not poets, that they can be considered with any plausibility as connected with the corruption of their age. Had that corruption availed so as to extinguish in them the sensibility to pleasure, passion, and natural scenery, which is imputed to them as an imperfection, the last triumph of evil would have been achieved. For the end of social corruption is to destroy all sensibility to pleasure; and, therefore, it is corruption. It begins at the imagination and the intellect as at the core, and distributes itself thence as a paralyzing venom, through the affections into the very appetites, until all become a torpid mass in which hardly sense survives. At the approach of such a period, poetry ever addresses itself to those faculties which are the last to be destroyed, and its voice is heard, like the footsteps of Astræa, departing from the world. Poetry ever communicates all the pleasure which men are capable of receiving: it is ever still the light of life; the source of whatever of beautiful or generous or true can have place in an evil time. It will readily be confessed that those among the luxurious citizens of Syracuse and Alexandria, who were delighted with the poems of Theocritus, were less cold, cruel, and sensual than the remnant of their tribe. But corruption must utterly have destroyed the fabric of human society before poetry can ever cease. The sacred links of that chain have never been entirely disjoined, which descending through the minds of many men is attached to those great minds, whence as from a magnet the invisible effluence is sent forth, which at once connects, animates, and sustains the life of all. It is the faculty which contains within itself the seeds at once of its own and of social renovation. And let us not circumscribe the effects of the bucolic and erotic poetry within the limits of the sensibility of those to whom it was addressed. They may have perceived the beauty of those immortal compositions, simply as fragments and isolated portions: those who are more finely organized, or born in a happier age, may recognize them as episodes to that great poem, which all poets, like the co-operating thoughts of one great mind, have built up since the beginning of the world.

The same revolutions within a narrower sphere had place in ancient Rome; but the actions and forms of its social life never seem to have been perfectly saturated with the poetical element. The Romans appear to have considered the Greeks as the selectest treasuries of the selectest forms of manners and of nature, and to have abstained from creating in measured language, sculpture, music, or architecture, anything which might bear a particular relation to their own condition, whilst it should bear a general one to the universal constitution of the world. But we judge from partial evidence, and we judge perhaps partially. Ennius, Varro, Pacuvius, and Accius, all great poets, have been lost. Lucretius is in the highest, and Vergil in a very high sense, a creator. The chosen delicacy of expressions of the latter are as a mist of light which conceal from us the intense and exceeding truth of his conceptions of nature. Livy is instinct with poetry. Yet Horace, Catullus, Ovid, and generally the other great writers of the Vergilian age, saw man and nature in the mirror of Greece. The institutions also, and the religion of Rome, were less poetical than those of Greece, as the shadow is less vivid than the substance. Hence poetry in Rome seemed to follow, rather than accompany, the perfection of political and domestic society. The true poetry of Rome lived in its institutions; for whatever of beautiful, true, and majestic, they contained, could have sprung only from the faculty which creates the order in which they consist. The life of Camillus, the death of Regulus; the expectation of the senators, in their godlike state, of the victorious Gauls; the refusal of the republic to make peace with Hannibal, after the battle of Cannæ, were not the consequences of a refined calculation of the probable personal advantage to result from such a rhythm and order in the shows of life, to those who were at once the poets and the actors of these immortal dramas. The imagination beholding the beauty of this order, created it out of itself according to its own idea; the consequence was empire, and the reward ever-living fame. These things are not the less poetry, *quia carent vate sacro.*[3] They are the episodes of that cyclic poem written by Time upon the memories of men. The Past, like an inspired rhapsodist, fills the theatre of everlasting generations with their harmony.

[3] "Because they lack the sacred bard."

At length the ancient system of religion and manners had fulfilled the circle of its revolutions. And the world would have fallen into utter anarchy and darkness, but that there were found poets among the authors of the Christian and chivalric systems of manners and religion, who created forms of opinion and action never before conceived; which, copied into the imaginations of men, became as generals to the bewildered armies of their thoughts. It is foreign to the present purpose to touch upon the evil produced by these systems: except that we protest, on the ground of the principles already established, that no portion of it can be attributed to the poetry they contain.

It is probable that the poetry of Moses, Job, David, Solomon, and Isaiah had produced a great effect upon the mind of Jesus and his disciples. The scattered fragments preserved to us by the biographers of this extraordinary person are all instinct with the most vivid poetry. But his doctrines seem to have been quickly distorted. At a certain period after the prevalence of a system of opinions founded upon those promulgated by him, the three forms into which Plato had distributed the faculties of mind underwent a sort of apotheosis, and became the object of the worship of the civilized world. Here it is to be confessed that "Light seems to thicken," and

> "The crow makes wing to the rocky wood,
> Good things of day begin to droop and drowse,
> And night's black agents to their preys do rouse."

But mark how beautiful an order has sprung from the dust and blood of this fierce chaos! how the world, as from a resurrection, balancing itself on the golden wings of Knowledge and of Hope, has reassumed its yet unwearied flight into the heaven of time. Listen to the music, unheard by outward ears, which is as a ceaseless and invisible wind, nourishing its everlasting course with strength and swiftness.

The poetry in the doctrines of Jesus Christ, and the mythology and institutions of the Celtic conquerors of the Roman Empire, outlived the darkness and the convulsions connected with their growth and victory, and blended themselves in a new fabric of manners and opinion. It is an error to impute the ignorance of the dark ages to the Christian doctrines or the predominance of the Celtic nations. Whatever of evil their agencies may have contained sprang from the extinction of the poetical principle, connected with the progress of despotism and superstition. Men, from causes too intricate to be here discussed, had become insensible and selfish: their own will had become feeble, and yet they were its slaves, and thence the slaves of the will of others: lust, fear, avarice, cruelty, and fraud, characterized a race amongst whom no one was to be found capable of *creating* in form, language, or institution. The moral anomalies of such a state of society are not justly to be charged upon any class of events immediately connected with them, and those events are most entitled to our approbation which could dissolve it most expeditiously. It is unfortunate for those who cannot distinguish words from thoughts, that many of these anomalies have been incorporated into our popular religion.

It was not until the eleventh century that the effects of the poetry of the Christian and chivalric systems began to manifest themselves. The principle of equality had been discovered and applied by Plato in his "Republic" as the theoretical rule of the mode in which the materials of pleasure and of power produced by the common skill and labor of human beings ought to be distributed among them. The limitations of this rule were asserted by him to be determined only by the sensibility of each, or the utility to result to all. Plato, following the doctrines of Timæus and Pythagoras, taught also a moral and intellectual system of doctrine, comprehending at once the past, the present, and the future condition of man. Jesus Christ divulged the sacred and eternal truths contained in these views to mankind, and Christianity, in its abstract purity, became the exoteric expression of the esoteric doctrines of the poetry and wisdom of antiquity. The incorporation of the Celtic nations with the exhausted population of the south impressed upon it the figure of the poetry existing in their mythology and institutions. The result was a sum of the action and reaction of all the causes included in it; for it may be assumed as a maxim that no nation or religion can supersede any other without incorporating into itself a portion of that which it supersedes. The abolition of personal and domestic slavery, and the emancipation of women from a great part of the degrad-

ing restraints of antiquity, were among the consequences of these
events.

The abolition of personal slavery is the basis of the highest political hope that it can enter into the mind of man to conceive. The
freedom of women produced the poetry of sexual love. Love became
a religion, the idols of whose worship were ever present. It was as if
the statues of Apollo and the Muses had been endowed with life and
motion, and had walked forth among their worshippers; so that
earth became peopled with the inhabitants of a diviner world. The
familiar appearance and proceedings of life became wonderful and
heavenly, and a paradise was created as out of the wrecks of Eden.
And as this creation itself is poetry, so its creators were poets; and
language was the instrument of their art: *"Galeotto fù il libro, e chi
lo scrisse."* [4] The Provençal trouveurs, or inventors, preceded Petrarch,
whose verses are as spells, which unseal the inmost enchanted fountains of the delight which is in the grief of love. It is impossible to
feel them without becoming a portion of that beauty which we contemplate: it were superfluous to explain how the gentleness and the
elevation of mind connected with these sacred emotions can render
men more amiable, more generous and wise, and lift them out of the
dull vapors of the little world of self. Dante understood the secret
things of love even more than Petrarch. His "Vita Nuova" is an
inexhaustible fountain of purity of sentiment and language: it is the
idealized history of that period, and those intervals of his life which
were dedicated to love. His apotheosis of Beatrice in Paradise, and
the gradations of his own love and her loveliness, by which as by
steps he feigns himself to have ascended to the throne of the Supreme
Cause, is the most glorious imagination of modern poetry. The
acutest critics have justly reversed the judgment of the vulgar, and
the order of the great acts of the "Divine Drama," in the measure of
the admiration which they accord to the Hell, Purgatory, and Paradise. The latter is a perpetual hymn of everlasting love. Love, which
found a worthy poet in Plato alone of all the ancients, has been
celebrated by a chorus of the greatest writers of the renovated world;
and the music has penetrated the caverns of society, and its echoes

---

[4] "The book, and he who wrote it, was a Galeotto" [*i. e.*, a pander], from the
episode of Paolo and Francesca in Dante's "Inferno," v. 137.

still drown the dissonance of arms and superstition. At successive intervals, Ariosto, Tasso, Shakespeare, Spenser, Calderon, Rousseau, and the great writers of our own age, have celebrated the dominion of love, planting as it were trophies in the human mind of that sublimest victory over sensuality and force. The true relation borne to each other by the sexes into which humankind is distributed has become less misunderstood; and if the error which confounded diversity with inequality of the powers of the two sexes has been partially recognised in the opinions and institutions of modern Europe, we owe this great benefit to the worship of which chivalry was the law, and poets the prophets.

The poetry of Dante may be considered as the bridge thrown over the stream of time, which unites the modern and ancient world. The distorted notions of invisible things which Dante and his rival Milton have idealized, are merely the mask and the mantle in which these great poets walk through eternity enveloped and disguised. It is a difficult question to determine how far they were conscious of the distinction which must have subsisted in their minds between their own creeds and that of the people. Dante at least appears to wish to mark the full extent of it by placing Rhipæus, whom Vergil calls *justissimus unus*,[5] in Paradise, and observing a most heretical caprice in his distribution of rewards and punishments. And Milton's poem contains within itself a philosophical refutation of that system, of which, by a strange and natural antithesis, it has been a chief popular support. Nothing can exceed the energy and magnificence of the character of Satan as expressed in "Paradise Lost." It is a mistake to suppose that he could ever have been intended for the popular personification of evil. Implacable hate, patient cunning, and a sleepless refinement of device to inflict the extremist anguish on an enemy, these things are evil; and, although venial in a slave, are not to be forgiven in a tyrant; although redeemed by much that ennobles his defeat in one subdued, are marked by all that dishonors his conquest in the victor. Milton's Devil as a moral being is as far superior to his God, as one who perseveres in some purpose which he has conceived to be excellent in spite of adversity and torture, is to one who in the cold security of undoubted triumph inflicts the

[5] "The one most just man."

most horrible revenge upon his enemy, not from any mistaken
notion of inducing him to repent of a perseverance in enmity, but
with the alleged design of exasperating him to deserve new torments.
Milton has so far violated the popular creed (if this shall be judged
to be a violation) as to have alleged no superiority of moral virtue to
his God over his Devil. And this bold neglect of a direct moral
purpose is the most decisive proof of the supremacy of Milton's
genius. He mingled as it were the elements of human nature as
colors upon a single pallet, and arranged them in the composition
of his great picture according to the laws of epic truth; that is,
according to the laws of that principle by which a series of actions
of the external universe and of intelligent and ethical beings is
calculated to excite the sympathy of succeeding generations of mankind. The "Divina Commedia" and "Paradise Lost" have conferred
upon modern mythology a systematic form; and when change and
time shall have added one more superstition to the mass of those
which have arisen and decayed upon the earth, commentators will
be learnedly employed in elucidating the religion of ancestral Europe,
only not utterly forgotten because it will have been stamped with
the eternity of genius.

Homer was the first and Dante the second epic poet: that is, the
second poet, the series of whose creations bore a defined and intelligible relation to the knowledge and sentiment and religion of the
age in which he lived, and of the ages which followed it, developing
itself in correspondence with their development. For Lucretius had
limed the wings of his swift spirit in the dregs of the sensible world;
and Vergil, with a modesty that ill became his genius, had affected
the fame of an imitator, even whilst he created anew all that he
copied; and none among the flock of mock-birds, though their notes
were sweet, Apollonius Rhodius, Quintus Calaber, Nonnus, Lucan,
Statius, or Claudian, have sought even to fulfil a single condition of
epic truth. Milton was the third epic poet. For if the title of epic
in its highest sense be refused to the "Æneid," still less can it be
conceded to the "Orlando Furioso," the "Gerusalemme Liberata,"
the "Lusiad," or the "Faerie Queene."

Dante and Milton were both deeply penetrated with the ancient
religion of the civilized world; and its spirit exists in their poetry

probably in the same proportion as its forms survived in the unreformed worship of modern Europe. The one preceded and the other followed the Reformation at almost equal intervals. Dante was the first religious reformer, and Luther surpassed him rather in the rudeness and acrimony than in the boldness of his censures of papal usurpation. Dante was the first awakener of entranced Europe; he created a language, in itself music and persuasion, out of a chaos of inharmonious barbarians. He was the congregator of those great spirits who presided over the resurrection of learning; the Lucifer of that starry flock which in the thirteenth century shone forth from republican Italy, as from a heaven, into the darkness of the benighted world. His very words are instinct with spirit; each is as a spark, a burning atom of inextinguishable thought; and many yet lie covered in the ashes of their birth, and pregnant with the lightning which has yet found no conductor. All high poetry is infinite; it is as the first acorn, which contained all oaks potentially. Veil after veil may be undrawn, and the inmost naked beauty of the meaning never exposed. A great poem is a fountain forever overflowing with the waters of wisdom and delight; and after one person and one age has exhausted all its divine effluence which their peculiar relations enable them to share, another and yet another succeeds, and new relations are ever developed, the source of an unforeseen and an unconceived delight.

The age immediately succeeding to that of Dante, Petrarch, and Boccaccio was characterized by a revival of painting, sculpture, and architecture. Chaucer caught the sacred inspiration, and the superstructure of English literature is based upon the materials of Italian invention.

But let us not be betrayed from a defence into a critical history of poetry and its influence on society. Be it enough to have pointed out the effects of poets, in the large and true sense of the word, upon their own and all succeeding times.

But poets have been challenged to resign the civic crown to reasoners and mechanists, on another plea. It is admitted that the exercise of the imagination is most delightful, but it is alleged that that of reason is more useful. Let us examine as the grounds of this distinction what is here meant by utility. Pleasure or good, in a general sense, is that which the consciousness of a sensitive and intelligent being seeks, and in which, when found, it acquiesces. There are two kinds of pleasure, one durable, universal, and permanent; the other transitory and particular. Utility may either express the means of producing the former or the latter. In the former sense, whatever strengthens and purifies the affections, enlarges the imagination, and adds spirit to sense, is useful. But a narrower meaning may be assigned to the word utility, confining it to express that which banishes the importunity of the wants of our animal nature, the surrounding men with security of life, the dispersing the grosser delusions of superstitions, and the conciliating such a degree of mutual forbearance among men as may consist with the motives of personal advantage.

Undoubtedly the promoters of utility, in this limited sense, have their appointed office in society. They follow the footsteps of poets, and copy the sketches of their creations into the book of common life. They make space, and give time. Their exertions are of the highest value, so long as they confine their administration of the concerns of the inferior powers of our nature within the limits due to the superior ones. But whilst the sceptic destroys gross superstitions, let him spare to deface, as some of the French writers have defaced, the eternal truths charactered upon the imaginations of men. Whilst the mechanist abridges, and the political economist combines labor, let them beware that their speculations, for want of correspondence with those first principles which belong to the imagination, do not tend, as they have in modern England, to exasperate at once the extremes of luxury and want. They have exemplified the saying, "To him that hath, more shall be given; and from him that hath not, the little that he hath shall be taken away." The rich have become richer, and the poor have become poorer; and the vessel of the State is driven between the Scylla and Charybdis of anarchy and despotism. Such are the effects which must ever flow from an unmitigated exercise of the calculating faculty.

It is difficult to define pleasure in its highest sense; the definition involving a number of apparent paradoxes. For, from an inexplicable defect of harmony in the constitution of human nature, the pain of the inferior is frequently connected with the pleasures of the superior portions of our being. Sorrow, terror, anguish, despair itself, are often the chosen expressions of an approximation to the highest good. Our sympathy in tragic fiction depends on this principle; tragedy delights by affording a shadow of the pleasure which exists in pain. This is the source also of the melancholy which is inseparable from the sweetest melody. The pleasure that is in sorrow is sweeter than the pleasure of pleasure itself. And hence the saying, "It is better to go to the house of mourning than to the house of mirth." Not that this highest species of pleasure is necessarily linked with pain. The delight of love and friendship, the ecstasy of the admiration of nature, the joy of the perception and still more of the creation of poetry, is often wholly unalloyed.

The production and assurance of pleasure in this highest sense is true utility. Those who produce and preserve this pleasure are poets or poetical philosophers.

The exertions of Locke, Hume, Gibbon, Voltaire, Rousseau,[6] and their disciples, in favor of oppressed and deluded humanity, are entitled to the gratitude of mankind. Yet it is easy to calculate the degree of moral and intellectual improvement which the world would have exhibited, had they never lived. A little more nonsense would have been talked for a century or two; and perhaps a few more men, women, and children burnt as heretics. We might not at this moment have been congratulating each other on the abolition of the Inquisition in Spain. But it exceeds all imagination to conceive what would have been the moral condition of the world if neither Dante, Petrarch, Boccaccio, Chaucer, Shakespeare, Calderon, Lord Bacon, nor Milton, had ever existed; if Raphael and Michael Angelo had never been born; if the Hebrew poetry had never been translated; if a revival of the study of Greek literature had never taken place; if no monuments of ancient sculpture had been handed down to us; and if the poetry of the religion of the ancient world had been extinguished together with its belief. The human mind could never, except by the intervention of these excitements, have been awakened to the invention of the grosser sciences, and that application of analytical reasoning to the aberrations of society,

---

[6] Although Rousseau has been thus classed, he was essentially a poet. The others, even Voltaire, were mere reasoners.—S.

which it is now attempted to exalt over the direct expression of the inventive and creative faculty itself.

We have more moral, political, and historical wisdom than we know how to reduce into practice; we have more scientific and economical knowledge than can be accommodated to the just distribution of the produce which it multiplies. The poetry in these systems of thought is concealed by the accumulation of facts and calculating processes. There is no want of knowledge respecting what is wisest and best in morals, government, and political economy, or at least, what is wiser and better than what men now practise and endure. But we let "*I dare not* wait upon *I would,* like the poor cat in the adage." We want the creative faculty to imagine that which we know; we want the generous impulse to act that which we imagine; we want the poetry of life; our calculations have outrun conception; we have eaten more than we can digest. The cultivation of those sciences which have enlarged the limits of the empire of man over the external world, has, for want of the poetical faculty, proportionally circumscribed those of the internal world; and man, having enslaved the elements, remains himself a slave. To what but a cultivation of the mechanical arts in a degree disproportioned to the presence of the creative faculty, which is the basis of all knowledge, is to be attributed the abuse of all invention for abridging and combining labor, to the exasperation of the inequality of mankind? From what other cause has it arisen that the discoveries which should have lightened, have added a weight to the curse imposed on Adam? Poetry, and the principle of Self, of which money is the visible incarnation, are the God and Mammon of the world.

The functions of the poetical faculty are twofold: by one it creates new materials of knowledge, and power, and pleasure; by the other it engenders in the mind a desire to reproduce and arrange them according to a certain rhythm and order which may be called the beautiful and the good. The cultivation of poetry is never more to be desired than at periods when, from an excess of the selfish and calculating principle, the accumulation of the materials of external life exceed the quantity of the power of assimilating them to the internal laws of human nature. The body has then become too unwieldy for that which animates it.

Poetry is indeed something divine. It is at once the centre and circumference of knowledge; it is that which comprehends all science, and that to which all science must be referred. It is at the same time the root and blossom of all other systems of thought; it is that from which all spring, and that which adorns all; and that which, if blighted, denies the fruit and the seed, and withholds from the barren world the nourishment and the succession of the scions of the tree of life. It is the perfect and consummate surface and bloom of all things; it is as the odor and the color of the rose to the texture of the elements which compose it, as the form and splendor of unfaded beauty to the secrets of anatomy and corruption. What were virtue, love, patriotism, friendship—what were the scenery of this beautiful universe which we inhabit; what were our consolations on this side of the grave—and what were our aspirations beyond it, if poetry did not ascend to bring light and fire from those eternal regions where the owl-winged faculty of calculation dare not ever soar? Poetry is not like reasoning, a power to be exerted according to the determination of the will. A man cannot say, "I will compose poetry." The greatest poet even cannot say it; for the mind in creation is as a fading coal, which some invisible influence, like an inconstant wind, awakens to transitory brightness; this power arises from within, like the color of a flower which fades and changes as it is developed, and the conscious portions of our natures are unprophetic either of its approach or its departure. Could this influence be durable in its original purity and force, it is impossible to predict the greatness of the results; but when composition begins, inspiration is already on the decline, and the most glorious poetry that has ever been communicated to the world is probably a feeble shadow of the original conceptions of the poet. I appeal to the greatest poets of the present day, whether it is not an error to assert that the finest passages of poetry are produced by labor and study. The toil and the delay recommended by critics can be justly interpreted to mean no more than a careful observation of the inspired moments, and an artificial connection of the spaces between their suggestions by the intertexture of conventional expressions; a necessity only imposed by the limitedness of the poetical faculty itself: for Milton conceived the "Paradise Lost" as a whole before he executed it in portions. We have his own authority also for the Muse having "dictated" to him the "unpremeditated song." And let this be an answer to those who would allege the fifty-six various readings of the first line of the "Orlando Furioso." Compositions so produced are to poetry what mosaic is to painting. This instinct and intuition of the poetical faculty are still more observable in the plastic and pictorial arts; a great statue or picture grows under the power of the artist as a child in a mother's womb; and the very mind which directs the hands in formation is incapable of accounting to itself for the origin, the gradations, or the *media* of the process.

Poetry is the record of the best and happiest moments of the happiest and best minds. We are aware of evanescent visitations of thought and feeling sometimes associated with place or person, sometimes regarding our own mind alone, and always arising unforeseen and departing unbidden, but elevating and delightful beyond all expression: so that even in the desire and the regret they leave, there cannot but be pleasure, participating as it does in the nature of its object. It is as it were the interpenetration of a diviner nature through our own; but its footsteps are like those of a wind over the sea, which the coming calm erases, and whose traces remain only as on the wrinkled sand which paves it. These and corresponding conditions of being are experienced principally by those of the most delicate sensibility and the most enlarged imagination; and the state of mind produced by them is at war with every base desire. The enthusiasm of virtue, love, patriotism, and friendship is essentially linked with such emotions; and whilst they last, self appears as what it is, an atom to a universe. Poets are not only subject to these experiences as spirits of the most refined organization, but they can color all that they combine with the evanescent hues of this ethereal world; a word, a trait in the representation of a scene or a passion will touch the enchanted chord, and reanimate, in those who have ever experienced these emotions, the sleeping, the cold, the buried image of the past. Poetry thus makes immortal all that is best and most beautiful in the world; it arrests the vanishing apparitions which haunt the interlunations of life, and veiling them, or in language or in form, sends them forth among mankind, bearing sweet news of kindred joy to those with whom their sisters abide—abide, because there is no portal of expression from the caverns of the spirit which they inhabit into the universe of things. Poetry redeems from decay the visitations of the divinity in man.

Poetry turns all things to loveliness; it exalts the beauty of that which is most beautiful, and it adds beauty to that which is most deformed; it marries exultation and horror, grief and pleasure, eternity and change; it subdues to union under its light yoke all irreconcilable things. It transmutes all that it touches, and every form moving within the radiance of its presence is changed by wondrous sympathy to an incarnation of the spirit which it breathes: its secret alchemy turns to potable gold the poisonous waters which flow from death through life; it strips the veil of familiarity from the world, and lays bare the naked and sleeping beauty, which is the spirit of its forms.

All things exist as they are perceived: at least in relation to the percipient. "The mind is its own place, and of itself can make a heaven of hell, a hell of heaven." But poetry defeats the curse which binds us to be subjected to the accident of surrounding impressions. And whether it spreads its own figured curtain, or withdraws life's dark veil from before the scene of things, it equally creates for us a being within our being. It makes us the inhabitants of a world to which the familiar world is a chaos. It reproduces the common universe of which we are portions and percipients, and it purges from our inward sight the film of familiarity which obscures from us the wonder of our being. It compels us to feel that which we perceive, and to imagine that which we know. It creates anew the universe, after it has been annihilated in our minds by the recurrence of impressions blunted by reiteration. It justifies the bold and true words of Tasso—"*Non merita nome di creatore, se non Iddio ed il Poeta.*"[7]

A poet, as he is the author to others of the highest wisdom, pleasure, virtue, and glory, so he ought personally to be the happiest, the best, the wisest, and the most illustrious of men. As to his glory, let time be challenged to declare whether the fame of any other institutor of human life be comparable to that of a poet. That he is the wisest, the happiest, and the best, inasmuch as he is a poet, is equally

[7] "No one merits the name of creator except God and the Poet."

incontrovertible: the greatest poets have been men of the most spotless virtue, of the most consummate prudence, and, if we would look into the interior of their lives, the most fortunate of men: and the exceptions, as they regard those who possessed the poetic faculty in a high yet inferior degree, will be found on consideration to confine rather than destroy the rule. Let us for a moment stoop to the arbitration of popular breath, and usurping and uniting in our own persons the incompatible characters of accuser, witness, judge, and executioner, let us decide without trial, testimony, or form, that certain motives of those who are "there sitting where we dare not soar," are reprehensible. Let us assume that Homer was a drunkard, that Vergil was a flatterer, that Horace was a coward, that Tasso was a madman, that Lord Bacon was a peculator, that Raphael was a libertine, that Spenser was a poet laureate. It is inconsistent with this division of our subject to cite living poets, but posterity has done ample justice to the great names now referred to. Their errors have been weighed and found to have been dust in the balance; if their sins "were as scarlet, they are now white as snow"; they have been washed in the blood of the mediator and redeemer, Time. Observe in what a ludicrous chaos the imputations of real or fictitious crime have been confused in the contemporary calumnies against poetry and poets; consider how little is as it appears—or appears as it is; look to your own motives, and judge not, lest ye be judged.

Poetry, as has been said, differs in this respect from logic, that it is not subject to the control of the active powers of the mind, and that its birth and recurrence have no necessary connection with the consciousness or will. It is presumptuous to determine that these are the necessary conditions of all mental causation, when mental effects are experienced unsusceptible of being referred to them. The frequent recurrence of the poetical power, it is obvious to suppose, may produce in the mind a habit of order and harmony correlative with its own nature and with its effects upon other minds. But in the intervals of inspiration, and they may be frequent without being durable, a poet becomes a man, and is abandoned to the sudden reflux of the influences under which others habitually live. But as he is more delicately organized than other men, and sensible to pain and pleasure, both his own and that of others, in a degree unknown to them, he will avoid the one and pursue the other with an ardor proportioned to this difference. And he renders himself obnoxious to calumny, when he neglects to observe the circumstances under which these objects of universal pursuit and flight have disguised themselves in one another's garments.

But there is nothing necessarily evil in this error, and thus cruelty, envy, revenge, avarice, and the passions purely evil have never formed any portion of the popular imputations on the lives of poets.

I have thought it most favorable to the cause of truth to set down these remarks according to the order in which they were suggested to my mind, by a consideration of the subject itself, instead of observing the formality of a polemical reply; but if the view which they contain be just, they will be found to involve a refutation of the arguers against poetry, so far at least as regards the first division of the subject. I can readily conjecture what should have moved the gall of some learned and intelligent writers who quarrel with certain versifiers; I confess myself, like them, unwilling to be stunned by the Theseids of the hoarse Codri of the day. Bavius and Mævius undoubtedly are, as they ever were, insufferable persons. But it belongs to a philosophical critic to distinguish rather than confound.

The first part of these remarks has related to poetry in its elements and principles; and it has been shown, as well as the narrow limits assigned them would permit, that what is called poetry, in a restricted sense, has a common source with all other forms of order and of beauty, according to which the materials of human life are susceptible of being arranged, and which is poetry in an universal sense.

The second part will have for its object an application of these principles to the present state of the cultivation of poetry, and a defence of the attempt to idealize the modern forms of manners and opinions, and compel them into a subordination to the imaginative and creative faculty. For the literature of England, an energetic development of which has ever preceded or accompanied a great and free development of the national will, has arisen as it were from a new birth. In spite of the low-thoughted envy which would undervalue contemporary merit, our own will be a memorable age in intellectual achievements, and we live among such philosophers and poets as surpass beyond comparison any who have appeared since the last national struggle for civil and religious liberty. The most unfailing herald, companion, and follower of the awakening of a great people to work a beneficial change in opinion or institution, is poetry. At such periods there is an accumulation of the power of communicating and receiving intense and impassioned conceptions respecting man and nature. The persons in whom this power resides, may often, as far as regards many portions of their nature, have little apparent correspondence with that spirit of good of which they are the ministers. But even whilst they deny and abjure, they are yet compelled to serve, that power which is seated on the throne of their own soul. It is impossible to read the compositions of the most celebrated writers of the present day without being startled with the electric life which burns within their words. They measure the circumference and sound the depths of human nature with a comprehensive and all-penetrating spirit, and they are themselves perhaps the most sincerely astonished at its manifestations; for it is less their spirit than the spirit of the age. Poets are the hierophants of an unapprehended inspiration; the mirrors of the gigantic shadows which futurity casts upon the present; the words which express what they understand not; the trumpets which sing to battle, and feel not what they inspire; the influence which is moved not, but moves. Poets are the unacknowledged legislators of the world.

MACHIAVELLI

BY
THOMAS BABINGTON MACAULAY

INTRODUCTORY NOTE

THOMAS BABINGTON MACAULAY (1800–1859) was the son of Zachary Macaulay, a Scotsman whose experience in the West Indies had made him an ardent Abolitionist. Thomas was an infant prodigy, and the extraordinary memory which is borne witness to in his writings was developed at an early age. He was educated at Cambridge, studied law, and began to write for the "Edinburgh Review" at twenty-five, his well-known style being already formed. He entered the House of Commons in 1830, and at once made a reputation as an orator. In 1834 he went to India as a member of the Supreme Council, and during his three and a half years there he proved himself a capable and beneficent administrator. On his return, he again entered Parliament, held cabinet office, and retired from political life in 1856.

Until about 1844 Macaulay's writings appeared chiefly in the "Edinburgh Review," the great organ of the Whig Party, to which he belonged. These articles as now collected are perhaps the most widely known critical and historical essays in the language. The brilliant antithetical style, the wealth of illustration, the pomp and picturesqueness with which the events of the narrative are brought before the eyes of the reader, combine to make them in the highest degree entertaining and informing. His "History of England," which occupied his later years, was the most popular book of its kind ever published in England, and owed its success to much the same qualities. The "Lays of Ancient Rome" and his other verses gained and still hold a large public, mainly by virtue of their vigor of movement and strong declamatory quality.

The essay on Machiavelli belongs to Macaulay's earlier period, and illustrates his mastery of material that might seem to lie outside of his usual field. But here in the Italy of the Renaissance, as in the England or the India which he knew at first hand, we have the same characteristic simplification and arrangement of motives and conditions that make his clear exposition possible, the same dash and vividness in bringing home to the reader his conception of a great character and a great epoch.

MACHIAVELLI[1]

THOSE who have attended to this practice of our literary tribunal are well aware, that, by means of certain legal fictions similar to those of Westminster Hall, we are frequently enabled to take cognizance of cases lying beyond the sphere of our original jurisdiction. We need hardly say, therefore, that, in the present instance, M. Périer is merely a Richard Roe, who will not be mentioned in any subsequent stage of the proceedings, and whose name is used for the sole purpose of bringing Machiavelli into court.

We doubt whether any name in literary history be so generally odious as that of the man whose character and writings we now propose to consider. The terms in which he is commonly described would seem to impart that he was the Tempter, the Evil Principle, the discoverer of ambition and revenge, the original inventor of perjury, and that, before the publication of his fatal "Prince," there had never been a hypocrite, a tyrant, or a traitor, a simulated virtue, or a convenient crime. One writer gravely assures us that Maurice of Saxony learned all his fraudulent policy from that execrable volume. Another remarks, that, since it was translated into Turkish, the sultans have been more addicted than formerly to the custom of strangling their brothers. Lord Lyttelton charges the poor Florentine with the manifold treasons of the house of Guise, and with the Massacre of St. Bartholomew. Several authors have hinted that the Gunpowder Plot is to be primarily attributed to his doctrines, and seem to think that his effigy ought to be substituted for that of Guy Fawkes, in those processions by which the ingenuous youth of England annually commemorate the preservation of the Three Estates. The Church of Rome has pronounced his works accursed

[1] Originally published as a review of a translation of the complete works of Machiavelli by J. V. Périès.

things. Nor have our own countrymen been backward in testifying their opinion of his merits. Out of his surname they have coined an epithet for a knave, and out of his Christian name a synonym for the Devil.

It is indeed scarcely possible for any person, not well acquainted with the history and literature of Italy, to read without horror and amazement the celebrated treatise which has brought so much obloquy on the name of Machiavelli. Such a display of wickedness, naked yet not ashamed, such cool, judicious, scientific atrocity, seemed rather to belong to a fiend than to the most depraved of men. Principles which the most hardened ruffian would scarcely hint to his most trusted accomplice, or avow, without the disguise of some palliating sophism, even to his own mind, are professed without the slightest circumlocution, and assumed as the fundamental axioms of all political science.

It is not strange that ordinary readers should regard the author of such a book as the most depraved and shameless of human beings. Wise men, however, have always been inclined to look with great suspicion on the angels and demons of the multitude; and, in the present instance, several circumstances have led even superficial observers to question the justice of the vulgar decision. It is notorious that Machiavelli was, through life, a zealous republican. In the same year in which he composed his manual of "Kingcraft," he suffered imprisonment and torture in the cause of public liberty. It seems inconceivable that the martyr of freedom should have designedly acted as the apostle of tyranny. Several eminent writers have, therefore, endeavored to detect in this unfortunate performance some concealed meaning, more consistent with the character and conduct of the author than that which appears at the first glance.

One hypothesis is, that Machiavelli intended to practise on the young Lorenzo de' Medici a fraud similar to that which Sunderland is said to have employed against our James II, and that he urged his pupil to violent and perfidious measures, as ⁺he surest means of accelerating the moment of deliverance and revenge. Another supposition, which Lord Bacon seems to countenance, is that the treatise was merely a piece of grave irony, intended to warn nations against the arts of ambitious men. It would be easy to show that neither of these solutions is consistent with many passages in "The Prince" itself. But the most decisive refutation is that which is furnished by the other works of Machiavelli. In all the writings which he gave to the public, and in all those which the research of editors has, in the course of three centuries, discovered; in his comedies, designed for the entertainment of the multitude; in his "Comments on Livy," intended for the perusal of the most enthusiastic patriots of Florence; in his history, inscribed to one of the most amiable and estimable of the popes; in his public despatches; in his private memoranda—the same obliquity of moral principle for which "The Prince" is so severely censured is more or less discernible. We doubt whether it would be possible to find, in all the many volumes of his compositions, a single expression indicating that dissimulation and treachery had ever struck him as discreditable.

After this, it may seem ridiculous to say that we are acquainted with few writings which exhibit so much elevation of sentiment, so pure and warm a zeal for the public good, or so just a view of the duties and rights of citizens, as those of Machiavelli. Yet so it is. And even from "The Prince" itself we could select many passages in support of this remark. To a reader of our age and country, this inconsistency is, at first, perfectly bewildering. The whole man seems to be an enigma, a grotesque assemblage of incongruous qualities, selfishness and generosity, cruelty and benevolence, craft and simplicity, abject villany and romantic heroism. One sentence is such as a veteran diplomatist would scarcely write in cipher for the direction of his most confidential spy: the next seems to be extracted from a theme composed by an ardent school-boy on the death of Leonidas. An act of dexterous perfidy and an act of patriotic self-devotion call forth the same kind and the same degree of respectful admiration. The moral sensibility of the writer seems at once to be morbidly obtuse and morbidly acute. Two characters altogether dissimilar are united in him. They are not merely joined, but interwoven. They are the warp and the woof of his mind; and their combination, like that of the variegated threads in shot silk, gives to the whole texture a glancing and ever-changing appearance. The explanation might have been easy if he had been a very weak or a very affected man. But he was evidently neither the one nor the other. His works prove, beyond all contradiction, that his understanding was strong, his taste pure, and his sense of the ridiculous exquisitely keen.

This is strange, and yet the strangest is behind. There is no reason whatever to think that those amongst whom he lived saw anything shocking or incongruous in his writings. Abundant proofs remain of the high estimation in which both his works and his person were held by the most respectable among his contemporaries. Clement VII patronized the publication of those very books which the Council of Trent, in the following generation, pronounced unfit for the perusal of Christians. Some members of the democratical party censured the secretary for dedicating "The Prince" to a patron who bore the unpopular name of Medici. But, to those immoral doctrines which have since called forth such severe reprehensions no exception appears to have been taken. The cry against them was first raised beyond the Alps, and seems to have been heard with amazement in Italy. The earliest assailant, as far as we are aware, was a countryman of our own, Cardinal Pole. The author of the "Anti-Machiavelli" was a French Protestant.

It is, therefore, in the state of moral feeling among the Italians of those times that we must seek for the real explanation of what seems most mysterious in the life and writings of this remarkable man. As this is a subject which suggests many interesting considerations, both political and metaphysical, we shall make no apology for discussing it at some length.

During the gloomy and disastrous centuries which followed the downfall of the Roman Empire, Italy had preserved, in a far greater degree than any other part of western Europe, the traces of ancient civilization. The night which descended upon her was the night of an Arctic summer. The dawn began to reappear before the last reflection of the preceding sunset had faded from the horizon. It was in the time of the French Merovingians and of the Saxon Heptarchy that ignorance and ferocity seemed to have done their worst. Yet even then the Neapolitan provinces, recognizing the authority of the Eastern Empire, preserved something of Eastern knowledge and refinement. Rome, protected by the sacred character of her pontiffs, enjoyed at least comparative security and repose. Even in those regions where the sanguinary Lombards had fixed their monarchy, there was incomparably more of wealth, of information, of physical comfort, and of social order, than could be found in Gaul, Britain, or Germany.

That which most distinguished Italy from the neighboring countries was the importance which the population of the towns, at a very early period, began to acquire. Some cities had been founded in wild and remote situations, by fugitives who had escaped from the rage of the barbarians. Such were Venice and Genoa, which preserved their freedom by their obscurity, till they became able to preserve it by their power. Other cities seem to have retained, under all the changing dynasties of invaders, under Odoacer and Theodoric, Narses and Alboin, the municipal institutions which had been conferred on them by the liberal policy of the Great Republic. In provinces which the central government was too feeble either to protect or to oppress, these institutions gradually acquired stability and vigor. The citizens, defended by their walls, and governed by their own magistrates and their own by-laws, enjoyed a considerable share of republican independence. Thus a strong democratic spirit was called into action. The Carlovingian sovereigns were too imbecile to subdue it. The generous policy of Otho encouraged it. It might perhaps have been suppressed by a close coalition between the Church and the empire. It was fostered and invigorated by their disputes. In the twelfth century it attained its full vigor, and, after a long and doubtful conflict, triumphed over the abilities and courage of the Swabian princes.

The assistance of the ecclesiastical power had greatly contributed to the success of the Guelfs. That success would, however, have been a doubtful good, if its only effect had been to substitute a moral for a political servitude, and to exalt the popes at the expense of the Cæsars. Happily the public mind of Italy had long contained the seeds of free opinions, which were now rapidly developed by the genial influence of free institutions. The people of that country had observed the whole machinery of the Church, its saints and its miracles, its lofty pretensions, and its splendid ceremonial, its worthless blessings and its harmless curses, too long and too closely to be duped. They stood behind the scenes on which others were gazing with childish awe and interest. They witnessed the arrangement of the pulleys, and the manufacture of the thunders. They saw the natural faces, and heard the natural voices, of the actors. Distant nations looked on the Pope as the vicegerent of the Almighty, the oracle of the All-Wise, the umpire from whose decisions, in the disputes either of theologians or of kings, no Christian ought to appeal. The Italians were acquainted with all the follies of his youth, and with all the dishonest arts by which he had attained power. They knew how often he had employed the keys of the Church to release himself from the most sacred engagements, and its wealth to pamper his mistresses and nephews. The doctrines and rites of the established religion they treated with decent reverence. But, though they still called themselves Catholics, they had ceased to be papists. Those spiritual arms which carried terror into the palaces and camps of the proudest sovereigns excited only contempt in the immediate neighborhood of the Vatican. Alexander, when he commanded our Henry II to submit to the lash before the tomb of a rebellious subject, was himself an exile. The Romans, apprehending that he entertained designs against their liberties, had driven him from their city; and, though he solemnly promised to confine himself for the future to his spiritual functions, they still refused to readmit him.

In every other part of Europe, a large and powerful privileged class trampled on the people, and defied the government. But, in the most flourishing parts of Italy, the feudal nobles were reduced to comparative insignificance. In some districts they took shelter under the protection of the powerful commonwealths which they were unable to oppose, and gradually sank into the mass of burghers. In other places, they possessed great influence; but it was an influence widely different from that which was exercised by the aristocracy of any trans-Alpine kingdom. They were not petty princes, but eminent citizens. Instead of strengthening their fastnesses among the mountains, they embellished their palaces in the market-place. The state of society in the Neapolitan dominions, and in some parts of the ecclesiastical State, more nearly resembled that which existed in the great monarchies of Europe. But the governments of Lombardy and Tuscany, through all their revolutions, preserved a different character. A people, when assembled in a town, is far more formidable to its rulers than when dispersed over a wide extent of country. The most arbitrary of the Cæsars found it necessary to feed and divert the inhabitants of their unwieldy capital at the expense of the provinces. The citizens of Madrid have more than once besieged their sovereign in his own palace, and extorted from him the most humiliating concessions. The sultans have often been compelled to propitiate the furious rabble of Constantinople with the head of an unpopular vizier. From the same cause, there was a certain tinge of democracy in the monarchies and aristocracies of northern Italy.

Thus liberty, partially indeed and transiently, revisited Italy; and with liberty came commerce and empire, science and taste, all the comforts and all the ornaments of life. The Crusades, from which the inhabitants of other countries gained nothing but relics and wounds, brought to the rising commonwealths of the Adriatic and Tyrrhene seas a large increase of wealth, dominion, and knowledge. The moral and the geographical position of those commonwealths enabled them to profit alike by the barbarism of the West and by the civilization of the East. Italian ships covered every sea. Italian factories rose on every shore. The tables of Italian money-changers were set in every city. Manufactures flourished. Banks were established. The operations of the commercial machine were facilitated by many useful and beautiful inventions. We doubt whether any country of Europe, our own excepted, has at the present time reached so high a point of wealth and civilization as some parts of Italy had attained 400 years ago. Historians rarely descend to those details from which alone the real estate of a community can be collected. Hence posterity is too often deceived by the vague hyperboles of poets and rhetoricians, who mistake the splendor of a court for the happiness of a people. Fortunately, John Villani has given us an example and precise account of the state of Florence in the early part of the fourteenth century. The revenue of the republic amounted to 300,000 florins, a sum which, allowing for the depreciation of the precious metals, was at least equivalent to £600,000 sterling—a larger sum than England and Ireland, two centuries ago, yielded annually to Elizabeth. The manufacture of wool alone employed 200 factories and 30,000 workmen. The cloth annually produced sold, at an average, for 1,200,000 florins—a sum fully equal, in exchangeable value, to £2,500,000 of our money. Four hundred thousand florins were annually coined. Eighty banks conducted the commercial operations, not of Florence only, but of all Europe. The transactions of these establishments were sometimes of a magnitude which may surprise even the contemporaries of the Barings and the Rothschilds. Two houses advanced to Edward III of England upwards of 300,000 marks, at a time when the mark contained more silver than fifty shillings of the present day, and when the value of silver was more than quadruple of what it now is. The city, and its environs contained 170,000 inhabitants. In the various schools about 10,000 children were taught to read, 1,200 studied arithmetic, 600 received a learned education.

The progress of elegant literature and of the fine arts was proportioned to that of the public prosperity. Under the despotic successors of Augustus all the fields of the intellect had been turned into arid wastes, still marked out by formal boundaries, still retaining the traces of old cultivation, but yielding neither flowers nor fruit. The deluge of barbarism came. It swept away all the landmarks. It obliterated all the signs of former tillage. But, it fertilized while it devastated. When it receded, the wilderness was as the garden of God, rejoicing on every side, laughing, clapping its hands, pouring forth, in spontaneous abundance, everything brilliant or fragrant or nourishing. A new language, characterized by simple sweetness and simple energy, had attained perfection. No tongue ever furnished more gorgeous and vivid tints to poetry; nor was it long before a poet appeared who knew how to employ them. Early in the fourteenth century came forth "The Divine Comedy," beyond comparison the greatest work of imagination which had appeared since the poems of Homer. The following generation produced indeed no second Dante, but it was eminently distinguished by general intellectual activity. The study of the Latin writers had never been wholly neglected in Italy. But Petrarch introduced a more profound, liberal, and elegant scholarship, had communicated to his countrymen that enthusiasm for the literature, the history, and the antiquities of Rome, which divided his own heart with a frigid mistress and a more frigid muse. Boccaccio turned their attention to the more sublime and graceful models of Greece.

From this time, the admiration of learning and genius became almost an idolatry among the people of Italy. Kings and republics, cardinals and doges, vied with each other in honoring and flattering Petrarch. Embassies from rival States solicited the honor of his instructions. His coronation agitated the Court of Naples and the people of Rome as much as the most important political transaction could have done. To collect books and antiques, to found professorships, to patronize men of learning, became almost universal fashions among the great. The spirit of literary research allied itself to that of commercial enterprise. Every place to which the merchant princes of Florence extended their gigantic traffic, from the bazars of the Tigris to the monasteries of the Clyde, was ransacked for medals and manuscripts. Architecture, painting, and sculpture were munificently encouraged. Indeed, it would be difficult to name an Italian of eminence, during the period of which we speak, who, whatever may have been his general character, did not at least affect a love of letters and of the arts.

Knowledge and public prosperity continued to advance together. Both attained their meridian in the age of Lorenzo the Magnificent. We cannot refrain from quoting the splendid passage in which the Tuscan Thucydides describes the state of Italy at that period. *"Ridotta tutta in somma pace e tranquillità coltivata non meno ne' luogti più montusoi e più sterili che nelle pianure e regioni più fertili, nè sottoposta ad altro imperio che de' suoi medesimi, non solo era abbondantissima d' abitatori e di ricchezze; ma illustrata sommamente dalla magnificenza di molti principi, dallo splendore di molte nobilissime e bellissime città, dalla sedia e maestà della religione, fioriva d' uomini prestantissimi nell' amministrazione delle cose pubbliche, e d' ingegni molto nobili in tutte le scienze, ed in qualunque arte preclara ed industriosa."*[2] When we peruse this just and splendid description, we can scarcely persuade ourselves that we are

[2] "Enjoying the utmost peace and tranquillity, cultivated as well in the most mountainous and barren places as in the plains and most fertile regions, and not subject to any other dominion than that of its own people, it not only overflowed with inhabitants and with riches, but was highly adorned by the magnificence of many princes, by the splendor of many renowned and beautiful cities, by the abode and majesty of religion, and abounded in men who excelled in the administration of public affairs and in minds most eminent in all the sciences and in every noble and useful art."— Guicciardini, "History of Italy," Book I., trans. Montague.

reading of times in which the annals of England and France present us only with a frightful spectacle of poverty, barbarity, and ignorance. From the oppressions of illiterate masters, and the sufferings of a degraded peasantry, it is delightful to turn to the opulent and enlightened States of Italy, to the vast and magnificent cities, the ports, the arsenals, the villas, the museums, the libraries, the marts filled with every article of comfort or luxury, the factories swarming with artisans, the Apennines covered with rich cultivation up to their very summits, the Po wafting the harvests of Lombardy to the granaries of Venice, and carrying back the silks of Bengal and the furs of Siberia to the palaces of Milan. With peculiar pleasure every cultivated mind must repose on the fair, the happy, the glorious Florence, the halls which rang with the mirth of Pulci, the cell where twinkled the midnight lamp of Politian, the statues on which the young eye of Michael Angelo glared with the frenzy of a kindred inspiration, the gardens in which Lorenzo meditated some sparkling song for the May-day dance of the Etrurian virgins. Alas for the beautiful city! Alas for the wit and the learning, the genius and the love!

> *"Le donne, e i cavalieri, gli affanni e gli agi,*
> *Che ne'nvogliava amore e cortesia*
> *Là dove i cuor son fatti sì malvagi."* [3]

A time was at hand when all the seven vials of the Apocalypse were to be poured forth and shaken out over those pleasant countries—a time of slaughter, famine, beggary, infamy, slavery, despair.

In the Italian States, as in many natural bodies, untimely decrepitude was the penalty of precocious maturity. Their early greatness, and their early decline, are principally to be attributed to the same cause—the preponderance which the towns acquired in the political system.

In a community of hunters or of shepherds every man easily and necessarily becomes a soldier. His ordinary avocations are perfectly compatible with all the duties of military service. However remote may be the expedition on which he is bound, he finds it easy to

---

[3] "The ladies and the knights, the toils and sports to which love and courtesy stirred our desire there where all hearts have grown so evil."—Dante, "Purgatorio," Canto 14, ll. 109–111.

transport with him the stock from which he derives his subsistence. The whole people in an army, the whole year a march. Such was the state of society which facilitated the gigantic conquests of Attila and Tamerlane.

But a people which subsists by the cultivation of the earth is in a very different situation. The husbandman is bound to the soil on which he labors. A long campaign would be ruinous to him. Still his pursuits are such as to give his frame both the active and the passive strength necessary to a soldier. Nor do they, at least in the infancy of agricultural science, demand his uninterrupted attention. At particular times of the year he is almost wholly unemployed, and can, without injury to himself, afford the time necessary for a short expedition. Thus the legions of Rome were supplied during its earlier wars. The season during which the fields did not require the presence of the cultivators sufficed for a short inroad and a battle. These operations, too frequently interrupted to produce decisive results, yet served to keep up among the people a degree of discipline and courage which rendered them not only secure but formidable. The archers and billmen of the Middle Ages, who, with provisions for forty days at their back, left the fields for the camp, were troops of the same description.

But when commerce and manufactures begin to flourish, a great change takes place. The sedentary habits of the desk and the loom render the exertions and hardships of war insupportable. The business of traders and artisans requires their constant presence and attention. In such a community there is little superfluous time; but there is generally much superfluous money. Some members of the society are, therefore, hired to relieve the rest from a task inconsistent with their habits and engagements.

The history of Greece is, in this, as in many other respects, the best commentary on the history of Italy. Five hundred years before the Christian era the citizens of the republics round the Ægean Sea formed perhaps the finest militia that ever existed. As wealth and refinement advanced, the system underwent a gradual alteration. The Ionian States were the first in which commerce and the arts were cultivated, and the first in which the ancient discipline decayed. Within eighty years after the battle of Platæa, mercenary troops were everywhere plying for battles and sieges. In the time of Demosthenes, it was scarcely possible to persuade or compel the Athenians to enlist for foreign service. The laws of Lycurgus prohibited trade and manufactures. The Spartans, therefore, continued to form a national force long after their neighbors had begun to hire soldiers. But their military spirit declined with their singular institutions. In the second century before Christ, Greece contained only one nation of warriors, the savage highlanders of Ætolia, who were some generations behind their countrymen in civilization and intelligence.

All the causes which produced these effects among the Greeks acted still more strongly on the modern Italians. Instead of a power like Sparta, in its nature warlike, they had amongst them an ecclesiastical state, in its nature pacific. Where there are numerous slaves, every freeman is induced by the strongest motives to familiarize himself with the use of arms. The commonwealths of Italy did not, like those of Greece, swarm with thousands of these household enemies. Lastly, the mode in which military operations were conducted during the prosperous times of Italy was peculiarly unfavorable to the formation of an efficient militia. Men covered with iron from head to foot, armed with ponderous lances, and mounted on horses of the largest breed, were considered as composing the strength of an army. The infantry was regarded as comparatively worthless, and was neglected till it became really so. These tactics maintained their ground for centuries in most parts of Europe. That foot-soldiers could withstand the charge of heavy cavalry was thought utterly impossible, till, towards the close of the fifteenth century, the rude mountaineers of Switzerland dissolved the spell, and astounded the most experienced generals by receiving the dreaded shock on an impenetrable forest of pikes.

The use of the Grecian spear, the Roman sword, or the modern bayonet, might be acquired with comparative ease. But nothing short of the daily exercise of years could train the man at arms to support his ponderous panoply, and manage his unwieldy weapon. Throughout Europe this most important branch of war became a separate profession. Beyond the Alps, indeed, though a profession, it was not generally a trade. It was the duty and the amusement of a large class of country gentlemen. It was the service by which they held their lands, and the diversion by which, in the absence of mental resources, they beguiled their leisure. But in the northern States of Italy, as we have already remarked, the growing power of the cities, where it had not exterminated this order of men, had completely changed their habits. Here, therefore, the practice of employing mercenaries became universal, at a time when it was almost unknown in other countries.

When war becomes the trade of a separate class the least dangerous course left to a government is to form that class into a standing army. It is scarcely possible that men can pass their lives in the service of one State, without feeling some interest in its greatness. Its victories are their victories. Its defeats are their defeats. The contract loses something of its mercantile character. The services of the soldier are considered as the effects of patriotic zeal, his pay as the tribute of national gratitude. To betray the power which employs him, to be even remiss in its service, are in his eyes the most atrocious and degrading of crimes.

When the princes and commonwealths of Italy began to use hired troops, their wisest course would have been to form separate military establishments. Unhappily this was not done. The mercenary warriors of the Peninsula, instead of being attached to the service of different powers, were regarded as the common property of all. The connection between the State and its defenders was reduced to the most simple and naked traffic. The adventurer brought his horse, his weapons, his strength, and his experience, into the market. Whether the King of Naples or the Duke of Milan, the Pope or the Signory of Florence, struck the bargain, was to him a matter of perfect indifference. He was for the highest wages and the longest term. When the campaign for which he had contracted was finished, there was neither law nor punctilio to prevent him from instantly turning his arms against his late masters. The soldier was altogether disjoined from the citizen and from the subject.

The natural consequences followed. Left to the conduct of men who neither loved those whom they defended, nor hated those whom they opposed, who were often bound by stronger ties to the army against which they fought than to the State which they served, who lost by the termination of the conflict, and gained by its prolongation, war completely changed its character. Every man came into the field of battle impressed with the knowledge, that, in a few days, he might be taking the pay of the power against which he was then employed, and fighting by the side of his enemies against his associates. The strongest interests and the strongest feelings concurred to mitigate the hostility of those who had lately been brethren in arms, and who might soon be brethren in arms once more. Their common profession was a bond of union not to be forgotten, even when they were engaged in the service of contending parties. Hence it was that operations, languid and indecisive beyond any recorded in history, marches and countermarches, pillaging expeditions and blockades, bloodless capitulations and equally bloodless combats, make up the military history of Italy during the course of nearly two centuries. Mighty armies fight from sunrise to sunset. A great victory is won. Thousands of prisoners are taken, and hardly a life is lost. A pitched battle seems to have been really less dangerous than an ordinary civil tumult.

Courage was now no longer necessary, even to the military character. Men grew old in camps, and acquired the highest renown by their warlike achievements, without being once required to face serious danger. The political consequences are too well known. The richest and most enlightened part of the world was left undefended to the assaults of every barbarous invader, to the brutality of Switzerland, the insolence of France, and the fierce rapacity of Aragon. The moral effects which followed from this state of things were still more remarkable.

Amongst the rude nations which lay beyond the Alps, valor was absolutely indispensable. Without it none could be eminent, few could be secure. Cowardice was, therefore, naturally considered as the foulest reproach. Among the polished Italians, enriched by commerce, governed by law, and passionately attached to literature, everything was done by superiority of intelligence. Their very wars, more pacific than the peace of their neighbors, required rather civil than military qualifications. Hence, while courage was the point of honor in other countries, ingenuity became the point of honor in Italy.

From these principles were deduced, by processes strictly analogous, two opposite systems of fashionable morality. Through the greater part of Europe, the vices which peculiarly belong to timid dispositions, and which are the natural defence of weakness, fraud, and hypocrisy, have always been most disreputable. On the other hand, the excesses of haughty and daring spirits have been treated with indulgence, and even with respect. The Italians regarded with corresponding lenity those crimes which require self-command, address, quick observation, fertile invention, and profound knowledge of human nature.

Such a prince as our Henry V would have been the idol of the North. The follies of his youth, the selfish ambition of his manhood, the Lollards roasted at slow fires, the prisoners massacred on the field of battle, the expiring lease of priestcraft renewed for another century, the dreadful legacy of a causeless and hopeless war bequeathed to a people who had no interest in its event—everything is forgotten but the victory of Agincourt. Francis Sforza, on the other hand, was the model of Italian heroes. He made his employers and his rivals alike his tools. He first overpowered his open enemies by the help of faithless allies: he then armed himself against his allies with the spoils taken from his enemies. By his incomparable dexterity, he raised himself from the precarious and dependent situation of a military adventurer to the first throne of Italy. To such a man much was forgiven—hollow friendship, ungenerous enmity, violated faith. Such are the opposite errors which men commit, when their morality is not a science, but a taste, when they abandon eternal principles for accidental associations.

We have illustrated our meaning by an instance taken from history. We will select another from fiction. Othello murders his wife; he gives orders for the murder of his lieutenant; he ends by murdering himself. Yet he never loses the esteem and affection of Northern readers. His intrepid and ardent spirit redeems everything. The unsuspecting confidence with which he listens to his adviser, the agony with which he shrinks from the thought of shame, the tempest of passion with which he commits his crimes, and the haughty fearlessness with which he avows them, give an extraordinary interest to his character. Iago, on the contrary, is the object of universal loathing. Many are inclined to suspect that Shakespeare has been seduced into an exaggeration unusual with him, and has drawn a monster who has no archetype in human nature. Now, we suspect that an Italian audience in the fifteenth century would have felt very differently. Othello would have inspired nothing but detestation and contempt. The folly with which he trusts the friendly professions of a man whose promotion he had obstructed, the credulity with which he takes unsupported assertions, and trivial circumstances, for unanswerable proofs, the violence with which he silences the exculpation till the exculpation can only aggravate his misery, would have excited the abhorrence and disgust of his spectators. The conduct of Iago they would assuredly have condemned, but they would have condemned it as we condemn that of his victim. Something of interest and respect would have mingled with their disapprobation. The readiness of the traitor's wit, the clearness of his judgment, the skill with which he penetrates the dispositions of others, and conceals his own, would have insured to him a certain portion of their esteem.

So wide was the difference between the Italians and their neighbors. A similar difference existed between the Greeks of the second century before Christ, and their masters, the Romans. The conquerors, brave and resolute, faithful to their engagements, and strongly influenced by religious feelings, were, at the same time, ignorant, arbitrary, and cruel. With the vanquished people were deposited all the art, the science, and the literature of the Western world. In poetry, in philosophy, in painting, in architecture, in sculpture, they had no rivals. Their manners were polished, their perceptions acute, their invention ready; they were tolerant, affable, humane; but of courage and sincerity they were almost utterly destitute. Every rude centurion consoled himself for his intellectual inferiority, by remarking that knowledge and taste seemed only to make men atheists, cowards and slaves. The distinction long continued to be strongly marked, and furnished an admirable subject for the fierce sarcasms of Juvenal.

The citizen of an Italian commonwealth was the Greek of the time of Juvenal and the Greek of the time of Pericles, joined in one. Like the former, he was timid and pliable, artful and mean. But, like the latter, he had a country. Its independence and prosperity were dear to him. If his character were degraded by some base crimes, it was, on the other hand, ennobled by public spirit and by an honorable ambition.

A vice sanctioned by the general opinion is merely a vice. The evil terminates in itself. A vice condemned by the general opinion produces a pernicious effect on the whole character. The former is a local malady, the latter a constitutional taint. When the reputation of the offender is lost, he, too, often flings the remains of his virtue after it in despair. The Highland gentleman, who, a century ago, lived by taking blackmail from his neighbors, committed the same crime for which Wild was accompanied to Tyburn by the huzzas of 200,000 people. But there can be no doubt that he was a much less depraved man than Wild. The deed for which Mrs. Brownrigg was hanged, sinks into nothing when compared with the conduct of the Roman who treated the public to one hundred pairs of gladiators. Yet we should greatly wrong such a Roman if we supposed that his disposition was as cruel as that of Mrs. Brownrigg. In our own country, a woman forfeits her place in society by what, in a man, is too commonly considered as an honorable distinction, and at worst as a venial error. The consequence is notorious. The moral principle of a woman is frequently more impaired by a single lapse from virtue than that of a man by twenty years of intrigues. Classical antiquity would furnish us with instances stronger, if possible, than those to which we have referred.

We must apply this principle to the case before us. Habits of dissimulation and falsehood, no doubt, mark a man of our age and country as utterly worthless and abandoned. But it by no means follows that a similar judgment would be just in the case of an Italian in the Middle Ages. On the contrary, we frequently find those faults which we are accustomed to consider as certain indications of a mind altogether depraved, in company with great and good qualities, with generosity, with benevolence, with disinterestedness. From such a state of society, Palamedes, in the admirable dialogue of Hume, might have drawn illustrations of his theory as striking as any of those with which Fourli furnished him. These are not, we well know, the lessons which historians are generally most careful to teach, or readers most willing to learn. But they are not therefore

useless. How Philip disposed his troops at Chæronea, where Hannibal crossed the Alps, whether Mary blew up Darnley, or Siquier
shot Charles XII, and the thousand other questions of the same
description, are in themselves unimportant. The inquiry may amuse
us, but the decision leaves us no wiser. He alone reads history aright,
who, observing how powerfully circumstances influence the feelings
and opinions of men, how often vices pass into virtues, and paradoxes
into axioms, learns to distinguish what is accidental and transitory
in human nature, from what is essential and immutable.

In this respect, no history suggests more important reflections than
that of the Tuscan and Lombard commonwealths. The character of
the Italian statesman seems, at first sight, a collection of contradictions, a phantom as monstrous as the portress of hell in Milton, half
divinity, half snake, majestic and beautiful above, grovelling and
poisonous below. We see a man whose thoughts and words have no
connection with each other, who never hesitates at an oath when he
wishes to seduce, who never wants a pretext when he is inclined to
betray. His cruelties spring, not from the heat of blood, or the
insanity of uncontrolled power, but from deep and cool meditation.
His passions, like well-trained troops, are impetuous by rule, and in
their most headstrong fury never forget the discipline to which they
have been accustomed. His whole soul is occupied with vast and
complicated schemes of ambition, yet his aspect and language exhibit
nothing but philosophical moderation. Hatred and revenge eat into
his heart; yet every look is a cordial smile, every gesture a familiar
caress. He never excites the suspicion of his adversaries by petty
provocations. His purpose is disclosed, only when it is accomplished.
His face is unruffled, his speech is courteous, till vigilance is laid
asleep, till a vital point is exposed, till a sure aim is taken; and then
he strikes for the first and last time. Military courage, the boast of
the sottish German, of the frivolous and prating Frenchman, of the
romantic and arrogant Spaniard, he neither possesses nor values. He
shuns danger, not because he is insensible to shame, but because, in
the society in which he lives, timidity has ceased to be shameful. To
do an injury openly is, in his estimation, as wicked as to do it
secretly, and far less profitable. With him the most honorable means
are those which are the surest, the speediest, and the darkest. He

cannot comprehend how a man should scruple to deceive those whom
he does not scruple to destroy. He would think it madness to declare
open hostilities against rivals whom he might stab in a friendly
embrace, or poison in a consecrated wafer.

Yet this man, black with the vices which we consider as most
loathsome, traitor, hypocrite, coward, assassin, was by no means
destitute even of those virtues which we generally consider as indicating superior elevation of character. In civil courage, in perseverance, in presence of mind, those barbarous warriors, who were foremost in the battle or the breach, were far his inferiors. Even the dan-
gers which he avoided with a caution almost pusillanimous never
confused his perceptions, never paralyzed his inventive faculties, never wrung out one secret from his smooth tongue and his inscrutable
brow. Though a dangerous enemy, and a still more dangerous
accomplice, he could be a just and beneficent ruler. With so much
unfairness in his policy, there was an extraordinary degree of fairness
in his intellect. Indifferent to truth in the transactions of life, he was
honestly devoted to truth in the researches of speculation. Wanton
cruelty was not in his nature. On the contrary, where no political
object was at stake, his disposition was soft and humane. The suscep-
tibility of his nerves and the activity of his imagination inclined him
to sympathize with the feelings of others, and to delight in the chari-
ties and courtesies of social life. Perpetually descending to actions
which might seem to mark a mind diseased through all its faculties,
he had nevertheless an exquisite sensibility, both for the natural and
the moral sublime, for every graceful and every lofty conception.
Habits of petty intrigue and dissimulation might have rendered him
incapable of great general views, but that the expanding effect of his
philosophical studies counteracted the narrowing tendency. He had
the keenest enjoyment of wit, eloquence, and poetry. The fine arts
profited alike by the severity of his judgment, and by the liberality
of his patronage. The portraits of some of the remarkable Italians
of those times are perfectly in harmony with this description. Ample
and majestic foreheads; brows strong and dark, but not frowning;
eyes of which the calm, full gaze, while it expresses nothing, seems
to discern everything; cheeks pale with thought and sedentary
habits; lips formed with feminine delicacy, but compressed with

more than masculine decision—mark out men at once enterprising
and timid, men equally skilled in detecting the purposes of others,
and in concealing their own, men who must have been formidable
enemies and unsafe allies, but men, at the same time, whose tempers
were mild and equable, and who possessed an amplitude and subtlety
of intellect which would have rendered them eminent either in
active or in contemplative life, and fitted them either to govern or to
instruct mankind.

Every age and every nation has certain characteristic vices, which
prevail almost universally, which scarcely any person scruples to
avow, and which even rigid moralists but faintly censure. Succeeding generations change the fashion of their morals, with the fashion
of their hats and their coaches; take some other kind of wickedness
under their patronage, and wonder at the depravity of their ancestors.
Nor is this all. Posterity, that high court of appeal which is never
tired of eulogizing its own justice and discernment, acts on such
occasions like a Roman dictator after a general mutiny. Finding the
delinquents too numerous to be all punished, it selects some of them
at hazard, to bear the whole penalty of an offence in which they are
not more deeply implicated than those who escape. Whether decima-
tion be a convenient mode of military execution, we know not; but
we solemnly protest against the introduction of such a principle into
the philosophy of history.

In the present instance, the lot has fallen on Machiavelli, a man
whose public conduct was upright and honorable, whose views of
morality, where they differed from those of the persons around him,
seemed to have differed for the better, and whose only fault was,
that, having adopted some of the maxims then generally received,
he arranged them more luminously, and expressed them more
forcibly, than any other writer.

Having now, we hope, in some degree cleared the personal character of Machiavelli, we come to the consideration of his works. As
a poet, he is not entitled to a very high place;[4] but the comedies
deserve more attention.

The "Mandragola," in particular, is superior to the best of Goldoni,

---

[4] In the original essay Macaulay had here some critical remarks on the poetry of
Machiavelli, but he omitted them on republication.

and inferior only to the best of Molière. It is the work of a man who, if he had devoted himself to the drama, would probably have attained the highest eminence, and produced a permanent and salutary effect on the national taste. This we infer, not so much from the degree as from the kind of its excellence. There are compositions which indicate still greater talent, and which are perused with still greater delight, from which we should have drawn very different conclusions. Books quite worthless are quite harmless. The sure sign of the general decline of an art is the frequent occurrence, not of deformity, but of misplaced beauty. In general, tragedy is corrupted by eloquence, and comedy by wit.

The real object of the drama is the exhibition of human character. This, we conceive, is no arbitrary canon, originating in local and temporary associations, like those canons which regulate the number of acts in a play, or of syllables in a line. To this fundamental law every other regulation is subordinate. The situations which most signally develop character form the best plot. The mother tongue of the passions is the best style.

This principle, rightly understood, does not debar the poet from any grace of composition. There is no style in which some man may not, under some circumstances, express himself. There is, therefore, no style which the drama rejects, none which it does not occasionally require. It is in the discernment of place, of time, and of person, that the inferior artists fail. The fantastic rhapsody of Mercutio, the elaborate declamation of Antony, are, where Shakespeare has placed them, natural and pleasing. But Dryden would have made Mercutio challenge Tybalt in hyperboles as fanciful as those in which he describes the chariot of Mab. Corneille would have represented Antony as scolding and coaxing Cleopatra with all the measured rhetoric of a funeral oration.

No writers have injured the comedy of England so deeply as Congreve and Sheridan. Both were men of splendid wit and polished taste. Unhappily, they made all their characters in their own likeness. Their works bear the same relation to the legitimate drama which a transparency bears to a painting. There are no delicate touches, no hues imperceptibly fading into each other: the whole is lighted up with a universal glare. Outlines and tints are forgotten in the common blaze which illuminates all. The flowers and fruits of the intellect abound; but it is the abundance of a jungle, not of a garden, unwholesome, bewildering, unprofitable from its very plenty, rank from its very fragrance. Every fop, every boor, every *valet,* is a man of wit. The very butts and dupes, Tattle, Witwould, Puff, Acres, outshine the whole Hotel of Rambouillet. To prove the whole system of this school erroneous, it is only necessary to apply the test which dissolved the enchanted Florimel, to place the true by the false Thalia, to contrast the most celebrated characters which have been drawn by the writers of whom we speak with the Bastard in "King John," or the Nurse in "Romeo and Juliet." It was not surely from want of wit that Shakespeare adopted so different a manner. Benedick and Beatrice throw Mirabel and Millamant[5] into the shade. All the good sayings of the facetious hours of Absolute and Surface might have been clipped from the single character of Falstaff without being missed. It would have been easy for that fertile mind to have given Bardolph and Shallow as much wit as Prince Hal, and to have made Dogberry and Verges retort on each other in sparkling epigrams. But he knew that such indiscriminate prodigality was, to use his own admirable language, "from the purpose of playing, whose end, both at the first and now, was, and is, to hold, as it were, the mirror up to nature."

This digression will enable our readers to understand what we mean when we say, that, in the "Mandragola," Machiavelli has proved that he completely understood the nature of the dramatic art, and possessed talents which would have enabled him to excel in it. By the correct and vigorous delineation of human nature, it produces interest without a pleasing or skilful plot, and laughter without the least ambition of wit. The lover, not a very delicate or generous lover, and his adviser the parasite, are drawn with spirit. The hypocritical confessor is an admirable portrait. He is, if we mistake not, the original of Father Dominic,[6] the best comic character of Dryden. But old Nicias is the glory of the piece. We cannot call to mind anything that resembles him. The follies which Molière ridicules are those of affectation, not those of fatuity. Coxcombs and

5 In Congreve's "Way of the World."   6 In Dryden's "Spanish Friar."

pedants, not absolute simpletons, are his game. Shakespeare has indeed a vast assortment of fools; but the precise species of which we speak is not, if we remember right, to be found there. Shallow is a fool. But his animal spirits supply, to a certain degree, the place of cleverness. His talk is to that of Sir John what soda-water is to champagne. It has the effervescence, though not the body or the flavor. Slender and Sir Andrew Aguecheek are fools, troubled with an uneasy consciousness of their folly, which, in the latter, produces meekness and docility, and in the former, awkwardness, obstinacy, and confusion. Cloten is an arrogant fool, Osric a foppish fool, Ajax a savage fool; but Nicias is, as Thersites says of Patroclus, a fool positive. His mind is occupied by no strong feeling; it takes every character, and retains none; its aspect is diversified, not by passions, but by faint and transitory semblances of passion, a mock joy, a mock fear, a mock love, a mock pride, which chase each other like shadows over its surface, and vanish as soon as they appear. He is just idiot enough to be an object, not of pity or horror, but of ridicule. He bears some resemblance to poor Calandrino, whose mishaps, as recounted by Boccaccio, have made all Europe merry for more than four centuries. He perhaps resembles still more closely Simon de Villa, to whom Bruno and Buffalmacco promised the love of the Countess Civillari. Nicias is, like Simon, of a learned profession; and the dignity with which he wears the doctoral fur renders his absurdities infinitely more grotesque. The old Tuscan is the very language for such a being. Its peculiar simplicity gives even to the most forcible reasoning and the most brilliant wit an infantine air, generally delightful, but to a foreign reader sometimes a little ludicrous. Heroes and statesmen seem to lisp when they use it. It becomes Nicias incomparably, and renders all his silliness infinitely more silly.

We may add, that the verses with which the "Mandragola" is interspersed appear to us to be the most spirited and correct of all that Machiavelli has written in metre. He seems to have entertained the same opinion, for he has introduced some of them in other places. The contemporaries of the author were not blind to the merits of this striking piece. It was acted at Florence with the greatest success. Leo X was among its admirers, and by his order it was represented at Rome.[7]

The "Clizia" is an imitation of the "Casina" of Plautus, which is itself an imitation of the lost κληρουμένοι of Diphilus.[8] Plautus was, unquestionably, one of the best Latin writers; but the "Casina" is by no means one of his best plays, nor is it one which offers great facilities to an imitator. The story is as alien from modern habits of life as the manner in which it is developed from the modern fashion of composition. The lover remains in the country and the heroine in her chamber during the whole action, leaving their fate to be decided by a foolish father, a cunning mother, and two knavish servants. Machiavelli has executed his task with judgment and taste. He has accommodated the plot to a different state of society, and has very dexterously connected it with the history of his own times. The relation of the trick put on the doting old lover is exquisitely humorous. It is far superior to the corresponding passage in the Latin comedy, and scarcely yields to the account which Falstaff gives of his ducking.

Two other comedies, without titles, the one in prose, the other in verse, appear among the works of Machiavelli. The former is very short, lively enough, but of no great value. The latter we can scarcely believe to be genuine. Neither its merits nor its defects remind us of the reputed author. It was first printed in 1796, from a manuscript discovered in the celebrated library of the Strozzi. Its genuineness, if we have been rightly informed, is established solely by the comparison of hands. Our suspicions are strengthened by the circumstance, that the same manuscript contained a description of the plague of 1527, which has also, in consequence, been added to the works of Machiavelli. Of this last composition, the strongest external evidence would scarcely induce us to believe him guilty. Nothing was ever written more detestable in matter and manner. The narrations, the reflections, the jokes, the lamentations, are all the very worst of their respective kinds, at once trite and affected, threadbare tinsel

---

[7] Nothing can be more evident than that Paulus Jovius designates the "Mandragola" under the name of the "Nicias." We should not have noticed what is so perfectly obvious, were it not that this natural and palpable misnomer has led the sagacious and industrious Bayle into a gross error.—M.

[8] A writer of the Greek "New Comedy," which followed that of Aristophanes.

from the Rag Fairs[9] and Monmouth-streets[9] of literature. A foolish schoolboy might write such a piece, and, after he had written it, think it much finer than the incomparable introduction of "The Decameron." But that a shrewd statesman, whose earliest works are characterized by manliness of thought and language, should, at near sixty years of age, descend to such puerility, is utterly inconceivable.

The little novel of "Belphegor" is pleasantly conceived, and pleasantly told. But the extravagance of the satire in some measure injures its effect. Machiavelli was unhappily married; and his wish to avenge his own cause, and that of his brethren in misfortune, carried him beyond even the license of fiction. Jonson seems to have combined some hints taken from this tale, with others from Boccaccio, in the plot of "The Devil is an Ass," a play which, though not the most highly finished of his compositions, is perhaps that which exhibits the strongest proofs of genius.

The political correspondence of Machiavelli, first published in 1767, is unquestionably genuine, and highly valuable. The unhappy circumstances in which his country was placed during the greater part of his public life gave extraordinary encouragement to diplomatic talents. From the moment that Charles VIII descended from the Alps the whole character of Italian politics was changed. The governments of the Peninsula ceased to form an independent system. Drawn from their old orbit by the attraction of the larger bodies which now approach them, they became mere satellites of France and Spain. All their disputes, internal and external, were decided by foreign influence. The contests of opposite factions were carried on, not as formerly in the Senate-house or in the market-place, but in the ante-chambers of Louis and Ferdinand. Under these circumstances, the prosperity of the Italian States depended far more on the ability of their foreign agents, than on the conduct of those who were intrusted with the domestic administration. The ambassador had to discharge functions far more delicate than transmitting orders of knighthood, introducing tourists, or presenting his brethren with the homage of his high consideration. He was an advocate to whose management the dearest interests of his clients were intrusted, a spy

[9] Old-clothes markets in London.

clothed with an inviolable character. Instead of consulting, by a reserved manner and ambiguous style, the dignity of those whom he represented, he was to plunge into all the intrigues of the court at which he resided, to discover and flatter every weakness of the prince, and of the favorite who governed the prince, and of the lackey who governed the favorite. He was to compliment the mistress, and bribe the confessor, to panegyrize or supplicate, to laugh or weep, to accommodate himself to every caprice, to lull every suspicion, to treasure every hint, to be everything, to observe everything, to endure everything. High as the art of political intrigue had been carried in Italy, these were times which required it all.

On these arduous errands Machiavelli was frequently employed. He was sent to treat with the King of the Romans and with the Duke of Valentinois. He was twice ambassador at the Court of Rome, and thrice at that of France. In these missions, and in several others of inferior importance, he acquitted himself with great dexterity. His despatches form one of the most amusing and instructive collections extant. The narratives are clear and agreeably written, the remarks on men and things clever and judicious. The conversations are reported in a spirited and characteristic manner. We find ourselves introduced into the presence of the men who, during twenty eventful years, swayed the destinies of Europe. Their wit and their folly, their fretfulness and their merriment, are exposed to us. We are admitted to overhear their chat, and to watch their familiar gestures. It is interesting and curious to recognize, in circumstances which elude the notice of historians, the feeble violence and shallow cunning of Louis XII; the bustling insignificance of Maximilian, cursed with an impotent pruriency for renown, rash yet timid, obstinate yet fickle, always in a hurry, yet always too late; the fierce and haughty energy which gave dignity to the eccentricities of Julius; the soft and graceful manners which masked the insatiable ambition and the implacable hatred of Cæsar Borgia.

We have mentioned Cæsar Borgia. It is impossible not to pause for a moment on the name of a man in whom the political morality of Italy was so strongly personified, partially blended with the sterner lineaments of the Spanish character. On two important occasions Machiavelli was admitted to his society—once, at the moment when

Cæsar's splendid villainy achieved its most signal triumph, when he caught in one snare, and crushed at one blow, all his most formidable rivals; and again when, exhausted by disease, and overwhelmed by misfortunes which no human prudence could have averted, he was the prisoner of the deadliest enemy of his house. These interviews between the greatest speculative and the greatest practical statesmen of the age are fully described in the "Correspondence," and form, perhaps, the most interesting part of it. From some passages in "The Prince," and perhaps also from some indistinct traditions, several writers have supposed a connection between those remarkable men much closer than ever existed. The envoy has even been accused of prompting the crimes of the artful and merciless tyrant. But, from the official documents, it is clear that their intercourse, though ostensibly amicable, was in reality hostile. It cannot be doubted, however, that the imagination of Machiavelli was strongly impressed, and his speculations on government colored, by the observations which he made on the singular character and equally singular fortunes of a man who, under such disadvantages, had achieved such exploits; who, when sensuality, varied through innumerable forms, could no longer stimulate his sated mind, found a more powerful and durable excitement in the intense thirst of empire and revenge; who emerged from the sloth and luxury of the Roman purple the first prince and general of the age; who, trained in an unwarlike profession, formed a gallant army out of the dregs of an unwarlike people; who, after acquiring sovereignty by destroying his enemies, acquired popularity by destroying his tools; who had begun to employ for the most salutary ends the power which he had attained by the most atrocious means; who tolerated within the sphere of his iron despotism no plunderer or oppressor but himself; and who fell at last amidst the mingled curses and regrets of a people of whom his genius had been the wonder, and might have been the salvation. Some of those crimes of Borgia which to us appear the most odious, would not, from causes which we have already considered, have struck an Italian of the fifteenth century with equal horror. Patriotic feeling also might induce Machiavelli to look with some indulgence and regret on the memory of the only leader who could have defended the independence of Italy against the confederate spoilers of Cambray.

On this subject, Machiavelli felt most strongly. Indeed, the expulsion of the foreign tyrants, and the restoration of that golden age which had preceded the irruption of Charles VIII, were projects which, at that time, fascinated all the master-spirits of Italy. The magnificent vision delighted the great but ill-regulated mind of Julius. It divided with manuscripts and saucers, painters and falcons, the attention of the frivolous Leo. It prompted the generous treason of Morone. It imparted a transient energy to the feeble mind and body of the last Sforza. It excited for one moment an honest ambition in the false heart of Pescara. Ferocity and insolence were not among the vices of the national character. To the discriminating cruelties of politicians, committed for great ends on select victims, the moral code of the Italians was too indulgent. But, though they might have recourse to barbarity as an expedient, they did not require it as a stimulant. They turned with loathing from the atrocity of the strangers who seemed to love blood for its own sake; who, not content with subjugating, were impatient to destroy; who found a fiendish pleasure in razing magnificent cities, cutting the throats of enemies who cried for quarter, or suffocating an unarmed population by thousands in the caverns to which it had fled for safety. Such were the cruelties which daily excited the terror and disgust of a people among whom, till lately, the worst that a soldier had to fear in a pitched battle was the loss of his horse and the expense of his ransom. The swinish intemperance of Switzerland; the wolfish avarice of Spain; the gross licentiousness of the French, indulged in violation of hospitality, of decency, of love itself; the wanton inhumanity which was common to all the invaders—had made them objects of deadly hatred to the inhabitants of the Peninsula. The wealth which had been accumulated during centuries of prosperity and repose was rapidly melting away. The intellectual superiority of the oppressed people only rendered them more keenly sensible of their political degradation. Literature and taste, indeed, still disguised with a flush of hectic loveliness and brilliancy the ravages of an incurable decay. The iron had not yet entered into the soul. The time was not yet come when eloquence was to be gagged, and reason to be hoodwinked, when the harp of the poet was to be hung on the willows of Arno, and the right hand of the painter to forget its cunning. Yet a discerning eye might even then have seen that genius and learning would not long survive the state of things from which they had sprung, and that the great men whose talents gave lustre to that melancholy period had been formed under the influence of happier days, and would leave no successors behind them. The times which shine with the greatest splendor in literary history are not always those to which the human mind is most indebted. Of this we may be convinced, by comparing the generation which follows them with that which had preceded them. The first-fruits which are reaped under a bad system often spring from seed sown under a good one. Thus it was, in some measure, with the Augustan age. Thus it was with the age of Raphael and Ariosto, of Aldus and Vida.

Machiavelli deeply regretted the misfortunes of his country, and clearly discerned the cause and the remedy. It was the military system of the Italian people which had extinguished their valor and discipline, and left their wealth an easy prey to every foreign plunderer. The secretary projected a scheme, alike honorable to his heart and to his intellect, for abolishing the use of mercenary troops, and for organizing a national militia.

The exertions which he made to effect this great object ought alone to rescue his name from obloquy. Though his situation and his habits were pacific, he studied with intense assiduity the theory of war. He made himself master of all its details. The Florentine government entered into his views. A council of war was appointed. Levies were decreed. The indefatigable minister flew from place to place in order to superintend the execution of his design. The times were, in some respects, favorable to the experiment. The system of military tactics had undergone a great revolution. The cavalry was no longer considered as forming the strength of an army. The hours which a citizen could spare from his ordinary employments, though by no means sufficient to familiarize him with the exercise of a man-at-arms, might render him a useful foot-soldier. The dread of a foreign yoke, of plunder, massacre, and conflagration, might have conquered that repugnance to military pursuits which both the industry and the idleness of great towns commonly generate. For a time the scheme promised well. The new troops acquitted themselves respectably in the field. Machiavelli looked with parental rapture on the success of his plan, and began to hope that the arms of Italy might once more be formidable to the barbarians of the Tagus and the Rhine. But the tide of misfortune came on before the barriers which should have withstood it were prepared. For a time, indeed, Florence might be considered as peculiarly fortunate. Famine and sword and pestilence had devastated the fertile plains and stately cities of the Po. All the curses denounced of old against Tyre seemed to have fallen on Venice. Her merchants already stood afar off, lamenting for their great city. The time seemed near when the sea-weed should overgrow her silent Rialto, and the fisherman wash his nets in her deserted arsenal. Naples had been four times conquered and reconquered by tyrants equally indifferent to its welfare, and equally greedy for its spoils. Florence, as yet, had only to endure degradation and extortion, to submit to the mandates of foreign powers, to buy over and over again, at an enormous price, what was already justly her own, to return thanks for being wronged, and to ask pardon for being in the right. She was at length deprived of the blessings, even of this infamous and servile repose. Her military and political institutions were swept away together. The Medici returned, in the train of foreign invaders, from their long exile. The policy of Machiavelli was abandoned; and his public services were requited with poverty, imprisonment, and torture.

The fallen statesman still clung to his project with unabated ardor. With the view of vindicating it from some popular objections, and of refuting some prevailing errors on the subject of military science, he wrote his "Seven Books on the Art of War." This excellent work is in the form of a dialogue. The opinions of the writer are put into the mouth of Fabrizio Colonna, a powerful nobleman of the ecclesiastical State, and an officer of distinguished merit in the service of the King of Spain. Colonna visits Florence on his way from Lombardy to his own domains. He is invited to meet some friends at the house of Cosimo Rucellai, an amiable and accomplished young man, whose early death Machiavelli feelingly deplores. After partaking of an elegant entertainment, they retire from the heat into the most shady recesses of the garden. Fabrizio is struck by the sight of some uncommon plants. Cosimo says, that, though rare in modern days, they are frequently mentioned by the classical authors, and that his grandfather, like many other Italians, amused himself with practising the ancient methods of gardening. Fabrizio expresses his regret that those who, in later times, affected the manners of the old Romans, should select for imitation the most trifling pursuits. This leads to a conversation on the decline of military discipline, and on the best means of restoring it. The institution of the Florentine militia is ably defended, and several improvements are suggested in the details.

The Swiss and the Spaniards were, at that time, regarded as the best soldiers in Europe. The Swiss battalion consisted of pikemen, and bore a close resemblance to the Greek phalanx. The Spaniards, like the soldiers of Rome, were armed with the sword and the shield. The victories of Flaminius and Æmilius over the Macedonian kings seem to prove the superiority of the weapons used by the legions. The same experiment had been recently tried with the same result at the battle of Ravenna, one of those tremendous days into which human folly and wickedness compress the whole devastation of a famine or a plague. In that memorable conflict, the infantry of Aragon, the old companions of Gonsalvo, deserted by all their allies, hewed a passage through the thickest of the imperial pikes, and effected an unbroken retreat, in the face of the *gendarmerie* of De Foix, and the renowned artillery of Este. Fabrizio, or rather Machiavelli, proposes to combine the two systems, to arm the foremost lines with the pike for the purpose of repulsing cavalry, and those in the rear with the sword, as being a weapon better adapted for every other purpose. Throughout the work, the author expresses the highest admiration of the military science of the ancient Romans, and the greatest contempt for the maxims which had been in vogue amongst the Italian commanders of the preceding generation. He prefers infantry to cavalry, and fortified camps to fortified towns. He is inclined to substitute rapid movements and decisive engagements for the languid and dilatory operations of his countrymen. He attaches very little importance to the invention of gunpowder. Indeed, he seems to think that it ought scarcely to produce any change in the mode of arming or of disposing troops. The general testimony of historians, it must be allowed, seems to prove that the ill-constructed and ill-served artillery of those times, though useful in a siege, was of little value on the field of battle.

On the tactics of Machiavelli we will not venture to give an opinion, but we are certain that his book is most able and interesting. As a commentary on the history of his times, it is invaluable. The ingenuity, the grace, and the perspicuity of the style, and the eloquence and animation of particular passages, must give pleasure, even to readers who take no interest in the subject.

"The Prince" and the "Discourses on Livy" were written after the fall of the republican government. The former was dedicated to the young Lorenzo de' Medici. This circumstance seems to have disgusted the contemporaries of the writer far more than the doctrines which have rendered the name of the work odious in latter times. It was considered as an indication of political apostasy. The fact, however, seems to have been, that Machiavelli, despairing of the liberty of Florence, was inclined to support any government which might preserve her independence. The interval which separated a democracy and a despotism Soderini and Lorenzo, seemed to vanish when compared with the difference between the former and the present state of Italy, between the security, the opulence, and the repose which she had enjoyed under its native rulers, and the misery in which she had been plunged since the fatal year in which the first foreign tyrant had descended from the Alps. The noble and pathetic exhortation with which "The Prince" concludes shows how strongly the writer felt upon this subject.

"The Prince" traces the progress of an ambitious man, the "Discourses" the progress of an ambitious people. The same principles on which, in the former work, the elevation of an individual is explained, are applied, in the latter, to the longer duration and more complex interest of a society. To a modern statesman the form of the "Discourses" may appear to be puerile. In truth, Livy is not a historian on whom implicit reliance can be placed, even in cases where he must have possessed considerable means of information. And the first Decade, to which Machiavelli has confined himself, is scarcely entitled to more credit than our Chronicle of British Kings who reigned before the Roman invasion. But the commentator is indebted to Livy for little more than a few texts which he might as easily have extracted from the Vulgate or "The Decameron." The whole train of thought is original.

On the peculiar immorality which has rendered "The Prince" unpopular, and which is almost equally discernible in the "Discourses" we have already given our opinion at length. We have attempted to show that it belonged rather to the age than to the man, that it was a partial taint, and by no means implied general depravity. We cannot, however, deny that it is a great blemish, and that it considerably diminishes the pleasure which, in other respects, those works must afford to every intelligent mind.

It is, indeed, impossible to conceive a more healthful and vigorous constitution of the understanding than that which these works indicate. The qualities of the active and the contemplative statesman appear to have been blended in the mind of the writer into a rare and exquisite harmony. His skill in the details of business had not been acquired at the expense of his general powers. It had not rendered his mind less comprehensive; but it had served to correct his speculations, and to impart to them that vivid and practical character which so widely distinguishes them from the vague theories of most political philosophers.

Every man who has seen the world knows that nothing is so useless as a general maxim. If it be very moral and very true, it may serve for a copy to a charity boy. If, like those of Rochefoucauld, it be sparkling and whimsical, it may make an excellent motto for an essay. But few indeed of the many wise apophthegms which have been uttered, from the time of the Seven Sages of Greece to that of "Poor Richard," have prevented a single foolish action. We give the highest and the most peculiar praise to the precepts of Machiavelli when we say that they may frequently be of real use in regulating conduct, not so much because they are more just or more profound than those which might be culled from other authors, as because they can be more readily applied to the problems of real life.

There are errors in these works. But they are errors which a writer, situated like Machiavelli, could scarcely avoid. They arise, for the most part, from a single defect which appears to us to pervade his whole system. In his political scheme, the means had been more deeply considered than the ends. The great principle, that societies and laws exist only for the purpose of increasing the sum of private happiness, is not recognized with sufficient clearness. The good of the body, distinct from the good of the members, and sometimes hardly compatible with the good of the members, seems to be the object which he proposes to himself. Of all political fallacies, this has perhaps had the widest and the most mischievous operation. The state of society in the little commonwealths of Greece, the close connection and mutual dependence of the citizens, and the severity of the laws of war, tended to encourage an opinion which, under such circumstances, could hardly be called erroneous. The interests of every individual were inseparably bound up with those of the State. An invasion destroyed his corn-fields and vineyards, drove him from his home, and compelled him to encounter all the hardships of a military life. A treaty of peace restored him to security and comfort. A victory doubled the number of his slaves. A defeat perhaps made him a slave himself. When Pericles, in the Peloponnesian war, told the Athenians, that, if their country triumphed, their private losses would speedily be repaired, but that, if their arms failed of success, every individual amongst them would probably be ruined, he spoke no more than the truth. He spoke to men whom the tribute of vanquished cities supplied with food and clothing, with the luxury of the bath and the amusements of the theatre, on whom the greatness of their country conferred rank, and before whom the members of less prosperous communities trembled; to men who, in case of a change in the public fortunes, would, at least, be deprived of every comfort and every distinction which they enjoyed. To be butchered on the smoking ruins of their city, to be dragged in chains to a slave-market, to see one child torn from them to dig in the quarries of Sicily, and another to guard the harems of Persepolis, these were the frequent and probable consequences of national calamities. Hence, among the Greeks, patriotism became a governing principle, or rather an ungovernable passion. Their legislators and their philosophers took it for granted, that, in providing for the strength and greatness of the State, they sufficiently provided for the happiness of the people. The writers of the Roman Empire lived under despots, into whose dominion a hundred nations were melted down, and whose gardens would have covered the little commonwealths of Phlius and Platæa. Yet they continued to employ the same language, and to cant about the duty of sacrificing everything to a country to which they owed nothing.

Causes similar to those which had influenced the disposition of the Greeks operated powerfully on the less vigorous and daring character of the Italians. The Italians, like the Greeks, were members of small communities. Every man was deeply interested in the welfare of the society to which he belonged, a partaker in its wealth and its poverty, in its glory and its shame. In the age of Machiavelli this was peculiarly the case. Public events had produced an immense sum of misery to private citizens. The Northern invaders had brought want to their boards, infamy to their beds, fire to their roofs, and the knife to their throats. It was natural that a man who lived in times like these should overrate the importance of those measures by which a nation is rendered formidable to its neighbors, and undervalue those which make it prosperous within itself.

Nothing is more remarkable in the political treatises of Machiavelli than the fairness of mind which they indicate. It appears where the author is in the wrong, almost as strongly as where he is in the right. He never advances a false opinion because it is new or splendid, because he can clothe it in a happy phrase, or defend it by an ingenious sophism. His errors are at once explained by a reference to the circumstances in which he was placed. They evidently were not sought out: they lay in his way, and could scarcely be avoided. Such mistakes must necessarily be committed by early speculators in every science.

The political works of Machiavelli derive a peculiar interest from the mournful earnestness which he manifests whenever he touches on topics connected with the calamities of his native land. It is difficult to conceive any situation more painful that that of a great man, condemned to watch the lingering agony of an exhausted country, to tend it during the alternate fits of stupefaction and raving which precede its dissolution, and to see the symptoms of vitality disappear one by one, till nothing is left but coldness, darkness, and corruption. To this joyless and thankless duty was Machiavelli called. In the energetic language of the prophet, he was "mad for the sight of his eyes which he saw"—disunion in the Council, effeminacy in the camp, liberty extinguished, commerce decaying, national honor sullied, an enlightened and flourishing people given over to the ferocity of ignorant savages. Though his opinions had not escaped the contagion of that political immorality which was common among his countrymen, his natural disposition seems to have been rather stern and impetuous than pliant and artful. When the misery and degradation of Florence, and the foul outrage which he had himself sustained, recur to his mind, the smooth craft of his profession and his nation is exchanged for the honest bitterness of scorn and anger. He speaks like one sick of the calamitous times and abject people among whom his lot is cast. He pines for the strength and glory of ancient Rome, for the fasces of Brutus and the sword of Scipio, the gravity of the curule chair, and the bloody pomp of the triumphal sacrifice. He seems to be transported back to the days when 800,000 Italian warriors sprung to arms at the rumor of a Gallic invasion. He breathes all the spirit of those intrepid and haughty Senators who forgot the dearest ties of nature in the claims of public duty, who looked with disdain on the elephants and on the gold of Pyrrhus, and listened with unaltered composure to the tremendous tidings of Cannæ. Like an ancient temple deformed by the barbarous architecture of a later age, his character acquires an interest from the very circumstances which debase it. The original proportions are rendered more striking by the contrast which they present to the mean and incongruous additions.

The influence of the sentiments which we have described was not apparent in his writings alone. His enthusiasm, barred from the career which it would have selected for itself, seems to have found a vent in desperate levity. He enjoyed a vindictive pleasure in outraging the opinions of a society which he despised. He became careless of the decencies which were expected from a man so highly distinguished in the literary and political world. The sarcastic bitterness of his conversation disgusted those who were more inclined to accuse his licentiousness than their own degeneracy, and who were unable to conceive the strength of those emotions which are concealed by the jests of the wretched, and by the follies of the wise.

The historical works of Machiavelli still remain to be considered.

The life of Castruccio Castracani will occupy us for a very short time, and would scarcely have demanded our notice had it not attracted a much greater share of public attention than it deserves. Few books, indeed, could be more interesting than a careful and judicious account, from such a pen, of the illustrious Prince of Lucca, the most eminent of those Italian chiefs, who, like Pisistratus and Gelon, acquired a power felt rather than seen, and resting, not on law or on prescription, but on the public favor and on their great personal qualities. Such a work would exhibit to us the real nature of that species of sovereignty, so singular and so often misunderstood, which the Greeks denominated tyranny, and which, modified in some degree by the feudal system, reappeared in the commonwealths of Lombardy and Tuscany. But this little composition of Machiavelli is in no sense a history. It has no pretensions to fidelity. It is a trifle, and not a very successful trifle. It is scarcely more authentic than the novel of "Belphegor," and is very much duller.

The last great work of this illustrious man was the history of his native city. It was written by command of the Pope, who, as chief of the house of Medici, was at that time sovereign of Florence. The characters of Cosimo, of Piero, and of Lorenzo, are, however, treated with a freedom and impartiality equally honorable to the writer and to the patron. The miseries and humiliations of dependence, the bread which is more bitter than every other food, the stairs which are more painful than every other ascent, had not broken the spirit of Machiavelli. The most corrupting post in a corrupting profession had not depraved the generous heart of Clement.

The history does not appear to be the fruit of much industry or research. It is unquestionably inaccurate. But it is elegant, lively, and picturesque, beyond any other in the Italian language. The reader, we believe, carries away from it a more vivid and a more faithful impression of the national character and manners than from more correct accounts. The truth is, that the book belongs rather to ancient than to modern literature. It is in the style, not of Davila and Clarendon, but of Herodotus and Tacitus. The classical histories may almost be called romances founded in fact. The relation is, no doubt, in all its principal points, strictly true. But the numerous little incidents which heighten the interest, the words, the gestures, the looks, are evidently furnished by the imagination of the author. The fashion of later times is different. A more exact narrative is given by the writer.

It may be doubted whether more exact notions are conveyed to the reader. The best portraits are perhaps those in which there is a slight mixture of caricature, and we are not certain that the best histories are not those in which a little of the exaggeration of fictitious narrative is judiciously employed. Something is lost in accuracy, but much is gained in effect. The fainter lines are neglected, but the great characteristic features are imprinted on the mind forever.

The history terminates with the death of Lorenzo de' Medici. Machiavelli had, it seems, intended to continue his narrative to a later period. But his death prevented the execution of his design, and the melancholy task of recording the desolation and shame of Italy devolved on Guicciardini.

Machiavelli lived long enough to see the commencement of the last struggle for Florentine liberty. Soon after his death monarchy was finally established, not such a monarchy as that of which Cosimo had laid the foundations deep in the institutions and feelings of his countrymen, and which Lorenzo had embellished with the trophies of every science and every art, but a loathsome tyranny, proud and mean, cruel and feeble, bigoted and lascivious. The character of Machiavelli was hateful to the new masters of Italy, and those parts of his theory which were in strict accordance with their own daily practice afforded a pretext for blackening his memory. His works were misrepresented by the learned, misconstrued by the ignorant, censured by the Church, abused with all the rancor of simulated virtue by the tools of a base government and the priests of a baser superstition. The name of the man whose genius had illuminated all the dark places of policy, and to whose patriotic wisdom an oppressed people had owed their last chance of emancipation and revenge, passed into a proverb of infamy. For more than two hundred years his bones lay undistinguished. At length an English nobleman paid the last honors to the greatest statesman of Florence. In the Church of Santa Croce a monument was erected to his memory, which is contemplated with reverence by all who can distinguish the virtues of a great mind through the corruptions of a degenerate age, and which will be approached with still deeper homage when the object to which his public life was devoted shall be attained, when the foreign yoke shall be broken, when a second Procida shall avenge the wrongs of Naples, when a happier Rienzi shall restore the good estate of Rome, when the streets of Florence and Bologna shall again resound with their ancient war-cry, *"Popolo; popolo; muoiano i tiranni!"*[10]

[10] "The people! the people! Death to the tyrants!"—Machiavelli's "History of Florence," Book III.